EPISTLE TO THE GALATIANS.

A

COMMENTARY,

CRITICAL AND GRAMMATICAL,

ON ST. PAUL'S

EPISTLE TO THE GALATIANS,

WITH A

REVISED TRANSLATION.

BY

CHARLES J. ELLICOTT, B.D.

PROFESSOR OF DIVINITY, KING'S COLLEGE, LONDON, AND LATE FELLOW OF ST. JOHN'S COLLEGE, CAMBRIDGE.

AND

An Introductory Notice,

BY

CALVIN E. STOWE, D.D.

PROFESSOR IN ANDOVER THEOLOGICAL SEMINARY.

ANDOVER:

WARREN F. DRAPER.

BOSTON: CROSBY, NICHOLS, LEE & Co.

NEW YORK: JOHN WILEY.

PHILADELPHIA: SMITH, ENGLISH & CO.

1865.

Andover:
Electrotyped and Printed by W. F. Draper.

INTRODUCTORY NOTICE

TO THE

AMERICAN EDITION.

THE Commentaries of Professor Ellicott, modest and unassuming as they are in tone, really mark an epoch in English sacred literature. They are as different from other English commentaries as De Wette's are from the Germans who preceded him ; and what De Wette has been to German exegesis, Ellicott is and will be to the English. I speak of scholarship and mode of exhibition mainly ; but the remark is also true in another respect, for, as De Wette was in his time the soundest and most favorable type of German rationalism as applied to the exposition of Scripture, Ellicott now most fitly represents the clear common sense and reverential piety so happily characteristic of the best biblical expositors in the English church. Protestant Germany only could have produced a De Wette, and Protestant England only, an Ellicott.

It is the professed object of both these writers, by a severe and purely grammatical analysis of the language of the sacred penmen, to ascertain precisely the ideas which they meant to convey ; and to express the results of this analysis in the simplest and briefest manner possible, without reference to theological systems, or ecclesiastical prepossessions, or practical inferences. This method must lie at the foundation of all true exegesis, and, to those who receive the Bible as the word of God, must form the basis of all Christian theology. Yet it is a method very seldom followed with any good degree of strictness, and it is not a method which is generally particularly interesting to theologians and preachers. It differs from the usual style of commentary as pure wheat differs from merchantable flour. Though the ascertainable purity of the wheat is acknowledged to be a great advantage, there is the trouble of grinding it before it can be made into bread. Theologizing and sermonizing commentary, though everywhere intermingled with the speculations and prepossessions of the commentator, is generally preferred to a severe and strictly linguistic exegesis, because, though less pure, it furnishes the material more ready for immediate use. But which method is it that really takes the Bible as the sufficient and only authoritative rule of Christian faith and practice, and follows out to its legitimate results the fundamental principle of Protestantism? There can be but one answer to this question; and it is this, the only truly biblical and Protestant method of commentary, which Professor Ellicott has conscientiously, consistently, and successfully pursued.

It is the crowning excellence of these commentaries, that they are exactly what they profess to be, *critical* and *grammatical*, and therefore, in the best sense of the term, *exegetical.* It is no part of the author's object to theologize or to sermonize, or to make proof-texts, or to draw inferences or to repel them, but simply to interpret the language of the sacred writers; and this object he accomplishes. He first, with the utmost care and the most conscientious laboriousness, gives the reader a correct text, by means of a widely extended comparison of original MSS., ancient translations, and the best editions. The amount of hard work evidently expended on this part of his undertaking is, to one who knows how to appreciate it, almost appalling. His results are worthy of all confidence. He is more careful and reliable than Tischendorf, slower and more steadily deliberate than Alford, and more patiently laborious than any other living New Testament critic, with the exception, perhaps, of Tregelles. Having thus ascertained the text, he then goes to work lexically and grammatically upon every word, phrase, and sentence which it offers; and here again is everywhere seen the real *labor limae* of the untiring and conscientious scholar. Nothing escapes his diligence, nothing wears out his patience. His exegetical conclusions are stated briefly and modestly, and with the utmost simplicity.

His references to other opinions and other writers, and to all the requisite authorities, are abundantly copious for the purposes of the most thorough study. The marginal indications of the course of thought are exceedingly judicious and helpful; and the full translations given at the close of each Commentary harmonize with all the other parts of the work. Here the constant marginal quotations from the older translators give the reader the best possible opportunity for an extensive comparison, which would otherwise, in most cases, be quite impossible, for want of access to the books.

The reader will be gratified to learn something of the history of the unpretending scholar who has already done so much, and who gives promise of so much more. CHARLES JOHN ELLICOTT is of an old Devonshire family, a branch of which early emigrated to America, and still has descendants here. He was born in 1819, the son of Rev. Charles Spencer Ellicott, Rector of Whitwell in Rutlandshire. He studied at the grammar schools of Oakham and Stamford, and afterwards entered St. John's College, Cambridge, of which society he became a Fellow in 1844. In 1848 he married and took the Rectorship of Pilton, in Rutlandshire, which he held till the beginning of 1856; when, for the sake of having access to large public libraries, he resigned his living and returned to Cambridge. In 1858 he was appointed one of the select preachers before the University, and prepared and published a volume of sermons on the "Destiny of the Creature" (Rom. 8:19 ff.). He received the same appointment again the next year, and was also made Hulsean Lecturer. In this capacity he delivered a course of lectures on the connection of the events in the life of Christ, which are now in press, and will soon be published. In 1858, also, he was appointed to succeed Professor Maurice in the professorship of Divinity at King's College, London, which office he still holds. On the 20th of February, 1860, while on a journey from Cambridge to London, in fulfilment of the duties of his office, he came very near losing his life by a shocking accident on the Eastern Counties Railway. Three persons in the same compartment with him were instantly killed, and he had both legs broken, and his arm and head were severely scalded. His life was saved by his throwing himself upon the bottom of the carriage at the moment when the shock was greatest. He has now recovered from his injuries and is pursuing his work with undiminished zeal and success. He has already published on all the epistles of Paul, except Corinthians and Romans, and these he has now in hand, and will in due time complete.

The American publisher will issue the successive volumes, as rapidly as circumstances will permit, in the same order with the English (the next being the epistle to the Ephesians), till the whole series is in the hands of our scholars. It is to be hoped also that the American publishers of Alford's work on the Greek Testament will speedily complete that, as the last volume is now in press in England. It is a different kind of commentary from Ellicott's, though equally useful in its own way. It includes the whole of the New Testament, and has more of what critics call *introduction* in the shape of extended and elaborate *prolegomena* to the several books, and is designedly of as popular a cast as, from the nature of the case, a scholarly commentary on a Greek book can be. The two works cannot at all interfere with each other. Both are an honor to the English theological literature of the present generation; each in its own sphere supplies an urgent want; and they both ought to be accessible to American students at as cheap a rate as possible.

C. E. STOWE.

THEOL. SEM., ANDOVER, MASS.
Aug. 30, 1860.

PREFACE TO THE FIRST EDITION.

THE following commentary is the first part of an attempt to elucidate St. Paul's Epistles, by systematically applying to the Sacred Text the present principles of grammar and criticism.

It is the result of several years' devotion to the study of biblical Greek, and owes its existence to the conviction that, in this country, the present very advanced state of philology has scarcely been applied with sufficient rigor to the interpretation of the New Testament. Our popular commentaries are too exclusively exegetical,[1] and presuppose, in the ordinary student, a greater knowledge of the peculiarities of the language of the New Testament than it is at all probable he possesses. Even the more promising student is sure to meet with two stumbling-blocks in his path, when he first maturely enters upon the study of the Holy Scripture.

In the first place, the very systematic exactitude of his former discipline in classical Greek is calculated to mislead him in the study of writers who belonged to an age when change had impaired, and conquest had debased the language in which they wrote; — his exclusive attention to a single dialect, informed, for the most part, by a single and prevailing spirit, ill prepares him for the correct apprehension of writings in which the tinge of nationalities, and the admixture of newer and deeper modes of thought are both distinctly recognizable; — his familiarity with modes of expression, which had arisen from the living wants of a living language, ill prepares him correctly and completely to understand their force when they are reproduced by aliens in kindred and customs, and strangers, and even more than strangers in tongue. Let all these diversities be fairly considered, and then, without entering into any more exact comparisons between biblical and classical Greek, it will be difficult not to admit that the advanced student in Attic Greek is liable to carry with him prejudices, which may, for a time at least, interfere with his full appreciation of the outward form in which the Sacred Oracles

1 I must explain the meaning in which, I use this word when in contradistinction to "grammatical." By a *grammatical* commentary, I mean one in which the principles of grammar are either exclusively or principally used to elucidate the meaning: by an *exegetical* commentary, one in which other considerations, such as the circumstances or known sentiments of the writer, etc., are also taken into account. I am not quite sure that I am correct in thus limiting "exegetical," but I know no other epithets that will serve to convey my meaning.

are enshrined. No better example of the general truth of these observations could be adduced than that of the illustrious Hermann, who, in his disquisition on the first three chapters of this very epistle, has convincingly shown, how even perceptions as accurate as his, and erudition as profound, may still signally fail, when applied, without previous exercise, to the interpretation of the New Testament.

A second stumbling-block that the classical student invariably finds in his study of the New Testament, is the deplorable state in which, till within the last few years, its grammar has been left. It is scarcely possible for any one unacquainted with the history and details of the grammar of the N. T. to form any conception of the aberrant and unnatural meanings that have been assigned to the prepositions and the particles; many of which cling to them in N. T. lexicons to this very day.[1] It requires a familiar acquaintance with the received glosses of several important passages to conceive the nature of the burdens hard to be borne, which long-suffering Hebraism — 'that hidden helper in all need,' as Lücke[2] calls it — has had to sustain; and how generations of excellent scholars have passed away without ever overcoming their Pharisaical reluctance to touch one of them with the tip of the finger. Then, again, grammatical figures have suffered every species of strain and distortion; enallage, hendyadys, metonymy, have been urged with a freedom in the N. T. which would never have been tolerated in any classical author, however ill-cared for, and however obscure. Here and there in past days a few protesting voices were raised against the uncritical nature of the current interpretations; but it is not, in Germany, till within a very few years, till the days of Fritzsche and Winer, that they have met with any response or recognition; and, among ourselves, even now, they have secured only a limited and critical audience.

It thus only too often happens, that, when a young man enters, for the first time, seriously upon the study of the N. T., it is with such an irrepressible feeling of repugnance to that laxity of language, which he is led to believe is its prevailing characteristic, that he either loses for the language of inspiration that reverence which its mere literary merits alone may justly claim; or else, under the action of a better though mistaken feeling, he shrinks from applying to it that healthy criticism to which all his previous education had inured his mind. The more difficult the portion of Scripture, the more sensibly are these evils felt and recognized.

It is under these feelings that I have undertaken a commentary on St. Paul's Epistles, which, by confining itself to the humbler and less ambitious

1 That this language is in no way overstrained may be easily seen by the notices in Winer's *Grammar*, on any leading preposition or conjunction. 'Ἐν is a difficult preposition in the N. T., but it would require a considerable amount of argument to make us believe it could ever, even in Heb. xiii. 9, bear the meaning of *ex!* See Winer, *Gr.* § 52, a, p. 466 (Ed. 5).

2 Lücke, *on John* iii. 20, vol. iii. p. 241.

sphere of grammatical details, may give the student some insight into the language of the New Testament, and enable him with more assured steps, to ascend the difficult heights of exegetical and dogmatical theology. My own studies have irresistibly impelled me to the conviction, that, without making any unnecessary distinctions between grammar and exegesis, we are still to recognize the necessity, — of first endeavoring to find out what the words actually convey, according to the ordinary rules of language; then, secondly, of observing the peculiar shade of meaning that the context appears to impart. Too often this process has been reversed; the commentator, on the strength of some 'received interpretation' or some dogmatical bias, has stated what the passage ought to mean, and then has been tempted, by the force of bad example, to coerce the words 'per Hebraismum,' or 'per enallagen,' to yield the required sense. This, in many, nay, most cases, I feel certain, has been done to a great degree *unconsciously*, yet still the evil effects remain. God's word, though innocently, has been dealt deceitfully with; and God's word, like His Ark of the Covenant, may not, with impunity, be stayed up by the officiousness of mortal aid.

I have, then, in all cases, striven, humbly and reverently, to elicit from the words their simple and primary meaning. Where that has *seemed* at variance with historical or dogmatical deductions, — where, in fact, exegesis has seemed to range itself on one side, grammar on the other, — I have never failed candidly to state it; where it has confirmed some time-honored interpretation, I have joyfully and emphatically cast my small mite into the great treasury of sacred exegesis, and have felt gladdened at being able to yield some passing support to wiser and better men than myself.[1] This, however, I would fain strive to impress upon my reader, to whatever party of the Church (alas! that there should be parties) he may chance to belong, that, as God is my witness, I have striven to state, in perfect candor and singleness of heart, all the details of interpretation with which I have come in contact. I have sought to support no particular party, I have desired to yield countenance to no peculiar views. I will candidly avow that on all the fundamental points of Christian faith and doctrine my mind is fully made up. It is not for me to sit in judgment upon what is called the liberal spirit of the age, but, without evoking controversies into which I have neither the will nor the abil-

1 Amidst all these details, I have, I trust, never forgotten that there is something higher than mere critical acumen, something more sure than grammatical exactitude; something which the world calls the "theological sense," but which more devout thinkers recognize as the assisting grace of the Eternal Spirit of God. Without this, without also a deeper and more mysterious sympathy with the mind of the sacred writer whom we are presuming to interpret, no mere verbal discussions can ever tend truly to elucidate, no investigation thoroughly to satisfy. I trust, indeed, that I have never been permitted to forget these golden words of him whom of all commentators I most honor and revere: — *οὐδὲ γὰρ δεῖ τὰ ῥήματα γυμνὰ ἐξετάζειν, ἐπεὶ πολλὰ ἕψεται τὰ ἀτοπήματα· οὐδὲ τὴν λέξιν καθ' ἑαυτὴν βασανίζειν, ἀλλὰ τῇ διανοίᾳ προσέχειν τοῦ γράφοντος.* Chrysost. tom. x. p. 674 B (ed. Bened.)

ity to enter, I may be permitted to say, that upon the momentous subject of the inspiration of Scripture, I cannot be so untrue to my own deepest convictions, or so forgetful of my anxious thoughts and investigations, as to affect a freedom of opinion which I am very far from entertaining. I deeply feel for those whom earth-born mist and vapor still hinder from beholding the full brightness and effulgence of divine truth; I entertain the most lively pity for those who still feel that the fresh fountains of Scripture are, in all the bitterness of the prophet's lamentation, only 'waters that fail;'— I feel it and entertain it, and I trust that no ungentle word of mine may induce them to cling more tenaciously to their mournful convictions, yet still I am bound to say, to prevent the nature of my candor being misunderstood, that throughout this commentary the full[1] inspiration of Scripture has been felt as one of those strong subjective convictions to which every hour of meditation adds fresh strength and assurance. Yet I have never sought to mask or disguise a difficulty: I have never advanced an explanation of the truth of which I do not, myself at least, feel convinced. I should shrink from being so untrue to myself, I should tremble at being so presumptuous towards God; as if He who sent the dream may not in His own good time send 'the interpretation thereof.' That there are difficulties in Scripture,— that there are difficulties in this deep Epistle, I both know and feel, and I have, in no case, shrunk from pointing them out; but I also know that there is a time,— whether in this world of unrest, or in that rest which remaineth to God's people, I know not,— when every difficulty will be cleared up, every doubt dispersed: and it is this conviction that has supported me, when I have felt and have been forced to record my conviction, that there are passages where the world's wisdom has not yet clearly seen into the depth of the deep things of God.

Before I wholly leave this momentous subject, I would fain plead its importance in regard to the method of interpretation which I have endeavored to follow. I am well aware that the current of popular opinion is now steadily setting against grammatical details and investigations. It is thought, I believe, that a freer admixture of history, broader generalizations, and more suggestive reflections, may enable the student to catch the spirit of his author, and be borne serenely along without the weed and toil of ordinary travel. Upon the soundness of such theories, in a general point of view, I will not venture to pronounce an opinion; I am not an Athanase, and cannot confront a world; but, in the particular sphere of Holy Scripture, I may, perhaps, be permitted to say, that if we would train our younger students to be reverential thinkers, earnest Christians, and sound divines, we must habituate them to a patient and thoughtful study of the words and language of

[1] I avoid using any party expressions. I would not wish, on the one hand, to class myself with such thinkers as Calovius, nor could I subscribe to the *Formula Consensus Helvetici;* but I am far indeed from recognizing that admixture of human imperfection and even error, which the popular theosophy of the day now finds in the Holy Scripture.

Scripture, before we allow them to indulge in an exegesis for which they are immature and incompetent. If the Scriptures are divinely inspired, then surely it is a young man's noblest occupation, patiently and lovingly to note every change of expression, every turn of language, every variety of inflection, to analyze and to investigate, to contrast and to compare, until he has obtained some accurate knowledge of those outward elements which are permeated by the inward influence and powers of the Holy Spirit of God. As he wearisomely traces out the subtle distinctions that underlie some illative particle, or characterize some doubtful preposition, let him cheer himself with the reflection that every effort of thought he is thus enabled to make, is (with God's blessing) a step towards the inner shrine, a nearer approach to a recognition of the thoughts of an Apostle, yea, a less dim perception of the mind of Christ.

No one who feels deeply upon the subject of inspiration will allow himself to be beguiled into an indifference to the mysterious interest that attaches itself to the very grammar of the New Testament.

I will then plead no excuse that I have made my notes so exclusively critical and grammatical. I rejoice rather that the awakening and awakened interest for theology in this country is likely to afford me a plea and a justification for confining myself to a single province of sacred literature. Already, I believe, theologians are coming to the opinion that the time for compiled commentaries is passing away. Our resources are now too abundant for the various details of criticism, lexicography, grammar, exegesis, history, archæology, and doctrine, to be happily or harmoniously blended in one mass. One mind is scarcely sufficiently comprehensive to grasp properly these various subjects; one judgment is scarcely sufficiently discriminating to arrive at just conclusions on so many topics. The sagacious critic, the laborious lexicographer, the patient grammarian, the profound exegete, the suggestive historian, and the impartial theologian, are, in the present state of biblical science, never likely to be united in one person. Excellence in any one department is now difficult; in all, impossible. I trust, then, that the time is coming when theologians will carry out, especially in the New Testament, the principle of the division of labor, and selecting that sphere of industry for which they are more particularly qualified, will, in others, be content to accept the results arrived at by the labors of their contemporaries.[1]

[1] In the present Epistle, there are distinct and instructive instances of the application of this principle. Hilgenfeld has published a recent edition of the Epistle to the Galatians, in which distinct prominence is given to historical and chronological investigations. Dr. Brown has lately devoted some expository discourses nearly exclusively to the doctrine and practical teaching of the Epistle; while Mr. Veitch has supplied him with grammatical annotations. Both of these works have their demerits as well as their merits, but, at any rate, they show that their authors had the good sense to confine themselves to those departments of interpretation for which they felt the greatest aptitude.

The most neglected portion of the New Testament literature is its lexicography; and this is the more inexcusable, as the excellent concordance of Bruder has been now twelve years before the world. I have here suffered greatly from want of sound help; and in addition to having frequently to draw solely from my own scanty resources in this department, and to leave my own more immediate subject to discuss points which I should have gladly found done to my hand, I have also had the thankless task of perpetually putting my readers on their guard against the overhasty and inaccurate classifications of Bretschneider and others. I have generally found Bretschneider's Lexicon the best; but the pages of my commentary will abundantly show how little reliance I have been able to place upon him. I rejoice to say that Dr. Scott, master of Baliol College, is engaged on a Lexicon to the N. T.; and those who know his eminent qualifications for the task must feel, as I do, the most perfect confidence in the way in which it will be executed. I regret that it was too little advanced to be of any use to me in this commentary. The general lexicon (beside that of Stephens) which I have chiefly used, is the edition of Passow's Lexicon by Palm and Rost, which I cannot help thinking is by very far the best lexicon, in a moderate compass, that we at present possess. The prepositions, in particular, are treated remarkably well, and very comprehensively.

The synonyms of the Greek Testament, a *most* important subject, have been greatly neglected. We have now a genial little volume, from one who always writes felicitously and attractively upon such subjects; but the agreeable author will not, I am sure, be offended when I say that it can scarcely be deemed otherwise than, as he himself modestly terms it, a slight contribution to the subject. We may fairly trust that an author who has begun so well will continue his labors in a more extended and comprehensive form. As Mr. Trench's work came too late into my hands, I have principally used the imperfect work of Tittman; but I perfectly agree with Mr. Trench in his estimate of its merits.

In the Grammar of the N. T. we are now in a fairly promising state. The very admirable work of Winer has completely rehabilitated the subject. It is a volume that I have studied with the closest attention, and to which I am under profound obligations. Still, it would not be candid if I did not admit that it has its weak points. I do not consider the treatment of the particles (a most important subject in St. Paul's epistles) at all equal to that of the prepositions, or by any means commensurate with our wants on this portion of grammar; the cases also might, perhaps, be more successfully handled. The great fault of the book is its superabundance of reference to the notes and commentaries on classical authors. In many cases these are of high importance; but, in a vast quantity of others, as I have often found to my cost, but little information is to be derived from the source to which the reader is referred. Mr. Green's *Grammar* I consider a work of great ability, but too short and unsystematic to be of the use it might otherwise have been to the student. I have, therefore, been obliged to use freely other grammatical subsidies than those which more particularly bear upon the New Testament.[1] My object has been throughout to make my references more to grammars and professed repertories of similar information, than to notes or commentaries on classical authors; for I am convinced that a *good* reference to a good grammar, though not a very showy evidence of research, is a truly valuable assistance; while a discursive note in an edition of a classic, from its want of a context, frequently supplies little real information. I have allowed myself greater latitude in references to the notes of commentators on the N. T., for here the similarity of language, and frequently of subject, constitutes a closer bond of union. In particular, I have used Fritzche's edition of the Romans nearly as a grammar, so full is it and so elaborate in all details of language. As a grammarian, I entertain for him the highest respect; but I confess my sympathy with him as a theologian is not great, nor can I do otherwise than deplore the unjust levity with which he often treats the Greek Fathers, and the tone of bitterness and asperity which he assumes towards the learned and pious Tholuck. It is a sad evidence of an untouched heart and unchastened spirit, when a commentator on the New Testament leaves the written traces of his bitterness on the margins of the Covenant of Love.

The same principle that has induced me to refer to repertories and systematic treatises on grammar, has also influenced me whenever I have been led into dogmatical questions. I have sought, in most cases, information from writers who have made the whole subject their study. I have freely used Bishop's Bull's *Harmonia Apostolica*, Waterland's *Works*, and such other of our great English divines as I have the good fortune to be acquainted with. I have used with profit the recent and popular treatise on St. Paul's doctrine by Usteri, and that by Neander in his *Planting of Christianity;* both of which, with, perhaps, some reservations, may be recommended to the student. I regret that I cannot speak with so much freedom of the discussions of the clever and critical Ferdinand Baur in his *Apostel Paulus.* I have referred to him in a few cases, for his unquestionable ability has seemed to demand it, but it has been always cautiously and warily; nor do I at all wish to commend him to the notice of any student except of

1 I have especially used the admirable and (in my opinion) wholly unrivalled syntax of Bernhardy, the good compendious syntax of Madvig, the somewhat heavy treatise on the same subject by Scheuerlein, Jelf's Grammar, and the small Greek grammar by Dr. Donaldson, which, though unpretending in form and succinct in its nature, will never be consulted, even by the advanced student, without the greatest advantage. On the particles, I have principally used the somewhat clumsy though useful work of Hartung, and the very able and voluminous notes of Klotz on *Devarius.* This latter work the student will rarely consult in vain. I have also derived some assistance from Thiersch's very good dissertation on the *Pentateuch.*

advanced knowledge and of fully fixed principles. The other books and authorities which I have cited will sufficiently speak for themselves.

I desire briefly, in conclusion, to allude to the general principles which I have adopted in the construction of the text, the compilation of the notes, and the revision of the translation, and to record my many obligations.

(I.) The text is substantially that of Tischendorf:[1] the only deviations from it that I have felt compelled to make form the subject of the critical notes which are, at intervals, appended to the text. Changes have been made in punctuation; but these, generally speaking, have not been such as to require special notice. I have here applied the principle of division of labor which I venture to advocate. It has always seemed to me that it is at least a very hazardous, if not a presumptuous undertkaing, for any man, however good a scholar, to construct an original text without eminent qualifications for that task. Years of patient labor must have been devoted to those studies; an unflagging industry in collecting, and a persistent sagacity in sifting evidence, must be united in the biblical critic, or his labors will be worse than useless. Those who have not these advantages will do well to rely upon others, reserving, however, to themselves (if they are honest men and independent thinkers) the task of scrutinizing, testing, and, if need be, of expressing dissent from the results arrived at by those whom they follow. I have humbly endeavored thus to act with regard to the text of the present epistle; where there has seemed reason to depart from Tischendorf (and he is *far* from infallible), I have done so, and have in all cases acted on fixed principles which time, and, above all, failures, have taught me. For a novice like myself to obtrude my critical canons on the reader would be only so much aimless presumption. I will only say that I can by no means assent to a blind adherence to external evidence, especially where the preponderance is not marked, and the internal evidence of importance; still, on the other hand, I regard with the greatest jealousy and suspicion any opposition to the nearly coincident testimony of the uncial MSS., unless the internal evidence be of a most strong and decisive character. I have always endeavored, first, to ascertain the exact nature of the diplomatic evidence; secondly, that of what I have termed *paradiplomatic* arguments (I must apologize for coining the word), by which I mean the apparent probabilities of erroneous transcription, permutation of letters, itacism, and so forth; thirdly and lastly, the internal evidence, whether resting on apparent deviations from the *usus*

[1] It was long with me a subject of anxious thought whether I should adopt the text of Lachmann (for whose critical abilities I have a profound respect), or that of Tischendorf. The latter I consider inferior to Lachmann in talent, scholarship, and critical acumen. But as a palæographer he stands infinitely higher, as a man of energy and industry he is unrivalled, and as a critic he has learnt from what he has suffered. Moreover, he is with us, still learning, still gathering, still toiling; while Lachmann's edition, with all its excellences and all its imperfections, must now remain as he has left it to us.

scribendi of the sacred author, or the *propensio*, be it *critica*, *dogmatica*, or *epexegetica*, on the part of the copyist. I have also endeavored to make the critical notes as perspicuous as the nature of the subject will permit, by grouping the separate classes of authorities, uncial manuscripts (MSS.), cursive manuscripts (mss.), versions (Vv.), and Fathers (Ff.), Greek and Latin, and in some measure familiarizing the uneducated eye to comprehend these perplexing, yet deeply interesting particulars. The symbols I have used are either those of Tischendorf (to whose cheap and useful edition I refer the reader), or else self-explanatory. I cannot leave this part of the subject without earnestly advising the younger student to acquire, at least in outline, a knowledge of the history and details of sacred criticism, and I can recommend him no better general instructor than Dr. Davidson, in the second volume of his excellent treatise on Biblical criticism.

(II.) With regard to the notes, I would wish first to remark, that they neither are, nor pretend to be, original. I have consulted all the best modern, and, I believe, the best ancient authorities, wherever they seemed likely to avail me in the line of interpretation I had marked out to myself. But as I have endeavored to confine myself principally to critical and grammatical details, numerous authors of high position and merit in other provinces of interpretation have unavoidably been, though not unconsulted, still not generally cited. Hence, though I entertain a deep reverence for the exegetical abilities of some of the Latin Fathers, I have never been able to place that reliance on their scholarship which I thankfully and admiringly recognize in the great Greek commentators. Many of our popular English expositors I have been obliged, from the same reasons, to pass over; for to quote an author merely to find fault with him, is a process with which I have no sympathy. I have studied to make my citations, *in malam partem*, on a fixed principle. In the first place, I hope I have always done it with that quick sense of my own weakness, imperfection, and errors, that is the strongest incentive to charitable judgments, and with that gentleness which befits a commentator on one whose affections were among the warmest and deepest that ever dwelt in mortal breast. In the second place, I have, I trust, rarely done it except where the contrast seemed more distinctly to show out what I conceived the true interpretation; where, in fact, the shadow was needed to enhance the light. Thirdly, I have sometimes felt that the allegiance I owe to Divine Truth, and the profound reverence I entertain for the very letter of Scripture, has required me to raise my voice, feeble as it is, against mischievous interpretations and rash criticism. The more pleasant duty of quoting *in bonam partem* has also been regulated by a system; first and foremost, of endeavoring to give every man his due; secondly, of supporting myself by the judgments and wisdom of others. I have, however, in no case sought to construct those catenæ of names, which it seems now the fashion of commentators[1] to link together in assent or dissent; for whenever I have examined one in detail, I have invariably found that the authors, thus huddled together, often introduced such countervailing statements as made their collective opinion anything but unanimous. This easy display of erudition, and of error, cannot be too much reprobated.

The portions upon which I have most dwelt are the particles, the cases, the prepositions, and, as far as I have been able, the compound verbs; but on this latter subject I have keenly felt the want of help, and have abundantly regretted that Winer never has completed the work he projected. If in the discussions on the particles I may have seemed wearisome or hypercritical, let me crave the reader's indulgence, and remind him of the excessive difficulties that have ever been felt and acknowledged in the connection of thought in St. Paul's Epistles. I hope no one will think my pains have here been misplaced. That my notes have visibly overlaid my text will, I fear, be urged against me. This I could have avoided by a more crowded page, or by disuniting the text and the notes; but I prefer bearing the charge to perplexing the reader's eye with close typography, or distracting his attention by references to an isolated text. The notes have been pared down, in some cases, to the very verge of obscurity; but in so difficult an epistle, after all possible curtailing, they must still be in disproportion to the text.

(III.) The last portion I have to notice is the translation. This it seemed desirable to append as a brief but comprehensive summary of the interpretations advanced in the notes. The profound respect I entertain for our own noble version would have prevented me, as it did Hammond, from attempting any performance of this nature, if I had not seen that a few corrections, made on a fixed principle, would enable the Authorized Version adequately to reflect the most advanced state of modern scholarship. The Authorized Version has this incalculable advantage, that it is a truly *literal* translation, —the only form of translation that can properly and reverently be adopted in the case of the holy Scriptures. Of the two other forms of translation, the idiomatic and the paraphrastic, I fully agree with Mr. Kennedy (*Preface to Transl. of Demosth.*) in the opinion that the former is most suitable for the general run of classical authors; while the latter may possibly be useful in some philosophical or political treatises, where the matter, rather than the manner, is the subject of study. But in the holy Scriptures every peculiar expression, even at the risk of losing an idiomatic turn, *must* be retained. Many words, especially the prepositions, have a positive dogmatical and theological significance, and to qualify them by a popular turn or dilute them by a paraphrase, is dangerous in the extreme. It is here that the excellence of our Authorized Version is so notably conspicuous; while it is studiedly close

[1] I regret to find that Professor Eadie, in his learned and laborious commentary on the Ephesians, has adopted this method; in some cases, e. g. p. 15, his authorities occupy five full lines of the commentary.

and literal, it also, for the most part, preserves the idiom of our language in the most happy and successful way. It has many of the merits of an idiomatic translation, and none of the demerits of what are popularly called literal translations, though they commonly only deserve the name of un-English metaphrases. A paraphrastic translation, such as that adopted by Messrs. Conybeare and Howson, I cannot but regard as in many ways unfitted for holy Scripture. I have, then, adopted the Authorized Version, and have only permitted myself to depart from it where it appeared to be *incorrect*, *inexact*, *insufficient*, or *obscure*, whether from accident or (as is alleged) from design. The citations I have appended from eight other versions will, perhaps, prove interesting, and will show the general reader what a "concordia discors" prevails among all the older English Versions,[1] and how closely and how faithfully the contributors to the Authorized Version adhered to their instructions to consult certain of the older translations, and not to depart from the Standard Version which had last preceded them except distinctly necessitated. Thus the Authorized Version is the accumulation, as well as the last and most perfect form of the theological learning of fully two hundred and thirty years. From such a translation, he must be a bold and confident man who would depart far, without the greatest caution and circumspection.

(IV.) Finally, I feel myself bound to specify a few of the commentators to whom I am more specially indebted.

Of the older writers I have paid the most unremitting attention to Chrysostom and Theodoret: for the former especially, often as a scholar, always as an exegete, I entertain the greatest respect and admiration. Of our older English commentators, Hammond has been of the greatest service to me; his scholarship is, generally speaking, very accurate, and his erudition profound. The short commentary of Bishop Fell I have never consulted without profit. Bengel's *Gnomon* has, of course, never been out of my hands. Of later writers I should wish to specify Dr. Peile, from whose commentary I have derived many valuable suggestions. I frequently differ from him in the explanation of *νόμος* without the article; but I have always found him an accurate scholar, and especially useful for his well-selected citations from Calvin. To the late lamented Professor Scholefield's *Hints for a New Translation* I have always attended. The translation of Conybeare and Howson has been of some use; but, as far as my experience goes, it appears the least happily executed portion of their valuable work. Dr. Brown's *Expository Discourses on the Galatians* is a book written in an excellent spirit, of great use and value in an exegetical point of view, but not always to be relied upon as a grammatical guide. I cannot pass over Dr. Bloomfield, though he has not been of so much use to me as I could have wished. To the recent Ger-

1 I have also consulted Abp. Newcome's, and all the later versions of any celebrity, even the Unitarian, but have derived from them no assistance whatever.

man commentators I am under the greatest obligations, both in grammar and exegesis, though not in theology. Meyer more as a grammarian, De Wette more as an exegete, command the highest attention and respect; to the former especially, though a little too Atticistic in his prejudices, my fullest acknowledgments are due. The commentaries of Winer and Schott are both excellent; to the latter, Meyer seems to have been greatly indebted. Usteri has generally caught most happily the spirit of his author; his scholarship is not profound, but his exegesis is very good. Rückert, more voluminous and more laborious, has always repaid the trouble of perusal. The two works in the best theological spirit are those of Olshausen and Windischmann: the latter, though a Romanist, and by no means uninfluenced by decided prejudices, always writes in a reverent spirit, and is commonly remarkable for his good sense, and not unfrequently his candor. Baumgarten-Crusius I have found of very little value. Hilgenfeld is very useful in historical questions, but has a bad tone in exegesis, and follows Meyer too closely to be of much use as an independent grammatical expositor.

These are not more than one-third of the expositors I have consulted, but are those which, for my own satisfaction, and the guidance of younger students, I should wish to specify.

I have now only to commit this first part of my work, with all its imperfections, faults, and errors, to the charitable judgment of the reader. I have written it, alone and unassisted, with only a country clergyman's scanty supply of books, in a neighborhood remote from large libraries and literary institutions; and though I have done my uttermost to overcome these great disadvantages, I can myself see and feel with deep regret how often I have failed. I commend myself, then, not only to the kind judgment, but I will also venture to add, the kind assistance of my readers; for I shall receive and acknowledge with great thankfulness any rectifications of errors or any suggestions that may be addressed to me at the subjoined direction.

I will conclude with earnest prayer to Almighty God, in the name of his ever-blessed Son, that He may so bless this poor and feeble effort to disclose the outward significance, the jots and tittles of His word, that He may make it a humble instrument of awakening in the hearts of others the desire to look deeper into the inward meaning, to mark, to read, and to understand, and with a lowly and reverent spirit to ponder over the hidden mysteries, the deep warnings, and the exhaustless consolations of the Book of Life.

To Him be all honor, all glory, and all praise.

C. J. ELLICOTT.

GLASTON, UPPINGHAM, SEPTEMBER, 1854.

PREFACE

TO THE SECOND EDITION.

The present edition is but little different from the first in the results arrived at, and in the statement of the principles on which those results mainly rest; but, in the details and construction of many of the notes, it will be found to involve changes both of diction and arrangement.

These changes have been found to be wholly unavoidable. The first edition was not only written with a scanty supply of books, and with a very limited knowledge of the contents of the Ancient Versions, but was constructed on principles which, though since found to be sound and trustworthy, do not appear in some cases to have been applied with sufficient ease and simplicity, or to have received a sufficiently extended range of application. It is useless to disguise the fact, that what at first professed to be only purely critical and purely grammatical, has by degrees become also exegetical; and has so far intruded into what is dogmatical, as to give systematic references to the leading treatises upon the points or subjects under discussion. The extremely kind reception that the different portions of this series have met with, has led in two ways to these gradual alterations. On the one hand, the not unnatural desire to make each portion more worthy of the approval that had been extended towards its predecessor, has been silently carrying me onward into widening fields of labor; on the other hand, the friendly criticisms that I have received from time to time have led me to retrench what has seemed unedifying, to dwell with somewhat less technicality of language on the peculiarities of grammar and construction, and yet at the same time to enter more fully upon all that has seemed to bring out the connection of thought and sequence of argument.

The latter portions of my work have been based on these somewhat remodelled principles, and — if I may trust the opinions of, perhaps, too partial and friendly judges — so far successfully, that I shall apparently be wise to keep them as the sort of standard to which, if God mercifully grant me life and strength, former portions of the series (wherever they may seem to need it) may be brought up, and future portions conformed.

The present edition, then, is an effort to make my earliest and decidedly most incomplete work as much as possible resemble those which apparently have some greater measures of maturity and completeness. It has involved, and I do not seek to disguise it, very great labor — labor, perhaps, not very much less than writing a new commentary. For though the notes remain *substantially* what they were before, and though I have found no reason to retract former opinions, except in about four or five debatable and contested passages,[1] I have still found that the interpolation of new matter, and the introduction of exegetical comments have obliged me, in many cases, to alter the arrangement of the whole note, and occasionally even to face the weary and irksome task of total re-writing, and reconstruction. I rejoice, however, now at length to feel that the reader of the later portions of this series will find no very appreciable difference when he turns back to this edition of the first portion. He will now no longer be without those invaluable guides, the Ancient Versions; he will, I trust, find but few links missing in the continuous illustration of the arrangement, scarcely any omission of a comment on important differences of reading, and on points of doctrinal difficulty no serious want of references to the best treatises and sermons of our great English divines. At the same time he will find the mode of interpretation and tenor of grammatical discussions precisely the same. Though the details may be often differently grouped, the principles are left wholly unchanged; and this, not from any undue predilection for former opinions, but simply from having found, by somewhat severe testing and trial, that they do appear to be sound and consistent.

For a notice of details, it will be now sufficient to refer to the prefaces to earlier portions of this series, more especially to those prefixed to the third, fourth, and fifth volumes, in which the different component elements of the notes above alluded to will be found noticed and illustrated at some length. This only may be added, that particular care has been taken to adjust the various references, especially to such authorities of frequent occurrence as Winer's *Grammar of the New Testament*, to the paging of the latest edition.[2] Where, from inability to obtain access to the last edition of works previously

1 These changes of opinion will be found noticed in their different places. I *believe* the only passages are chap. ii. 6, προσανέθεντο; iii. 4, ἐπάθετε; iii. 19 (in part), iv. 17, ἐκκλεῖσαι; vi. 17 (slightly), βαστάζω.

2 I have also retained the references to the *translation* of Neander's *Planting*, as published by Mr. Bohn, and of Müller's *Doctrine of Sin*, as published by Messrs. Clark, simply because the presence of these volumes in two justly popular series makes it probable that many readers may have these works, who have not, and, perhaps, may not be in the habit of consulting the originals. The translation of the latter of these works has, I believe, been somewhat severely criticized. I fear I am unable to defend it; but, as the allusions to Müller in my notes relate more to general principles than to individual passages, I do not think the general reader will suffer much from the inaccuracies or harshness of the translation.

quoted, this has not been done, the reader will commonly find some allusion to the continued use of the authority in its earlier form.[1]

I may also remark that, in deference to the wishes of some of my critics, I have prefixed to the Epistle a few sentences of introduction, giving a summary account of the results of recent historical criticism. This portion of sacred literature has been so fully treated, both by Dr. Davidson and Dean Alford, and has farther received so much valuable illustration from the excellent *Life of Saint Paul* by Messrs. Conybeare and Howson, that I feel it now unnecessary to do more than to group together a few remarks for the benefit, not of the critical scholar, but of the general student, to whom these brief notices sometimes prove acceptable and suggestive.

I must not conclude without expressing my hearty sense of the value of several commentaries that have appeared since the publication of my first edition. I desire particularly to specify those of my friends, Dean Alford, and Mr. Bagge, and the thoughtful commentary of my kind correspondent, Dr. Turner, of New York. Of the great value of the first of these it is unnecessary for me to speak; my present notes will show how carefully I have considered the interpretations advanced in that excellent work, and how much I rejoice to observe that the results at which we arrive are not marked by many differences of opinion. The edition of Mr. Bagge will be found very useful in critical details, in the careful and trustworthy references which it supplies to the older standard works of lexicography, and in what may be termed phraseological annotations. The third of these works differs so much from the present in its plan and general construction, as to make the points of contact between us so much fewer than I could wish; but I may venture to express the opinion, that the reader who finds himself more interested in general interpretation than in scholastic detail, will rarely consult the explanatory notes without profit and instruction. The recent edition of Professor Jowett has not been overlooked; but after the careful and minute examination of his *Commentary on the Thessalonians*, which I made last year, I have been reluctantly forced into the opinion that our systems of interpretation are so radically different, as to make a systematic reference to the works of this clever writer not so necessary as might have been the case if our views on momentous subjects had been more accordant and harmonious.

Before I draw these remarks to a close, I must not fail gratefully to return my heartfelt thanks for the numerous kind and important suggestions which I have received from private friends and from public criticism. By

[1] In the note on ὀρθοποδοῦσιν (chap. ii. 14), I have still been unable to verify the references to Theodorus Studita. The best edition, I believe, is that of Sirmond, and this I have used, as well as one or two others, but without effect. I should be glad if some reader, experienced in Bibliography, could direct me to the edition probably referred to.

this aid I have been enabled to correct whatever has seemed doubtful or erroneous; and to these friendly comments the more perfect form in which this commentary now appears before the student is, in many respects, justly due. From my readers, and those who are interested in these works, I fear I must now claim some indulgence as to the future rate of my progress. While I may presume to offer to them the humble assurance that, while life and health are spared to me, the onward course of these volumes will not be suspended, I must not suppress the fact, that the duties to which it has now pleased God to call me are such as must necessarily cause the appearance of future commentaries to take place at somewhat longer intervals. Those who are acquainted with studies of this nature, will, I feel sure, agree with me, that it is impossible to hurry such works; nay, more, I am convinced that all sober thinkers will concur in the opinion, that there is no one thing for which a writer will have hereafter to answer before the dread tribunal of God with more terrible strictness, than for having attempted to explain the everlasting Words of Life with haste and precipitation. When we consider only the errors and failures that mark every stage in our most deliberate and most matured progress, even in merely secular subjects, we may well pause before we presume to hurry through the sanctuary of God, with the dust and turmoil of worldly, self-seeking, and irreverent speed.

May the great Father of Lights look down with mercy on this effort to illustrate His word, and overrule it to His glory, His honor, and His praise.

CAMBRIDGE, 28TH JANUARY, 1859.

INTRODUCTION.

This animated, argumentative, and highly characteristic Epistle would appear to have been written by St. Paul not very long after his journey through Galatia and Phrygia (Acts xviii. 23), and as the ταχέως (ch. i. 6) *seems* to suggest (but comp. notes, and see contra, Conyb. and Hows. *St. Paul*, Vol. II. p. 164, ed. 2), towards the commencement of the lengthened abode at Ephesus (Autumn 54 or 55 to Pentecost 57 or 58; comp. Acts xix. 10, xx. 31, 1 Cor. xvi. 8), forming apparently the first of that series of Epistles (Gal., 1 Cor., 2 Cor., Rom.) which intervenes between the Epp. to the Thessalonians and the four Epp. of the first captivity (Col., Eph., Philem., Phil.). It was addressed to the churches of the province of Galatia (ch. i. 2), — a province of which the inhabitants could not only boast a Gallic origin, but also appear to have retained some of the peculiarities of the Gallic character; see notes on ch. i. 6, iii. 1. The Epistle was not improbably encyclical in its character (see Olshaus. on ch. i. 2, and notes on ch. vi. 17), and was called forth by the somewhat rapid lapse of the Galatians into the errors of Judaism, which were now being disseminated by unprincipled and self-seeking teachers (comp. ch. vi. 12, 13) with a dangerous and perhaps malignant activity. Against these errors the Apostle had already solemnly protested (ch. i. 9), but, as this Epistle shows, with at present so little abiding effect, that the Judaizing teachers in Galatia, possibly recruited with fresh emissaries from Jerusalem, were now not only spreading dangerous error, but assailing the very apostolic authority of him who had founded these churches (comp. ch. iv. 13), and who loved them so well (ch. iv. 19, 20).

In accordance with this the Epistle naturally divides itself into *two* controversial portions, and a concluding portion which is more directly hortatory and practical. The *first* portion (ch. i. ii.) the Apostle devotes to a *defence* of his office, and especially to a proof of his divine calling and of his independence of all human authority (ch. i. 11—ii. 10), — nay, his very opposition to it in the person of St. Peter, when that Apostle had acted with inconsistency (ch. ii. 11—21). In the *second*, or what may be called the *polemical* portion (ch. iii. iv.), the Apostle, both by argument (ch. iii. 1, sq.), appeal (ch. iv. 12—20), and illustration (ch. iv. 1—7, 21—30), establishes the truth of the fundamental positions that justification is by faith, and not by the deeds of the law (ch. iii. 5, 6), and that they alone who are of faith are the inheritors of the promise, and the true children of Abraham; comp. notes on ch. iii. 29. The *third* portion (ch. v. vi.) is devoted to hortatory warning (ch. iv. 31—v. 6), illustrations of what constitutes a *real* fulfilment of the law (ch. v. 13—26), practical instructions (ch. vi. 1—10), and a vivid recapitulation (ch. vi. 11—16).

The genuineness and authenticity are supported by distinct external testimony (Irenæus, *Hær.* III. 7. 2, Tertull. *de Præscr.* § 6; see Lardner, *Credibility*, Vol. II. p. 163 sq., Davidson, *Introduction*, Vol. II. p. 318 sq.), and, as we might infer from the strikingly characteristic style of the Epistle, have never been doubted by any reputable critic; comp. Meyer *Einleit.* p. 8.

Sample Pages.

THE EPISTLE TO THE GALATIANS.

CHAPTER I. 1.

Apostolic address and salutation, concluding with a doxology.

ΠΑΥΛΟΣ ἀπόστολος, οὐκ ἀπ' ἀνθρώπων οὐδὲ δι' ἀνθρώπου, ἀλλὰ διὰ Ἰησοῦ

1. ἀπόστολος] '*an Apostle*,' in the higher and more especial meaning of the word; and as such (particularly when enhanced by the succeeding clause), a forcible protest against the Judaists, who probably refused to apply it in this particular sense to any out of the significant number of the Twelve; comp. Hilgenf. *Galaterbrief*, p. 107. It may be observed (comp. Maurice, *Unity of N. T.* p. 402) that the question involved more than mere personal slander (τὴν γεγενημένην διαβολήν, Theod.): in asserting the preëminence of the Twelve over St. Paul, they were practically denying Christ's perpetual rule over His church. With regard to the meaning of ἀπόστολος in St. Paul's Epp., we may remark that in a few instances (*e. g.* 2 Cor. viii. 23, and most probably Phil. ii. 25, see notes *in loc.*), it appears to be used in its simple etymological sense. In 2 Cor. xi. 13, 1 Thess. ii. 6, the meaning may be thought doubtful; but in Rom. xvi. 7, οἵτινές εἰσιν ἐπίσημοι ἐν τοῖς ἀποστόλοις (commonly cited in this sense, Conyb. and Hows. *St. Paul*, Vol. I. p. 463), the correct translation appears certainly that of Fritzsche, 'quippe qui in Apostolorum collegio bene audiant:' compare Winer, *RWB.* s. v. *Apostel*, Vol. I. p. 69, note 2. The various applications of this word in eccles. writers are noticed by Suicer, *Thesaur.* s. v. Vol. I. p. 475 sq., Hamm. *on Rom.* xvi. 7. οὐκ ἀπ' ἀνθρώπων οὐδὲ δι' ἀνθρώπου] '*not from men nor by man*,' 'not from men as an ultimate, nor through man as a mediate authority,' — the prep. ἀπὸ here correctly denoting the *causa remotior* (Winer, *Gr.* § 47. b, p. 331, Bernhardy, *Syntax*, v. 12, p. 222), διά, the *causa medians;* see Winer, § 50. 6, p. 372, Green, *Gr.* p. 299. 'Ἀπὸ is thus not 'for ὑπό,' Brown *in loc.* (comp. Rück., Olsh.), as the use of ἀπὸ for ὑπό, especially after passives, though found apparently in some few instances in earlier writers (Poppo, *Thucyd.* I. 17, Vol. I. p. 158), occasionally in later (Bernhardy, *Synt.* v. 12, p. 224), and frequently in Byzantine Greek, does not appear in St. Paul's Epistles, nor in any *decisive* instance in the N. T.; comp. Winer, *Gr.* § 47. b, p. 332, note. In all cases the distinction between the prepp. seems sufficiently clear: ὑπὸ points to an action which results from

Χριστοῦ καὶ Θεοῦ πατρὸς τοῦ ἐγείραντος αὐτὸν ἐκ νεκρῶν,

a more immediate and *active*, ἀπὸ to a less immediate and more *passive* cause; comp. Herm. Soph. *Elect.* 65, and see Rom. xiii. 1 (*Lachm., Tisch.*), where St. Paul's correct use of these prepp. may be contrasted with that of Chrysost. *in loc.* There are, indeed, few points more characteristic of the Apostle's style than his varied but accurate use of prepp. esp. of two or more in the same or in immediately contiguous clauses (*e. g.* εἰς . . . ἐπί, Rom. iii. 22; ἐξ . . . διὰ . . . εἰς, xi. 36; ἐπὶ . . . διὰ . . . ἐν, Eph. iv. 6; ἐν . . . διὰ . . . εἰς, Col. i. 16), for the purpose of more precise definition or limitation; comp. Winer, *Gr. l. c.*, p. 372. δι' ἀνθρώπου] '*through man,*' οὐκ ἀνθρώπῳ χρησάμενος ὑπουργῷ, Theod., — not with any studied force in the singular as pointing to any particular individual (Mosheim, *Reb. ante Constant.* p. 70), nor yet for solemnity's sake, as more exclusive (Alf.), but simply as thus forming a more natural antithesis to the following διὰ Ἰησοῦ Χριστοῦ. καὶ Θεοῦ πατρός] '*and God the Father;*' in noticeably close union with Ἰησ. Χρ., both being under the vinculum of the single preposition διά; comp. verse 3. We might here not unnaturally have expected καὶ ἀπὸ Θεοῦ πατρός, as forming a more exact antithesis to what precedes, and as also obviating a ref. of διὰ to the *causa principalis* (Gal. i. 15); comp., however, 1 Cor. i. 9, and see Winer, *Gr.* § 47. i. p. 339, and the list in Fritz. *on Rom.* i. 5, Vol. I. 15, — but exclude from it 1 Pet. ii. 13, 14. In the present case the use of διὰ seems due partly to a brevity of expression, which is obviously both natural and admissible where it is not necessary to draw strict lines between agency, origin, and medium (comp. Rom. xi. 34, and even Plato, *Sympos.* p. 186 E, διὰ τοῦ θεοῦ κυβερνᾶται), and partly to an instinctive association of the two Persons of the blessed Trinity in his choice and calling as an Apostle. To urge this as a *direct* evidence for the ὁμοουσία of the Father and the Son (Chrys., Theod.) may perhaps be rightly deemed precarious; yet still there *is* something *very* noticeable in this use of a common preposition with both the first and second Persons of the Trinity, by a writer so cumulative, and yet for the most part so exact, in his use of prepositions as St. Paul. Θεοῦ πατρός] '*God the Father;*' not in the ordinary inclusive reference to all men (De W., Alf.), nor with more particular reference to Christians, scil. 'our Father' (Ust. al.), but, as the associated clause seems rather to suggest, with special and exclusive reference to the preceding subject, our Lord Jesus Christ; so, perhaps too expressly, Syr. ܐܒܘܗܝ [patrem ejus]; comp. Pearson, *Creed*, Art. I. Vol. I. p. 42, (ed. Burt.).

τοῦ ἐγείραντος κ. τ. λ.] '*who raised Him from the dead.*' The addition of this designation has been very differently explained. While there may probably be a *remote* reference to the fact that it is upon the resurrection of Jesus Christ that our faith rests (1 Cor. xv. 17; comp. Usteri, *Paul. Lehrbegr.* II. I. I, p. 97, 98), and from it all gifts of grace derived (Alf.), the context seems clearly to suggest that the more *immediate* reference is to the fact that the Apostle's call was received from Christ in His exalted and glorified position (1 Cor. ix. 1, 1 Cor. xv. 8); 'verax etiam novissimus Apostolus qui per Jesum Christum totum jam Deum post resurrectionem ejus missus est,' August. *in loc.*; see Brown, *Galatians*, p. 22. The article with νεκρῶν appears regularly omitted in this and similar phrases, except Eph. v. 14, and (with ἀπὸ) Matth. xiv. 2, xxviii. 7, al.; see Winer, *Gr.* § 19, p. 112.

[2] καὶ οἱ σὺν ἐμοὶ πάντες ἀδελφοί, ταῖς ἐκκλησίαις τῆς Γαλατίας.
[3] χάρις ὑμῖν καὶ εἰρήνη ἀπὸ Θεοῦ πατρὸς καὶ Κυρίου ἡμῶν Ἰησοῦ
Χριστοῦ, [4] τοῦ δόντος ἑαυτὸν περὶ τῶν ἁμαρτιῶν ἡμῶν, ὅπως

2. πάντες] Emphatic: 'ceteros qui secum erant *omnes* commotos adversus eos ostendit,' Ps. Ambr. St. Paul frequently adds to his own name that of one or more of his companions, *e. g.* Sosthenes, (1 Cor. i. 1), Timothy, (2 Cor. i. 1, Phil. i. 1, Col. i. 1), Silvanus and Timothy, (1 Thess. i. 1, 2 Thess. i. 1): here, however, to add weight to his admonitions, and to show the unanimity (Chrysost.) that was felt on the subject of the Epistle, he adopts the inclusive term πάντες ἀδελφοί, defining it more closely by οἱ σὺν ἐμοί (Phil. iv. 21),—'all the brethren who are my present companions in my travels and my preaching.' There is, then, no necessity for restricting ἀδελφοὶ to 'official brethren' (Brown, comp. Beza), nor for extending οἱ σὺν ἐμοὶ to the whole Christian community of the place from which the Epistle was written (Erasm., Jowett): in this latter case we should certainly have expected 'with whom I am,' rather than 'who are with me;' see Usteri *in loc.* ταῖς ἐκκλησίαις τῆς Γαλ.] '*to the churches of Galatia;*' plural, and with a comprehensive reference, (πανταχοῦ γὰρ εἷρψεν ἡ νόσος, Theod., comp. Chrys.), the epistle probably being an encyclical letter addressed to the different churches (of Ancyra, Pessinus, Tavium, and other places) throughout the province. The omission of the usual titles of honor or affection seems undoubtedly *intentional* (Chrys.), for in the only other Epistles where the simple τῇ ἐκκλησίᾳ is used, (1 Cor. i. 2, 2 Cor. i. 1, 1 Thess. i. 1, 2 Thess. i. 1), there is in the two former passages the important and qualifying addition τοῦ Θεοῦ, and in the two latter ἐν Θεῷ πατρὶ κ. τ. λ.

3. χάρις ὑμῖν καὶ εἰρήνη] '*Grace to you and peace:*' not *merely* a union of two ordinary forms of Jewish salutation (Fritz. *Rom.* i. 7, Vol. I. p. 23), or of the Greek χαίρειν, and the Hebrew שָׁלוֹם לְךָ, but a greeting of full spiritual significance; χάρις, as Olsh. observes, being the divine love manifesting itself to man, εἰρήνη the state that results from a reception of it. The Oriental and Occidental forms of salutation are thus blended and spiritualized in the Christian greeting; see notes *on Eph.* i. 2, and comp. Koch *on* 1 *Thessal.* p. 60. καὶ Κυρίου κ. τ. λ.] '*and (from) our Lord Jesus Christ.* Strictly speaking, Christ is the mediating imparter of grace, God the direct giver; but just as in verse 1, διὰ was applied both to the Father and the Son, so here, in this customary salutation see *on Phil.* i. 4), ἀπὸ is applied both to the Son and the Father. Olshausen (*on Rom.* i. 7) justly remarks that nothing speaks more decisively for the divinity of our Lord than these juxtapositions with the Father, which pervade the whole language of Scripture.

4. τοῦ δόντος ἑαυτόν] '*who gave Himself,*' scil. to death; more fully expressed 1 Tim. ii. 6, ὁ δοὺς ἑαυτὸν ἀντίλυτρον, comp. Tit. ii. 14. The participial clause serves at the very outset to specify the active principle of the error of the Galatians. The doctrine of the atoning death of Jesus Christ, and a recurrence to the laws of Moses, were essentially incompatible with each other. περὶ τῶν ἁμαρτ. ἡμῶν] '*for our sins,*' scil. to atone for them, Rom. iii. 25, Gal. iii. 13. The reading ὑπὲρ (*Rec*) has but little external support, and is, perhaps, due to dogmatical correction, or to that interchange of περὶ and ὑπὲρ (Fritz. *Rom.* Vol. I. p. 28) of which the MSS. of the

ἐξέληται ἡμᾶς ἐκ τοῦ ἐνεστῶτος αἰῶνος πονηροῦ κατὰ τὸ θέλημα

N. T. present so many traces. Strictly speaking, ὑπέρ, in its ethical sense, retains some trace of its local meaning, 'bending over to protect' (μάχεσθαι ὑπέρ τινος; Donalds. *Gr. Gr.* § 480), and thus points more immediately to the action, than to the object or circumstance from which the action is supposed to spring. The latter relation is more correctly defined by περί, — *e. g.* φοβεῖσθαι περί τινος; see Winer, *Gr.* § 47. e, p. 334, Schæfer. *Demosth.* Vol. I. p. 189, 190. Περί will thus be more naturally used with the thing, 'sins,' ὑπὲρ with the person, 'sinners;' and this, with a few exceptions (*e. g.* 1 Cor. xv. 3, Heb. v. 3), appears the usage of the N. T.; comp. 1 Pet. iii. 18, where both forms occur. Still it must be admitted that both in the N. T., and even in classical Greek (Buttm., *Ind. ad Mid.* p. 188) the distinction between these two prepp. is often scarcely appreciable; see notes *on Eph.* vi. 19, and *on Phil.* i. 7. ὅπως ἐξέληται] '*in order that he might deliver us;*' not 'eximeret,' Beza, but 'eriperet,' Vulg., — the verb ἐξαιρεῖσθαι (only here in St Paul's Epp.) deriving from the context the idea of *rescuing* (δύναμιν σημαίνει τοῦ ῥυσαμένου, Theod. Mops.) as from danger, etc.; comp. Acts xii. 11, xxiii. 27, and appy. xxvi. 17, and see Elsner. *Obs.* Vol. II. p. 170. On the force of ὅπως in the N. T., and its probable distinction from ἵνα, see notes *on* 2 *Thess.* i. 12. ἐκ τοῦ ἐνεστῶτος κ. τ. λ.] '*out of the present evil world;*' not exactly ἐκ τῶν πράξεων τῶν πονηρῶν, Chrysost., still less τοῦ παρόντος βίου, Theod., but simply, — 'the present evil state of things,' see notes *on Eph.* i. 21, where the meaning of αἰών is briefly discussed. It is doubtful whether ὁ ἐνεστὼς αἰὼν is (*a*) simply equivalent to ὁ νῦν αἰών (2 Tim. iv. 10, Tit. ii. 12, see notes), and therefore in opposition to ὁ αἰὼν ὁ μέλλων (comp. Clem. *Cor.* II. 6, ἔστιν δὲ οὗτος ὁ αἰὼν καὶ ὁ μέλλων δύο ἐχθροί), or whether (*b*) it denotes in a more restricted sense 'the commencing age,' the age of faithlessness and the developing powers of Antichrist that had already begun; see Meyer *in loc.* The participle ἐνεστὼς will appy. admit either meaning (comp. Rom. viii. 38, 1 Cor. iii. 22, with 2 Thess. ii. 2, and see exx. in Rost u. Palm, *Lex.*, s. v. Vol. I. p. 929, Schweigh. *Lex. Polyb.* s. v.); the order of the words, however, — not τοῦ πον. αἰῶνος τοῦ ἐνεστ., — and the general and undogmatical character of the passage seem decidedly in favor of (*a*): so distinctly Syr. ܥܠܡܐ ܗܢܐ [hoc sæculo], Vulg., Clarom., 'præsenti sæculo,' and sim. the best of the remaining Vv. In either case the influence of the article appears to extend only to ἐνεστ.; αἰῶνος πονηροῦ forming an explanatory apposition, in effect equivalent to a tertiary predication (Donalds. *Gr.* § 489), 'an evil age as it is,' and pointing out either (*a*) more generally, or (*b*) more specifically, the corrupting influences of the world and its works: see esp. Donalds. *Journal of Sacr. and Class. Philol.* No. II., p. 223. The reading αἰῶνος τοῦ ἐνεστ., adopted by *Lachm.*, has but weak external support [AB; 39; Orig. (3), Did. al.], and is internally suspicious as a grammatical correction.

Θεοῦ καὶ πατρὸς ἡμῶν] '*God and our Father,*' 'Dei et patris nostri,' Vulg., — not 'God, even our Father' (Brown), καί being only the simple copula; see Middleton, *Greek Art.* p. 292, 367 (ed. Rose), and comp. notes *on* 1 *Thess.* iii. 11. The august title ὁ Θεὸς καὶ πατὴρ occurs several times in the N. T., both alone (1 Cor. xv. 24, Col. iii. 17, James i. 27), and with a dependent genitive, viz. (*a*) τοῦ Κυρίου ἡμῶν 'I. X., Rom. xv. 6, Eph. i. 3, 2 Cor. i. 3, xi. 31, Col. i. 3,

τοῦ Θεοῦ καὶ πατρὸς ἡμῶν,
5 ᾧ ἡ δόξα εἰς τοὺς αἰῶνας τῶν αἰώνων· ἀμήν.

I marvel at your speedy lapse to another gospel, which if an angel were to preach, let him be anathema. It is not man but God whom I strive to please.

6 Θαυμάζω ὅτι οὕτως ταχέως μετατίθεσθε

1 Pet. i. 3, and (*b*) ἡμῶν only, as here, Phil. iv. 20, 1 Thess. i. 1, iii. 11, 13, and 2 Thess. ii. 16. Whether in these latter formulæ the gen. depends on both, or only on the latter of the two nouns, cannot be positively decided. No *grammatical* arguments based on the absence of the article are here applicable, as πατὴρ is anarthrous according to rule (Middl. *Gr. Art.* III. 4, § 2, Winer, *Gr.* § 19, 4, p. 116); nor will the most careful investigation of the separate passages afford any *sure* grounds for deciding on *exegetical* principles; contr. Fritz. *Rom.* Vol. III. p. 234. This, however, may be said, that as the term πατὴρ conveys necessarily a *relative* idea, which in theological language admits of many applications (see Suicer, *Thesaur.* s. v. Vol. II. p. 629 sq.), while Θεὸς conveys only one *absolute* idea, it would not seem improbable that the connection of thought in the mind of the inspired writer might lead him in some passages to add a defining gen. to πατὴρ which he did not intend necessarily to be referred to Θεός. The Greek commentators, whose opinion on such a point would be of great value, do not appear to be unanimous: Theod. Mops. *in loc.* and Theodoret, *on Rom.* xvi. 6, refer the gen. to the last nom.; Chrys. *on Eph.* i. 3, leaves it doubtful; see notes *on Eph.* i. 3.

5. ἡ δόξα] '*the glory*,' scil. εἴη not ἔστω; see *on Eph.* i. 2. In this and similar forms of doxology, — excepting that of the angels, Luke ii. 14, and of the multitude, Luke xix. 38, — δόξα regularly takes the article when used alone, *e. g.* Rom. xi. 36, xvi. 27, Eph. iii. 21, Phil. iv. 20, 2 Tim. iv. 18, Heb. xiii. 21, 2 Pet. iii. 18. When joined with one or more substantives it appears sometimes with the art. (1 Pet. iv. 11, Rev. i. 6, vii. 12), sometimes without it (Rom. ii. 10, 1 Tim. i. 17, Jude 25). It is thus difficult to determine whether we have here (*a*) the 'rhetorical' form of the article (Bernhardy, *Synt.* VI. 22, p. 315), 'the glory which especially and alone belongs to God' (comp. Winer, *Gr.* § 18. 1, p. 97), or (*b*) whether δόξα takes the article as an abstract noun (Middl. *Gr. Art.* V. 1). On the whole, (*a*) seems the most natural, and best suited to the context. αἰῶνας τῶν αἰώνων] '*the ages of the ages*,' 'sæcula sæculorum,' Vulg., less precisely Syr. ܠܥܠܡ ܥܠܡܝܢ [sæculum sæculorum]; a semi-Hebraistic expression for a duration of time superlatively (infinitely) long; comp. Winer, *Gr.* § 36. 2, p. 220. The same words occur, Phil. iv. 20, 1 Tim. i. 17, 2 Tim. iv. 18, and frequently in the Apocalypse. Occasionally we meet with the singular αἰὼν τῶν αἰώνων (Eph. iii. 21, comp. Dan. vii. 18), and the perhaps more distinctly Hebraistic αἰὼν τοῦ αἰῶνος, Heb. i. 8 (quotation), Psalm cxi. 10, — but with scarcely any appreciable difference of meaning; see notes *on Eph.* iii. 21. Vorst. (*de Hebraismis N. T.*, p. 325) investigates both this and the similar expression γενεὰς γενεῶν; but his remarks must be received with caution, as on the subject of Hebraisms he cannot now be considered a safe guide.

6. θαυμάζω] '*I marvel*;' 'manifestatis beneficiis, mirari se dicit quod ab Illo potuerint separari,' Ps. Jerome. The idea of wondering at something *blameworthy* is frequently implied in this word: see Rost u. Palm. *Lex.* s. v., and compare Mark vi. 6, John vii. 21, 1 John iii. 13. The further idea which Chrys.

ἀπὸ τοῦ καλέσαντος ὑμᾶς ἐν χάριτι Χριστοῦ εἰς ἕτερον εὐαγγέλιον,

finds in the address, οὐ μόνον ἐντρέπων ..... ὁμοῦ δὲ καὶ δεικνὺς οἵαν ἔχει περὶ αὐτῶν ὑπόνοιαν, ὅτι μεγάλην τινὰ καὶ ἐσπουδασμένην, — does not seem intended. οὕτως ταχέως] '*so quickly*.' After what? In our ignorance of the exact time when the Galatians were converted, as well as the circumstances of their defection, this question cannot be satisfactorily answered. Of the proposed answers, — (*a*) their conversion, Mey., Alf.; (*b*) the Apostle's last visit, Beng., Flatt; or (*c*) the entry of the false teachers, Chrys., Theoph., — the first appears the least, and the last the most probable, as the following verse seems to show who the Apostle had in his thoughts. At any rate the reference of the adverb seems decidedly rather to *time* than *manner* (2 Thess. ii. 2, 1 Tim. v. 22, compare Conyb. and Hows. *in loc.*), however that time be defined. Still all historical deductions from such a passage (Wieseler, *Chronol.* p. 285, Davids. *Introduct.* Vol. II. p. 297) must obviously be debatable and precarious. Grotius appositely cites, in illustration of the levity of the Gallic character, Cæsar, *Bell. Gall.* iv. 5, 'sunt (Galli) in consiliis capiendis mobiles, et novis plerumque rebus student;' comp. *ib.* II. 1, III. 10, 19: see Elsner, *Observ. Sacr.* Vol. II. p. 172.

μετατίθεσθε] '*are going over from, are falling away from*:' present (οὐκ εἶπε μετέθεσθε, ἀλλά, μετατίθεσθε, Chrys., — the defection was still going on), and middle, not passive, as Theod. Mops. (μετάγεσθε, ὡς ἐπὶ ἀψύχων; comp. Heb. vii. 12), Vulg., Clarom., al. While in earlier writers μετατίθεμαι is used both with and without an accusative (γνώμην), in the sense of 'changing an opinion' (see exx. in Rost u. Palm, *Lex.* s. v.), it is as frequently used in later writers in the sense 'descisco,' with prepp. εἰς, πρός, ἐπὶ of the party, etc., *to whom* — *e. g.* Polyb. III. 118, 8, μετατίθεσθαι πρὸς τοὺς Καρχηδονίους — and ἐκ, ἀπό (or a simple gen., Diod. Sic. XVI. 31), of the party, etc., *from whom* the defection has taken place; so Appian, *Bell. Mithr.* 41, ἀπὸ Ἀρχελάου πρὸς Σύλλαν μετατίθεσθαι: comp. 2 Macc. vii. 24, and see further exx. in Kypke, *Obs.* Vol. II. p. 273, and in Wetst. *in loc.* τοῦ καλέσαντος] '*Him who called you*,' scil. God the *Father* (Chrys., Theod.), to whom the calling of Christians appears regularly ascribed by St. Paul (verse 15, Rom. viii. 30, ix. 24, 25, 1 Cor. i. 9, vii. 15, 17, 1 Thess. ii. 12, 2 Thess. ii. 14, 2 Tim. i. 9), — not '*Christ* who called you,' Syr., Jerome, al., the correct theological distinction being, ἡ μὲν κλῆσίς ἐστι τοῦ Πατρός, τῆς δὲ κλήσεως ἡ αἰτία, τοῦ Υἱοῦ, Chrys.: comp. Rom. v. 15. Brown (p. 39), excepts Rom. i. 7, but scarcely with sufficient reason; see Fritz. and De W. *in loc.*, and comp. Reuss, *Théol. Chrét.* IV. 15, Vol. II. p. 144, Usteri, *Lehrb.* II. 2, 3, p. 269, 279 sq. The passages cited by Alford *on Rom. l. c.*, viz. John v. 25, 1 Tim. i. 12, do not seem fully in point. ἐν χάριτι] '*by the grace of Christ*;' holy instrument of the divine calling, the prep. ἐν being here used in its instrumental sense (Eph. ii. 13, vi. 14, al.), and marking not so much the element *in* which, as the principle *by* which (immanent instrumentality, Jelf, *Gr.* § 622. 3, comp. notes *on Eph.* ii. 13) the calling was vouchsafed unto mankind; see notes *on* 1 *Thess.* iv. 18, and comp. Winer, *Gr.* § 48. a, p. 347. De Wette and Meyer both adduce 1 Cor. vii. 15, ἐν δὲ εἰρήνῃ κέκληκεν ἡμᾶς ὁ Θεός, but not pertinently, as both there and in the two other passages in which καλεῖν is joined with ἐν, viz., Eph. iv. 4, 1 Thess. iv. 7 (see notes *in loc.*), the prep. retains its simple and primary force 'of permanence in,' and marks, as it were, the element *in which*

7 ὃ οὐκ ἔστιν ἄλλο, εἰ μή τινές εἰσιν οἱ ταράσσοντες ὑμᾶς καὶ

we are called to move. In the present case, however, the *dogmatical* consideration, that the Grace of Christ, in the sense it here appears used by St. Paul, denotes an active and energizing influence rather than a passive element, seems distinctly to suggest the instrumental sense; comp. Rom. v. 15, and see Meyer and Hilgenf. in *h. l.* The usual explanation, according to which ἐν is used 'in sensu prægnanti' for εἰς ('vocavit in gratiam,' Vulg., Auth.), is more than doubtful, as καλέω implies no idea of motion (comp. Winer, *Gr.* § 50. 4. a, p. 367), while that of Wieseler (*Chronol.* p. 285, note), according to which ἐν χάρ. = χάριν (ch. iii. 19), is alike inconsistent with the usage of ἐν, and the regular meaning of χάρις Χριστοῦ.

ἕτερον] '*another sort of*,' Fell. If we compare the very similar passage, 2 Cor. xi. 4, in which ἕτερος and ἄλλος occur in juxtaposition, and apparently in senses exactly identical with those in the present passage, it will not seem necessary to lay any stress on ἕτερον as implying either (*a*) 'bad,' 'perverted' (comp. Plato, *Phileb.* 13 A, ἕτερον ὄνομα, Pind. *Pyth.* III. 34 [60] δαίμων ἕτερος; see Rost u. Palm. *Lex.* s. v. Vol. I. p. 1202, Wetst. *on* 1 *Tim.* v. 25), or even (*b*) 'strange,' Scholef. *Hints*, p. 88 (ed. 3), comp. Jude 7,—as both here and 2 Cor. *l. c.* ἕτερος appears only to refer to distinction of *kind*, ἄλλος of *individuality*; 'ἕτερος non tantum alium sed diversum significat,' Tittm. *Synon.* p. 155; comp. Plato, *Sympos.* 186 B, ἕτερόν τε καὶ ἀνόμοιον. It must be admitted, however, that this distinction is not always kept up in the N. T.; see Matth. xi. 3, 1 Cor. xv. 39.

7. ὃ οὐκ ἔστιν ἄλλο εἰ μή κ.τ.λ.] '*which is* NOT *another, save that*,' etc. The various interpretations of these words turn mainly on the antecedent assigned to ὅ; this may be (*a*) the whole sentence, ὅτι—εὐαγγέλιον, '*quod quidem* (scil. vos deficere a Christo) non est aliud nisi,' Winer; (*b*) the preceding εὐαγγέλιον, 'which Gospel is, admits of being, no other,' De W. (compare Syr., Chrys., Theod.), and appy. the majority of expositors; (*c*) the preceding compound expression ἕτερον εὐαγγέλιον, Meyer, Alf. Of these (*c*) is clearly to be preferred, as best preserving the natural and grammatical sequence of the words, and the distinction between ἕτερος and ἄλλος. To prevent the words ἕτερον εὐαγγέλιον being misconstrued into the admission that there could *really* be any other gospel than the one preached to them, St. Paul more fully explains himself, using ἄλλος rather than the ambiguous ἕτερος, and throwing the emphasis on οὐκ: 'which (ἕτερον εὐαγγέλιον) is *not* another (a second) GOSPEL, except (only in this sense, that) there are some who trouble you,' *i. e.*, the Judaists bring you another gospel, but it is really no GOSPEL at all; comp. Hamm. and Meyer *in loc.* In a word, as Hilgenf. correctly observes, the seeming paradox lies in this fact, that εὐαγγέλιον is understood after ἄλλο in its strictest meaning, but expressed after ἕτερον in one more lax. εἰ μή] '*save that*.' The gloss εἰ μή = ἀλλά can be distinctly impugned in even what seem the strongest passages, *e. g.* Matth. xii. 4 (see Fritz. *in loc.*), 1 Cor. vii. 17 (see Meyer *in loc.*): consult Klotz, *Devar.* Vol. II. p. 524, Hartung, *Partik.* μή, 3. 6, Vol. II. p. 120, compared with Dindorf in Steph. *Thes.* Vol. III. p. 190. The first *distinct* evidences of this interchange appear only in very late writers.

οἱ ταράσσοντες] '*who are troubling you*;' 'qui vos conturbant,' Vulg. The definite article might at first sight seem inconsistent with the indef. τινες: when thus used, however, it serves to particularize, and in the present case specifies,

θέλοντες μεταστρέψαι τὸ εὐαγγέλιον τοῦ Χριστοῦ. 8 ἀλλὰ καὶ ἐὰν ἡμεῖς ἢ ἄγγελος ἐξ οὐρανοῦ εὐαγγελίζηται ὑμῖν παρ' ὃ εὐηγγε-

the τινὲς as those whose *characteristic* was troubling the Galatians, 'some who are your troublers;' comp. Luke xviii. 9, τινὰς τοὺς πεποιθότας, Col. ii. 8, μή τις ὑμᾶς ἔσται ὁ συλαγωγῶν. Winer (*Gr.* § 18. 3, p. 100) adduces some exx. from classical Greek, and compares the common expression εἰσιν οἱ λέγοντες: see also Bernhardy, *Synt.* VI. 23, p. 318. We cannot, therefore, with Rückert definitely pronounce this as an instance of Asiatic Hellenism. The article must, of course, be carried on to θέλοντες; see Kühner's valuable note on Xen. *Mem.* I. 1. 20.

τὸ εὐαγγέλιον τοῦ Χριστοῦ] It is doubtful whether Χριστοῦ is the gen. *subjecti*, 'the Gospel preached by Christ,' or the gen. *objecti*, 'the Gospel of or concerning Christ.' From the fuller expression, Rom. i. 3, εὐαγγέλ. τοῦ Θεοῦ περὶ τοῦ υἱοῦ αὐτοῦ, we may, perhaps, here decide on the latter interpretation: see Winer, *Gr.* § 30. 1, p. 160. According to Meyer (*on Mark* i. 1), when the gen. after εὐαγγέλ. is σωτηρίας, βασιλείας, κ.τ.λ. it is gen. *objecti*; when Θεοῦ, gen. *subjecti*; but when Χριστοῦ, gen. *objecti* or *subjecti*, to be determined only by the context.

8. καὶ ἐάν] '*even if*;' not, however, necessarily 'supposing a case which has never occurred' (Alf.), but, as usual, conveying the idea of condition with the assumption of *objective* possibility; see Herm. *de Partic.* ἄν, 2. 7, p. 95, and esp. the very clear distinctions of Schmalfeld, *Synt. d. Gr. Verb.* § 93, 94. It may be further observed that, as the order shows, καὶ belongs not to ἡμεῖς or to the sentence, but to ἐάν (*etiam si*), to which it gives force and prominence; see Herm. *Viger*, No. 307, Hartung, *Partic.* καί, 3. 3, Vol. I. p. 141, and notes *on Phil.* ii. 17.

ἡμεῖς] '*we*.' Though ἡμεῖς here seems to refer mainly to St. Paul, and is frequently so used elsewhere, yet, as οἱ σὺν ἐμοὶ π. ἀδελ. may very reasonably be here included (Mey.), it does not seem desirable, with De W., Conyb., and others, to limit the term specially to the Apostle. The use of ἡμεῖς, or of the simple plural, must always depend on the context; comp. notes *on* 1 *Thess.* i. 2.

παρ' ὃ] '*contrary to that which*.' The meaning of the prep. has been the subject of considerable controversy; the Lutherans having urged the meaning *præterquam* (Vulg., and appy. Chrys.), the Romanists that of *contra* (Theod., al.). This latter meaning is perfectly correct (opp. to Brown, p. 45; see Donalds. *Gr.* § 485, and exx. in Winer, *Gr.* § 49. g, p. 360, esp. Xen. *Mem.* I. 1. 18, where παρὰ τοὺς νόμους and κατὰ τ. ν. are in antithesis), and is appy. required by the context and tenor of the argument. The Apostle implies throughout the Epistle that the Judaical gospel was in the strict sense of the words an ἕτερον εὐαγγ., and in its very essence *opposed* to the true Gospel. ἀνάθεμα] '*accursed*;' strictly considered, nothing more than the Hellenistic form of the Attic ἀνάθημα, Moeris (cited by Lobeck, *Phryn.* p. 249), the original meaning of both forms being τὸ ἀφιερωμένον Θεῷ, Theodoret *on Rom.* ix. 3. The prevailing use, however, of ἀνάθεμα *in malam partem* compared with the command, Lev. xvii. 29, seems (esp. in the LXX and the N. T.) to have gradually led to a distinction in meaning; ἀνάθημα being used in the sense of *donarium* (2 Macc. ix. 16, Luke xxi. 25), ἀνάθεμα (Rom. ix. 3, 1 Cor. xii. 3, xvi. 22) as '*aliquid divinæ iræ sacratum*;' Hesych. ἀνάθεμα· ἐπικατάρατος, ἀκοινώνητος. ἀνάθημα· κόσμημα. This distinction, though very generally, is still

λισάμεθα ὑμῖν, ἀνάθεμα ἔστω. 9 ὡς προειρήκαμεν, καὶ ἄρτι
πάλιν λέγω, εἴ τις ὑμᾶς εὐαγγελίζεται παρ' ὃ παρελάβετε, ἀνά-

not universally observed: see Theod. and esp. Chrys. *on Rom.* ix. 3, who, even while he asserts two distinct meanings, seems to regard the forms as interchangeable. In the eccles. writers (see Suicer, *Thes.* Vol. I. p. 268, Bingham, XVI. 2), ἀνάθεμα, like the Hebrew חֵרֶם (see Winer, *RWB*, Art. *Bann*) was applied to excommunication; though even here, it may be observed, accompanied sometimes with distinct *execration;* see Bingham, *ib.* 2. 17. This milder sense has been frequently maintained in the present passage (Hammond *in loc.*, Waterland, *Doct. Trin.* ch. 4, Vol. III. p. 458), but is distinctly opposed to the usage of the N. T.; compare ἐπικατάρατος, ch. iii. 10, κατάρα, ch. iii. 13. For further reff. see the good note of Fritz. *Rom.* ix. 3, Vol. II. p. 253 sq.

9. προειρήκαμεν] '*we have said before.*' To what does πρὸ here refer? Is it (*a*) solely to the preceding verse, as Chrys., Theod., Jerome (comp. Neander, *Planting*, Vol. I. p. 214, Bohn), or (*b*) to a declaration made at the Apostle's last visit, as Syr. (appy.), and recently, Ust., De W., Mey., al.? Grammatical considerations do not contribute to a decision: for neither, on the one hand, can the use of the perfect rather than the aor. προείπομεν (ch. v. 21, 1 Thess. iv. 6) be pressed in favor of (*a*), — εἴρηκα at most only marking the continuing validity of what was said (comp. 2 Cor. xii. 9, and Winer, *Gr.* § 40. 4, p. 243), — nor, on the other hand, can the reference to what has just been said be urged as inconsistent with the usage of πρό (Ust.), for see 2 Macc. iii. 7, προειρημένων χρημάτων (where the subject referred to is mentioned no further back than the beginning of the preceding verse), 3 Macc. vi. 35, and compare 2 Cor. vii. 3 with 2 Cor. vi. 12. *Contextual* reasons, however, viz. the insertion of ἄρτι as marking an antithesis to what was distinctly *past*, and the apparent identity of time marked by the two plural verbs εὐαγγελ., προειρ. (Alf.), seem so distinctly in favor of (*b*), that in this case we do not hesitate to maintain that reference even in opposition to the opinion of the Greek expositors; comp. 2 Cor. xiii. 2. This passage has been pressed into the controversy relative to the state of the Galatian church at the Apostle's second visit; see Davidson, *Introd.* Vol. II. p. 305.

καὶ ἄρτι κ.τ.λ.] '*so now I say again:*' undoubtedly a consecutive sentence. Rückert and B. Crus., by making it part of the antecedent sentence, retain the more Attic meaning of ἄρτι, but suppose an intolerably harsh ellipsis before εἴ τις. Ἄρτι is not used in Attic Greek for purely present time, — comp. Plato, *Meno*, 89, where ἐν τῷ νῦν is in opp. to ἐν τῷ ἄρτι, — but is not uncommonly so used in later Greek; see esp. Lobeck, *Phryn.* p. 18 sq.

εἰ . . . εὐαγγελίζεται] '*if any one preacheth;*' simply and purely conditional ('εἰ cum indic. nihil significat præter conditionem,' Klotz, *Devar.* Vol. II. p. 455), 'if, as a matter of fact, preaching is a course of action pursued by any one,' be such an assumption reasonable or the contrary; see esp. Schmalfeld, *Syntax*, § 91, p. 195. This change from the more restricted ἐὰν with subj., verse 8, *appears* here intentional; comp. Acts v. 38, 39. Still such distinctions must not be overpressed, as there is abundant evidence to show that not only in later, but even sometimes in earlier writers, they were not always carefully observed; see Madvig, *Gr.* § 125. 1. It is certainly noticeable that, in Euclid (*e. g.* Book I. Prop. 4), ἐὰν with subj. is nearly always

θεμα ἔστω. 10 ἄρτι γὰρ ἀνθρώπους πείθω ἢ τὸν Θεόν; ἢ ζητῶ ἀνθρώποις ἀρέσκειν; εἰ ἔτι ἀνθρώποις ἤρεσκον, Χριστοῦ δοῦλος οὐκ ἂν ἤμην.

used in mathematical hypotheses, where there can be *no* accessory idea, but where experience must prove the truth or fallacy of the supposition: see Winer, *Gr.* § 41. 2, p. 260, note. This use of εὐαγγελίζομαι with an accus. *personæ*, is an ἅπαξ λεγόμ. in St. Paul's Epp., but occurs elsewhere both in the N. T. (Luke iii. 18, Acts viii. 25, 40, xiii. 22, xiv. 15, 21, xvi. 10, 1 Pet. i. 12), and in later writers: comp. Winer, *Gr.* § 32. 1, p. 199, and Lobeck, *Phryn.* p. 267 sq.

10. ἄρτι γάρ] '*For now;*' not contrasting his present conduct and former Pharisaism (Neander, *Planting*, Vol. I. p. 222 [Bohn], Wieseler, *Chronol.* p. 178), but emphatically repeating the ἄρτι of the preceding verse, and calling especial attention to his present words; —'*Now*, — when I am using such unhesitating language.' The exact force of γὰρ seems more open to question: it may be plausibly taken as in abrupt and ironical reference to the charges of the Judaists; 'well! am I now,' etc. (on this idiomatic use of γάρ, see esp. Klotz, *Devar.* Vol. II. p. 245), but is perhaps more naturally regarded as *argumentative*, — not, however, so much with reff. to the seeming harshness of his previous words (Mey., Alf.), as to their *unquestionable truth*, the best proof of which lay in his being one who was making God his friend, and not men; see Olsh. and Hilgenf. *in loc.* πείθω] '*am I persuading*,' ܗܘ ܡܦܝܣ [sum persuadens] Syr., 'suadeo,' Vulg., Clarom.; scil. '*am I making friends of;*' the slight modification of meaning, viz. 'persuadendo mihi concilio,' as suggested by the latter words of the clause, being easily supplied from the context; see Acts xii. 20, 2 Macc. iv. 45, and comp. πεῖσαι τὸν Θεόν (with inf.), Joseph. *Antiq.* IV. 6. 5, VI. 5. 6, VIII. 10. 3. The usual comment, that πείθω is here used *de conatu* (Ust., al.), is *very* questionable. Of the passages cited in support of this meaning, Acts xxviii. 23, certainly proves nothing, and Ælian, *Var. Hist.* II. 6, is not to the point, 'attempt' being implied not by the verb but its tense. The same obs. seems applicable to Xenoph. *Hell.* VI. 5, 16, Polyb. *Hist.* IV. 64. 2, cited in Steph. *Thess.* s. v. ἢ ζητῶ, κ. τ. λ.] '*or am I seeking to please*,' etc; not merely a different (De W.), but a more general and comprehensive statement of the preceding clause. The student will find a sound sermon on this verse by Farindon, *Serm.* XXI. Vol. II. p. 139 (ed. 1849). ἔτι ἀνθρ. ἤρεσκον] '*were still pleasing men.*' It is not necessary either to press the use of the imperf. *de conatu*, or to modify the meaning of ἀρέσκω, 'studeo placere,'— a meaning which it never bears; see Fritz. *Rom.* xv. 2, Vol. III. p. 221, note. The apostle says, 'I am not pleasing men; and a clear proof is, that I am Christ's servant, whose service is incompatible with that of man.' The emphasis thus rests on ἔτι (Mey., Brown) which is not merely logical (De Wette), but *temporal*, with ref. to the preceding ἄρτι. The *Rec.* inserts γὰρ after εἰ, with D[3]EJK; Syr., and other Vv.; Chrys., Theod., al., — but with but little plausibility, as the authority for the omission is strong [ABD[1]FG; 5 mss.; Vulg., Clarom., Copt., Arm.; Cyr. (3), Dam.], and the probability of interpolation to assist the argument, by no means slight.
ἤμην] This form of the imperf., so common in later writers, is found, Xen. *Cyr.* VI. 1. 9, Lysias, III. 17, but is unequivocally condemned by the Atticists. Buttm.

The Gospel I preach is not of man; and I will confirm this by stating my mode of life before my conversion.

[11] Γνωρίζω δὲ ὑμῖν, ἀδελφοί, τὸ εὐαγγέλιον τὸ εὐαγγελισθὲν ὑπ' ἐμοῦ, ὅτι οὐκ ἔστιν κατὰ ἄνθρωπον· [12] οὐδὲ γὰρ ἐγὼ παρὰ ἀνθρώπου

11. δέ] *Tisch.* γάρ. The external authorities for δὲ are AD³EJK; many Vv. (Æth.-Pol. and others omit entirely); Chrys., Theod., al.; Ambrst. (*Rec.*, *Griesb.*, *Scholz.*, *Lachm.*, *De W.*, *Mey.*). For γάρ, BD¹FG; 17. al. . . . Vulg., Clarom.; Dam., Hier. Aug., al. (*Tisch.*; commended by *Griesb.*). The permutation of δὲ and γὰρ is so common that *internal* considerations become here of some importance. The question is, does St. Paul here seem to desire to carry out further his previous remarks, to explain, or to prove them? In the first case we could only have, as Rück observes, δέ; in the second, γὰρ or δέ (δὲ retaining a faint oppositive force, Klotz, *Devar.* Vol. II. p. 3); in the third, only γάρ. The context seems decisively in favor of the first hypoth., and therefore of δέ.

remarks that it is commonly found when in combination with ἄν; this, however, is doubtful; so Lobeck, *Phryn.* p. 152.

11. γνωρίζω δέ] '*Now I certify, make known unto you;*' commencement of what may be termed the apologetic portion of the epistle, ch. i. 11—ch. ii. 21. The present formula, Usteri observes, is always used by St. Paul as the prelude of a more deliberate and solemn avowal of his opinion; comp. 1 Cor. xv. 1, 2 Cor. viii. 1, 1 Cor. xii. 3 (διὸ γν.). Δὲ is consequently here (see crit. note) what is termed μεταβατικόν, Bekk. *Anecd.* p. 958 (cited by Hartung, Vol. I. p. 165), *i. e.*, it indicates a *transition* from what has been already said, to the fresh aspects of the subject which are now introduced. For examples of the very intelligible attraction τὸ εὐαγγ. . . . . ὅτι, see Winer, *Gr.* 66. 6, p. 551. οὐκ ἔστιν κατὰ ἄνθρωπον] '*is not after man,*' *i. e.*, 'is of no human strain:' 'κατὰ complectitur vim prepositionum ἀπὸ (?), διὰ et παρά,' Bengel. This remark, if understood exegetically rather than grammatically, is perfectly correct. Κατὰ ἄνθρ., taken *per se*, implies 'after the fashion, after the manner of man' (Winer, *Gr.* § 49. d, p. 358), but in the present context amounts to the more comprehensive declaration that the εὐαγγέλιον was not ἀνθρώπινον, either in its essence or object; οὐχ ὑπὸ ἀνθρωπίνων σύγκειται λογισμῶν, Theod.: compare Plato, *Phileb.* 12, τὸ δ' ἐμὸν δέος . . . . . οὐκ ἔστι κατὰ ἄνθρ.; where the true qualitative nature of the expression is shown by the further explanation, ἀλλὰ πέρα τοῦ μεγίστου φόβου. The different shades of meaning under which this formula appears in St. Paul's Epp. (ch. iii. 15, Rom. iii. 5, 1 Cor. iii. 3, ix. 8, xv. 32) must be referred to the context, not to the preposition; see Fritz. *Rom.* iii. 5, Vol. I. p. 159 sq. and comp. Suicer, *Thesaur.* Vol. I. p. 351.

12. οὐδὲ γὰρ ἐγὼ] '*for neither did I receive it, etc.;*' proof of the preceding assertion. The true force of οὐδὲ has here been frequently misunderstood, but may be properly preserved, if we only observe (1) that in all such cases as the present (comp. John v. 22, viii. 42, Rom. viii. 7), the particle must receive its *exact* explanation from the context ('adsumptâ extrinsecus aliquâ sententiâ,' Klotz, *Devar.* Vol. II. p. 707), and (2) that οὐδὲ γάρ, in negative sentences, stands in strict parallelism and bears corresponding meanings with καὶ γὰρ in positive sentences; see Hartung, *Partik.* οὐδέ, 2. B. 2, Vol. I. p. 211, and comp. Ellendt, *Lex. Soph.* s. v. Vol. II. p. 21 sq. We may thus correctly translate, either (*a*) *nam ne ego quidem*, 'even

παρέλαβον αὐτὸ οὔτε ἐδιδάχθην, ἀλλὰ δι' ἀποκαλύψεως Ἰησοῦ

I who so naturally might have been taught of men,' Hilgenf., Winer *in loc.*, and *Gr.* § 55. 6, p. 436; or (*b*) *neque enim ego*, 'I as little as the other Apostles' (Olsh.); or perhaps a little more inclusively, '*I* (distinctly emphatic)—as little as any others, whether Χριστοδίδακτοι or ἀνθρωποδίδακτοι.' Of these (*b*) is to be preferred not only from contextual but even grammatical reasons; for independently of seeming too concessive, (*a*) would also have been most naturally expressed by οὐδὲ ἐγὼ γάρ, or καὶ γὰρ οὐδ' ἐγώ (Rück). This last objection Meyer considers invalid on account of the normal position of γάρ,—but inexactly; for though γάρ generally occupies the 2nd place, yet when the 1st and 2nd words are closely united (which would here be the case) it occupies the 3rd: see Klotz, *Devar.* Vol. II. p. 251. παρὰ ἀνθρώπου] '*from man;*' not synonymous with ἀπὸ ἀνθρώπου, the distinction between these prepositions after verbs of receiving, etc. (παρὰ more *immediate*, ἀπὸ more *remote* source), being appy. regularly maintained in St. Paul's Epp.: comp. 1 Cor. xi. 23, παρέλαβον ἀπὸ τοῦ Κυρίου, on which Winer (*de Verb. Comp.* Fasc. II. p. 7) rightly observes, 'non παρὰ τοῦ Κυρίου, propterea quod non ipse Christus præsentem docuit;' see Schulz, *Abendm.* p. 218 sq. οὔτε ἐδιδάχθην] '*nor was I taught it;*' slightly different from the preceding παρέλαβον, the ἐδιδ. pointing more to *subjective* appropriation, while παρέλ. only marks *objective* reception (Windischm.): so appy. Beng., 'alterum (παρέλ.) fit *sine* labore, alterum *cum* labore discendi.' On the sequence οὐδὲ—οὔτε, see Winer, *Gr.* § 55. 6, p. 436, and esp. Hartung, *Partik.* οὔτε, I. 9, Vol. I. p. 201 sq., where this unusual, but (in cases like the present) defensible collocation is fully explained. In all such passages, δὲ refers to the foregoing words or sentences, so that οὔτε is used as if οὐ or οὐκ had preceded; δέ, in negative sentences, having often much of the force and functions which καὶ has in affirmative sentences; see especially Wex. *Antig.* Vol. II. p. 157, and comp. Klotz. *Devar.* Vol. II. p. 711. The reading οὐδὲ (*Rec.* and even *Lachm.*) is only supported by AD[1]FG; a few mss.; Eus., Chrys., al., and, as a likely repetition of the preceding οὐδέ, or a correction of a supposed solecism, is more than doubtful. Ἰησοῦ Χριστοῦ] '*from Jesus Christ;*' gen. *subjecti*; forming an antithesis to the preceding παρά ἀνθρ.; Christ was the *source* and author of it (Fell. Hamm.): comp. 2 Cor. xii. 1, and notes *on* 1 *Thess.* 1. 6. In expressions similar to the present (comp. εἰρήνη Θεοῦ, εὐαγγ. τοῦ Χριστοῦ), it is only from the context that the nature of the gen., whether *subjecti* or *objecti*, can be properly determined; see Winer, *Gr.* § 30 1, p. 168, and comp. notes on ver. 7. The peculiar revelation here alluded to may be, as Aquinas supposes, one vouchsafed to the Apostle *soon* after his conversion, by which he was fitted to become a preacher of the Gospel; comp. Eph. iii. 3, where, however, ἐγνωρίσθη (*Lach.*, *Tisch.*) is less decisive than *Rec.* ἐγνώρισε. It is a subject of continual discussion whether the teaching of St. Paul was the result of one single illumination, or of progressive development; comp. Reuss. *Théol.*, *Chrét.* IV. 4, Vol. II. p. 42, sq. Thiersch, *Apost. Age*, Vol. I. p. 110 sq. (Transl.) The most natural opinion would certainly seem to be this; that as, on the one hand, we may reverently presume that all the fundamental truths of the Gospel would be *fully* revealed to St. Paul before he commenced preaching; so, on the other, it might have been ordained,

Χριστοῦ. 13 ἠκούσατε γὰρ τὴν ἐμὴν ἀναστροφήν ποτε ἐν τῷ Ἰουδαϊσμῷ, ὅτι καθ' ὑπερβολὴν ἐδίωκον τὴν ἐκκλησίαν τοῦ Θεοῦ καὶ
ἐπόρθουν αὐτήν. 14 καὶ προέκοπτον ἐν τῷ Ἰουδαϊσμῷ ὑπὲρ πολ-

that (in accordance with the laws of our spiritual nature) its deepest mysteries and profoundest harmonies should be seen and felt through the practical experiences of his apostolical labors. The question is partially entertained by Augustine, *de Gestis Pelag.* ch. XIV. (32), Vol. x. p. 339 sq. (ed. Migne, Par. 1845).

13. ἠκούσατε γάρ] *'For ye heard;'* historical proof, by an appeal to his former *well known* (ἠκούσ. emphatic) zeal for Judaism, that it was no human influence or human teaching that could have changed such a character; οὐ γάρ ἄν, εἰ μὲ Θεὸς ἦν ὁ ἐκκαλύπτων, οὕτως ἀθρόαν ἔσχον μεταβολήν, Chrys. τὴν ἀναστροφήν ποτε, κ. τ. λ.] *'my conversation in time past,'* etc. Auth. Vers. These words are taken by most interpreters as simply equivalent to τήν ποτε (προτέραν) ἀναστ. This is not critically exact. As Dr. Donaldson suggests, the position of ποτε is due to the verb included in ἀναστροφήν: as St. Paul would have said ἀνεστρεφόμην ποτε, he allows himself to write τὴν ἐμὴν ἀναστροφήν ποτε. Meyer aptly cites Plato, *Leg.* III. 685 D, ἡ τῆς Τροίας ἅλωσις τὸ δεύτερον.

τῷ Ἰουδαϊσμῷ] *'the Jews' religion,' i. e. 'Judaism;'* see 2 Macc. ii. 21, xiv. 38, 4 Macc. iv. 26. On the specializing force of the art. with abstract nouns, see Scheuerlein, *Syntax.* § 26. 2. c, p. 219.

ἐπόρθουν] *'was destroying it,'* 'expugnabam,' Vulg., Clarom.: see Acts ix. 21, ὁ πορθήσας ἐν Ἱερουσαλὴμ τοὺς ἐπικαλουμένους, and comp. Æsch. *Sept.* 176. It is not necessary either to modify the meaning of πορθεῖν with Syr. (ܡܚܪܒ ܗܘܝܬ eram vastans), Copt. (desolabam), and other Vv., or to explain the imperf. as *de conatu* (σβέσαι ἐπεχείρει, Chrys.), with the Greek commentators. As Meyer justly observes, St. Paul previous to his conversion was actually engaged in the work of *destruction:* he was not a *Verwüster* merely, or a *Verstörer*, but a *Zerstörer:* comp. Acts xxii. 4, ἐδίωξα ἄχρι θανάτου. The imperfects accurately denote the course of the Apostle's conduct, which commenced and continued during the time of his Judaism, but, owing to his conversion, *was never carried out;* contrast ἐδίωξα, Acts, *l. c.*, 1 Cor. xv. 9, and see Bernhardy, *Synt.* x. 3, p. 372 sq., where the three principal uses of the imperf. (simultaneity, duration, and *non-completion*) are perspicuously stated, and comp. the more elaborate notice of Schmalfeld, *Synt.* § 55, pp. 97—111.

14. συνηλικιώτας] *'contemporaries.'* Συνηλ. is an ἅπαξ λεγόμ. in the N. T., and is only found occasionally in a few later writers, *e. g.* Diod. Sic. I. 53, Dion. Halic. x. 49; see Wetst. *in loc.* and the exx. collected by Dindorf and Hase in Steph. *Thesaur.* s.v. Vol. VII. p. 1378. The compound form (compare συμμέτοχος, Eph. iii. 6, v. 7; συγκοινωνός, 1 Cor. ix. 23) is condemned by the Atticists; Attic writers using only the simple form; see Thomas Mag. p. 208 (ed Bern.), Herodian, p. 433 (ed Koch.)

περισσοτ. ζηλωτὴς ὑπάρχ.] *being from the first more exceedingly a zealot* or *contender;* modal participial clause serving to define more particularly the peculiar nature of the advance which St. Paul made in Judaism. The comparison περισσ. is obviously with those just mentioned, the πολλοὶ συνηλ. ἐν τῷ γένει μου. τῶν πατρικῶν μοῦ παραδόσεων] *'for the traditions of my fathers;'* gen. *objecti* after ζηλωτής,

λοὺς συνηλικιώτας ἐν τῷ γένει μου, περισσοτέρως ζηλωτὴς ὑπάρχων τῶν πατρικῶν μου παραδόσεων.

I will confirm this by a recital of the places where I abode, and the countries in which I travelled. The churches of Judea knew of me only by report.

15 Ὅτε δὲ εὐδόκησεν ὁ Θεός, ὁ ἀφορίσας με
ἐκ κοιλίας μητρός μου καὶ καλέσας διὰ τῆς
χάριτος αὐτοῦ,
16 ἀποκαλύψαι τὸν υἱὸν αὐτοῦ

15. ὁ Θεὸς] ℵADEJK; mss.; many Vv., but Syr. (Philox.) with ast.; Orig. (1) Chrys. (1), Theod. (3), al.; Iren. (1), Aug., al. (*Rec.*, *Griesb.*, but om. om., *Scholz*, [*Lachm.*] *Mey.*). *Tisch.* omits these words with BFG; some mss.; Boern., Vulg., Syr.; Orig. (2), Chrys. (1), Theodoret (2), Iren. (1), Orig. (interp.), Faust. ap. Aug., Ambrst., Hier., al. (*De W.*, approved by *Mill*, Prolegom. p. 47). The accidental omission, however, seems probable on paradiplomatic considerations (see Pref. p. x[illegible]i), Θ having O immediately before, and soon after it.

— object about which the ζῆλος was displayed; comp. Acts xxi. 20, xxii. 3, 1 Cor. xiv. 12, Tit. ii. 14. The insertion of μου qualifies the more general term πατρικός, making it equivalent to the more special πατροπαράδοτος, and thus certainly seeming here to limit the παραδόσεις to the special ancestral traditions of the sect to which the Apostle belonged (Meyer), *i. e.*, to *Pharisaical* traditions; comp. Acts xxiii. 6, Φαρισαῖος, υἱὸς Φαρισαίων, and more expressly Acts xxii. 3, κατὰ τὴν ἀκριβεστάτην αἵρεσιν τῆς ἡμετέρας θρησκείας ἔζησα Φαρισαῖος.

15. ὅτε δὲ εὐδόκ. κ. τ. λ.] '*But when it pleased God;*' notice of the time *subsequent* to his conversion, in which the Apostle might have been thought to have conferred with men, but did not. On the meaning of εὐδοκέω, — here marking the free, unconditioned, and gracious will of God, see notes *on* 1 *Thess.* ii. 8, and on its *four* constructions in the N. T., notes *on Col.* i. 19. ἐκ κοιλίας μητρός μου] '*from my mother's womb,*' *i. e.* 'from the moment I was born,'— not as Calv., 'nondum genitum,' Jer. i. 5; ἐκ being temporal both here and Matth. xix. 12, Luke i. 15, Acts iii. 2, xiv. 8, and marking the point from which the temporal series is reckoned: see Winer, *Gr.* § 47. b, p. 328. The verb ἀφορίσας, as Jowett observes, has two meanings, the first physical (Æth.-Pol.), the second and predominant one, ethical and spiritual ('segregavit,' Vulg., Clarom.); comp. Rom. i. 1. καὶ καλέσας κ. τ. λ.] '*and called me by means of His grace;*' scil. at the Apostle's conversion (Acts ix. 3 sq.), — not with any reference to a calling, undefined in time, which depended on the counsels of God, as Rückert *in loc.*: compare Rom. viii. 30, where the temporal connection between προώρισε and ἐκάλεσε (on the force of the aorists see Fritz. *in loc.*) is exactly similar to that between ἀφορίσας and καλέσας in the present passage. The κλῆσις in both cases has a distinct origin in time; αὐτόν [Θεὸν] ἄφη καὶ πρὸ αἰώνων προεγνωκέναι καὶ μετὰ ταῦτα κεκληκέναι καθ' ὃν καιρὸν ἐδοκίμασε, Theod.; comp. Usteri, *Lehrb.* II. 2. 2, p. 269. διὰ τῆς χαρ. αὐτοῦ] '*by means of His grace:*' grace was the 'causa *medians*' of the Apostle's call; πανταχοῦ τῆς χάριτος εἶναί φησι τὸ πᾶν καὶ τῆς φιλανθρωπίας αὐτοῦ τῆς ἀφάτου, Chrys. The *moving* cause of the call was the Divine εὐδοκία, the *mediating* cause, the boundless grace of God, the *instrument*, the heaven-sent voice; comp. Winer, *Gr.* § 47, p. 337.

16. ἀποκαλύψαι] '*to reveal;*' dependent on the preceding εὐδόκησεν, not

ἐν ἐμοί, ἵνα εὐαγγελίζωμαι αὐτὸν ἐν τοῖς ἔθνεσιν, εὐθέως οὐ προσ-

on the participles (Est.), — a connection that would involve the unexampled construction (in the N. T.) εὐδόκ. — ἵνα εὐαγγ., and would impair the force of ἵνα. ἐν ἐμοί] '*within me;*' not 'per me,' Grot., 'in my case,' Green, or 'coram me,' Peile, but simply 'in me,' Vulg., *i. e.* 'in my soul; Χριστὸν εἶχεν ἐν ἑαυτῷ λαλοῦντα, Chrys. It may be admitted, that, owing partly to linguistic (see *on* 1 *Thess.* ii. 16), and partly to dogmatical reasons (Winer, *Gr.* § 47. 2. obs., p. 322), there is some difficulty in satisfactorily adjusting all St. Paul's varied uses of the preposition ἐν; still, wherever the primary meaning gives a sense which cannot be objected to dogmatically or exegetically, we are bound to abide by it. Here this meaning is especially pertinent. Both *subjectively*, by deep inward revelations, as well as *objectively*, by outward manifestations, was the great apostle prepared for the work of the ministry; see Chrysost. *in loc.* On the arbitrary meanings assigned to ἐν in the N. T., see Winer, *Gr.* § 48. a, p. 348. εὐαγγελίζωμαι] Present: the action was still going on. εὐθέως οὐ προσανεθέμην] '*straightway I addressed,*' etc.; the εὐθέως standing prominently forward and implying that he not only avoided conference with men, but did so from *the very first; οὐκ εἶπεν ἁπλῶς, 'οὐ προσανεθέμην,' ἀλλ' 'εὐθέως, κ. τ. λ,'* Chrys. According to the common explanation, εὐθέως is to be connected in sense with ἀπῆλθον, though in immediate structure with προσανεθέμην; 'Apostolus, — quæ fuit ejus alacritas, interponit negativam sententiam quæ ipse in mentem venit,' Winer, comp. Jowett, and Alf. It seems more correct to say that εὐθέως belongs to the whole sentence, from οὐ προσαν. to Ἀραβίαν, which, by means of the antithesis between its component negative and affirmative clauses, in fact expresses one single thought; 'immediately I avoided all conference and intercourse with man;' comp. Meyer *in loc.* οὐ προσανεθέμην] '*I addressed no communication to;*' not exactly 'non acquievi,' Vulg., Clarom., nor quite so much as ܠܐ ܓܠܝܬ [non revelavi] Syr., but more simply, οὐκ ἀνεκοινωσάμην, Theod., 'I made no communication to, and held no counsel with,' 'non contuli,' Beza. The prep. πρὸς does not imply that the Apostle 'did not *in addition to that* confer,' (comp. Ust.), but, as not uncommonly in composition, simply indicates *direction* towards: compare προσανατίθεσθαι τοῖς μάντεσι (Diod. Sic. XVII. 116) with προσαναφέρειν τοῖς μάντεσι (ib. ib.), in which latter verb the idea of direction is made more apparent; see Fritz., *Fritzsch. Opusc.* p. 204. σαρκὶ καὶ αἵματι] '*flesh and blood;*' a Hebrew circumlocution for man, — generally with the accessory idea of *weakness* or *frailty;* see Hammond and Lightfoot *on Matt.* xvi. 17. The expression occurs four times in the N. T., apparently under the following modifications of meaning: (*a*) Man, in his mere corporeal nature, 1 Cor. xv. 50, Heb. ii. 14; (*b*) Man in his weak intellectual nature, contrasted with God, Matt. xvi. 17 (contr. Mey.), comp. Chrys. Vol. x. 675 E, ed. Ben.; (*c*) Man, in his feeble human powers, contrasted with spiritual natures and agencies, Eph. vi. 12. The present passage seems to belong to (*b*); the apostle took not weak men for his advisers or instructors, but communed in stillness with God. Chrys., in referring the words to the Apostles, himself seemed

ανεθέμην σαρκὶ καὶ αἵματι,
[17] οὐδὲ ἀπῆλθον εἰς Ἱεροσόλυμα
πρὸς τοὺς πρὸ ἐμοῦ ἀποστόλους ἀλλὰ ἀπῆλθον εἰς Ἀραβίαν, καὶ

to feel the application too limited, as he adds, εἰ δὲ καὶ περὶ πάντων ἀνθρώπων τοῦτό φησιν, οὐδὲ ἡμεῖς ἀντεροῦμεν.

17. οὐδὲ ἀπῆλθον] 'nor did I go away,' scil. from Damascus, — to which place the mention of his conversion naturally leads his thoughts. It does not here seem necessary to press οὐδὲ in translation ('nor yet did I,' etc., Conyb.), as the context does not seem climactic; see notes *on* 1 *Thess.* ii. 3. (*Transl.*) In the present case it has appy. only that *quasi*-conjunctive force (see notes ver. 12), by which it appends one negation to another, — 'non apte connexa, sed potius fortuito concursu accedentia,' Klotz, *Devar.* Vol. II. p. 707; see notes *on Eph.* iv. 27, Winer, *Gr.* § 55. 6, p. 432, and esp. Francke, *de Part. Neg.* II. 2, p. 6. The reading ἀνῆλθον [*Rec.* with AJK; mss.; Copt., Syr.-Philox.; Chrys., Theod.] seems obviously a correction, and is rejected by all the best editors. ἀλλά] The particle has here its usual force after a negation, and implies such an opposition between the negative and affirmative clauses, that the first is, as it were, obliterated and absorbed by the second; see Klotz, *Devar.* Vol. II. p. 11, Fritz. *Mark*, Excurs. 2, p. 773. Schrader is thus *perhaps* justified in pressing the opposition between οὐ προσαν. and ἀλλὰ ἀπῆλθ., as an evidence that St. Paul went into Arabia for *seclusion;* contr. Anger, *Rat. Temp.* ch. IV. p. 123. In estimating, however, the force of ἀλλὰ in negative sentences, caution must always be used, as οὐκ — ἀλλὰ (not δὲ) is the *regular* sequence, like 'nicht — sondern' (not 'aber') in German; see Donalds. *Cratyl.* § 201. εἰς Ἀραβίαν] '*into Arabia;*' possibly the Arabian desert in the neighborhood of Damascus, Ἀραβία being a term of somewhat vague and comprehensive application; see Conyb. and Hows. *St. Paul,* Vol. I. p. 105, and for the various divisions of Arabia, Forbiger, *Alt. Geogr.* § 102, Vol. II. p. 728 sq. This brief, but circumstantial, recapitulation of St. Paul's early history is designed to show that, in the early period after his conversion he was never in any place where he could have learned anything from the other apostles. A discussion of the *object* (probably religious meditation), and of the *duration* (probably a large portion of three years) of this abode in Arabia, — both, especially the latter, greatly contested points, will be found in Schrader, *Paulus,* Part I. p. 54 sq., Wieseler, *Chronol.* p. 141 sq., Davidson, *Introd.* Vol. II. p. 75, 80. Δαμασκόν] '*Damascus.*' This most ancient city certainly existed as early as the days of Abraham (Gen. xiv. 15, xv. 2), and is supposed, even at that remote period, to have had an independent government (see L. Müller, *Orig. Regni Damasc.* in Iken, *Thesaur.* Vol. I. p. 721 sq.) After being subdued by David (2 Sam. viii 5, 6), it revolted under Solomon (1 Kings xi. 24), formed the seat of a very widely extended government (comp. 1 Kings xx. 1), was recovered by Jeroboam, the son of Joash (2 Kings xiv. 28), united in alliance with the kingdom of Israel, but was afterwards taken by Tiglath Pileser (2 Kings xvi. 9). After falling successively under that of the Babylonian, Persian, and Seleucid sway, it passed at last under that of the Romans (B. C. 64; see Diod. Sic. XXXIX. 30), and at the time of the Apostle formed a part of the dependent kingdom of Aretas (2 Cor. xi. 32). For further notices of the history of this ancient city, see Winer, *RWB.* Vol. I. p. 244 sq., Pauly, *Real-Encycl.* Vol. II.

πάλιν ὑπέστρεψα εἰς Δαμασκόν. [18] ἔπειτα μετὰ ἔτη τρία ἀνῆλθον εἰς Ἱεροσόλυμα ἱστορῆσαι Κηφᾶν, καὶ ἐπέμεινα πρὸς αὐτὸν

p. 847 sq., Conyb. and Howson, *St. Paul*, Vol. I. p. 105.

18. ἔτη τρία] '*three years*;' scil. after his *conversion*, that being the obvious and natural *terminus a quo* to which all the dates in the narrative are to be referred; see notes on ch. ii. 1. How much of this time was spent in Damascus, and how much in Arabia is completely uncertain. The only note of time in Acts ix. 23, ἡμέραι ἱκαναί, which *appears* to include this stay in Arabia, has by recent expositors been referred solely to the time of preaching at Damascus, — though appy. with less probability; see Anger, *Rat. Temp.* p. 122, Wieseler, *Chronol.* p. 143.

ἱστορῆσαι] '*to visit, to become acquainted with*;' scarcely so little as 'videre,' Vulg., Syr., Copt., al., but more in the sense of 'coram cognoscere,'— to visit and make a personal acquaintance with. As the meaning of this verb has been somewhat contested, we may remark that it is used by later writers with reference to (*a*) *places, things*, — in the sense of 'visiting,' 'making a journey to see;' Plutarch, *Thes.* 30, *Pomp.* 40, Polyb. *Hist.* III. 48. 12; comp. Chrysost. ὅπερ οἱ τὰς μεγάλας πόλεις καὶ λαμπρὰς καταμανθάνοντες λέγουσιν: (*b*) *persons* — in the sense of 'seeing,' 'making the acquaintance of;' Joseph. *Antiq.* VIII. 2. 5, ἱστορῆσαι Ἐλεάσαρον; *Bell.* VI. 1. 8, ὃν ἐγὼ ἱστόρησα; somewhat curiously, in reference to the pillar of salt into which Lot's wife was changed, *Antiq.* I. 22, ἱστόρηκα δὲ αὐτήν: see, also, Clem. *Hom.* VIII. 24 (p. 196, ed. Dressel), ἱστορῆσαι τοὺς τῆς θεραπείας ἐπιτυγχονόντας, ib. I. 9, p. 32; XIX. 6, p. 376; and exx. collected by Hilgenf. *Gal.* p. 122, note. There is thus no lexical necessity for pressing the primary meaning (Hesych. ἱστορεῖ, ἐρωτᾷ) advocated by Bagge *in loc.* The reading Πέτρον (*Rec.*), instead of Κεφᾶν [A B; a few mss.; Syr., Copt., Sahid., Syr.-Phil. in marg., Æth., al.], is supported by preponderating external authority [D E F G J K; mss.; Vulg., Clarom., al.; many Ff.], but is rightly rejected by most modern editors as a probable explanatory gloss.

ἐπέμεινα πρὸς αὐτόν] '*I tarried with him*; comp. chap. ii. 5, διαμείνῃ πρὸς ὑμᾶς; Matth. xxvi. 55, πρὸς ὑμᾶς ἐκαθεζόμην (*Lachm.*); 1 Cor. xvi. 6, πρὸς ὑμᾶς δὲ τυχὸν παραμενῶ, ver. 7, ἐπιμεῖναι πρὸς ὑμᾶς, al., usually with persons; 'sæpe nostri scriptores, ut ipsorum Græcorum poetæ passim, πρὸς cum accus., adjecto verbo quietis, sic collocant, ut non sit nisi *apud*, i. q., παρὰ cum dativo,' Fritz. *Mark* i. 18, p. 202. We may compare with this the legal forms, πρὸς διαιτητὴν λαχεῖν, Demosth. p. 22. 28; δίκας εἶναι πρὸς τοὺς ἄρχοντας, ib. 43, 71, etc., where the original notion of 'going to,' etc., has passed into that of mere direction. The ἐπὶ in ἐπέμεινα is not *per se* 'intensive' (Alf. *on Col.* i. 23), but appy. denotes *rest* at a place; see Rost u. Palm, *Lex.* s. v. ἐπί, C. 3, Vol. I. p. 1045. The verb itself has two constructions in the N. T., — with a simple dative (Rom. vi. 1, xi. 22, 23, Col. i. 23, 1 Tim. iv. 16), and with prepp. ἐπί, πρός, ἐν (Acts xxviii. 14, Phil. i. 24); see notes *on Col.* i. 23, and Winer, *Verb. Comp.* II. p. 11.

ἡμέρας δεκαπέντε] The reason for this *shortness* of St. Paul's stay is mentioned, Acts ix. 29. The apostle specifies the exact time of his stay at Jerusalem, to show convincingly how very slight had been his opportunities of receiving instruction from St. Peter or any one else there.

ἡμέρας δεκαπέντε· 19 ἕτερον δὲ τῶν ἀποστόλων οὐκ εἶδον εἰ μὴ
Ἰάκωβον τὸν ἀδελφὸν τοῦ Κυρίου. 20 ἃ δὲ γράφω ὑμῖν, ἰδοὺ ἐνώ-

19. εἰ μὴ Ἰάκωβον] '*save James*,' *i. e.*, no other ἀπόστολον save him. It may be fairly said, that every principle of grammatical perspicuity requires that, after these words, not merely εἶδον, but εἶδον τὸν ἀπόστολον be supplied; comp. 1 Cor. i. 14, οὐδένα ὑμῶν ἐβάπτισα εἰ μὴ Κρίσπον καὶ Γάϊον. This is distinctly admitted both by Mey., Hilgenf., and the best recent commentators, even though they differ in their deductions: so very clearly Chrys. St. James, then, was an ἀπόστολος (whatever be the meaning assigned to the word), — a fact somewhat confirmed by the use of ἀποστόλους, Acts ix. 28. The additional title, ὁ ἀδελφὸς τοῦ Κυρίου (τὸ σεμνολόγημα, as Chrys. terms it), was probably added (Ust.) to distinguish this James from the son of Zebedee, who was then living. Whether it follows from this passage, that Jacobus *Frater* and Jacobus *Alphæi* are identical (*by no means* such a fiction as Meyer somewhat hastily terms it), and that James was thus one of the Twelve, is a question which falls without the scope of this commentary. This consideration only may be suggested; whether in a passage so circumstantial as the present, where St. Paul's whole object is to prove that he was no emissary from the *Apostles* (comp. ver. 17), the use of ἀδελφός, in its less proper sense (Κυρίου ἀνεψιός, Theod.), is not more plausible than the similar one — of ἀπόστολος. The most weighty counter-argument is derived from John vii. 5, οὐδὲ γὰρ οἱ ἀδελφοὶ αὐτοῦ ἐπίστευον εἰς αὐτόν; but it deserves careful consideration whether ἐπίστευον really means more than a proper, intelligent, and rightful belief; see even De Wette *on John l. c.*, and comp. John vi. 64, where οὐ πιστεύειν is predicated of some of the μαθηταί, and where ver. 67 implies some doubt even of οἱ δώδεκα. The student who desires to examine this difficult question, may profitably consult Mill, *on the Brethren of our Lord*, Schneckenburger, *on St. James*, p. 144, sq., Arnaud, *Recherches sur l'Epître de Jude*, and the review of it by Deitlein in Reuter, *Repert.* (Aug. 1851), Neander, *Planting*, Vol. I. p. 351, note (Bohn); Blom's *Disputation*, (in Volbeding, *Thesaur. Comment.* Vol. I.); Credner, *Einleitung*, Vol. I. p. 571; Wieseler, *Stud. u. Krit.* (Part I. 1842); and Hilgenf. *Galaterbr.* p. 219. The most recent monographs are those by Schaff, Berlin, 1842; and Goy, Mont. 1845.

20. ἃ δὲ γράφω κ. τ. λ.] '*but as to what I write unto you*;' not parenthetical, but a strong and reiterated assurance of the little he had received from the Apostles, ἃ δὲ γράφω ὑμῖν being an emphatic anacoluthon; comp. Wannowski, *Constr. Abs.* p. 54 sq., where this and similar constructions are fully discussed. ὅτι οὐ ψεύδομαι] '*(I declare) that I lie not*;' strong confirmatory asseveration of the truth, — not of ver. 12 sq. (Winer), but of ver. 17, 18. In passages marked with this sort of abruptness and pathos (see Lücke *on* 1 *Joh.* iii. 20, p. 245, ed. 2), a verb consonant with the context is commonly supplied before ὅτι; comp. Acts xiv. 22. Accordingly, in the present case, γράφω (Mey.), λέγω (De W.), ἐστὶ (Rück.), ὄμνυμι (Ust.), have been proposed as suppletory; the first three are, however, obviously too weak, the last too strong — ἐνώπιον τοῦ Θεοῦ not being any more than לִפְנֵי יְהוָֹה, a formal oath (Olsh.). *If* any definite word was in the Apostle's thoughts, it was perhaps διαμαρτύρομαι (Acts x. 42, with ὅτι); especially as, in three out of the five places in which

πιον τοῦ Θεοῦ ὅτι οὐ ψεύδομαι. 21 ἔπειτα ἦλθον εἰς τὰ κλίματα
τῆς Συρίας καὶ τῆς Κιλικίας. 22 ἤμην δὲ ἀγνοούμενος τῷ προσώπῳ
ταῖς ἐκκλησίαις τῆς Ἰουδαίας ταῖς ἐν Χριστῷ, 23 μόνον δὲ ἀκούοντες

ἐνώπ. τοῦ Θεοῦ occurs, this verb (though in slightly different senses and constructions) is found joined with it; see 1 Tim. v. 21, 2 Tim. ii. 14, iv. 1. On this use of ὅτι in asseverations, see Fritz. *Rom.* ix. 2, Vol. II. p. 242.

21. τὰ κλίματα] *'the regions;'* 'regiones,' Vulg., 'partes,' Clarom.; a word only used in the N. T. by St. Paul, here and Rom. xv. 23, 2 Cor. xi. 10. The primary meaning, as derivation indicates, is 'inclinatio' or 'declivitas,' *e. g.* κλίματα ὀρῶν, Eustath. p. 1498. 47 (comp. Polyb. *Hist.* VII. 6. 1), thence with ref. to the inclination of the heavens to the poles, 'a tract of the sky,' κλῖμα οὐρανοῦ, Herodian, XI. 8, and lastly, — its most usual meaning, — a tract of the earth, whether of greater (comp. Athen. XII. p. 523 E) or, as in the present case, of more limited extent; comp. Polyb. *Hist.* v. 44. 6, x, 1. 3. On its accentuation (usually κλίμα, but more correctly κλῖμα), see Lobeck, *Paralip.* p. 418. The journey here mentioned is appy. identical with that briefly noticed in Acts ix. 30; see Conyb. and Hows. *St. Paul*, Vol. I. p. 115.

Συρίας] Not the *lower* part of Syria, called Phœnice (Winer, Ust., al.), but 'Syria proper' (ἡ ἄνω Συρία, Strabo), as St. Paul's object is to show the *distance* he was from any quarter where he could have received instruction from the Apostles; see Meyer *in loc.* In Acts xxi. 3, Συρία is used merely in a general way to denote the Roman province bearing that name: on its divisions, see Forbiger, *Handb. Geogr.* Vol. II. p. 640.

τῆς Κιλικίας] Occasionally mentioned in combination with Συρία (Acts xv. 23, 41) as geographically conterminous (Alf.), and as serving to define what portion of the larger province is especially alluded to. For a general notice of this province, see Strabo, *Geogr.* XIV. 5, p. 668 sq., Mannert, *Geogr.* VI. 3, p. 32 sq., Forbiger, *Alt. Geogr.* § 67, Vol. II. p. 271 sq.

22. τῷ προσώπῳ] *'in respect of personal appearance,'* scil. *'by face;'* οὐδὲ ἀπὸ ὄψεως γνώριμος ἦν αὐτοῖς, Chrys. The general limiting nature of the dative (Scheuerl. *Synt.* § 20, Donalds. *Gr.* § 458) may here be fully recognized: the Apostle was not unknown to the Churches in every sense, but only in regard to his outward appearance. This particular dative, commonly called the dative 'of reference to,' must be carefully distinguished both from the *instrumental* and the *modal* dat. (1 Cor. xi. 5), and may be best considered as a *local* dative ethically used. Here, for instance, the Apostle's appearance was not *that by which*, but as it were *the place in which*, their ignorance was evinced; see esp. Scheuerl. *Synt.* § 22. a, p. 179, and comp. Winer, *Gr.* § 31. 6, p. 193, Bernhardy, *Synt.* III. 8, p 84.

τῆς Ἰουδαίας] The Church of Jerusalem is, however, to be excepted, as there the Apostle was εἰσπορευόμενος καὶ ἐκπορευόμενος, παῤῥησιαζόμενος ἐν τῷ ὀνόματι τοῦ Κυρίου, Acts ix. 28.

ταῖς ἐν Χριστῷ] Not merely a periphrasis for the adjective 'the Christian churches,' but *'the churches which are in Christ;' i. e.*, which are incorporated with Him who is the Head: comp. Eph. i. 22, 23.

23. ἀκούοντες ἦσαν] *'they were hearing;'* scil. the members of these Churches; see Winer, *Gr.* § 67. 1, p. 555. This periphrasis, which probably owes its prevalence in the New Testa-

ἦσαν ὅτι ὁ διώκων ἡμᾶς ποτὲ νῦν εὐαγγελίζεται τὴν πίστιν ἥν
ποτε ἐπόρθει· 24 καὶ ἐδόξαζον ἐν ἐμοὶ τὸν Θεόν.

When I went up to Jerusalem, I communicated my Gospel both in public and private: I resisted the false brethren, and was accredited by the Apostles.

II. Ἔπειτα διὰ δεκατεσσάρων ἐτῶν πάλιν

ment to the similar formula in Aramaic (ܫܡܥܝܢ ܗܘܘ), serves to express the idea of *duration* more distinctly than the simple tense; see Winer, *Gr.* § 45. 5, p. 311. In the LXX it seems principally limited to those cases in which the participle is used in the original; see Thiersch. *de Pent.* III. 11, p. 113. Examples are found in Attic Greek (see Jelf, *Gr.* § 375. 4), but commonly under the limitation that the participle expresses some property or quality inherent in the subject; see Stalbaum, Plato, *Rep.* VI. 492 A.

ὅτι ὁ διώκων κ. τ. λ.] '*our former persecutor;*' the participle being here, by means of the art., turned into a species of subst., and losing all temporal force; see the exx. collected by Winer, *Gr.* § 57, p. 317, and comp. the very bold form, τὸν ἑαυτῆς ἔχοντα, Plato, *Phædr.* 244, E, cited by Bernhardy, *Synt.* VI. 22. obs. p. 316. Ὅτι is here not the 'ὅτι recititavum' (Schott), — a use of the particle not found in St. Paul's Epp., except in citations from the O. T. (Mey.), — but preserves its usual relatival force, the 'oratio indirecta' which it introduces, passing afterwards into the 'oratio directa' in the pronoun. This latter assumption Mey. deems unnecessary, as St. Paul might call himself, being now a Christian, '*our* former persecutor.' This, however, seems forced and artificial. τὴν πίστιν] '*the faith,*' objectively represented as a rule of life (De W.); comp. ch. iii. 23, 1 Tim. i. 19, iv. 1, al. In the Eccles. writers πίστις is frequently used in the more distinctly objective sense, 'the Christian doctrine,' 'doctrina *fidem* postulans' (*e. g.*, Ignat. *Eph.* § 16, πίστιν Θεοῦ ἐν κακῇ διδασκαλίᾳ φθείρῃ; Concil. Laod. can. 46, πίστιν ἐκμανθάνειν; see Suicer, *Thes.* s. v. πίστις, 2. a), but it seems *very* doubtful whether this sense ever occurs in the N. T. In Acts vi. 7, ὑπακούειν τῇ πίστει seems certainly very similar to ὑπακούειν τῷ εὐαγγελίῳ, Rom. x. 16 (see Fritz. Vol. I. 17), but even there 'the faith,' as the inward and outward rule of life (see Meyer *in loc.*), yields a very satisfactory meaning. On the various uses of πίστις, see Usteri, *Lehrb.* II. 1. 2, p. 91 sq.

24. ἐν ἐμοί] '*in me,*' not 'on account of me' (Brown), or 'for what he had done in me' (Jowett), but simply 'in me' Vulg., Clarom.), 'ut qui *in me* invenissent celebrationis materiam,' Winer *in loc.:* comp. Exod. xiv. 4, ἐνδοξασθήσομαι ἐν Φαραῷ. God, as Windisch. observes, was working *in* St. Paul, and so was praised *in* him. The prep., in such cases as the present, points to the object as being as it were the *sphere* in which (Eph. i. 17), or the *substratum* on which (1 Cor. vii. 14, see Winer, *Gr.* p. 345; compare Andoc. *de Myster.* p. 33, ed. Schiller) the action takes place. The transition from this to the common usage of ἐν in the sense of 'dependence on,' is easy and obvious; see exx. in Rost u. Palm, *Lex.* s. v. A. 2. b, Vol. I. p. 909, and comp. Bernhardy, *Synt.* v. 8. b. p. 210.

CHAPTER II. 1. διὰ δεκατεσσάρων ἐτῶν] '*after an interval of,*' 'post,' Vulg., Clarom., Copt., Armen.; δεκατεσσάρων παρελθόντων ἐτῶν, Chrys.: comp. Acts xxiv. 17, δι' ἐτῶν πλειόνων. The meaning of the prep. has here been unduly pressed to suit preconceived his-

ἀνέβην εἰς Ἱεροσόλυμα μετὰ Βαρνάβα, συμπαραλαβὼν καὶ Τίτον· ² ἀνέβην δὲ κατὰ ἀποκάλυψιν, καὶ ἀνεθέμην αὐτοῖς

torical views. Διά, in its temporal sense, denotes an action enduring *through and out of* a period of time; and may thus be translated *during*, or *after*, according as the nature of the action makes the idea of duration through the whole of the period (Heb. ii. 15, διὰ παντὸς τοῦ ζῆν), or occurrence at the end of the period most prominent. Thus διὰ πολλοῦ χρόνου σε ἑώρακα is correctly explained by Fritz. (*Fritzsch. Opusc.* p. 163, note), 'longo temporis spatio decurso (quo te non vidi) te vidi;' comp. Herm. *on Vig.* No. 377, b. This is the correct use of διά. There are, however, a few indisputable instances of a more lax use of the prep. in the N. T., to denote an action which took place *within*, not during *the whole of* a period; *e. g.* Acts v. 19, διὰ τῆς νυκτὸς ἤνοιξε, where both the tense and the occurrence preclude the possibility of its being 'throughout the night' (contr. Meyer), — so also Acts xvi. 9—xvii. 10 is perhaps doubtful; see Fritz. *Opusc.* p. 165, Winer, *Gr.* § 57. i. p. 337. Grammatical considerations, then, *alone* are not sufficient to justify Dr. Peile's paraphrase, 'not till after;' but on *exegetical* grounds it may be fairly urged that the mention of fourteen years, thus undefined by a terminus *ad quem* as well as *a quo*, would be singularly at variance with the circumstantial nature of the narrative. With regard to the great historical difficulties in which the passage is involved, it can here only briefly be said; — (1) The terminus *a quo* of the fourteen years, being purely a subjective epoch, does certainly seem that time which must have ever been present to the Apostle's thoughts, — the time of his *conversion* (Anger, Wieseler); especially as the ἔτη τρία, ch. i. 18, appear so reckoned. (2) Exegetical as well as grammatical (πάλιν) considerations seem to show it was St. Paul's *second* journey; — for how, when misconstruction was so possible, could it be passed over? and how can St. Peter's conduct be explained? But (3) chronolog. arguments, based on historical coincidences, make it impossible to doubt that Irenæus (*Hær.* III. 13) and Theodoret (*in loc.*) are right in supposing this the journey mentioned Acts xv., and therefore, according to St. Luke's account, *the third.* In a commentary of this nature it is impossible to allude to the various efforts (even to the invalidation of an unquestionable text) to reconcile (2) and (3): it may be enough to say that both chronological and historical deductions seem so certain, that (2) must give way: see the sensible explanation and remarks of Thiersch. *Apost. Age*, Vol. I. p. 120 sq. (Transl.). A complete discussion will be found in the chronological works of Anger and Wieseler, Davidson, *Introd.* Vol. II. p. 112 sq., Winer, *RWB.* Art. 'Paulus,' Conyb. and Howson, *St. Paul*, ch. vii.: see also Meyer *in loc.*, Alford, Vol. II. Prolegom. p. 26. συμπαραλαβὼν καὶ Τίτον] '*having taken with me also Titus;*' the ascensive καὶ perhaps alluding to his being uncircumcised; comp. Acts xv. 2, Παῦλον καὶ Βαρνάβαν καὶ τινας ἄλλους ἐξ αὐτῶν. St. Paul was now the principal person (συμπαραλαβών); at the preceding (second) visit Barnabas seems to have taken the lead; see Meyer *in loc.*

2. ἀνέβην δέ] '*I went up too;*' δὲ having its 'vim exponendi' (Fritz. *in loc.*), or, as we might perhaps more exactly say, its *reiterative* force (Klotz, *Devar.* Vol. II. p. 361, Hartung, *Partik.* δέ, 2. 7, Vol. I. p. 168), and repeating, not without a slight opposition, the preceding ἀνέβην. The native force of

τὸ εὐαγγέλιον ὃ κηρύσσω ἐν τοῖς ἔθνεσιν, κατ' ἰδίαν δὲ τοῖς

the particle may just be traced in the faint contrast which the explanation and introduction of fresh particulars give rise to. κατὰ ἀποκάλυψιν] '*by*, scil. *in accordance with*, *revelation*,— not for my own purposes;' κατὰ as usual implying the rule, the '*norman* agendi;' see Bernhardy, *Synt.* v. 20. b, p. 239, 241. Hermann's translation 'explicationis causâ' must, on exegetical, and *perhaps* even on grammatical grounds (see Fritzsch. *Opusc.* p. 169), *certainly* be rejected. For (1) ἀποκάλυψις is never used in this lower sense, either by St. Paul or any other of the sacred writers; and (2) the current of the Apostle's argument is totally at variance with such an explanation. His object is here to show that his visit to Jerusalem was not to satisfy any doubts of his own, nor even any suggestions of his converts, but in obedience to the command of God. The objection, that the current translation would require κατά τινα ἀποκάλυψιν (Herm.), may be neutralized by the observation that κατὰ ἀποκάλυψιν is in effect used nearly adverbially; see Eph. iii. 3. ἀνεθέμην] '*I communicated;*' 'contuli cum eis,' Vulg., Clarom., compare Syr. [patefeci]; 'enarravi,' Fritz.; 'ipsa collatio unam doctrinæ speciem exclusâ omni varietate monstrabat,' Beza. The meaning assigned by Green (*Gramm. N. T.* p. 82) 'to leave altogether in the hands of, or at the pleasure of another,' is more than doubtful; in the only other place in the N. T. where the word occurs, Acts xxv. 4, τῷ βασιλεῖ ἀνέθετο τὰ κατὰ τὸν Παῦλον, the meaning is clearly, as here, 'communicated:' see Fritz. *Opusc.* p. 169, and the exx. in Wetst. *in loc.* αὐτοῖς] '*to them*,' scil. to the inhabitants of Ἱεροσόλυμα (ver. 1), or rather (as the sense obviously requires a certain limitation), to the Christians residing there,—'Christianis gregariis' (Fritz.), as opp. to τοῖς δοκοῦσιν, the Apostles; comp. Matth. xii. 15, Luke v. 17, and see Winer, *Gr.* § 22. 3. 1, p. 131, Bernhardy, *Synt.* VI. 11. b, p. 288. The reference to the Apostles collectively (Schott, Olsh.), or to the Elders of the Church, is not by any means probable. κατ' ἰδίαν δέ] '*but privately*,' *i. e.* in a private conference; comp. Mark iv. 34; the Apostle communicated his εὐαγγέλιον to the Christians at Jerusalem openly and unreservedly, *but* κατ' ἰδίαν (between me and them, ܒܝܢܝ ܘܠܗܘܢ, Syr.) entered probably more into its doctrinal aspects; compare Theod. *in loc.* The meaning assigned to δὲ ('I mean') by Alf., who appy. denies any second and separate communication, seems *here* very doubtful (see ver. 4), and that to κατ' ἰδίαν ('preferably,' 'specially,') by Olsh., distinctly untenable, as κατ' ἰδίαν occurs sixteen times in the N. T., and in all cases is used in a directly, or (as here) indirectly *local* sense; see Mark ix. 28, xiii. 3, Luke x. 23, etc., and compare Neand. *Plant.* Vol. I. p. 104. (Bohn). τοῖς δοκοῦσιν] '*to those who were high in reputation*,' Scholef. *Hints*, p. 88; see Eurip. *Hec.* 292 (where οἱ δοκοῦντες is opp. to οἱ ἀδοξοῦντες), and the exx. collected by Kypke and Elsner, esp. Eur. *Troad.* 608, and Herodian, VI. 1, τοὺς δοκοῦντας καὶ ἡλικίᾳ σεμνοτάτους,—in all of which οἱ δοκ. appears simply equivalent to ἐπίσημοι (Theod.). There is not then, as Olsh. conceives, any shade of blame or irony (Alf.) in the expression, but as Chrys. correctly observes, 'τοῖς δοκοῦσι,' φησί, μετὰ τῆς ἑαυτοῦ καὶ τὴν κοινὴν ἁπάντων λέγων ψῆφον: see Œcum. *in loc.* μή πως εἰς κενὸν τρέχω, ἢ ἔδραμον] '*lest I might be running, or have (already) run in vain;*' *i. e.* 'lest I might lose my past or present labor' (Hamm.),

δοκοῦσιν, μή πως εἰς κενὸν τρέχω, ἢ ἔδραμον. 3 Ἀλλ' οὐδὲ
Τίτος ὁ σὺν ἐμοί, Ἕλλην ὤν, ἠναγκάσθη περιτμηθῆναι·

by leaving others to deem that it was fruitless and unaccredited. This passage presents combined grammatical and exegetical difficulties, both of which must be briefly noticed, (α) τρέχω. By comparing the very similar passage 1 Thess. iii. 5, μήπως ἐπείρασεν . . . καὶ εἰς κενὸν γένηται κ. τ. λ., it would certainly seem that τρέχω is pres. subj. (see Winer, *Gr.* § 56. 2, p. 448, where both passages are investigated); but there is a difficulty both in mood and tense. The former may be explained away by the observable tendency of the New Testament and later writers to lapse from the optat. into the subjunct. (Winer, § 41. b. 1, p. 258, Green, *Gr.* p. 72); the latter, either by considering τρέχω a 'then-present,' opp. to ἔδραμον, a 'then-past,' or as pointing to the continuance of the action. (β) μή πως then, is not *num forte* (an opinion formerly held by Fritzsche, and still by Green, p. 82, but well refuted by Dr. Peile), but *ne forte.* (γ) ἔδραμον may be explained in two ways; either (with Fritz.) as an indic. after a non-realized etc. hypoth. (Herm. *de Partic.* ἄν, 1. 10, p. 54), — a structure at which, strange to say, Hilgenf. seems to stumble, — or indic. after μήπως (fearing lest), the change of mood implying that the event apprehended had now taken place; see Winer, *Gr.* § 56. 2, p. 446: compare Scheuerl. *Synt.* § 34. a. p. 364, Matth. *Gr.* § 520. 8. We have then two possible translations; (1) Purpose; ἀνεθέμην . . . μήπως ἔδραμον, *I communicated . . . that I might not perchance have run in vain* (as I should have done if I had not, etc.) (2) Apprehension; ἀνεθέμην . . . (φοβούμενος) μήπως ἔδραμον, *I communicated . . being apprehensive lest perchance I might really have,* etc.; the verb 'timendi' being idiomatically omitted; see Gayler, *de Part. Neg.* p. 327, Schmalfeld, *Synt.* § 152. Of these (2) seems most in accordance with St. Paul's style; see 1 Thess. *l. c.*, and ch. iv. 11. To both translations, however, there are very grave objections; to (1) on logical, to (2) on exegetical grounds: to (1), because it was not on the communication or non-communication of his Gospel that St. Paul's running in vain really hinged, but on the assent or dissent of the Apostles: to (2), because it is incredible that he who went up κατ' ἀποκάλυψιν could have felt any doubt about his own course. To escape these difficulties we must adopt one of two explanations (neither wholly free from objections); either we must refer the words, *objectively,* to the danger St. Paul's converts might have run of being rejected by the Church if he had not communicated; or (which is most probable), *subjectively,* with the Greek commentators, *to the opinions of others;* ἵνα διδάξω τοὺς ταῦτα ὑποπτεύοντας ὅτι οὐκ εἰς κενὸν τρέχω, Chrys.; see Hammond *in loc.* If others deemed St. Paul's past and present course fruitless, it really must in that respect have amounted to a loss of past and present labor.

3. ἀλλ' οὐδέ] '*But* (to distinctly prove, *à fortiori,* that I had not run in vain) *not even,*' etc. The emphasis rests on Τίτος, — Titus, whom the apostles might have required to be circumcised, even while in general terms they approved of St. Paul's preaching. On this gradational force of ἀλλ' οὐδέ ('*at ne — quidem,*' 'indicant, silentio oblitteratâ re leviore, afferri graviorem'), see Fritz. *in loc.* (*Opusc.* p. 178), and comp. Luke xxiii. 15, Acts xix. 2. The true separative force of ἀλλὰ ('aliud jam esse quod sumus dicturi,' Klotz, *Devar.*

4 διὰ δὲ τοὺς παρεισάκτους ψευδαδέλφους, οἵτινες παρεισῆλθον κατασκοπῆσαι τὴν ἐλευθερίαν ἡμῶν ἣν ἔχομεν ἐν Χριστῷ Ἰησοῦ,

Vol. II. p. 2) is here distinctly apparent. Ἕλλην ὤν) '*being a Greek*' scil. inasmuch as, or though he was a Greek,' καίτοι Ἕλλην ὤν, Theodoret; not 'and was a Greek,' Alf., the appended participial clause not being predicative, but *concessive*, or suggestive of the reason why the demand was made; compare Donalds. *Cratyl.* § 305, *Gr.* 492 sq.

ἠναγκάσθη] '*was compelled.*' The choice of this word seems clearly to imply that the circumcision of Titus was strongly pressed on St. Paul and St. Barnabas; see Baur, *Paulus*, p. 121. It does not, however, by any means appear that the *Apostles* were party to it; in fact, if we assume the identity of this journey with the third, the language of Acts xv. 5 seems distinctly to imply the contrary.

4. διὰ δὲ τοὺς παρεισάκτους ψευδαδέλφους] '*and that*, or *now it was, because of the false brethren insidiously brought in*,' scil. οὐκ ἠναγκάσθη περιτμηθῆναι; explanatory statement (δὲ explicative; see below) why Titus was not compelled to be circumcised, viz., because the ψευδάδελφοι were making it a party matter. The construction is not perfectly perspicuous, but it does not appear necessary either to regard it as a positive anacoluthon (Rink, *Lucubr. Crit.* p. 171, Hilgenf. *in loc.*), or an anacol. arising from two blended constructions (Winer, *Gr.* § 63, p. 502, still less a connection of ver. 4 with ver. 2 (Bagge, al.). The difficulty, as the Greek expositors seem to have felt, is really in the δέ: this, however, is neither περιττός (Theod. compare Theod. M.), nor equivalent to οὐδέ (compare Chrys., Theoph., Œcum.), but simply *explicative* ('declarat et intendit,' Beng.), and faintly ratiocinative; see Klotz, *Devar.* Vol. II. p. 362. Alford comp. δέ, ver. 2, but the uses seem clearly different; there the insertion of αὐτοῖς naturally suggests a *contrast*, while here the naked statement οὐκ ἠναγκ. περιτμ. as naturally prepares us for a restrictive *explanation*.

παρεισάκτους] '*insidiously brought in*,' Scholef. This word appears to have two meanings, (*a*) *advena, adventitius*, ἀλλότριος (Hesych., Suid., Phot.); comp. Georg. Al. *Vit. Chrys.* 40 (cited by Hase, Steph. *Thes.* Vol. VIII. p. 187). παρείσακτε τῆς πόλεως ἡμῶν; (*β*) *irreptitius;* compare Prol. Sirach, πρόλογος παρείσακτος, — a meaning still further enhanced by παρεισῆλθον; compare 2 Pet. ii. 1, Jude 4. The compound ψευδάδελφοι designates those who did not acknowledge the great principle of faith in Christ being the only means of salvation (Neander, *Plant.* Vol. II. p. 114, Bohn), while their *intrusive* character is well marked by the compounds παρεισῆλθον and παρεισάκτους; compare Polyb. *Hist.* I. 18, 3, παρεισάγεσθαι καὶ παρεισπίπτειν εἰς τὰς πολιορκουμένας πόλεις.

οἵτινες] '*men who*,' 'a set of men who,' —not simply equivalent to οἵ (Ust.). but specifying the *class* to which they belonged; see Matth. *Gr.* § 483, Jelf, *Gr.* § 816, and notes on ch. iv. 24, where the uses of ὅστις are more fully discussed. The translation of Fritz., 'quippe qui' (comp. Herm. *Œd. R.* 688), is here unduly strong; even in classical Greek, what is commonly termed a *causal*, may be more correctly considered an *explicative* sense; see Ellendt, *Lex. Soph.* s. v. 3, Vol. II. p. 383. This, too, is the prevailing sense in the later writers; see Dindorf in Steph. *Thesaur.* s. v.

κατασκοπῆσαι] '*to spy out*,' ܕܢܪܓܠܘܢ [ut explorarent] Syr., 'explorare,' Vulg.; not 'ut dolose eripiant libertatem Christianam,' (Dindorf, Steph. *Thes.* s. v.

ἵνα ἡμᾶς καταδουλώσουσιν· 5 οἷς οὐδὲ πρὸς ὥραν εἴξαμεν τῇ ὑπο-
ταγῇ, ἵνα ἡ ἀλήθεια τοῦ εὐαγγελίου διαμείνῃ πρὸς ὑμᾶς. 6 ἀπὸ

5. οἷς οὐδέ] These words are omitted by the first hand of D (Tisch. *Cod. Clarom.* p. 568) E; Irenæus (p. 200, ed. Bened.), and, according to Jerome, in some *Latin* manuscripts: Tertullian and Ambrose appear only to have rejected the relative; see *adv. Marc.* v. 3. It is obvious that such an omission would greatly simplify the structure, but this very fact in a critical point of view makes it suspicious. When to this we add the immense preponderance of external authority, we can entertain but little doubt that οἷς οὐδέ is genuine; see Bagge *in loc.*, who has well discussed this reading.

Vol. IV. p. 1232), κατασκοπ. being here used in the same (hostile) sense as κατασκοπεῦσαι, Josh. ii. 2; ὁρᾷς πῶς καὶ τῇ τῶν κατασκόπων προσηγορίᾳ ἐδήλωσε τὸν πόλεμον ἐκείνων, Chrys. ἐν Χριστῷ] Not '*per Christum*,' a meaning it *may* bear (Fritz. p. 184) but in the fuller and deeper sense '*in Christ;*' see notes on ver. 17. ἵνα ἡμᾶς καταδουλώσουσιν] '*that they may succeed in enslaving us;*' the tense pointing to the result, the compound to the completeness of the act; comp. 2 Cor. xi. 20. Although this reading is confirmed by a decided preponderance of uncial authority [ABCDE], and the improbability of a correction very great, still the instances of ἵνα with a future are so very few (Gayler, *Part. Neg.* p. 169), and these, too, so reducible in number (Klotz, *Devar.* Vol. II. p. 631), that we are not justified in saying more than this, that the future *appears* used to convey the idea of *duration* (Winer), or perhaps, rather, of issue, *sequence* (Schmalfeld, *Synt.* § 142; comp. Alf.), more distinctly than the more usual aorist subj. Though excessively doubtful in classical writers (Herm. *Partic.* ἄν, II. 13, p. 134), a few instances are found in later authors; see Winer, *Gr.* § 41, b. 1, p. 259.

5. τῇ ὑποταγῇ] '*by yielding them the subjection they claimed;*' dative of manner; see Winer, *Gr.* § 31. 7. p. 194, comp. Scheuerl. *Synt.* § 22. 6, p. 180. The article is not merely the article with abstract nouns (Green, *Gr.* p. 146), but is used to specify the obedience which the false brethren (not the Apostles, Fritz.) demanded in this particular case. ἡ ἀλήθεια τοῦ εὐαγγελίου] '*the truth of the Gospel;*' the true teaching of the Gospel, as opposed to the false teaching of it as propagated by Judaizers, *i. e.*, as in verse 16, the doctrine of justification by faith. The distinction drawn by Winer (*Gr.* § 34. 3, p. 211) between such expressions as the present, — where the governing noun is a distinct element pertaining to the governed, and such as πλούτου ἀδηλότης, 1 Tim. vi. 17, καινότης ζωῆς, Rom. vi. 4, — where it is more a rhetorically expressed attribute, though denied by Fritz. *Rom.* Vol. I. p. 368, seems perfectly just. A doctrinal import is contained in ἡ ἀλήθεια τοῦ εὐαγγ., which is entirely lost by explaining it as merely τὸ ἀληθὲς εὐαγγέλιον. διαμείνῃ πρὸς ὑμᾶς] '*might remain steadfast with you,*' 'permaneat[-eret]' Vulg., Clarom.; the διὰ obviously being *intensive*, as in Heb. i. 11, 2 Pet. iii. 4; comp. Chrys., ἵνα . . . τοῦτο διὰ τῶν ἔργων βεβαιώσωμεν. πρὸς ὑμᾶς] See on ch. i. 18.

6. ἀπὸ δὲ τῶν δοκούντων εἶναί τι κ. τ. λ.] '*But from those who were high in reputation;*' — interrupted declaration of his independence of the οἱ δοκοῦντες. The meaning of this verse

δὲ τῶν δοκούντων εἶναι τι (ὁποῖοί ποτε ἦσαν οὐδέν μοι διαφέρει· πρόσωπον Θεὸς ἀνθρώπου οὐ λαμβάνει) ἐμοὶ γὰρ οἱ δοκοῦντες

is perfectly clear, but the structure is somewhat difficult. According to the common explanation, ἀπὸ—εἶναί τι is a sentence that would naturally have terminated with οὐδὲν ἔλαβον or προσελαβόμην (not ἐδιδάχθην, Winer, § 47. p. 331), or more correctly still, οὐδέν μοι προσανετέθη; owing, however, to the parenthesis ὁποῖοι—λαμβάνει, the natural structure is interrupted, and the sentence, commenced *passively*, is concluded *actively* with ἐμοὶ γὰρ κ. τ. λ.; see Winer, *Gr.* § 63. 1. 1, p. 502. The real difficulty of the sentence, however, lies in the following γάρ. That it is (*a*) merely *resumptive*, Scholef. (*Hints*, p. 74), Peile, al., is indemonstrable; as, of the passages usually cited in favor of this force, viz. Acts xvii. 28, 1 Cor. ix. 19, 2 Cor. v. 4, Rom. xv. 27, the first three are clearly instances of the argumentative force (see Winer, *Gr.* § 53. 10. 3, p 403, Meyer *on Cor. ll.cc.*), while in the fourth the words εὐδόκησαν γὰρ are merely emphatically repeated. That it is (*b*) *argumentative*, either as giving a reason for οὐδέν μοι διαφέρει κ. τ. λ. (Alf.), or for πρόσωπον Θεὸς κ. τ. λ. (Mey.), is logically and contextually improbable, as parenthetical and non-parenthetical parts would thus be confused and intermingled. If, however, γὰρ be regarded as (*c*) *explicative*, the whole seems clear and logical. To avoid the words δοκούντων εἶναί τι being misunderstood, and supposed to assign an *undue* preëminence to these Apostles, St. Paul hastily introduces the parenthetical comment, leaving the former sentence incomplete: then, feeling that its meaning was still so far obvious as to need some justification, he reverts to it, slightly qualifying it by the emphatic ἐμοί, slightly justifying it by the explicative γάρ, '*to me* (whatever they might have done for others) *it is certainly a fact that*,' etc. On this explicative force of γάρ, see Donalds. *Gr.* § 618, Klotz. *Devar.* Vol. II. p 233 sq., Hartung, *Partik.* γάρ § 2, and comp. Lücke, *John* iv. 44. Of the other interpretations of this difficult passage, none appear to deserve special notice except that of the Greek writers (Chrys., however, is silent, and Theod. has here a *lacuna*), who connect ἀπὸ τῶν δοκούντων immediately with οὐδέν μοι διαφέρει in the sense of οὐδεμία μοι φροντὶς περὶ τῶν δοκ. (Theoph.), but thus assign an untenable meaning to ἀπό, and dislocate the almost certain connection of ὁποῖοί ποτ' ἦσαν with what follows. Further details will be found in Meyer, De Wette, and Fritzsche (*Opusc.* p. 201 sq.). The Vv. are for the most part perplexingly literal (comp. Vulg.); the Syr., however, by its change of γὰρ into ܕܝܢ seems certainly in accordance with the general view adopted above.

τῶν δοκούντων εἶναί τι] '*who were deemed to be somewhat*,' ܕܡܬܚܫܒܝܢ [qui reputati erant] Syr., 'qui videbantur,' Vulg.; used with reference to the judgment of *others* (contrast ch. vi. 2), and so, perfectly similar in meaning to τοῖς δοκοῦσιν, ver. 2; comp. Plato, *Gorg.* 572 A, ὑπὸ πολλῶν καὶ δοκ. εἶναί τι; *Euthyd.* 303 C, τῶν σεμνῶν καὶ δοκ. τι εἶναι. ὁποῖοί ποτε] '*qualescumque*;' ποτε not being temporal, 'olim,' Beza (perhaps suggested by the 'aliquando' of Vulg.), but connected with ὁποῖοι, which it serves to render more general and inclusive; compare Demosth. *Or. de Pace*, IV. 15 (p. 60), ὁποία ποτ' ἐστὶν αὕτη, cited by Bloomf. and Fritz. *in. loc.* ἦσαν *may* certainly refer to the period of the Apostles' lives when they were uncon-

οὐδὲν προσανέθεντο, [7] ἀλλὰ τοὐναντίον ἰδόντες ὅτι πεπίστευμαι τὸ εὐαγγέλιον τῆς ἀκροβυστίας καθὼς Πέτρος τῆς περιτομῆς

verted, or when they were in attendance on our Lord (a view strongly supported by Hilgenf.); it seems, however, far more natural to refer the tense to a past, relative to the time of writing the words. οὐδέν μοι διαφ.] '*it maketh no matter to me.*' For examples of this less usual, but fully defensible insertion of the dative, see Lobeck, *Phryn.* p. 384, and comp. Wetst. *in loc.* πρόσωπον Θεὸς κ. τ. λ.] '*God accepteth no man's person*'—πρόσωπον put forward with emphasis, while Θεὸς and ἀνθρ. form a suggestive contrast (Mey.); 'God looketh not to the outward as men do, and judgeth on no partial principles, and no more did I his servant.' This and the equiv. expression βλέπειν εἰς πρόσωπ. ἀνθρ. are in the N. T. always used with a bad reference; see Matth. xxii. 16, Mark xii. 14, Luke xx. 21. The corresponding expression in the O. T. נָשָׂא פָנִים (translated sometimes θαυμάζειν πρόσωπον; comp. Jude 16) is used *occasionally* in a good sense; see Gen. xix. 21, and comp. Fritz. and Schott *in loc.* προσανέθεντο] '*communicated nothing,*' '*addressed no communication to;*' 'contulerunt,' Vulg., Clarom., and more distinctly 'dixerunt,' Æth.-Pol. 'notum fecerunt,' Arm.; as in ch. i. 16. In spite of the authority of the Greek expositors (μάθοντες τὰ ἐμὰ οὐδὲν προσέθηκαν, οὐδὲν διώρθωσαν, Chrys.), and appy of Syr. (ܐܘܣܦܘ adjecerunt), Copt. [*ououah.*], Goth. ('anaïnsokun'), al., it still seems more safe to retain the same meaning in both passages. There is weight in the argument urged in ed. 1 (see, too, Wieseler, *Chronol.* p. 195 note), that προσανέθ. here may seem to specify *addition*, as in contrast with ἀνεθέμην ver. 2, still the tendency of later Greek to compound forms (compare notes on ch. iii. 13), and the perfect parallelism of this with the *similarly negative* formula in ch. i. 16, are tacit arguments which seem *slightly* to preponderate. In the passage commonly referred to (Xen. *Mem.* II. 1. 8), προσαναθέσθαι merely implies 'etiam sibi adjungere, scil. *suscipere*' (see Kühner *in loc.*), and so proves nothing, except that Bretschn., Olsh., Rück., al., must be incorrect in translating 'nihil mihi præterea *imposuerunt,*' as this expresses a directly opposite idea. Under any circumstances, there is nothing either in this word, or in the whole paragraph, to substantiate the extraordinary position of Baur, that the Apostles only yielded to St. Paul's views after a long struggle.

7. ἀλλὰ τοὐναντίον] '*but on the contrary;*' scil. so far from giving instructions to me, they practically added the weight of their approval: τὸ ἐναντίον τοῦ μέμψασθαι τὸ ἐπαινέσαι, Chrys. Surely this was not exactly leaving St. Paul 'to fight his own battle,' Jowett, Alf. πεπίστευμαι] The principal instances in the New Testament of this well-known structure will be found, Winer, *Gr.* § 32. 5, p. 204. On the use of the perfect as indicating *permanence, duration,* 'concreditum mihi habeo,' see ib. § 40. 4, p. 242. Usteri calls attention to the accurate use of the perf. here, compared with the aorist in Rom. iii. 2, ἐπιστεύθησαν ('Ιουδαῖοι) τὰ λόγια τοῦ Θεοῦ. τῆς ἀκροβυστίας] '*of the uncircumcision,*' scil. τῶν ἀκροβύστων; οὐ τὰ πράγματα λέγων αὐτά ἀλλὰ τὰ ἀπὸ τούτων γνωριζόμενα ἔθνη, Chrys.; comp. Rom. iii. 30. The derivation of ἀκροβ. (not ἄκρον, βύω, but an Alexandrian corruption of ἀκροποσθία) is discussed by Fritzsche, *Rom.* ii. 26, Vol. I. p. 136. καθὼς Πέ-

8 (ὁ γὰρ ἐνεργήσας Πέτρῳ εἰς ἀποστολὴν τῆς περιτομῆς ἐνήργησεν
κἀμοὶ εἰς τὰ ἔθνη), 9 καὶ γνόντες τὴν χάριν τὴν δοθεῖσάν μοι,
Ἰάκωβος καὶ Κηφᾶς καὶ Ἰωάννης, οἱ δοκοῦντες στῦλοι εἶναι, δεξ-

τρος κ. τ. λ.] '*even as Peter was of the circumcision.*' St. Peter here appears as the representative of the 'Judenapostel' (Meyer; comp. Grot.), on the principle that 'a potiori fit denominatio;' for though originally chosen out as the first preacher to the Gentiles (Acts xv. 7), his subsequent labors appear to have been more among Jews; compare 1 Pet. i. 1. On the use of καθώς, see notes on ch. iii. 6, and on its most suitable translation, compare notes *on* 1 *Thess.* i. 5 (*Transl.*).

8. ὁ γὰρ ἐνεργ. κ. τ. λ.] '*For He who wrought (effectually) for Peter,*' ܠܦܛܪܘܣ Syr., 'Petro,' Vulg., Clarom.; not '*in* Petro,' Grot.; historical confirmation of what precedes, added parenthetically. There are four constructions of ἐνεργέω in St. Paul's Epp.; (*a*) ἐνεργέω τι, 1 Cor. xii. 11; (*b*) ἐνεργέω ἔν τινι, Eph. ii. 2; (*c*) ἐνεργέω τι ἔν τινι, ch. iii. 5; (*d*) ἐνεργέω τινι εἴς τι, here; comp. Prov. xxxi. 12. In this latter case the dative is not governed by ἐνεργέω, as the verb is not a pure compound [there is no form ἐργέω], but is the dat. *commodi.* Ὁ ἐνεργήσας, it may be observed, is not Christ (Chrys., Aug.), but God (Jerome); for, in the first place, St. Paul always speaks of his Apostleship as given *by* God (Rom. xv. 15, 1 Cor. xv. 10, Eph. iii. 2) *through* Christ (Rom. i. 5; compare ib. xv. 18, and ch. i. 1); and secondly, this ἐνεργεῖν is distinctly ascribed to God, 1 Cor. xii. 6, Phil. ii. 13. εἰς ἀποστολήν] '*for* or *towards the Apostleship,*' *i. e.* for the successful performance of it (Hamm.), not merely 'in respect of it' (Mey.), — a meaning lexically admissible both in classical writers (Rost u. Palm, *Lex.* s. v. εἰς, v. 2, Vol. I. p. 804), and in the N. T. (Winer, *Gr.* § 49. a, p. 354) but here contextually insufficient, as the sense seems almost obviously to require the more definite notion of *purpose*, or contemplated object; compare 2 Cor. ii. 12, εἰς τὸ εὐαγγέλιον (to preach the Gospel), Col. i. 29. The second εἰς is joined with τὰ ἔθνη by what is called 'comparatio compendiaria,' Jelf, *Gr.* § 781.

9. καὶ γνόντες] '*and having become aware;*' continuation of the interrupted narrative; ἰδόντες (Ver. 7) . . . . καὶ γνόντες. The former participle appears to refer to the mental impression produced, when the nature and success of St. Paul's preaching was brought before them; the latter, to the result of the actual information they derived from him; but see notes ch. iv. 9.

Ἰάκωβος] '*James,*' the Brother of our Lord (ch. i. 9), Bishop of Jerusalem, — and as such placed first in order in the recital of acts that took place in that Church. Irenæus (*Haer.* III. 12, ad fin.) in noticing this subject, uses the strong expression 'qui circa Jacobum Apostoli;' see Grabe *in loc.* The reading Πέτρ. καὶ Ἰάκ. has but weak external support [DEFG; Clarom., Goth., Theod. (4), Greg. Nyss., al.], and on internal grounds is highly suspicious. οἱ δοκοῦντες κ. τ. λ.] '*who have the reputation of being,*' οὓς πάντες πανταχοῦ περιφέρουσιν, Chrys.; δοκέω not being pleonastic, but retaining its usual and proper meaning; see exx. in Winer, *Gr.* § 65. 7, p. 540. The metaphor is illustrated by Suicer *Thes.* s. v. στῦλος, Vol. II. 1044, Wetst. *in loc.*, and (from Rabbinical writers) by Schoettg. *Hor. Hebr.* Vol. I. p. 728, 729.

ιὰς ἔδωκαν ἐμοὶ καὶ Βαρνάβᾳ κοινωνίας· ἵνα ἡμεῖς εἰς τὰ ἔθνη,
αὐτοὶ δὲ εἰς τὴν περιτομήν· 10 *μόνον τῶν πτωχῶν ἵνα μνημονεύω-*
μεν, ὃ καὶ ἐσπούδασα αὐτὸ τοῦτο ποιῆσαι.

The most apposite quotations are perhaps, Clem. *Rom.* I. 5, οἱ δικαιότατοι στῦλοι, Euseb. *Hist.* VI. 41, στεῤῥοὶ καὶ μακάριοι στῦλοι. δεξιὰς . . . κοινωνίας] '*right hands of fellowship*,' scil. in the Apostolic office of teaching and preaching; comp. Schulz, *Abendm.* p. 190 sq. The remark of Fritzs. (*Opusc.* p. 220, comp. Mey.), — 'articulum τὰς δεξιὰς τῆς κοινωνίας non desiderabit, qui δεξ. κοιν. *dextras sociales, i. e.* dextras ejusmodi, quibus societas confletur valere reputaverit,' is scarcely necessary. As δεξιὰς in the phrase δεξιὰς διδόναι (1 Macc. xi. 50, 62, xiii. 50) is usually anarthrous, the principle of correlation (Middleton, *Gr. Art.* III. 33) causes it to be omitted with κοινωνίας; compare Winer, *Gr.* § 18. 2. 6, p. 142. The separation of the gen. from the subst. on which it depends occurs occasionally in St. Paul's Epistles, and is usually due either to explanatory specification (Phil. ii. 10), correction (1 Thess. ii. 13), emphasis (1 Tim. iii. 6), or, as appy. here, merely structural reasons, — the natural union of δεξιὰς and ἔδωκαν, and of ἔδωκαν and its dative; comp. Winer, *Gr.* 30. 3. 2, p. 172. ἵνα ἡμ. εἰς τὰ ἔθνη] '*that we — to the Gentiles*,' not εὐαγγελιζώμεθα (Winer, *Gr.* p. 518), as this verb is not found with εἰς in St. Paul's Epp. (Mey.), but either simply πορευθῶμεν, or perhaps better ἀπόστολοι γενώμεθα, 'apostulatu fungeremur,' Beza. It is scarcely necessary to add that this compact was intended to be rather general than specific, and that the terms ἔθνη and περιτομὴ have more of a *geographical* than a merely personal reference. St. Paul knew himself to be the Apostle of the Gentiles (comp. Rom. xi. 13); but this did not prevent him (κατὰ τὸ εἰωθός, Acts xvii. 2), while in Gentile lands, preaching *first* to the Jews; see Acts xvii. 10, xviii. 5, xix. 8. The insertion of μὲν after ἡμεῖς [with ACDE; more than thirty mss.; Copt., Syr.-Philox.; Chrys. al.] seems certainly a grammatical insertion.

10. μόνον τῶν πτωχῶν κ. τ. λ.] '*only that we should remember the poor*;' limiting clause dependent on δεξιὰς ἔδωκαν and expressive of the condition attached to the general compact: 'we were to go to the Gentiles, they to the circumcision, with this stipulation only, that we were not to forget the poor in Judæa;' comp. Rom. xv. 26, 27, 1 Cor. xvi. 3. There is thus no ellipsis of αἰτοῦντες, παρακαλοῦντες, or indeed of any verb; the μόνον carries its own explanation; 'imperium ipsâ voce μόνον adsignificatum, ut id sit quod καὶ παρήγγειλαν,' Fritzsche, *Matth.* Excurs. I. p. 839. ὃ καὶ ἐσπούδασα κ. τ. λ.] '*which very thing I was also forward to do*,' literally 'which, namely, this very thing, I was also,' etc.; αὐτὸ τοῦτο (ܗܝ ܗܕܐ Syr.) not being redundantly joined with ὅ, 'per Hebraismum' (Rück., B. Crus., and even Conyb.), but simply forming an emphatic epexegesis of the preceding relative; see Winer, *Gr.* § 22. 4, p. 134. Occasionally in the N. T. (Mark i. 7, vii. 25, Rev. vii. 2 al., and (as might be conceived) not uncommonly in the LXX., there seem to be clear instances of a Hebraistic redundancy of the simple αὐτός, but appy. never of this stronger form αὐτὸς οὗτος; see Winer, *Gr. l. c.*, and comp. Bornem. *Schol. Luc.* p. LIV. ἐσπούδασα] '*I was forward*,' 'I evinced σπουδή;' with an appended object-infin.; comp.

When Peter dissembled, I withstood and rebuked him, urging that to observe the law as a justifying principle is to make void the grace of God.

11 Ὅτε δὲ ἦλθεν Κηφᾶς εἰς Ἀντιόχειαν,

Eph. iv. 3, 1 Thess. ii. 17. The aor. is here correctly used, not for the perfect (Conyb.), nor even for the pluperf., nor yet exactly as expressing the *habit* (compare Alf.), — this usage being somewhat doubtful in the N. T. (see Winer, *Gr.* § 40. 5. 1, p. 248, and notes *on Eph.* i. 3), — but simply an historical fact that belongs to the past, without its being affirmed or denied that it may not continue to the present; See Fritz. *de Aor. Vi*, p. 17, and *on* 1 *Thess.* ii. 16.
The passages usually adduced (Rom. xv. 27, 1 Cor. xvi. 1 sq., 2 Cor. viii. 1 sq., compare Acts xi. 17 sq., xxiv. 17) illustrate the practice, but not the tense, being subsequent to the probable date of this Epistle. All historical deductions from this passage, except, *perhaps*, that Barnabas had recently left St. Paul (hence the sing.; see Winer, *in loc.*), seem very precarious.

11. ὅτε δὲ ἦλθεν Κηφᾶς] '*But when Cephas came,*' etc. Still further proof of the Apostle's independence by an historical notice of his opposition to, and even reproval of St. Peter's inconsistent conduct at Antioch: see some good remarks on this subject in Thiersch. *History of Church*, Vol. I. p. 123 sq. (Transl.). The reading Πέτρος (*Rec.*) is fairly supported [DEFGJK; Demid., Goth.; mss.; Chrys., al.], but still even in external authority inferior to Κηφᾶς, [*Lachm.*, *Tisch.*, with ABCH; a few mss.; Syr., Copt., Sahid.; Clem., al.], not to mention the high probability of Πέτρος having been an explanatory change.
κατὰ πρόσωπον] '*to the face,*' Auth. 'in faciem,' Vulg., ܒܐܦܘܗܝ [in faciem ejus] Syr., — not 'coram omnibus, aperto Marte' (Elsn., Conyb., al.), this being specified in ἔμπροσθεν πάντων, ver. 14: comp. Acts xxv. 16, and perhaps ib. iii. 13, κατὰ πρόσωπον Πιλάτου, 'to the face of Pilate.' The preposition has here its secondary local meaning, '*e regione;*' the primary idea of horizontal direction (Donalds. *Gr.* § 479) passing naturally into that of local opposition. This may be very clearly traced in the descriptions of the positions of troops, etc., by the later military writers; *e. g.* Polyb. *Hist.* I. 34. 5, οἱ κατὰ τοὺς ἐλέφαντας ταχθέντες; *ib. ib.* 9, οἱ κατὰ τὸ λαιόν; with πρόσωπον, *ib.* III. 65, 6, XI. 14. 6: see Bernhardy, *Synt.* v. 20, b, p. 240, Dobree, *Advers.* Vol. I. p. 114. The gloss κατὰ σχῆμα (in appearance, — not in reality) adopted by Chrys., Jerome, and several early writers, is wholly untenable, and due only to an innocent though mistaken effort to salve the authority of St. Peter, appy. first suggested by Origen [*Strom.* Book x.]: see Jerome, *Epist.* 86—97, esp. 90, the appy. unanswerable objections of Augustine (*Epist.* 8—19), the sensible remarks of Bede *in loc.*, and for much curious information on the whole subject, Deyling, *Obs. Sacr.* Vol. II. p. 520 sq. (No. 45). ὅτι κατεγνωσμένος ἦν] '*because he had been condemned;*' not 'reprehensibilis,' Vulg., nor 'even '*reprehensionem* incurrerat,' Winer, but simply 'reprehensus erat,' Clarom., Goth., Syr.-Phil. (Syr. paraphrases), al.
As this clause has been much encumbered with glosses, it will be best to notice separately both the meaning of the verb and the force of the participle. (1) Καταγιγνώσκειν (generally with τινός τι, more rarely, τινά τινος) has two principal meanings; (α) '*to note accurately;*' usually in a bad sense, *e. g.*, '*detect,*' Prov. xxviii. 11 (Aquil. ἐξιχνιάσει) '*think ill of,*' Xen. *Mem.* I. 3, 10: (β) '*to note judicially,*' — either in the lighter sense of *accuse* (probably 1 John iii. 20; see

κατὰ πρόσωπον αὐτῷ ἀντέστην, ὅτι κατεγνωσμένος ἦν. 12 πρὸ
τοῦ γὰρ ἐλθεῖν τινας ἀπὸ Ἰακώβου μετὰ τῶν ἐθνῶν συνήσθιεν·
ὅτε δὲ ἦλθον, ὑπέστελλεν καὶ ἀφώριζεν ἑαυτόν, φοβούμενος τοὺς ἐκ

Lücke *in loc.*), or the graver of *condemn* (the more usual meaning). (2) The perf. part. pass. *cannot* be used as a pure verbal adjective. The examples adduced by Elsner *in loc.* will all bear a different explanation; and even those in which the use of the participle *seems* to approach that of the Hebrew part. (Gesen. *Gr.* § 131. 1), such as Rev. xxi. 8 (perf. part.), Jude 12 (aor.), or Heb xii. 18 (pres.), can all be explained grammatically; see Winer, *Gr.* § 45. 1, p. 307. The only tenable translations, then, are (*a*) '*he had been accused*,' or (*b*) '*he had been condemned*;' and of these (*b*) seems obviously most in accordance with the context and the nature of the case. As St. Peter's conduct had been condemned, not merely by himself (Alf.), but, as seems more natural, generally by the sounder body of Christians at Antioch, St. Paul, as the representative of the anti-Judaical party, feels himself authorized to rebuke him, and that too (ver. 14), publicly.

12. τινὰς ἀπὸ Ἰακώβου *may* be connected together, and grammatically translated, 'some of the followers of James;' see Jelf, *Gr.* 620. 3, Bernhardy, *Synt.* v. 12, p. 222. As, however, in the New Testament, this mode of periphrasis (οἱ ἀπὸ κ. τ. λ.) appears mainly confined to *places* (Mark xiii. 22, Acts vi. 9, xxvii. 24, al.), or abstract substantives (Acts xv. 5), it will seem most exact to connect ἀπὸ Ἰακ. with ἐλθεῖν. So distinctly Æth.-Pol., omitting, however, the τινές: the other Vv. mainly preserve the order of the Greek. We certainly cannot deduce from this that they were '*sent* by James' (Theoph., Mey., Alf.), for though this use of ἀπὸ does occur (comp. Matth. xxvi. 47 with Mark xv. 43, and see Fritz. *Matth.* Vol. I. p. 779), yet the common meaning of the prep. in such constructions is *local* rather than *ethical*, — separation rather than mission from: compare Knapp, *Script. Var. Argum.* p. 510. The men in question probably represented themselves as rigid followers of St. James, and are thus briefly noticed as having come ἀπὸ Ἰακώβου, rather than ἀπὸ Ἱεροσολύμων. συνήσθιεν] '*was eating with them*,' *i. e.* again followed that course which in the case of Cornelius similarly called forth the censure of οἱ ἐκ περιτομῆς (Acts xiii. 3), but was then nobly vindicated. Of the two following verbs ὑπέστ. and ἀφώρ. (both governing ἑαυτόν), the first does not mark the *secret*, the second the *open* course (Matth.), but simply the *initial* and *more completed* acts, respectively; the second was the result of the first, De Wette *in loc.* The reading ἦλθεν (*Lachm.*) has insufficient external authority [BD[1]FG; 2 mss.; Clarom.], and is a not improbable confirmation to the sing. which follows. φοβούμενος] '*fearing*,' '*because he feared*,' ܡܛܠ ܕܕܚܠ ܗܘܐ [quia timebat]; causal participle explaining the feeling which led to the preceding acts; 'timens ne culparetur ab illis,' Irenæus, *Hær.* III. 12 (ad fin.). The Greek commentators [there is a lacuna in Theod.] and others (see Poli *Synops. in loc.*) have endeavored to modify the application of this word, but without lexical authority. As on a different occasion (Matth. xiv. 30), so here again the apostle drew back from a course into which his first and best feelings had hastily led him. Some strongly-ex-

περιτομῆς· 13 καὶ συνυπεκρίθησαν αὐτῷ καὶ οἱ λοιποὶ Ἰουδαῖοι,
ὥστε καὶ Βαρνάβας συναπήχθη αὐτῶν τῇ ὑποκρίσει. 14 ἀλλ'

14. Ἰουδαϊκῶς ζῇς] This order is maintained by ABCFG; 37. 73. 80; Boern., Am., Demid. (three other mss.), Amit.; Or., Phil. (Carp.); many Lat. Ff. (but καὶ οὐκ Ἰουδ. omitted in Clarom., Sang., Ambrst. Sedul., Agap.): so *Lachm.*, *Meyer*. *Tisch.* reads ἐθν. ζῇς καὶ οὐκ Ἰουδ.; with DEJK; nearly all mss.; majority of Vv.; Chrys., Theod., Dam., Theophyl., Œcum., (*Rec.*, *Scholz*, *Alf.*) External authority thus appears decidedly in favor of the text, and is but little mollified by internal arguments, for a correction of the perspicuity (ἐθν. ζῇς) is quite as probable as the assumed one 'for elegance.' (*Alf.*) πῶς] It is difficult to imagine

pressed remarks on this subject will be found in South, *Serm.* XXVIII. Vol. II. p. 476 (Tegg).

13. συνυπεκρ. αὐτῷ] '*joined with him in dissimulation;*' result of the bad example, — the secession of the rest of the Jewish Christians at Antioch from social communion with the Gentile converts. The meaning of συνυπεκρ. is softened down by Syr. (subjecerunt se cum illo) Clarom. ('consenserunt cum illo'), al., but without reason; these very Christians of Antioch were the first who knew and *rejoiced* at (Acts xv. 31) the practically contrary decision of the Council. A good 'prælectio' on this text will be found in Sanderson, *Works*, Vol. IV. p. 44 (ed. Jacobs). ὥστε] '*so that,*' — as a simple matter of fact. In this form of the consecutive sentence the distinction between ὥστε with the indic. and the infin. can scarcely be maintained in translation. The latter (the *objective* form, as it is termed by Schmalfeld), is used when the result is a necessary and logical consequence of what has previously been enunciated; the former, when it is stated by the writer (the *subjective* form) as a simple and unconditioned fact; see Klotz, *Devar.* Vol. II. p. 772, and esp. Schmalfeld, *Synt.* § 155 sq., and Ellendt, *Lex. Soph.* s. v. Vol. II. p. 1101 sq., where the uses of this particle are well discussed. Here, for example, St. Paul notices the lapse of Barnabas as a fact, without implying that it was a necessary consequence of the behavior of the others. This distinction, however, is appy. not always observed in the N. T., nor indeed always in classical writers; comp. Winer, *Gr.* § 41. 5. 1, p. 269.

συναπήχθη αὐτῶν τῇ ὑποκρίσει] '*was carried away with them by their dissimulation,*' scil. into dissimulation: 'cum dativo personæ συναπάγ. *simul cum aliquo abduci,*' etc., declarat; cum dativo rei, *simul per rem abduci*, etc., significat,' Fritz. *Rom.* xii. 16, Vol. III. p. 88 sq. Σὺν thus refers to the companions in the τὸ ἀπάγεσθαι; ὑποκρίσει to the instrument *by which*, — not 'rei ad quam' (Bretsch., comp. Alf.), a questionable construction even in poetry (Bernhardy, *Synt.*, III. 12, p. 95), — and, by obvious *inference*, the state *into which* they were carried away; see 2 Pet. iii. 17. Fritzsche cites Zosim. *Hist.* v. 6, καὶ αὐτὴ δὲ ἡ Σπάρτη συναπήγετο τῇ κοινῇ τῆς Ἑλλάδος ἁλώσει κ. τ. λ.: add Clem. Alex. *Strom.* I. p. 311, τῇ ἡδονῇ συναπαγόμενος. Ὑπόκρισις is well paraphrased by Wieseler (*Chronol.* p. 197), as 'a practical denial of their better [spiritual] insight,' — and (we add) of their better feelings and knowledge; see above, on συνυπεκρ.

14. ὀρθοποδοῦσιν] '*walk uprightly;*' an ἅπαξ λεγόμ. in the N. T., and *very* rare elsewhere; Dindorf and

ὅτε εἶδον ὅτι οὐκ ὀρθοποδοῦσιν πρὸς τὴν ἀλήθειαν τοῦ εὐαγγελίου, εἶπον τῷ Κηφᾷ ἔμπροσθεν πάντων Εἰ σὺ Ἰουδαῖος ὑπάρθων ἐθνικῶς καὶ οὐκ Ἰουδαϊκῶς ζῇς, πῶς τὰ ἔθνη ἀναγκάζεις Ἰουδαΐζειν;

why *Tisch.* rejected this reading, supported as it is by ABCDEFG; mss.; majority of Vv.; Or., Dam., and Lat. Ff. (*Griesb. Scholz, Lachm., De Wette, Meyer,* approved by *Mill*, Prolegom. p. 123.) For τί, which seems very much like an interp., the authorities are JK; great majority of mss.; Syr.-Phil., al.; Chrys. Theod., Theophyl., Œcum. (*Rec., Tisch.*)

Jacobs in Steph. *Thesaur.* s. v. cite a few instances from later writers, *e. g.* Theodor. Stud. p. 308 B, 443 D, 473 D, 509 D, 575 E; but I have not succeeded in verifying the quotations. The meaning, however, is sufficiently obvious, and rightly expressed by the 'recte ambulare' of Vulg., Syr., and the best Vv.: comp. ὀρθόπους (Soph. *Antig.* 972), the similar verb ὀρθοτομεῖν, 2 Tim. ii. 15, and notes *in loc.* On the idiomatic use of the present in the narration of a past event, when 'continuance' or 'process' is implied, see Winer, *Gr.* § 40. 2. c, p. 239, and esp. Schmalfeld, *Synt.* § 54. 6, p. 96. πρὸς τὴν ἀλήθ.] '*according to the truth,*' *i. e.* 'according to the rule of;' the prep. here seeming to mark not so much the *aim* or *direction* (Hamm., Mey., Alf.), as the *rule* or *measure* of the ὀρθοποδεῖν; comp. 2 Cor. v. 10, κομίσηται, ... πρὸς ἃ ἔπραξεν, and see Winer, *Gr.* § 49. h, p. 361. The objection of Meyer, that St. Paul always expresses 'rule,' 'measure,' etc., after verbs *eundi* by κατά, not πρός, does not here fully apply; as motion is much more obscurely expressed in ὀρθοποδεῖν than περιπατεῖν (St. Paul's favorite verb of moral motion), which appears in all the instances that Meyer has adduced, viz. Rom. viii. 4, xiv. 15; 1 Cor. iii. 3. ἔμπροσθεν πάντων] '*before all men;*' 'publicum scandalum non poterat private curari,' Jerome; compare 1 Tim. v. 20. The speech which follows (ver. 14—21) is appy. rightly regarded as the *substance* of what was said by the Apostle on this important occasion; see on ver. 15. ἐθνικῶς ζῇς] '*livest after a Gentile fashion,*' scil. in thy general and habitual way of living. The tense must not be overpressed. St. Peter was not at that *exact* moment living ἐθνικῶς; his former conduct, however (μετὰ τῶν ἐθνῶν συνήσθιεν, ver. 12), is justly assumed by St. Paul as his regular and proper course of living (comp. Neand. *Planting*, Vol. II. p 83, Bohn), and specified as such to give a greater force to the reproof; see Usteri *in loc.* ἀναγκάζεις] '*constrainest thou;*' not 'invitas exemplo,' Grot., nor even 'wouldest thou constrain,' Conyb., but simply and plainly 'cogis,' Vulg., ܐܠܨ Syr., with reference to the moral influence and practical constraint (Hamm., Fell) which the authority and example of an Apostle like St. Peter could not fail to have exercised on the Christians at Antioch. To suppose that the Apostle joined with οἱ ἀπὸ Ἰακ. in actual outward coercion (Wieseler, *Chronol.* p. 198), is neither required by the word (see remarks in Sturz, *Lex. Xenoph.* Vol. I. p. 186) nor in any way to be inferred from the context. Ἰουδαΐζειν] '*to Judaize,*' 'Judaizare,' Vulg., Clarom., 'ïudaiviskon,' Goth.; not merely synonymous with Ἰουδαϊκῶς ζῆν (Schott, comp. Syr.), but probably a little more definite and inclusive, and carrying with it the idea of a more studied imitation and obedience; compare Esth. viii. 17.

15 ἡμεῖς φύσει Ἰουδαῖοι καὶ οὐκ ἐξ ἐθνῶν ἁμαρτωλοί· 16 εἰδότες δὲ

16. πίστεως Χριστοῦ] *Tisch.* omits Χριστοῦ, with FG; Boern.; Tert. Theod. (1), — but here again on insufficient external authority, and not without the omission seeming to be intentional, to avoid the thrice-repeated Χρ. in one verse. In favor of the text are ABCDE; mss.; Clarom., Vulg., al.; Chrys. (2), (*Rec.*, *Griesb.*, *Scholz*, *Lachm.*, *De W.*).

15. ἡμεῖς κ. τ. λ.] '*We,*' scil. 'you and I, and others like us;' κοινοποιεῖ τὸ λεγόμενον, Chrys. St. Paul here begins, as Meyer observes, with a concessive statement: 'We, I admit, have this advantage, that by birth we are Jews, not Gentiles, and consequently (καὶ *consecutive*, comp. notes *on* 1 *Thess.* iv., 1 and Klotz, *Devar.* Vol. I. p. 107) as such, sinners.' In the very admission, however, there seems a gentle irony; 'born Jews — yes, and nothing more — sinners of the Jews at best;' comp. Stier, *Ephes.* Vol. I. p. 257. With regard to the construction, it seems best with Herm. to supply ἐσμὲν to this verse, which thus constitutes a concessive protasis, ver. 16 (εἰδότες δὲ κ. τ. λ.) supplying the apodosis. It is now scarcely necessary to add, that in sentences of this nature there is no *ellipsis* of μέν: 'recte autem ibi non ponitur (μὲν) ubi aut non sequitur membrum oppositum, aut scriptores oppositionem addere nondum constituerant, aut loquentes alterius membri oppositionem quâcunque de causâ non indixerunt,' Fritz. *Rom.* x. 19, Vol. II. p. 423; compare Jelf, *Gr.* § 770, and Buttmann, *Mid.* (Excurs. XII.) p. 148. This verse and what follows have been deemed as addressed to the Galatians either directly (Calv. Grot.), or indirectly, in the form of meditative musings (Jowett), — but with but little plausibility. The speech seems clearly continued to the end of the chapter (Chrys., Theod., Jerome), and to be the *substance* of what was said: it is not, however, unnatural also to suppose that it may here be expressed in a slightly altered *form*, and in a shape calculated to be more intelligible, and more immediately applicable to the Apostle's present readers. For a paraphrase, see notes to *Transl.*, and also Usteri, *Lehrb.* II. 1. 2, p. 161.

φύσει] '*by nature;*' not merely by habit and custom as the proselytes; ἐκ γένους καὶ οὐ προσήλυτοι, Theod. Mops. This passage is important as serving to fix the meaning of φύσις in *loci dogmatici*, such as Eph. ii. 3: see esp. Stier, *Ephes.* Vol. I. p. 257. ἁμαρτωλοί] The point of view from which a Jew must naturally consider them (Eph. ii. 12); perhaps with slight irony (Stier, *Red. Jes.* Vol. VI. p. 307). That they were so regarded needs no other proof than such expressions as τελῶναι καὶ ἁμαρτωλοί; comp. Tobit xiii. 6.

16. εἰδότες δέ] '*but as we know,*' ܡܛܠ ܕܝܕܥܝܢܢ [quia novimus] Syr.; causal participle (Jelf, *Gr.* § 697, Schmalfeld, *Synt.* § 207) attached to ἐπιστεύσαμεν, and introducing the apodosis to the concessive sentence. Reconsideration seems still to show that of the many explanations of this difficult passage, this is appy. the simplest. According to the common interpret., εἰδ. δὲ .... Χριστοῦ forms an interposed sentence between ver. 15 and the latter part of ver. 16; but here δὲ is a serious obstacle, as its proper force can only be brought out by supplying *although* (De W.) to ver. 15, unless, indeed, with Alf. we venture on the somewhat doubtful translation 'nevertheless,' or fall back [with AD^{3}K; some Vv.; Greek Ff. (*Rec.*)] on the still more doubtful omis-

ὅτι οὐ δικαιοῦται ἄνθρωπος ἐξ ἔργων νόμου ἐὰν μὴ διὰ πίστεως Ἰησοῦ Χριστοῦ, καὶ ἡμεῖς εἰς Χριστὸν Ἰησοῦν ἐπιστεύ-

sion. δικαιοῦται] '*is justified*,' 'Deo probatus redditur;' τὸ δικαιοῦσθαι being in antithesis to τὸ εὑρίσκεσθαι ἁμαρτωλόν, ver. 17; see Schott *in loc.*, where the different meanings of δικαιοῦσθαι are explained with great perspicuity. The broad distinction to be observed is between (*a*) the *absolute* use of the verb, whether with regard to God (Luke vii. 29), Christ (1 Tim. iii. 16), or men (Rom. iv. 2, James ii. 21); and (*b*) the *relative* use ('ratione habitâ vel controversiæ, cui obnoxius fuerit, vel peccatorum, quæ vere commiserit'). In this latter division we must again distinguish between the purely *judicial* meaning (Matth. xii. 37) and the far wider *dogmatical* meaning, which involves the idea not only of forgiveness of past sins (Rom. vi. 7), but also of a spiritual change of heart through the in-working power of faith. See more in Schott *in loc.*, and in Bull, *Harm. Apost.* Ch. I. § 2 (with Grabe's notes), and on the whole subject consult *Homily on Salv.* III. 1, Jackson, *Creed*, Book IV. 6, 7, Waterland *on Justif.* Vol. VI. p. 1 sq. and esp. the admirable explanations and distinctions of Hooker, *Serm.* II. Vol. III. p. 609 sq. (ed. Keble). ἐξ ἔργων νόμου] '*by the works of the law*;' as the cause of the δικαιοῦσθαι; comp. Bull, *Harm. Apost.* Ch. I. § 8, with the notes of Grabe, p. 16 (ed. Burt.). With regard to the exact force of ἐκ, it may be observed that in its primary ethical sense it denotes (α) *origin* (more immediate, ἀπὸ more remote); from which it passes through the intermediate ideas of (β) *result from*, and (γ) *consequence of*, to that of (δ) nearly direct *causality* (Rost u. Palm, *Lex.* ἐκ, IV. 1), thus closely approximating to ὑπὸ with a gen. (a common use in Herod.) and διὰ with a gen. (Fritz. *Rom.* v. 16, Vol. I. p. 332). In many cases it is hard to decide between these different shades of meaning, especially in a writer so varied in his use of prepp. as St. Paul: here, however, we are guided both by the context and by the analogy of Scripture. From both it seems clear that ἐκ is here in its simple *causal* sense; the whole object of the speech being to show that the works of the law have no 'causalis ἐνέργεια' in man's justification. On the contrary, in the antithetical passage in St. James (ch. ii. 24) just as δικαιοῦσθαι has a slightly different (more inclusive) meaning (see Hooker, *Serm.* II. 20), so also has the prep., — which proportionately recedes from ideas of more *direct*, to those of more *remote* causality (causa sine quâ non); comp. Hamm., *Pract. Catech.* p. 78 (A. C. L.). νόμου] Gen. *objecti*: 'deeds by which the requisitions of the law are fulfilled,' 'eorum præstationem quæ lex præcipit' (Beza), — the מַעֲשִׂים הַתּוֹרִיִּם of the Rabbinical writers, and the directly antithetical expression to ἁμαρτήματα νόμου, Wisdom ii. 12 (Mey.); see exx. in Winer, *Gr.* § 30. 1, p. 167. The νόμος here, it need scarcely be said, is not merely the *ceremonial* (Theod., al.), but the *whole* law, — the Mosaic law in its widest significance; see Fritz. *Rom.* III. 20, Vol. I. p. 179. ἐὰν μή] Two constructions here seem to be blended, οὐ δικ. ἄνθρ. ἐξ ἔργων νόμου, and οὐ δικ. ἄνθρ. ἐὰν μὴ διὰ πίστεως Ἰ. Χ. The two particles, though apparently equivalent in meaning to ἀλλά, never lose their proper *exceptive* force: see Fritz. *Rom.* xiv. 14, Vol. III. p. 195, and notes on ch. i. 7. διὰ πίστεως Ἰησοῦ Χριστοῦ] '*by faith in* or *on Jesus Christ*;' 'per fidem in Jesu

σαμεν, ἵνα δικαιωθῶμεν ἐκ πίστεως Χριστοῦ καὶ οὐκ ἐξ ἔργων νόμου, διότι ἐξ ἔργων νόμου οὐ δικαιωθήσεται πᾶσα σαρξ.

Christo collocatam,' Rom. iii. 22. Stier (*Ephes.* Vol. I. p. 447) explains πίστ. Ἰησ. Χρ. both here and (esp.) ch. iii. 22, in a deeper sense, 'faith which belongs to, has its foundation *in* Christ' (comp. Mark xi. 22, Ephes. iii. 12), the gen. Ἰησ. Χρ. being the gen. *subjecti.* This view may deserve consideration in other places, but here certainly the context and preceding antithesis seem decidedly in favor of the more simple gen. *objecti.* It may be observed that διὰ here closely approximates in meaning to ἐκ below, the same idea of causality being (as Meyer suggests) expressed under two general forms, *origin* and *means.* We must be careful, then, not to press unduly the distinction between the prepp.: the antithesis is here not so much between the modes of operation, as between the very nature and essence of the principles themselves. As to the doctrinal import of διὰ πίστεως, Waterland (*on Justif.* p. 22) well remarks, that 'faith is not the mean by which grace is wrought or conferred, but the mean whereby it is accepted or received;' it is 'the only hand,' as Hooker appropriately says, 'which putteth on Christ to justification,' *Serm.* II. 31: consult also Forbes, *Consid. Mod.* Book I. 3. 10—13.

The order Χριστοῦ Ἰησοῦ is adopted by *Lachm.*, but on external authority [AB; Aug.] that cannot be deemed sufficient.

καὶ ἡμεῖς] '*we also;*' '*nos etiam* quanquam natalibus Judæi, legi Mosis obnoxii,' Schott. ἐπιστεύσαμεν εἰς Χρ. Ἰησ.] '*put our faith in Jesus Christ;*' not 'have become believers,' Peile, but simply aoristic, the tense pointing to the particular time when this act of faith was first manifested: see Windischm. *in loc.* In the formula πιστεύειν εἰς with acc., — less usual in St. Paul's Epp. (Rom. x. 14, i. 29), but very common in St. John, — the preposition retains its proper force, and marks not the mere direction of the belief (or object *toward* which), but the more strictly theological ideas of *union* and *incorporation with;* compare notes on ch. iii. 27, Winer, *Gr.* § 31. 5, p. 191, and for the various constructions of πιστεύω in the New Testament, notes on 1 *Tim.* i. 17, and Reuss, *Théol. Chret.* IV. 14, Vol. II. p. 129. The distinction drawn by Alf. between Χρ. Ἰησ. in this clause and Ἰησ. Χρ. above seems very precarious, esp. in a passage where there is so much diff. of reading.

διότι] '*because that,*' 'propter quod,' Vulg., ܡܛܠ ܕ Syr.; scarcely 'for' (it is an axiom that), Alf., — for though διότι [properly *quam ob rem,* and then *quoniam*] is often used by later writers in a sense little, if at all, differing from ὅτι (see Fritz. *Rom.* i. 19, Vol. I. 57), it does not also appear to be interchangeable with γάρ, but always to retain some trace of its proper *causal* force; comp. notes on 1 *Thess.* ii. 8. The reading is doubtful. The text is supported by CD[3]EJK; very many mss., Vv., and Ff., — and is perhaps to be preferred, as ὅτι [*Lachm.* with ABD[1]FG; 5 mss.] seems more probably a correction of the longer διότι, than the reverse.

οὐ δικαιωθήσεται κ. τ. λ. '*shall* NOT *be justified,*' 'non justificabitur omnis caro,' Vulg.; Rom. iii. 20, comp. Psalm cxliii. 2, οὐ δικαιωθήσεται ἐνώπιόν σου πᾶς ζῶν: a somewhat expressive Hebraism (see Ewald, *Gr.* p. 657), according to which οὐ is to be closely associated with the verb, and the predication regarded as comprehensively and emphatically negative; non-justification is

17 εἰ δὲ ζητοῦντες δικαιωθῆναι ἐν Χριστῷ εὑρέθημεν καὶ αὐτοὶ

predicated of all flesh; see Winer, *Gr.* § 26. 1, p. 155, Vorst, *de Hebraismis*, p. 519, Fritz. *Rom.* iii. 20, Vol. I. p. 179, and comp. Thol. *Beiträge*, No. 15, p. 79. The future is here *ethical, i. e.* it indicates not so much mere futurity as moral possibility, — and with οὐ, something that neither can nor will ever happen: see esp. Thiersch, *de Pent.* III. 11, p. 148 sq., where this and similar uses of the future are well illustrated; comp. Bernhardy, *Synt.* x. 5, p. 377, Winer, *Gr.* § 40. 6, p. 251. On the doctrinal distinctions in St. Paul's Epp. between the pres., perf., and fut. of δικαιοῦσθαι with πίστις, see Usteri, *Lehrb.* II. 1. 1, p. 90; compare Peile, *Append.* Vol. II. note D. The order οὐ δικ. ἐξ ἔργων νομ. (*Rec.*) is only found in JK; mss.; Goth., al.; Theod. (1), al., and is rejected by all recent critics.

17. εἰ δέ] '*But if*, in accordance with these premises of thine, assuming the truth of these thy retrogressive principles; συλλογίζεται τὰ εἰρημένα, Theod. ζητοῦντες] '*quærentes — inventi sumus*;' nervosum antitheton, Beng. ἐν Χριστῷ] '*in Christ*;' not 'through Christ,' (Peile), but '*in* Christ,' — in mystical union with him; see Winer, *Gr.* § 48. a, p. 346, note. It is right to notice that this distinction between ἔν τινι and διά τινος is strongly opposed by Fritz. (*Opusc.* p. 184, note), and considered merely grammatically, his objections deserve consideration; but here, as only too often (comp. *Rom.* Vol. II. p. 82 sq.), he puts out of sight the *theological* meaning which appears regularly attached to ἐν Χριστῷ. In the present passage the meaning is practically the same, whichever translation be adopted; but in the one the deep significance of the formula (union, fellowship, with Christ) is kept in view, in the other it is obscured and lost sight of; comp. notes *on Eph.* i. 3, ii. 6. εὑρέθημεν] '*were found to be*, after all our *seeking*;' not either a Hebraism, or a periphrasis of the verb substantive (Kypke, *Obs.* Vol. I. p. 2). The verb εὑρισκ. has always in the N. T. its proper force, and indicates not merely the existence of a thing, but the manifestation or acknowledgment of that existence; 'if we are found (deprehendimur), in the eyes of God and men, to be sinners;' comp. Matth. i. 18, Luke xvii. 18, Acts viii. 40, Rom. vii. 10, al., and see esp. Winer, *in loc.*, and *Gr.* § 65. 8, p. 542. καὶ αὐτοί] '*ourselves also*,' as much as those whom we proudly regard only as Gentiles and *sinners*.

ἆρα] '*ergone*'? 'are we to say, as we must on such premises?' ironical and interrogative: — not ἄρα (Chrys., Ust. al.); for though in two out of the three passages in which ἆρα occurs (Luke xviii. 8, Acts viii. 38) it anticipates a *negative*, and not as here, an *affirmative* answer, it must still be retained in the present case, as μὴ γένοιτο in St. Paul's Epp. is never found except after a question. The particle has here probably an *ironical* force, 'are we to say pray,' *i. e.* in effect, 'we are to say, I suppose,' see Jelf, *Gr.* 873. 2. It is thus not *for* ἄρ' οὐ — at all times a *very* questionable position, as in most if not all of such cases, it will be found that there is a faint irony or politely assumed hesitation, which seems to have suggested the use of the dubitative ἆρα, even though it is obvious that an affirmative answer is fully expected. The same may be said of 'ne' for 'nonne:' see esp. Kühner, Xen. *Mem.* II. 6, and ib. *Tuscul. Disput.* II. 11, 26; compare Stalb. Plato, *Rep.* VIII. 566 A. The original identity of ἆρα and ἄρα (Klotz, *Devar.* Vol. II. p. 180) is impugned (appy. with doubtful success) by Dunbar, *Class. Museum*, Vol. V. p. 102 sq., see Shepherd, *ib.* Vol. V. p. 470 sq.

ἁμαρτωλοί, ἆρα Χριστὸς ἁμαρτίας διάκονος; μὴ γένοιτο. 18 εἰ
γὰρ ἃ κατέλυσα ταῦτα πάλιν οἰκοδομῶ, παραβάτην ἐμαυτὸν

ἁμαρτίας διάκονος] '*a minister of sin;*' scil., in effect, a promoter, a furtherer of it (comp. 2 Cor. xi. 15), one engaged in its service; ἁμαρτία being almost personified, and, as its position suggests, emphatically echoing the preceding ἁμαρτωλοί, — 'of *sin* (not of righteousness), — of a dispensation which not only leaves us where we were before, but causes us, when we exclusively follow it, to be for this very reason accounted sinners?' Εἰ δὲ ὅτι τὸν νόμον καταλιπόντες τῷ Χριστῷ προσεληλύθαμεν .... παράβασις [or rather, ἁμαρτία] τοῦτο νενόμισται, εἰς αὐτὸν ἡ αἰτία χωρήσει τὸν δεσπότην Χριστόν, Theod.; comp. Chrys. *in loc.* The argument is in fact a *reductio ad absurdum*: if seeking for justification in Christ is only to lead us to be accounted sinners, — not merely as being without law and in the light of Gentiles (Mey.), but as having wilfully neglected an appointed means of salvation, — then Christ, who was the cause of our neglecting it, must needs be, not only negatively but positively, a minister of sin; see De Wette *in loc.* μὴ γένοιτο] '*be it not so,*' '*far be it,*' 'absit,' Vulg., ܚܣ [propitius fuit; compare Matth. xvi. 22] Syr., *i. e.* in effect (esp. in a context like the present), '*God forbid,*' Auth. This expressive formula, though not uncommon in later writers (see exx. in Raphel, *Annot.* Vol. II. p. 249, compare Sturz. *Dial. Maced.* p. 204), only occurs in the N. T. in St. Paul's Epp.; viz. Rom. iii. 4, 6, 31, vi. 2, 15, vii. 7, 13, ix. 14, xi. 1, 11, 1 Cor. vi. 15, Gal. iii. 21. In all these cases it is interjectional, and in all, except the last, rebuts (as Conyb. has remarked) an inference drawn from St. Paul's doctrine by an adversary. The nature of the inference makes the revulsion of thought (ταχέως ἀποπηδᾷ, Dam.) either more or less apparent, and will usually suggest the best mode of translation.

18. εἰ γάρ] '*For if;*' direct confirmation of the immediately preceding μὴ γένοιτο (Usteri, *Lehrb.* II. 1. 2, p. 162, note), and indirect and allusive expansion of the εὑρέθημεν ἁμαρτωλοί: 'I say μὴ γένοιτο in ref. to Christ, for it is not in seeking to be justified in Him, but in seeking to rebuild the *same* structure that I have destroyed (though nobler materials now lie around) that my sin, my transgression of the law's own principles really lies. In the change to the *first* person sing. there *may* be a delicate application to St. Peter personally, which 'clementiæ causâ' is expressed in this rather than in the *second* person (Alf., Mey.); it must not be forgotten, however, that the fervor as well as the introspective character of St. Paul's writings leads him frequently to adopt this μετασχηματισμὸς εἰς ἑαυτόν, see esp. Rom. vii. 7 sq.; so also 1 Cor. iii. 5 sq. iv. 3 sq. vi. 12, x. 29, 30, xiii. 11, 12, etc.: comp. Knapp, *Scripta Var. Argum.* No. 12, p. 431, 437. ταῦτα] '*these* — and nothing better in their place,' Meyer. The emphasis rests on ταῦτα, not on ἐμαυτόν (Olsh.), the position of which [παραβ. ἐμαυτόν, not ἐμαυτ. παραβ.] shows it clearly to be unemphatic. παραβάτην] '*a transgressor,*' scil. τοῦ νόμου; ܥܒܪ ܥܠ ܦܘܩܕܢܐ [transgressor mandati] Syr. But in what particular manner? Surely not, 'in having formerly neglected what I now reassert' (De W., Alf.), — a somewhat weak and anticlimactic reference to εὑρέθημεν ἁμαρτωλοί, — but, as the following γάρ, and the unfolding argu-

συνιστάνω. [19] ἐγὼ γὰρ διὰ νόμου νόμῳ ἀπέθανον ἵνα Θεῷ ζήσω.

ment seem clearly to require, 'in reconstructing what I ought to perceive is only temporary and preparative. Reconstruction of the same materials is, in respect of the law, not only a tacit avowal of an ἁμαρτία (εὑρέθ. ἁμαρτ.) in having pulled it down, but is a real and definite παράβασις of all its deeper principles. So, very distinctly, Chrys., ἐκεῖνοι δεῖξαι ἐβούλοντο, ὅτι ὁ μὴ τηρῶν τὸν νόμον παραβάτης· οὗτος εἰς τοὐναντίον περιέτρεψε τὸν λόγον, δεικνὺς ὅτι ὁ τηρῶν τὸν νόμον, παραβάτης, οὐ τῆς πίστεως ἀλλὰ καὶ αὐτοῦ τοῦ νόμου. The counter-argument that the *I* of ver. 18 has 'given up' faith in Christ, and so could never consider the law as preparative (Alf.), is of no real force; for in the first place the ἐγὼ had not *given it up*, but had only added to it, and in the next place, even had he done so, he might equally show himself a *real* though unconscious παραβάτην.

ἐμαυτὸν συνιστάνω] '*set myself forward*,' '*demonstrate myself to be*:' Hesych. συνιστάνειν· ἐπαινεῖν, φανεροῦν, βεβαιοῦν, παρατιθέναι. This meaning, 'sinceris Atticis ignotum,' Fritz, *Rom.* iii. 5, Vol. I. p. 159, deduces from the primary notion *componendi;* 'ut esset συνίστημί τι, compositis collectisque quæ rem contineant argumentis aliquid doceo:' see exx. in Wetst. *Rom.* iii. 5, Schweigh. *Lex. Polyb.* s. v. The form συνίστημι (*Rec.*), only found in D[3](E?)JK; mss. and Ff., seems a mere grammatical gloss.

19. ἐγὼ γὰρ] '*For I truly*:' explanatory confirmation of the preceding assertion; the *explicative* γὰρ showing how this rehabilitation of the law actually amounts to a transgression of its true principles, while the emphatic ἐγὼ adds the force and vitality of *personal* experience. In the retrospective reference of παραβάτης adopted by De W. and Alf. (see above), the γὰρ loses all its force; it must either be referred, most awkwardly, to μὴ γένοιτο (D. W.), or, still worse, be regarded as merely transitional.

διὰ νόμου νόμῳ ἀπέθανον] '*through the law died to the law*.' Of the many explanations of these obscure words the following (derived mainly from Chrys.) appears by far the most tenable and satisfactory. The result may be summed up in the following positions: — (1) Νόμος in each case has the same meaning. (2) That meaning, as the *context* requires, must be the *Mosaic* law (ver. 16), no grammatical arguments founded on the absence of the article (Middleton *in loc.*) having any real validity; comp. exx. in Winer, *Gr.* § 19, p. 112. (3) The law is regarded under the same aspect as in Rom. vii. 6—13, a passage in strictest analogy with the present. (4) Διὰ νόμου must not be confounded with διὰ νόμον or κατὰ νόμον; it was *through* the instrumentality of the law (διὰ τ. ἐντολῆς, Rom. vii. 8) that the sinful principle worked within and brought death upon all. (5) Ἀπέθανον is not merely 'legi valedixi' (comp. κατηργήθην ἀπὸ τοῦ νόμου), but expresses *generally* what is afterwards more *specifically* expressed in ver. 20 by συνεσταύρωμαι. (6) Νόμῳ is not merely the dative 'of reference to,' but a species of dative 'commodi;' the expressions ζῆν τινι and ἀποθαν τινι having a wide application; see Fritz. *Rom.* xiv. 7, Vol. III. p. 176; —'I died not only as concerns the law, but as the law required.' The whole clause then may thus be paraphrased: '*I, through the law*, owing to sin, was brought under its curse; but having undergone this, with, and in the person of Christ (ch. iii. 13, compare 2 Cor. v. 14), I *died to the law* in the fullest and deepest sense, — being both free from its claims, and having satisfied its

20 Χριστῷ συνεσταύρωμαι· ζῶ δὲ οὐκέτι ἐγώ, ζῇ δὲ ἐν ἐμοὶ Χριστός. ὃ δὲ νῦν ζῶ ἐν σαρκί, ἐν πίστει ζῶ τῇ τοῦ υἱοῦ τοῦ Θεοῦ,

curse.' The difference between this and the common interpretations lies principally in the fuller meaning assigned to ἀπέθανον, and its reference to συνεστ. A careful investigation will be found in Usteri, *Lehrb.* II. 1. 2, p. 164 sq.

ζήσω] '*may live;*' not a future (Alf.), — an anomalous usage (see notes on ver. 4) that it is surely unnecessary to obtrude on the present passage — but the regular *aor. subj.* (1 Thess. v. 10), the tense of the dependent clause being in idiomatic accordance with that of the leading member; compare Schmalfeld, *Synt.* § 144. 1, p. 296.

20. Χριστῷ συνεστ. '*I have been and am crucified with Christ;*' more exact specification of the preceding ἀπέθανον. This συνεσταύρ. it need scarcely be said, did not consist merely in the crucifixion of the lusts (ch. v. 24, Grot.), but in that union with Christ according to which the believer shares the death of his crucified Lord; ἐπείδη ἐν τῷ βαπτίσματι τοῦ τε θανάτου καὶ τῆς ἀναστάσεως τύπον ἐπλήρουν, συσταυροῦσθαι ἐλέγοντο τῷ Χριστῷ, Theod. Mops. *in loc.* ζῶ δὲ οὐκέτι ἐγώ] '*I live however no longer myself,*' *i. e.* my old self; see Rom. vi. 6, and compare Neand. *Plant.*, Vol. I. p. 422 (Bohn). The familiar but erroneous punctuation of this clause (ζῶ δέ, οὐκέτι ἐγώ, ζῇ δὲ κ. τ. λ.) has been rightly rejected by all recent editors except Scholz. The only passing difficulty is in the use of δέ: it does not simply continue (Rück., Peile), or expand (Ust.) the meaning of Χρ. συνεστ. but reverts with its proper adversative force to ἵνα Θεῷ ζήσω, συνεστ., being not so much a link in the chain of thought, as a rapid and almost parenthetical epexegesis of ἀπέθανον.

ζῇ δὲ] The δὲ does not introduce any opposition to the preceding negative clause (it would then be ἀλλά), but simply marks the emphatic repetition of the same verb (Hartung, *Partik.* δέ, 2. 17, Vol. I. p. 168), just retaining, however, that *sub-adversative* force which is so common when a clause is added, expressing a new, though not a dissimilar thought; see Klotz, *Devar.* Vol. II. p. 361. On the doctrinal import of ζῇ ἐν ἐμοὶ Χρ. ('Christ and His Spirit dwelling in them, and as the soul of their souls moving them unto such both inward and outward actions, as in the sight of God are acceptable'), see Hooker, *Serm.* III. 1, Vol. III. p. 764 sq. (ed. Keble.) ὃ δὲ νῦν ζῶ] '*yes, the life which now I live;*' explanatory and partially concessive clause, obviating the possible objection arising from the seeming incompatibility of the assertion ζῇ ἐν ἐμοὶ Χρ. with the fact of the actual ζῆν ἐν σαρκί: 'it is true,' says the Apostle, 'I do yet live in the flesh, an earthly atmosphere is still around me, *but* even thus I live and breathe in the pure element of faith, — faith in him who loved me, yea and (καὶ) gave such proofs of his love.' With regard to the construction it is only necessary to observe that ὃ is not 'quod attinet ad id quod' (Winer), but simply the accus. *objecti* after ζῶ, scil. τὴν δὲ ζωὴν ἣν νῦν ζῶ: comp. Rom. vi. 10, ὃ γὰρ ἀπέθανε, and see Fritz. *in loc.*, Vol. I. p. 393. δὲ is thus not merely continuative (De W.), but serves both to limit and explain the preceding words (comp. 1 Cor. i. 16, and Winer, *Gr.* § 53. 7. b, p. 393), its true oppositive force being sufficiently clear when the suppressed thought (see below) is properly supplied; see Klotz, *Devar.* Vol. II. p. 366. νῦν] The refer-

τοῦ ἀγαπήσαντός με καὶ παραδόντος ἑαυτὸν ὑπὲρ ἐμοῦ. 21 οὐκ
ἀθετῶ τὴν χάριν τοῦ Θεοῦ· εἰ γὰρ διὰ νόμου δικαιοσύνη, ἄρα
Χριστὸς δωρεὰν ἀπέθανεν.

ence of this particle is doubtful. It *may* specify the period since the Apostle's conversion, but is much more plausibly referred by Chrys., Theod., al. to the present life in the flesh, 'hæc vita mea terrestris;' see Phil. i. 22. In the former case the qualitative and tacitly contrasting ἐν σαρκὶ ('earthly existence,' 'life in the phenomenal world,' αἰσθητὴ ζωή, Chrys.; comp. Müller, *on Sin*, Vol. I. p. 453, Clark) would seem wholly superfluous. ἐν πίστει] '*in faith.*' The instrumental sense, '*by* faith,' adopted by Theodoret, and several ancient as well as modern expositors, is, though inexact, not grammatically untenable. The deeper meaning of the words is, however, thus completely lost. On this '*life* in faith' see the middle and latter portion of a profound paper, '*Bemerk. zum Begriffe der Religion*,' by Lechler, *Stud. u. Kritik.* for 1851, Part IV. τῇ τοῦ υἱοῦ τοῦ Θεοῦ] '*namely that of the Son of God;*' distinctive, and with solemn emphasis, — the insertion of the article serving both to specify and enhance, 'in fide, eâque Filii dei' (see notes *on* 1 *Tim.* i. 13, and on 2 *Tim.* i. 13), while the august title, by intimating the true fountain of life (John v. 26) tends to add confirmation and assurance; ὅταν περὶ τοῦ Υἱοῦ νοεῖν ἐθέλῃς, μαθὼν τίνα ἐστὶ τὰ ἐν τῷ Πατρὶ ταῦτα καὶ ἐν τῷ Υἱῷ εἶναι πίστευε, Athan. *on Matth.* xi. 27, Vol. I. p. 153, (ed. Bened.). The reading of *Lachm.* τῇ τοῦ θεοῦ καὶ Χριστοῦ, τοῦ ἀγ. is supported by BD[1]FG; Clarom., — but has every appearance of being a gloss; see Meyer (critical notes), p. 29. καὶ παραδόντος κ.τ.λ.] '*and* (as a proof of his love) *gave Himself,*' *etc.;* the καὶ being ἐξηγητικόν, and illustratively subjoining the practical proof; see Fritz. *Rom.* ix. 23, Vol. II. p. 339, and on this and other uses of καί, notes *on Phil.* iv. 12. ὑπὲρ ἐμοῦ] '*for me,*' 'pro me,' Vulg.; to atone for me and to save me. On the dogmatical meaning of this prep., see notes on ch. iii. 13.

21. οὐκ ἀθετῶ] '*I do not make void,*' '*nullify;*' not 'abjicio,' Vulg., still less ἀτιμάζω, Theod., — but 'non *irratam* facio,' scil. 'ut dicam per legem esse justitiam,' Aug.: compare 1 Cor. i. 19, τὴν σύνεσιν τῶν συνετῶν ἀθετήσω; ch. iii. 15, ἀθετεῖ (διαθήκην); so 1 Macc. xv. 27, ἠθέτησε πάντα ὅσα συνέθετο αὐτῷ; and frequently in Polyb., see Schweigh. *Lex.* s. v. The verb is sometimes found in the milder sense of 'despising,' 'rejecting,' etc. — with *persons* (Luke x. 16, John xii. 48, 1 Thess. iv. 8); but this obviously falls short of the meaning in the present context. τὴν χάριν τοῦ Θεοῦ] '*the grace of God,*' as shown in the death of Christ, and our justification by faith in Him; not 'the Gospel,' as Hamm. *on Heb.* xiii. 9. In our justification, as it is well said in the *Homilies*, there are *three* things which go together, — on God's part His *grace* and mercy; upon Christ's part the satisfaction of God's justice; and upon our part true and lively faith in the merits of Jesus Christ, *on Salvat.* Part I. γὰρ explains and justifies the preceding declaration; 'I say οὐκ ἀθετῶ, *for* it is an immediate inference that if the law could have been the medium of δικαιοσ., Christ's death would have been purposeless.'

διὰ νόμου] '*by means of the law,*' as a medium of δικαιοσύνη: emphatic, as the position shows, and antithetical to

O foolish Galatians, is not the Spirit which ye have received an evidence that justification is by faith, and not by the works of the law?

III. Ὦ ἀνόητοι Γαλάται, τίς ὑμᾶς ἐβάσ-

Χριστὸς in the succeeding clause. In the present verse it is in effect asserted that the νόμος is not a *medium* of δικαιοσύνη (εἰς κτῆσιν δικαιοσύνης ἀρκεῖ, Theod.); in ch. iii. 11, it is asserted not to be the *sphere* of it, and in ch. iii. 21, not the *origin*. δικαιοσύνη] '*righteousness*,' ܙܕܝܩܘܬܐ Syr., 'justitia,' Vulg.; not equivalent to δικαίωσις (Whately, *Dangers*, etc., § 4) nor yet, strictly considered, the result of it, but appy. in the most inclusive meaning of the term—*righteousness*, whether imputed, by which we are accounted δίκαιοι, or infused and inherent, by which we could be found so; see Hooker, *Serm.* II. 3, 21, where the distinction between justifying and sanctifying righteousness is drawn out with admirable perspicuity. On the meaning of the word, see Andrewes, *Serm.* V. Vol. V. p 114 (A. C. L.), Waterland, *Justif.* Vol. VI. p. 4, and for some acute remarks on its lexical aspects, Knox, *Remains*, Vol. II. p. 276. ἄρα] '*then*,' *i. e.* 'the obvious *inference* is.' On the meaning of ἄρα, see notes, ch. v. 11. δωρεάν] '*for nought, without cause*;' not here 'frustra' (Grot.), 'sine effectu,'—but '*sine justâ causâ*,' Tittm. *Synon.* I. p. 161; περιττὸς ὁ τοῦ Χριστοῦ θάνατος, Chrys., 'superflue mortuus est Chr.,' Jerome: comp. John xv. 25, ἐμίσησάν με δωρεάν; Psalm xxxiv. (xxxv.) 7, δωρεὰν ἔκρυψάν μοι διαφθοράν (Symm. ἀναιτίως). So חִנָּם, which the LXX frequently translate by δωρεάν, has the meaning 'in nullum bonum finem,' as well as 'gratis' and 'frustra:' comp. Gesen. *Lex.* s. v., Vorst, *de Hebraism.* VII. 6, p. 228, 229.

CHAPTER III. 1. ἀνόητοι Γαλ.] '*foolish Galatians*;' fervid and indignant application of the results of the preceding demonstration to the case of his readers. The epithet ἀνόητος is used in three other passages by St. Paul,—Rom. i. 14, opp. to σοφός; 1 Tim. vi. 9, joined with βλαβερός; Tit. iii. 3, with ἀπειθής and πλανώμενος,—and in all seems to mark not so much a dulness in ('insensati,' Vulg.), as a *deficiency in*, or rather an *insufficient application of*, the νοῦς; comp. Syr. ܚܣܝܪܝ ܪܥܝܢܐ [destituti mente], and Luke xxiv. 15, where while βραδὺς τῇ καρδίᾳ denotes the defect in *heart*, ἀνόητος seems to mark the defect in *head*; comp. Tittm. *Synon.* I. p. 144, where this word is defined somewhat artificially, but rightly distinguished from ἄφρων and ἀσύνετος which seem to point respectively rather to 'senselessness' and 'slowness of understanding.' It cannot then be asserted (Brown) that the Galatians were proverbially *stupid*; compare Callim. *H. Del.* 184, ἄφρονι φύλῳ. Themistius, who himself spent some time in the (then extended Forbig. *Geogr.* Vol. II. p. 364) province, gives a very different character: οἱ δὲ ἄνδρες ἴστε ὅτι ὀξεῖς καὶ ἀγχίνοι καὶ εὐμαθέστεροι τῶν ἄγαν Ἑλλήνων· καὶ τριβωνίου παραφανέντος ἐκκρέμαντι εὐθύς, ὥσπερ τῆς λίθου τὰ σιδήρια, *Orat.* 23, ad fin. p. 299 (ed. Harduin). Versatility and inconstancy, as the Epistle shows (comp. notes on ch. i. 6), were the true characteristics of the Galatian. Foolishness must have been often, as in the present case, not an unnatural concomitant. ὑμᾶς ἐβάσκανεν] '*did bewitch you*,' 'fascinavit vos,' Vulg, Clarom. The verb βασκαίνω is derived from βάζω, βάσκω (Pott. *Etym. Forsch.* Vol. I. p. 271), and perhaps signified originally 'malâ linguâ nocere;' comp. Benfey, *Wurzellex.* Vol. II. p. 104. Here, however, the reference appears rather to

κανεν, οἷς κατ' ὀφθαλμοὺς Ἰησοῦς Χριστὸς προεγράφη ἐν ὑμῖν ἐσταυρωμένος; [2] τοῦτο μόνον θέλω μαθεῖν ἀφ' ὑμῶν, ἐξ

the bewitching influence of the evil eye (compare Ecclus. xiv. 8, βασκαίνων ὀφθαλμῷ, and see Elsner, *in loc.*, Winer, *RWB.* Art. 'Zauberei') though not necessarily 'the evil eye of *envy*,' (Chrys.; comp. Syr. [Syriac]) as in this latter sense βασκ. is commonly with a *dat.* (but in Ecclus. xiv. 6, Ignat. *Rom.* 3, with accus.); see Lobeck, *Phryn.* p. 462, Pierson, *Herodian*, p. 470. The addition, τῇ ἀληθείᾳ μὴ πείθεσθαι [*Rec.* with CD³E²JK; mss.; Vulg. (but not all mss.), Æth.-Pol., al.; Ath., Theod.], is rightly rejected by most modern editors, both as deficient in external authority [omitted in ABD¹E¹FG; 2 mss.; Syr., and nearly all Vv.], and as an apparent gloss from ch. v. 7. προεγράφη] '*was openly set forth*,' 'proscriptus est,' Vulg., Clarom. The meaning of this word has been much discussed. The ancient (comp. Syr.) and popular gloss is ἐζωγραφήθη (Theoph., Œcum., and appy. Chrys., Theod.), but without any lexical authority: for common as is the use of γράφω in a pictorial sense, there appears no *certain* instance of προγράφω being ever so used; see Rettig, *Stud. u. Krit.* 1830, p. 96 sq. We can then only safely translate προεγράφη either (α) '*antea scriptus est*,' or (β) '*palam scriptus est*.' Between these it is difficult to decide. Considered *lexically* (α) seems the most probable; for though (β) is appy. the more common meaning in Hellenic writers (Plutarch, *Camill.* § 11, comp. Polyb. *Hist.* XXXII. 21. 12, al.), yet in the three other passages *in the N. T.* in which προγράφω occurs, viz., Rom. xv. 4, Eph. iii. 3, Jude 4, it is used in the former sense. Both meanings occur in the LXX: (α) in 1 Esdr. vi. 32 (*Ald.*) (β) in 1 Macc. x. 36. *Contextual* considerations seem, however, in favor of (β); as not only does this meaning harmonize best with the prominent and purely local κατ' ὀφθαλμούς (compare κατ' ὄμματα, Soph. *Antig.* 756), but also best illustrate the peculiar and suggestive ἐβάσκανεν, — which thus gains great force and point; 'who could have bewitched you by his gaze, when you had only to fix your eyes on Christ to escape the fascination;' comp. Numb. xxi. 9. ἐν ὑμῖν] '*among you*;' not a Hebraistic pleonasm ('construi debet ἐν οἷς ὑμῖν,' Grot.), but a regular local predicate appended to προεγράφη, and appy. intended to enhance the preceding οἷς κατ' ὀφθ. by a still more studied specification of place: not only had the truth been presented to them, but preached *among them*, with every circumstance of individual and local exhibition. According to the usual connection ἐν ὑμῖν is joined with ἐσταυρ. (comp. Chrys.), but in that case both perspicuity and emphasis would have required the order ἐσταυρ. ἐν ὑμῖν, while in the present the isolation of ἐσταυρ. is in accordance with the natural order, and adds greatly to the pathos and emphasis; see 1 Cor. i. 23, and compare 1 Cor. ii. 2. On the force of the perf. part. as implying the permanent character of the action, see Winer, *Gr.* § 45. 1, p. 305, Green, *Gr.* p. 308. It may be observed that *Lachm.* (*Griesb.* om. om.) omits ἐν ὑμῖν with ABC; 10 mss.; Amit., Tol., Syr., al., — but with but little probability, as the omission of such a seemingly superfluous clause can easily be accounted for, but not the insertion.

2. τοῦτο μόνον] '*this only*,' — not to mention other arguments which might be derived from your own admissions;

ἔργων νόμου τὸ Πνεῦμα ἐλάβετε ἢ ἐξ ἀκοῆς πίστεως; 3 οὕτως ἀνόητοί

'de eo quod promptum est sciscitor,' Jerome. μαθεῖν ἀφ' ὑμῶν] '*to learn of you*,' Auth. Ver.; not for παρὰ ὑμῶν (Rück.) which would imply a more immediate and direct communication, but with the proper force of ἀπό, which, as a general rule (Col. i. 7, *seems* an exception), indicates a source less active and more remote; contrast 2 Tim. iii. 14, and see Winer, *Gr.* § 47, ἀπό, p. 331 note; comp. notes also on ch. i. 12. For exx. of this use of μαθεῖν, not 'to learn as a disciple,' with an ironical reference (Luth., Beng.), but simply 'to arrive at a knowledge,' see exx. in Rost u. Palm, *Lex.* s. v., and compare Acts xxiii. 27. τὸ Πνεῦμα] '*the Spirit*,' τὴν τοσαύτην ἰσχύν, Chrys.; 'de Spiritu miraculorum loqui hic apostolum patet,' Bull, *Harm. Ap.* Part II. 11. 8. Is it not, however, necessary to understand this as the exclusive meaning, much less to explain it, with Baur, *Apost. Paulus*, p. 515, as 'das Christliche Bewusstseyn:' see next verse.

ἀκοῆς πίστεως may be translated, either (α) '*the hearing of faith*,' *i. e.* the reception of the Gospel (Brown), or (β) '*the report* or *message of faith*,' *i. e.* the preaching which related to, had as its subject πίστις (gen. *objecti*), according as ἀκοὴ is taken in an active or passive sense. The former might seem to preserve a better antithesis to ἔργων νόμου, —'hearing the doctrine of faith, opp. to doing the works of the law' (Schott, Peile; comp. Æth.), but is open to the decided *lexical* objection that ἀκοὴ appears always used in the N. T. in a passive sense (so both in Rom. x. 17 [see Fritz.], and in 1 Thess. ii. 13, where see notes), and to the *contextual* objection that the real opposition is not between the doing and the hearing, but between the two principles, faith and the law,— the question in effect being, ὁ νόμος ὑμῖν ἔδωκεν τοῦ θείου Πνεύματος ἐνέργειαν, ἢ μόνη ἡ ἐπὶ τὸν Κύριον πίστις, Theod. We may, then, with some confidence, adopt (β); so Goth. ('gahauseins'), Arm., and recently De Wette, Meyer, and the best modern commentators.

3. οὕτως ἀνόητοι] '*to so high a degree, so very foolish*,'—with reference to what follows: 'quum οὕτως cum adjectivo nomini aut adverbio copulatur, reddes non solum 'ita,' 'adeo,' verum etiam 'usque adeo,'' Steph. *Thesaur.* s. v. Vol. v. p. 2433, where several exx. are cited; *e. g.* Isoc. *Paneg.* 43 D, οὕτω μεγάλας, Xen. *Cyr.* II. 216, οὕτω πολέμιον. ἐναρξάμενοι] '*after having begun*;' temporal participle referring to the *previous* fact of their first entrance into Christian life. On the temporal force of the participle, see notes *on Eph.* iv. 8, but reverse the accidentally transposed 'subsequent to' and 'preceding;' and on the force of the compound (more directly concentrated action), see notes *on Phil.* i. 6.

Πνεύματι] '*with the Spirit*;' dat. of the manner (*modal* dat.) in which the action took place; see Winer, *Gr.* § 31. 6, p. 193, Bernhardy, *Synt.* III. 14, p. 100, Jelf, *Gr.* § 603. The meaning of πνεῦμα and σὰρξ in this verse has been the subject of considerable discussion. Of the earlier expositors, Theodoret paraphrases πν. by ἡ χάρις, σὰρξ by ἡ κατὰ νόμον πολιτεία (so Waterl. *Distinct. of Sacr.* II. § 10, Vol. v. p. 262), while Chrys. finds in σὰρξ a definite allusion to the circumcision; comp. Eph. ii. 11. Alii alia. The most satisfactory view is that taken by Müller, *Doct. of Sin*, ch. 2, Vol. I. 355 sq. (Clark),—viz., that when πνεῦμα is thus in ethical contrast with σάρξ, it is to be understood of *the Holy Spirit*, regarded as the governing and directing principle in man, σάρξ, on the contrary, as *the worldly tendency*

ἔστε; ἐναρξάμενοι Πνεύματι νῦν σαρκὶ ἐπιτελεῖσθε; [4] τοσαῦτα

of human life, 'the life and movement of man in things of the phenomenal world.' If this be correct πν. and σὰρξ are here used, not to denote Christianity and Judaism *per se*, but as it were the essence and active principle of each.

ἐπιτελεῖσθε] '*are ye brought to completion?*' Not middle, as often in Hellenic Greek (see Schweigh. *Lex. Polyb.* s. v.), but *pass.* (Vulg., Clarom., Chrys.), as in 1 Pet. v. 9, comp. Phil. i. 6. The meaning of the compound must not be neglected; it does not merely imply 'finishing' (Ust., Peile), as opposed to 'beginning,' but appears always to involve the idea of bringing to a *complete* and *perfect* end; comp. 1 Sam. iii. 12, ἄρξομαι καὶ ἐπιτελέσω; see further exx. in Bretsch. *Lex.* s. v., and the good collection in Rost u. Palm. *Lex.* s. v. Vol. I. p. 1123, — the most definite of which seems, Herod. IX. 64, ἡ δίκη τοῦ φόνου ἐκ Μαρδονίου ἐπετελέετο.

4. ἐπάθετε] '*Did ye suffer*,' 'passi estis,' Vulg., Clarom., ܣܝܒܪܬܘܢ [sustinuistis] Syr., Æth. (both). The meaning of this word has been much discussed. The apparent tenor of the argument, as alluding rather to benefits than to sufferings, has led Kypke (*Obs.* Vol. II. p. 277, compare Schoettg. *Hor.* Vol. I. p. 731) and others to endeavor to substantiate by exx. that πάσχειν is not only a word of neutral meaning, but, even without εὖ or ἀγαθόν, actually signifies '*beneficiis affici*,' — a usage, however, of which Steph. (*Thes.* s. v.) rightly says 'exemplum desidero.' For the *neutral* meaning ('experienced,' ed. 1), as including a reference to all the spiritual dispensations, whether sufferings or blessings, which had happened to (Arm.), or had been vouchsafed to the Galatians, much may be said, both lexically and contextually, — still, on the one hand, the absence of any *direct* instance in the N. T. [even in Mark v. 26, there is an idea of suffering in the background], and, on the other, the authority of the ancient Vv. and Greek expositors lead us *now* to revert to the regular meaning, *suffered*, and to refer it to the labors (Copt.), and persecutions which, in one form or other, must have certainly tried the early converts of Galatia; see Chrys., Jerome, and the good note of Alford *in loc.* All these sufferings were a genuine evidence of the ἐναρξάμενοι Πνεύματι, and would be regarded and alluded to by the Apostle as blessed tokens of the Spirit's influence; comp. 1 Thess. ii. 13 sq., and the remarks of August. *in h. l.*

εἴγε καὶ εἰκῆ] '*if indeed*,' or, '*if at least, it really be in vain.*' The sense of this clause has been obscured by not attending to the true force of εἴγε and καί.

εἴγε must not be confounded with εἴπερ (Tholuck, *Beiträge*, p. 146): the latter, in accordance with the extensive, or perhaps rather *intensive* force of περ (Donalds. *Crat.* § 178, compare Klotz. *Devar.* Vol. II. p. 723), implies '*si omnino*;' the former (εἴγε), in accordance with the restrictive γέ, is '*si quidem*,' and if resolved, *tum certe, si*; ('γὲ ita tantummodo ad tollendam conditionem facit, quia *tum certe, si quid fiat, aliud esse* significat, non ut ipsam conditionem confirmet,' Klotz, *Devar.* Vol. II. p. 308), comp. p. 528. No inference, however, of the Apostle's real opinion can be drawn merely from the γε (εἴγε 'usurpatur de re quæ jure sumpta,' Herm. *Vig.* No. 310), as it is the sentence and not the particle which determines the rectitude of the assumption.

καὶ must closely be joined with εἰκῆ, and either (*a*), with its usual *ascensive* force ('quasi ascensionem ad eam rem quo pertineat particula;' Klotz, *Devar.*

ἐπάθετε εἰκῇ; εἴ γε καὶ εἰκῇ. 5 ὁ οὖν ἐπιχορηγῶν ὑμῖν τὸ Πνεῦμα
καὶ ἐνεργῶν δυνάμεις ἐν ὑμῖν, ἐξ ἔργων νόμου ἢ ἐξ ἀκοῆς πίστεως;
6 Καθὼς Ἀβραὰμ ἐπίστευσεν τῷ Θεῷ, καὶ

As Abraham was justified by faith; so shall his spiritual children be justified, and share his blessing.

Vol. II. p. 638), gives to the clause the meaning, 'if at least it amount to, *i. e.* be really in vain,' or (*b*), with what may be termed its *descensive* force (*Odyss.* I. 58, see Hartung, *Partik.* καί, § 2. 8, Vol. I. p. 136), serves to imply, 'if at least it be only in vain, *i. e.* has not proceeded to a more dangerous length, 'videndum ne ad perniciem valeat,' August., Cocceius. Of these (*b*) is the most emphatic and pungent (so Mey.; De W.), but (*a*) most characteristic of the large heart of the Apostle, and of the spirit of love and tenderness to his converts (ch. iv. 19), which is blended even with the rebukes of this Epistle; so Chrys., and the Greek expositors; comp. Brown, p. 112.

5. ὁ οὖν ἐπιχορηγῶν] '*He then who is bestowing*,' etc.: resumption by means of the *reflexive* οὖν (see below, and notes *on Phil.* ii. 1) of the subject of ver. 2; ver. 3 and 4 being in effect parenthetical. The subject of this verse is not St. Paul (Lomb. Erasm., al.), but, as the context, the meaning of δυνάμεις, the nature of the action specified (ἐπιχορηγῶν), and the permanence of the action implied by the tense pres. ἐπιχορηγῶν (comp. Winer, *Gr.* § 45. 1, p. 304, Schmalfeld, *Synt.* § 202, p. 405), all obviously suggest, — *God:* ὁ Θεός, φησιν, ὁ ἐπιχορηγῶν ὑμῖν τὸ Πνεῦμα, Theoph. The force of ἐπὶ in ἐπιχορ. does not appear *additive*, but *directive* (see Rost u. Palm, *Lex.* s. v., and *ib.* s. v. ἐπί, C. 3. cc), any idea of the freedom or ample nature of the gift (Winer, Peile), being due solely to the primary meaning of the simple verb; see notes *on Col.* ii. 19, and compare 2 Cor. ix. 10, where both χορηγέω and ἐπιχορηγέω occur in the same verse, and appy. in the same sense *quantitatively* considered. For exx. of the use of ἐπιχορ. in later writers see the collection of Hase, in Steph. *Thes.* s. v. Vol. III. p. 1902. On the present resumptive use of οὖν after a (logical) parenthesis, which has been incorrectly pronounced rare in Attic writers, see Klotz, *Devar.* Vol. II. p. 718, Hartung, *Partik.* οὖν, 3. 5, Vol. II. p. 22. It may be remarked that, as a general rule, οὖν is *continuative* and *retrospective* rather than illative, and is in this respect to be distinguished from ἄρα (Donalds. *Gr.* § 604), but it must not also be forgotten that as in the New Testament the use of οὖν is to that of ἄρα nearly as 11 to 1, the force of the former particle must not be unduly restricted. In St. Paul's Epp. where the proportion is not quite 4 to 1, the true distinction between the two particles may be more safely maintained; see, however, notes *on* 1 *Tim.* ii. 1 (*Transl.*)

δυνάμεις] '*miraculous powers*,' ܚܝ̈ܠܐ [virtutes] Syr., 'virtutes,' Vulg., Clarom. This more restricted meaning, which may be supported by 1 Cor. xii. 28, and probably Matth xiv. 2, seems best to accord with the context. Καί is then ἐξηγητικόν, and ἐν ὑμῖν retains its natural meaning with ἐνεργέω, 'in you,' '*within* you;' comp. Matth. *l. c.* αἱ δυνάμεις ἐνεργοῦσιν ἐν αὐτῷ. ἐξ ἔργων νόμου] '*from the works of the law*;' not *exactly* 'as following upon,' Alf. 2, — but, in more strict accordance with the primary force of the prep. 'from,' 'out of' ('ex,' Vulg.), as the *originating* or moving cause of the ἐπιχορήγησις; compare notes *on Gal.* ii. 16.

6. καθώς] '*Even as*.' The answer

ἐλογίσθη αὐτῷ εἰς δικαιοσύνην. [7] γινώσκετε ἄρα ὅτι οἱ ἐκ πίσ-

is so obvious, that St. Paul proceeds as if it had been expressed. The compound particle καθὼς is not found in the purer Attic writers, though sufficiently common in later writers; see exx. collected by Lobeck, *Phryn.* p. 426. Em. Moschop., the Byzantine Grammarian, cited by Fabricius, *Bibl. Græca*, Vol. VI. p. 191 (ed. Harles), remarks that this is an Alexandrian usage; τὸ καθὰ οἱ Ἀττικοὶ χρῶνται, τὸ δὲ καθώς οὐδέποτε, ἀλλ' ἡ τῶν Ἀλεξανδρέων διάλεκτος καθ' ἣν ἡ θεία γραφὴ γέγραπται: see esp. Sturz *de Dialecto Maced.* § 9, s. v. (Steph. *Thes.* ed. Valpy, p. clxx.) On the most suitable translation, compare notes *on* 1 *Thess.* i. 5 (*Transl.*). ἐλογίσθη αὐτῷ εἰς δικαιοσύνην] '*it was accounted for to him,*' or '*was reckoned to him, as righteousness,*' scil. τὸ πιστεῦσαι; see Winer, *Gr.* § 49. 2, p. 427 (ed 5). The phrase λογίζεταί τι εἰς τι, Acts xix. 27, Rom. ii. 26, iv. 3, ix. 8, is explained by Fritzsche (*Rom.* Vol. I. p. 137), as equivalent to λογίζεταί τι εἰς τὸ εἶναί τι, 'ita res æstimatur ut res sit,' h. e. 'ut pro re valeat;' hence 'tribuitur alicui rei vis ac pondus rei.' In such cases, the more exact idea conveyed by εἰς, of *destination* for any object or thing (Rost u. Palm, *Lex.* s. v. εἰς, v. 1), is blended with that of simple predication of it. In later writers this extended so far that εἰς, is often used as a mere *index* of the accus., having lost all its prepositional force; *e. g.* ἄγειν εἰς γυναῖκα: see Bernh. *Synt.* v. 11. b. 2, p. 219. With the present semi-Hebraistic use of λογίζ. εἰς, it is instructive to contrast Xen. *Cyr.* III. 1. 33, χρήματα εἰς ἀργύριον λογισθέντα, where εἰς has its primary ethical meaning of *measure, accordance to.*

On the doctrinal meaning of ἐλογίσθη κ. τ. λ., see Bull, *Harm. Apost.* II. 12. 22, and for an able comparison of the faith of Abraham with that of Christians, Hammond, *Pract. Catech.* Book I. 8.

7. γινώσκετε ἄρα] '*Know ye therefore,*' ܕܥܘ [cognoscite] Syr., Vulg., Clarom., Armen., — not *indicative*, as Jerome, Ps. Ambr., al., and most recently Alf.: the *imper.* is not only more animated, but more logically correct, for the declaration in the verse is really one of the points which the Apostle is laboring to prove; ἐν κεφαλαίῳ διδάσκει τὸν Ἀβραὰμ ἐκ πίστεως δικαιωθέντα, καὶ τοὺς τροφίμους τῆς πίστεως υἱοὺς τοῦ Ἀβραὰμ χρηματίζοντας, Theod.; see Olsh. *in loc.* The objections of Rück., and even of Alf. to the use of ἄρα with the imper. are distinctly invalid; not only is the union of the imperative with ἄρα logically admissible, and borne out by usage (comp. Hom. *Il.* x. 249), but further, in perfect harmony with the true lexical force of the particle: '*rebus ita comparatis* (Abraham's faith being reckoned to him as righteousness) *cognoscite*,' etc.; see Klotz. *Devar.* Vol. II. p. 167. οἱ ἐκ πίστεως] '*they who are of faith,*' not 'they who rest on faith' (Green, *Gr.* p. 288), but, in accordance with the primary meaning of *origin*, 'they who are spiritually descended from, whose source of spiritual life is — πίστις: comp. Rom. ii. 8, οἱ ἐξ ἐριθείας, 'qui a malarum fraudum machinatione originem ducunt,' 'qui malitiam tanquam parentem habent,' Fritz. *in loc.*, Vol. I. p. 105. οὗτοι] '*these (and none other than these),*' 'exclusis ceteris Abrahamo natis,' Beng.; see James i. 25. This retrospective and emphatic use of the pronoun is illustrated by Winer, *Gr.* § 23. 4, p. 144; see also Bernhardy, *Synt.* VI. 8. d, p. 283, Jelf, *Gr.* § 658.

τεως, οὗτοί εἰσιν υἱοὶ Ἀβραάμ. 8 προϊδοῦσα δὲ ἡ γραφὴ ὅτι ἐκ
πίστεως δικαιοῖ τὰ ἔθνη ὁ Θεός, προευηγγελίσατο τῷ Ἀβραὰμ
ὅτι ἐνευλογηθήσονται ἐν σοὶ πάντα τὰ ἔθνη. 9 ὥστε οἱ ἐκ πίστεως, εὐλογοῦνται σὺν τῷ πιστῷ Ἀβραάμ.

8. προϊδοῦσα δὲ ἡ γραφή] '*Moreover the Scripture foreseeing:*' further statement that the faithful, who have already been shown to be the true children of Abraham, are also the only and proper participators in his blessing. This sort of personification is noticed by Schoettg. (*Hor. Hebr.* Vol. I. p. 732) as a 'formula Judæis admodum solemnis,' *e. g.*, מָה רָאָה הַכָּתוּב 'Quid vidit scriptura?' מָה רָאָה הוּא 'Quid vidit ille, *h. e.* quidnam ipsi in mentem venit?' see also Surenhus. Βίβλ. Καταλλ. p. 6, sq. In such cases ἡ γραφὴ stands obviously for the Author of the Scriptures — God, by whose inspiration they were written; compare Syr., where ܐܠܗܐ [Aloha] is actually adopted in the translation. δὲ appears to be here μεταβατικόν, *i. e.* indicative of *transition* (Hartung, *Partik.* δέ, 2. 3, Vol. I. p. 165, Winer, *Gr.* § 53. 7. b, p. 393); it does not merely connect this verse with the preceding (Auth. Ver., Peile, Conyb., al.), but implies a further consideration of the subject under *another* aspect; 'δὲ eam ipsam vim habet ut abducat nos ab eâ re quæ proposita est, transferatque ad id, quod, missâ illâ priore re, jam pro vero ponendum esse videatur,' Klotz, *Devar.* Vol. II. p. 353. The exact force of δέ, which is never *simply* connective (Hartung, *Partik.* Vol. I. p. 163) and never loses *all* shades of its true oppositive character, deserves almost more attentive consideration in these Epp. than any other particle, and will often be found to supply the only true clue to the sequence and evolution of the argument.

δικαιοῖ] '*justifieth;*' not 'would justify,' Auth. ('præsens pro futuro,' Grot.), nor present with ref. to what is *now* taking place (De W.), but what is termed the *ethical* present, with significant reference to the eternal and immutable counsels of God; ἄνωθεν ταῦτα καὶ ὥρισε καὶ προηγόρευσεν ὁ Θεός, Theod.; comp. Matth. xxvi. 2, παραδίδοται; see Winer, *Gr.* § 40. 2, p. 237, and for the rationale of this usage, Schmalfeld, *Synt.* § 54. 2, p. 91.

προευηγγελίσατο] '*made known the glad tidings beforehand;*' compare Gen. xii. 3, xviii. 18, xxii. 18. The compound προευαγγ. is somewhat rare; it occurs in Schol. Soph. *Trach.* 335, Philo, *de Opif.* § 9. Vol. I. p. 7, *de Mut. Nom.* § 29, Vol. I. p. 602 (ed. Mang.) and the eccles. writers.

ὅτι ἐνευλογ.] '*shall be blessed in;*' quotation, by means of the usual ὅτι *recitativum*, from Gen. xii. 3 (compare ch. xviii. 18, xxii. 18), though not in the exact words; the here more apposite but practically synonymous πάντα τὰ ἔθνη being used (perhaps from ch. xviii. 18) instead of the πᾶσαι αἱ φυλαὶ τῆς γῆς of the LXX: compare Surenhus. Βιβλ. Καταλλ. p. 567. The simple form εὐλογηθ. is adopted by *Elz.* (not *Steph.*), but only with FG and cursive mss.

ἐν σοί] '*in thee,*' as the spiritual father of all the faithful; not 'per te,' Schott, but simply and plainly 'in te,' Vulg., Clarom., — the prep. with its usual force specifying Abraham as the *substratum, foundation,* on which, and in which, the blessing rests; compare 1 Cor. vii. 14, and Winer, *Gr.* § 48. a, p. 345.

9. ὥστε] '*So then,*' '*Consequently,*' see notes on ch. ii. 13. Ὥστε states the

They who are of the works of the Law lie under a curse, from which Christ has freed us; having ensured to all in Himself the blessing of Abraham.

10 Ὅσοι γὰρ ἐξ ἔργων νόμου εἰσίν, ὑπὸ
κατάραν εἰσίν· γέγραπται γὰρ ὅτι ἐπικατάρατος
πᾶς ὃς οὐκ ἐμμένει ἐν πᾶσιν τοῖς γεγραμμένοις

result from the emphatic ἐνευλογ. (συλλογιζόμενος ἐπήγαγεν, Chrys.): it is from the fact of the blessing having been promised to Abraham and his children, that οἱ ἐκ πίστεως share it, inasmuch as they are true children (ver. 7) of Abraham; εὐλογημένοι εἰσὶν οἱ . . . τῇ πίστει προσιόντες, ὥσπερ καὶ ὁ πιστὸς Ἀβρ. ηὐλόγητο, Theoph. σύν] '*together with;*' not 'similiter,' Grot., but, in accordance with the regular meaning of the prep., 'with,' 'in *association* with' (Winer, *Gr.* § 48. b, p. 349), the πιστῷ serving to hint (Mey., Alf.) at that to which this association is truly to be referred; εἴ τις τοίνυν τῆς ἐκείνου συγγενείας ἀξιωθῆναι ποθεῖ, τὴν ἐκείνου πίστιν ζηλούτω, Theod. The change of prep. introduces a corresponding change in the aspect in which Abraham is regarded: under ἐν he is regarded as the Patriarch, the spiritual ancestor *in whom*,—under σὺν he is regarded as the illustriously faithful individual *with whom*, all οἱ ἐκ πίστ. share the blessing; see Windischm. *in loc.* Schott cites a similar use of μετά (with Gen.) Psalm cv. 6, ἡμάρτομεν μετὰ τῶν πατέρων; Eccles. ii. 16, ἀποθανεῖται ὁ σοφὸς μετὰ τοῦ ἄφρονος; but in both cases a similarity of lot rather than a strict community and fellowship in it, seems implied; as a general rule, μετά τινος implies rather *coëxistence*, σύν τινι, *coherence;* see Krüger, *Sprachl.* § 68. 13. 1, and comp. notes *on Eph.* vi. 23.

10. ὅσοι γὰρ κ. τ. λ.] Proof of the justice of the conclusion in ver. 9 with regard to οἱ ἐκ πίστεως; γὰρ introducing *e contrario*—a confirmatory notice of the acknowledged state of the other class, οἱ ἐξ ἔργων νόμου: not only are they not blessed with Abraham, but they are actually under a curse. St. Paul's love of proving all his assertions has been often noticed; comp. Davidson, *Introd.* Vol. II. p. 145. οἱ ἐξ ἔργων νόμου] '*they who are of*, *i. e.* appertain to, rest upon, *the works of the law*,' 'qui in lege justitiam quærunt,' Bull, *Harm. Ap.* II. 7. 12; the primary force of ἐκ, owing to the nature of the expression, being here slightly less obvious than in ver. 8, and suggesting more the secondary and derivative idea of *dependence on* than of direct origination from; see Winer *in loc.*, and comp. 1 Cor. xii. 16, οὐκ εἰμὶ ἐκ τοῦ σώματος. ὑπὸ κατάραν] '*under a curse;*' not 'under *the* curse,' but almost simply and generally, '*under curse*' = ἐπικατάρατος; comp. ὑφ' ἁμαρτίαν, Rom. iii. 9: the proof drawn from the O. T. becomes thus more cogent. Ὑπὸ, it may be remarked, has appy. here no quasi-*physical* sense (κατάρα being viewed in the light of a burden, Rück., Windschm.), but its common *ethical* sense of 'subjection to;' see Winer, *Gr.* § 49. k, p. 362. With regard to the argument, it is only necessary to observe that the whole obviously rests on the admission, which it was impossible not to make, that no one of οἱ ἐξ ἔργων νόμου can fulfil all the requisitions of the law; see esp. Bull, *Harm. Apost.* II. 7. 11, and comp. with it Usteri, *Lehrb.* I. 4. B, p. 60. γέγραπται γάρ] Confirmation from Scripture of the preceding words. The quotation is from Deut. xxvii. 26, though not in the exact words either of the Heb. or LXX; comp. Surenhus. Βίβλος Καταλλ., p. 569, and Bagge *in loc.* The following ὅτι is omitted by *Rec.*, but only with JK; mss.. and some

ἐν τῷ Βιβλίῳ τοῦ νόμου, τοῦ ποιῆσαι αὐτά. 11 ὅτι δὲ ἐν νόμῳ
οὐδεὶς δικαιοῦται παρὰ τῷ Θεῷ δῆλον, ὅτι ὁ δίκαιος ἐκ πίστεως,

Ff. τοῦ ποιῆσαι αὐτά] '*to do them*,' 'ut faciat ea,' Vulg., Clarom.; purpose contemplated and involved in the ἐμμένει. This use of the infin. to denote *design*, *intention*, is (with the exception of a few instances from the other writers in the N. T., Mark iv. 3 [*Rec.*], James v. 17) confined to St. Paul and St. Luke; see Fritz. *Matth.* Excurs. II. p. 485, Winer, *Gr.* § 45. 4. b, p. 377. The construction is not, properly considered, Hebraistic, but belongs to later Greek, and may be correctly explained as an amplification of the use of the gen., which serves first to mark the *result* or *product* (*e. g. Il.* β. 397, κύματα παντοίων ἀνέμων, Scheuerl. *Synt.* § II. 1, p. 79), then further, the *purpose* of the working object, and lastly (*e. g.* in LXX, where the Hebr. idiom would naturally cause this development) becomes little more than *explanatory* and *definitive*; comp. Gen. iii. 6, ὡραῖόν ἐστι τοῦ κατανοῆσαι, Exod. ii. 18, ἐταχύνατε τοῦ παραγενέσθαι. In this latter case the first verb commonly marks a more general action, the second, one more limiting and special; comp. Gen. xxxiv. 17, εἰσακούειν ἡμῶν τοῦ περιτεμέσθαι, and see esp. Thiersch, *de Pent.* III. 12, p. 173 sq., where this usage is well investigated. The progress of this structure in classical Greek is briefly noticed by Bernhardy, *Synt.* IX. 2, p. 357.

11. ὅτι δὲ κ. τ. λ.] '*But (further) that in the law*,' etc.:' continuation of the reasoning; δὲ subjoining to the 'argumentum e contrario,' — that those of the law are under the curse (ver. 10), — the supplementary argument derived from Scripture that *no one* under any circumstances is justified by the law. The oppositive force of δὲ may thus be felt in the incidental reply which the verse affords to a deduction that might have been obviously made from ver. 10; 'but — lest any one should imagine that if a man *did* so ἐμμένειν κ. τ. λ. he would be blessed — let me add,' etc.; compare De Wette *in loc.* ἐν νόμῳ] '*under the law*;' *i. e.* in the sphere and domain of the law; Acts xiii. 39, Rom. ii. 12, iii. 19. The instrumental meaning is grammatically tenable (object existing in the means, Jelf, *Gr.* § 622. 3, see notes *on* 1 *Thess.* iv. 18), and even contextually plausible, owing to the prominence of ἐν νόμῳ and its apparent opposition to Χριστός, ver. 13 (see Meyer): as, however, owing to the inversion of the syllogism, the opposition between the clauses is much obscured, the simpler and more usual meaning is here to be preferred: comp. notes *on* 1 *Thess.* ii. 3. The more inclusive ἐν is thus perhaps chosen designedly, as the Apostle's object is appy. to show that the idea of justification falls wholly *out of the domain* of the law, and is incompatible with its very nature and character. παρὰ τῷ Θεῷ] '*in the sight of*;' *i. e.* 'in the judgment of God' (Rom. ii. 13, xii. 16, 1 Pet. ii. 20), the idea of locality suggested by the prep. being still retained in that of judgment at a tribunal; see notes *on* 2 *Thess.* i. 6. This usage is sufficiently common in classical writers; see Bernhardy, *Synt.* v. 17. b, p. 257, and exx. in Palm u. Rost, *Lex.* s. v. παρά, II. 2, Vol. II. p. 667. ὅτι ὁ δίκαιος κ. τ. λ.] '*because, The just shall live by faith*,' Habak. ii. 4, again cited in Rom. i. 17, Heb. x. 38, — this second ὅτι being causal, the first simply declarative. It is *extremely* difficult to decide whether ἐκ πίστ. is to be joined with ὁ δίκ. ('the just by faith'), or with the verb. The

ζήσεται· 12 ὁ δὲ νόμος οὐκ ἔστιν ἐκ πίστεως, ἀλλ' ὁ ποιήσας
αὐτὰ ζήσεται ἐν αὐτοῖς. 13 Χριστὸς ἡμᾶς ἐξηγόρασεν ἐκ τῆς

former is perfectly correct in point of grammar, though doubted by Bp. Middl. (see Winer, *Gr.* § 20. 2, p. 123), and is adopted by Hammond, Meyer, and other careful expositors. As, however, it seems certain (opp. to Baumg.-Crus.) that the original Hebrew (see Hitzig *in loc.*, *Kl. Prophet.* p. 263, 264) does *not* bear this meaning, — as St. Paul is quoting the words in the order in which they stand in the LXX, not in that (ὁ ἐκ πίστ. δίκ.) most favorable to such a transl., — as the argument seems best sustained by the other construction (see Middl. *in loc.*, and comp. Bull, *Exam. Cens.* Animadv. III. 5), — and lastly, as ζήσεται ἐκ πίστ. thus stands in more exact opposition to ζήσ. ἐν αὐτοῖς, it seems best with Copt., Arm. (appy.), Chrys. (appy.), and the bulk of the older expositors, to connect ἐκ πίστεως with ζήσεται.

12. ὁ δὲ νόμος κ. τ. λ.) '*but the law is not of faith*,' scil. does not spring from it, has no connection with it in point of principle or origin; *propositio minor* of the syllogism, ὁ δίκ. ἐκ πίστ. ζήσ. being the *prop. major*, ἐν νόμ. οὐδ. δικ. the *conclusion*. The Auth. Vers. by translating δὲ 'and' obscures the argumentation. ὁ ποιήσας αὐτά] '*he who hath done them*,' scil. τὰ προστάγματα and τὰ κρίματα, mentioned in the former part of the verse here referred to, — Lev. xviii. 5. Ποιήσας is emphatic ('præcepta legis non sunt de credendis, sed de faciendis,' Aquin.), and is prefaced by the adversative ἀλλ' as expressing a sentiment directly opposite to what has preceded. There is thus no ellipse of γέγραπται (Schott) or λέγει (Bagge); comp. Fritz. *Rom.* Vol. II. p. 284. The insertion of ἄνθρωπος after αὐτὰ (*Rec.*) has only the authority of D³EJK and mss., and is rightly rejected by most modern editors.

ἐν αὐτοῖς] '*in them*,' *i. e.*, as Winer paraphrases, 'ut in his legibus, vitæ fons quasi insit.'

13. Χριστὸς ἡμᾶς κ. τ. λ.] '*Christ ransomed us*,' etc.; vivid and studiedly abrupt contrast to the declaration involved in the two preceding verses; the law condemned us, Christ ransomed us; 'non dissimile asyndeton, Col. iii. 4, ubi item de Christo,' Beng.

ἡμᾶς] Jews; not Jews *and* heathens; 'Judæos præcipue pressit maledictio,' Beng., compare Chrys. For (1) the whole context implies that the law is the Mosaic law: see Usteri *in loc.* (2) This law had, strictly speaking, no force over the Gentiles, but was, in fact, the μεσότοιχος between the Jews and Gentiles: Eph. ii. 14, 15. For a further discussion of this, consult Meyer and Usteri *in loc.*, and Brown *Galat.* p. 129 sq. The doctrinal deductions made from this and similar passages, though perfectly just and true (comp. Neand. *Plant.* Vol. I. p. 438, Bohn), cannot be urged against the more limited meaning which the context seems obviously to require. ἐξηγόρασεν] '*ransomed*,' '*redeemed*.' Christ ransomed the Jews from the curse of the law, by having taken it upon Himself for their sakes and in their stead. An accurate explanation of this, and the cognate idea ἀπολύτρωσις, will be found in Ust. *Lehrb.* II. 1. 1, p. 107, and II. 1. 3, p. 202. The force of the preposition (ἐκ) need not be very strongly pressed, *e. g.* 'emtione nos *inde* eruit,' Beng.: see Polyb. *Hist.* III. 42. 2, ἐξηγόρασε παρ' αὐτῶν τά τε μονόξυλα πλοῖα κ. τ. λ., where the prep. has no marked meaning. This tendency to use verbs com-

καταρας τοῦ νόμου γενόμενος ὑπὲρ ἡμῶν κατάρα, ὅτι γέγραπται
Ἐπικατάρατος πᾶς ὁ κρεμάμενος ἐπὶ ξύλου, 14 ἵνα εἰς τὰ ἔθνη ἡ

pounded with prepp. without any obvious increase of meaning, is one of the characteristics of later Greek; Thiersch, *de Pentat. Vers. Alex.* II. 1, p. 83.

γενόμενος ὑπὲρ ἡμῶν κατ.] '*by having become a curse for us*;' dependent participle expressing the *manner* of the action, which again is more distinctly elucidated in the quotation; λέγει δὲ καὶ τὸν τρόπον, Theod. The abstract κατάρα (not, 'an accursed thing,' Peile, — which dilutes the antithesis) is probably chosen, as Meyer suggests, instead of the concrete, to express with more force the completeness of the satisfaction which Christ made to the law. On the doctrinal import of the expression (κατάρα ἤκουσε δι' ἐμέ, ὁ τὴν ἐμὴν λύων κατάραν, Greg. Naz.) see the quotations in Suicer, *Thes.* s. v. κατάρα, Vol. II. p. 57 sq., and for a few words of great force and eloquence on the 'maledictum crucis,' Andrewes, *Serm.* III. Vol. II. p. 174 (A. C. Libr.). ὑπὲρ ἡμῶν] '*for us*,' 'salutis nostræ reparandæ causâ,' Schott. In this and similar passages the exact meaning of the prep. has been much contested. Is it (α) '*in commodum (alicujus)*,' or (β) '*in loco (alicujus)?*' The following seems the most simple answer. Ὑπέρ, in its ethical sense, has principally and primarily (see note, ch. i. 4) the *first* meaning, especially in doctrinal passages, where the atoning death of Christ is alluded to, *e. g.* 2 Cor. v. 21, τὸν μὴ γνόντα ἁμαρτίαν ὑπὲρ ἡμῶν ἐποίησεν ἁμαρτίαν. But as there are general passages in the N. T. where ὑπὲρ has eminently the *second* meaning, *e. g.* Philem. 13, ἵνα ὑπὲρ σοῦ μοι διακονῇ (comp. Plato, *Gorg.* 515 C, ἐγὼ ὑπὲρ σοῦ ἀποκρινοῦμαι), — so are there doctrinal passages (as here) where ὑπὲρ may admit the second meaning *united* with the first, when the context (*e. g.* in 1 Cor. xv. 3 it would be inadmissible), and nature of the argument seem to require it, though probably never (Winer *Gr.* § 48. 1, p. 342) the second *exclusively*: see Magee, *Atonement*, No. 30, Vol. I. p. 245 sq., and Usteri, *Lehrb.* III. 1, p. 115 sq., where the meaning of the prep. is briefly discussed.

ὅτι γέγραπται] '*forasmuch as it is written*;' parenthetical confirmation of the assertion involved in the preceding participial clause, γενόμ. κ. τ. λ. The passage in Deut. (ch. xxi. 23) here adduced does not allude to crucifying, but to exposure after death on stakes or crosses (Josh. x. 26), but is fully pertinent as specifying the 'ignominious particularity to which the legal curse belonged,' and which our Redeemer by hanging dead on the cross formally fulfilled; see esp. Pearson, *Creed*, Art. IV. Vol. I. p. 248 sq. (Burt.). It is interesting to notice that the dead body was not hanged by the neck, but *by the hands*, and not on a tree, but on a piece of wood ('non ex arbore sed ligno,' Dassov.); see the treatise of Dassovius in *Thesaur. Theolog.-Philol.* Vol. II. p. 614, Jahn, *Archæol.* § 258, and Bähr, *Stud. u. Krit.* for 1849, p. 924 sq.

The reading of *Rec.*, γέγραπται γάρ, has only the support of D³EJK; mss.; Syr. (both) Copt., al., and bears every appearance of a confirmation to the more usual mode of citation, ver. 10.

14. ἵνα εἰς τὰ ἔθνη] '*in order that unto the Gentiles*:' divine purpose involved in the ἐξηγόρασεν ἐκ τῆς κατάρας κ. τ. λ. The first purpose was the ransom of the *Jews* from the curse; the second, which was involved in the first (ὅτι ἡ σωτηρία ἐκ τῶν Ἰουδαίων ἐστί, John iv. 22), was the extension of Abraham's blessing to the *Gentiles*, but that,

εὐλογία τοῦ Ἀβραὰμ γένηται ἐν Χριστῷ Ἰησοῦ, ἵνα τὴν ἐπαγγελίαν τοῦ Πνεύματος λάβωμεν διὰ τῆς πίστεως.

Even the customs of men must show that the promise of God to Abraham cannot be annulled by the law which was so long afterwards.

15 Ἀδελφοί, κατὰ ἄνθρωπον λέγω· ὅμως

not through the law but in Jesus Christ. Εἰς with accus. is here neither simply identical with dat. (comp. Winer, *Gr.* § 31. 5, p. 191), nor in its more lax sense of 'in reference to' (Piele; comp. Bern. *Synt.* v. 11, p. 219), but retains its proper *local* meaning, with reference to the metaphorical arrival of the εὐλογία; see Winer, *Gr.* § 49. a, p. 353. ἡ εὐλογία τοῦ Ἀβρ.] '*the blessing of Abraham*,' scil. the blessing announced to and vouchsafed to Abraham (ver. 8), ἡ εὐλογία ἡ ἐκ πίστεως, Theoph.; the gen. being the gen. *objecti;* comp. Rom. xv. 8, τὰς ἐπαγγελίας τῶν πατέρων, and see Winer, *Gr.* § 30. 1. p. 167 sq., Krüger, *Sprachl.* § 47. 7, 1 sq. ἐν Χριστῷ Ἰησ.] '*in Christ Jesus*,' 'in Christo Jesu,' Vulg., Clarom., Copt., Arm.; not 'propter,' Æth., or for διά, Grot. (comp. Chrys.), as this instrumental use of ἐν with persons, though found in a few passages (comp. Matth. ix. 34, ἐν τῷ ἄρχοντι, — he was the *causa efficiens*), is here certainly not necessary. It was '*in* Christ,' in the knowledge of Him and in His death, that the Gentiles received the blessing. ἵνα τὴν κ. τ. λ.] '*in order that we might receive;*' second statement of purpose, not subordinated to, but coordinate with the preceding one. Meyer cites as instances of a similar parallelism of ἵνα, Rom. vii. 13, 2 Cor. ix. 3, Eph. vi. 19. The Apostle advances with his subject, till at last under λάβωμεν he includes all; '*nos*, omnium gentium homines, sive Judæi, sive Barbari.' τὴν ἐπαγγελίαν τοῦ Πνεύματος] '*the promise of the Spirit;*' not merely τὸ ἐπαγγελθὲν Πνεῦμα (Fritz. *Rom.* vi. 4, Vol. I. p. 368), but 'the realization of the promise of the Spirit,' ἐπαγγ. being taken in a partially *concrete* sense; comp. Luke xxiv. 49, Heb. x. 36, and see Winer, *Gr.* § 34. 3, p. 211. Grammatically considered, τοῦ Πνεύμ. may be a *gen. subjecti*, sc. 'promissionem a Spiritu profectam,' or a *gen. objecti*, as above. Doctrinally considered, however, the latter is distinctly to be preferred; the Spirit being usually represented by the Apostle as not so much the source, as the pledge of the fulfilment of the promise; see Usteri, *Lehrb.* II. 1. 2, p. 174 note. After a wondrous chain of arguments, expressed with equal force, brevity, and profundity, the Apostle comes back to the subject of ver. 2; the gift of the Holy Ghost came through faith in Jesus Christ.

15. ἀδελφοὶ κ. τ. λ.] Proof that the promise was not abrogated by the law: οὕτω δείξας τὴν πίστιν πρεσβυτέραν τοῦ νόμου, διδάσκει πάλιν ὡς ὁ νόμος ἐμποδὼν οὐ δύναται γενέσθαι ταῖς Θεοῦ ἐπαγγελίαις, Theod. κατὰ ἄνθρωπον] '*after the manner of men;*' ἐξ ἀνθρωπίνων παραδειγμάτων, Chrys., ἀνθρωπίνοις πράγμασι κέχρημαι, Theod.; see notes, ch. i. 11. With this expression the Apostle here introduces an argument which rests on mere human analogies, and which he uses as men might ('tanquam inter homines,' Syr.), one to another: 'affero exemplum ex hominum vitâ depromptum,' Fritz. *Rom.* iii. 5, Vol. I. 160, — where the various meanings of this formula will be found briefly noticed. ὅμως ἀνθρώπου κ. τ. λ.] '*though it be but a man's covenant, yet when confirmed*,' etc.: logically inexact, but not idiomatically uncommon

ἀνθρώπου κεκυρωμένην διαθήκην οὐδεὶς ἀθετεῖ ἢ ἐπιδιατάσσεται.
16 τῷ δὲ Ἀβραὰμ ἐρρέθησαν αἱ ἐπαγγελίαι, καὶ τῷ σπέρματι

transposition of ὅμως, which, as the sense shows, really belongs to οὐδείς. Both ὅμως and other adverbs (*e. g.* ἀεί, πολλάκις, ἔτι), are occasionally thus, as it were, attracted out of their logical order, when the meaning is otherwise distinct; see Winer, *Gr.* § 61. 4, p. 488, and Ellendt, *Lex. Soph.* s. v. ὅμως, who observes that this transposition is most frequently found with participles; 'ὅμως cum participio ita componitur, ut inclusum protasi tamen ad apodosin pertineat,' Vol. II. p. 318: compare Plato, *Phædo*, 91 C. φοβεῖται μὴ ἡ ψυχὴ ὅμως καὶ θειότερον καὶ κάλλιον ὂν τοῦ σώματος προαπολλύηται, and see Stalbaum, *in loc.* διαθήκην] '*a covenant.*' It may be true, doctrinally considered, that it is not of much moment whether διαθ. be interpreted '*contractum* an *testamentum*' (Calv.); considered however exegetically, it is obvious that (*a*) the order of the words, and (*b*) the comparison between the διαθήκη of man and the διαθήκη of God (ver. 17), tacitly instituted by the emphatic position of ἀνθρώπου (sing. to make the antithesis more apparent), both require exclusively the former meaning; so Æth. *(kidan)*, and appy. Theoph. διαθήκην καὶ συμφωνίαν: the other Vv. either adopt διαθήκη (Syr., Copt.), or are ambiguous. A paper on the uses of this word in the N. T. will be found in the *Classical Museum*, Vol. VII. p. 299; see also Bagge *in loc.* ἐπιδιατάσσεται] '*adds new conditions,*' 'superordinat,' Vulg., Clarom., 'novas addit constitutiones,' Bretsch. *Lex.* s. v., or, in effect, as it is neatly paraphrased by Herm., 'additamentis vitiat; comp. Joseph. *Antiq.* XVII. 9, 4, and esp. *Bell. Jud.* II. 2. 3, ἀξιῶν τῆς ἐπιδιαθήκης τὴν διαθήκην εἶναι κυριωτέραν.

16. τῷ δὲ Ἀβραάμ] '*Now to Abraham;*' parenthetical argument designed to make the application of this particular example to the general case perfectly distinct, and to obviate every misapprehension. The Apostle seems to say; 'this, however, is not a case merely of a διαθήκη, but of an ἐπαγγελία, — yea, of ἐπαγγελίαι; nor was it made merely to a man Abraham (ἀνθ. διαθ.), but to Christ. According to the usual interpretation, δὲ introduces the *prop. minor* of a syllogism, which is interrupted by the parenthetical comment οὐ λέγει . . . Χριστός, but resumed in ver. 17, '*atqui* Abraamo et semini,' etc., Herm. To this, however, the objection of Meyer seems very just, that in that case St. Paul would have undoubtedly given a greater logical prominence to the *divine* nature of the promises to Abraham by some such term as Θεὸς δὲ τῷ Ἀβρ. κ. τ. λ.; see also Alf. *in loc.* αἱ ἐπαγγελίαι] '*the promises;*' plural, as being several times repeated (Est.), and couched in different forms of expression; comp. Gen. xiii. 15, xv. 18, xvii. 8, xxvi. 4, xxviii. 14. They involved, as Bengel well observes, not only earthly but heavenly blessings, 'terræ Canaan et mundi, et divinorum bonorum omnium. The latter were more distinctly future, the former paulo-post-future. On the exact spiritual nature of these promises, see Hengstenberg, *Christol.* Vol. I. p. 38 (Clark).

The so-called Ionic form ἐρρέθησαν has the support of the best uncial MSS., and is adopted by most of the recent editors; see Lobeck, *Phryn.* p. 447. καὶ τῷ σπέρματι αὐτοῦ] '*and to his seed;*' emphatic, as pointing to Christ, and forming as it were the fulcrum of the argument which follows.

αὐτοῦ. οὐ λέγει Καὶ τοῖς σπέρμασιν, ὡς ἐπὶ πολλῶν, ἀλλ' ὡς ἐφ' ἑνός Καὶ τῷ σπέρματί σου, ὅς ἐστιν Χριστός.

The passages of Scripture referred to are here appy. Gen. xiii. 15, and xvii. 8, but not Gen. xxii. 18; so Iren. v. 32, Origen *on Rom.* iv. Vol. v. p. 276 (ed. Lomm.). We may here pause to make a brief remark on the great freedom with which so many commentators have allowed themselves to characterize St. Paul's argument as either artificial ('Schulkunst,' Ewald) or Rabbinical (Mey.; comp. Surenhus. Βίβλ. Καταλλ. p. 84), or, as Baur, *Apost. Paul.* p. 665, has even ventured to assert, 'plainly arbitrary and incorrect.' It may be true that similar arguments occur in Rabbinical writers (Schoettg. *Hor.* Vol. I. p. 736); it may be true that σπέρμα (like זֶרַע) is a collective noun, and that when the plural is used, as in Dan. i. 12, 'grains of seed' are implied. All this may be so, — nevertheless, we have here an interpretation which the Apostle, writing under the illumination of the Holy Ghost has deliberately propounded, and which, therefore (whatever difficulties may at first appear in it), is profoundly and indisputably true. We hold, therefore, that there is as certainly a mystical meaning in the use of זֶרַע in Gen. xiii. 15, xvii. 8, as there is an argument for the resurrection in Exod. iii. 6, though in neither case was the writer necessarily aware of it. As זֶרַע in its simple meaning generally (except Gen. iv. 25, 1 Sam. i. 11) denotes not the mere progeny of a man, but his posterity viewed as one organically-connected whole; so here in its mystical meaning it denotes not merely the spiritual posterity of Abraham, but Him in whom that posterity is all organically united, the πλήρωμα, the κεφαλή, even Christ. This St. Paul endeavors faintly to convey to his Greek readers by the use of σπέρμα and σπέρματα: see Olsh. and Windischm. *in loc.*, both of whom may be consulted with profit.

οὐ λέγει] '*He saith not;*' not ἡ γραφή (Bos, *Ellips.* p. 54), as in Rom. xv. 10, — where this subst. is supplied from γέγραπται, ver. 9, — or τὸ πνεῦμα (Rück., Winer, *Gr.* § 39. 1), which appears arbitrary, but the natural subject ὁ Θεός, as in Eph. iv. 8, v. 14, and (φησὶ) 1 Cor. vi. 16, Heb. viii. 5. So appy. Syr., which here inserts ܗܘ [illi] after λέγει.

ὡς ἐπὶ πολλῶν] '*as (speaking) of many.*' Apparently a solitary instance in the N. T. of this meaning of ἐπὶ with *gen.* after verbs 'dicendi,' etc. (2 Cor. vii. 14 [Rück.], is not in point, as ἐπὶ Τίτου is there 'coram Tito'), though not uncommon in classical Greek; compare Plato, *Charm.* 155 D, ἐπὶ τοῦ καλοῦ λέγων παιδός, and *ib. Gorg.* 453 E, πάλιν δ' εἰ ἐπὶ τῶν αὐτῶν τεχνῶν λέγομεν. In this use of ἐπί, a trace of the local meaning (*superposition*, Donalds. *Gr.* § 483) may be distinctly perceived, the gen. representing as it were the *substratum* on which the action rests; comp. John vi. 2; and see Bernhardy, *Synt.* v. 23, p. 248, Winer, *Gr.* § 47. g, p. 335, and for a comprehensive notice of this prep., Wittmann, *de Naturâ* etc. ἐπί (Schweinf. 1846).

ὅς ἐστιν Χριστός] '*Christ (Jesus),*' not Christ and his Church, as Hammond *in loc.*: this appears evident from the emphasis which St. Paul lays on the use of the singular; σπέρμα δὲ αὐτοῦ κατὰ σάρκα ἐστὶν ὁ Χριστός, Chrys. Some useful remarks on this passage will be found in the *Theol. Critic*, No. IV. p. 494 sq.

17 τοῦτο δὲ λέγω· διαθήκην προκεκυρωμένην ὑπὸ τοῦ Θεοῦ [εἰς
Χριστὸν] ὁ μετὰ τετρακόσια καὶ τριάκοντα ἔτη γεγονὼς νόμος οὐκ

17. εἰς Χριστόν] '*for Christ,*' *i. e.*, to be fulfilled in Christ: not 'usque ad tempora Christi,' or 'in reference to Christ' (Peile), but as in ver. 24. These words are omitted by ABC; 17. 23*. 67**. 80; Vulg., Copt., Æth. (both); Cyr. (2), Dam.; Jerome, Aug. (often), Pel., Bed. (*Lachm.*, *Tisch.*, *Mey.*), — and it must be fairly owned have *some* appearance of being a gloss, still the authority for the insertion, — viz., DEFGJK; most mss.; Syr. (both), Clarom., Arm. [correct *Griesb.*]; Chrys., Theod., Theoph., Œcum. (*Rec.*, *Scholz*), is so strong that we seem justified in an insertion in brackets. See Bagge *in loc.* (p. 95), who has argued with ability in favor of the Received Text.

17. τοῦτο δὲ λέγω] '*This, however, I say,*' 'hoc autem dico,' Vulg., Clarom. Instead of using the collective οὖν, which might obscure the exact position which ver. 16 holds in the argument, St. Paul uses the explanatory formula τοῦτο δὲ λέγω. The δὲ thus serves to resume the argument (σαφηνείας χάριν ἀναλαμβάνει τὸν λόγον, Œcum.) after the short digression, κατ' ἄνθρ. λέγω — τοῦτο δὲ λέγω, and also to mark the application of the particular case to the general principle. ὁ μετὰ τετρακόσια κ. τ. λ.] '*which came (so long a time as) four hundred and thirty years afterwards;*' μετὰ πλεῖστον χρόνον, Theod. The chronological difficulty involved in this passage, when compared with Gen. xv. 13, Exod. xii. 40, and Acts vii. 6, can only be briefly noticed. Here the period from the promise to the exodus is stated to be 430 years; but in Exod. *l. c.* the same period, and in Gen. and Acts *l. c.* the round number 400 is assigned to the sojourn in Egypt alone. The ancient mode of explanation seems perfectly satisfactory, — viz., that the 430 years include the sojourn in Canaan (about 215 years) as well as that in Egypt; the whole period of abode ἐν γῇ οὐκ ἰδίᾳ (Gen. xv. 13); comp. August. *Quæst. in Heptat.* II. 47 (Vol. III. p. 611, Migne), Usher, *Chronol. Sacr.* ch. 8. This is confirmed by the addition of the words καὶ ἐν γῇ Χαναάν (Exod. *l. c.*) in the LXX, and Samar. Pent.: see Petav. *Rat. Temp.* II. Book 2, 4, Vol. II. p. 71, Hales, *Chron.* Vol. II. p. 153 (ed. 1811). It may be observed that the records of the family of Levi appear to render so long a sojourn in Egypt as 430 years impossible. Amram, grandson of Levi, marries his father's sister Jochebed (Exod. vi. 20; comp. Exod. ii. 1, Numb. xxvi. 59). Now, as it appears probable by a comparison of dates that Levi was born when Jacob was about 87, Levi would have been 43 when he came into Egypt; there he lives 94 years (Exod. vi. 16). Assuming, then, even that Jochebed was born in the last year of Levi's life, she must at least have been 256 years old when Moses was born, if the sojourn in Egypt be 430 years: see Windischm. *in loc.* The transposition ἔτη τετρακ. κ. τ. λ. (*Rec.*) has against it the authority of all the uncial MSS. except J K, and is certainly to be rejected.

εἰς τὸ καταργῆσαι κ. τ. λ.] '*that it should render the promise of none effect,*' ad evacuandam promissionem,' Vulg., Clarom. (compare Æth., Syr.-Philox); εἰς τὸ with the infinitive here retaining its usual primary force of *object* or *intention*: τὸ καταργ. was the object aimed at by the invalidation. It may be remarked that as the prep. alone may point to *consequence* as

ἄκυροῖ, εἰς τὸ καταργῆσαι τὴν ἐπαγγελίαν. 18 εἰ γὰρ ἐκ νόμου ἡ
κληρονομία, οὐκέτι ἐξ ἐπαγγελίας· τῷ δὲ Ἀβραὰμ δι' ἐπαγγελίας
κεχάρισται ὁ Θεός.

The law was to bring the conviction of sin (positive answer): and was not against the promises of God (negative answer), to which it was a preparative institution.

19 Τί οὖν ὁ νόμος; τῶν παραβάσεων

well as *intention* (see exx. in Rost. u. Palm, *Lex.* s. v. ἐπὶ v. 1), we must not abruptly deny what is termed the 'ecbatic' force of εἰς τό: still usage seems to show that in St. Paul's Epp. the *final* εἰς τὸ so much predominates (opp. to Jelf, *Gr.* § 625. 3. a), that even in passages like 2 Cor. viii. 6, we must not conceive all idea of *purpose* wholly obliterated; compare Winer, *Gr.* § 44. 6, p. 294 sq., and see notes *on* 1 *Thess.* ii. 12.

18. εἰ γὰρ ἐκ νόμου] Confirmatory expansion of the preceding words; 'I say advisedly, εἰς τὸ καταργ. κ. τ. λ.; for if the inheritance be of the law, the promise must plainly be reduced to inoperativeness and invalidity; see Theoph. *in loc.* The prep. ἐκ here preserves its primary meaning of *origin* under the slight modification of *result* or *consequence;* see notes on ch. ii. 16. ἡ κληρονομία] '*the inheritance;*' here used by the Apostle in its higher meaning to denote that inheritance of the blessings of the Messiah's kingdom, — the inheritance of the heavenly Canaan, which was typified by the lower and primary meaning, the inheritance of the earthly Canaan; comp. Acts vii. 5, Heb. xi. 4, and see Brown p. 147. οὐκέτι ἐξ ἐπαγγελίας] '*it is no more of promise;*' the latter supposition is excluded by the former; comp. Rom. vii. 20, xi. 6, and see Winer, *Gr.* § 66. 10, p. 545. Οὐκέτι is thus used in its simple *logical* sense without any temporal reference. δι' ἐπαγγελίας] '*by means of promise;*' not 'in the form of a promise' (Peile, Rück.), nor as uniting with κεχάρ. as a mere equivalent to ἐπηγγείλατο (Æth., both), but simply and plainly 'per promissionem,' Beza, 'by virtue and by means of promise.' The enjoyment of the inheritance depended on no conditions, came through no other medium, save that of promise.' κεχάρισται] '*hath freely given it,*' 'gratis dedit,' Copt.; 'notanda est emphasis in voce κεχ. quæ a χάρις deducitur, adeoque a Bezâ (?) recte vertitur *gratificatus est,* confer Rom. iv. 13, 14, 15,' Bull, *Harm. Ap.* II. 5. 5. Κεχάρ. *may* be translated intransitively, 'Abrahamo grata fecit Deus' (Schott, Olsh., Bretsch.); but as the verb is nearly always used transitively in the N. T., and as logical perspicuity requires that the subject of the first member of the conditional syllogism (Beng.) should be supplied in the second, it appears most natural to tacitly supply κληρονομίαν as the obvious object-accusative. With the present use of the perf., implying the *duration* of the χάρις, contrast Phil. ii. 9, ἐχαρίσατο αὐτῷ ὄνομα, where the action is represented as a simple historical fact.

19. τί οὖν ὁ νόμος] '*What then is the law,*' *i. e.* 'what is the meaning, the object of the law?' Answer to the not unnatural objection, — that the Law must according to the Apostle's reasoning, be deemed a useless institution (περιττῶς ἐτέθη, Theod.), — by a statement of its real use, office, characteristics, and relation to the covenant of grace: ἵνα μή τις νομίσῃ περιττὸν τὸν νόμον, καὶ τοῦτο διορθοῦται τὸ μέρος, δεικνὺς ὅτι οὐκ εἰκῇ, ἀλλὰ πανὺ χρησίμως

χάριν προσετέθη, ἄχρις οὗ ἔλθῃ τὸ σπέρμα ᾧ ἐπήγ-

ἐδόθη, Chrys. Τί is not for διὰ τί (Schott, Brown), but is the idiomatic neuter expressive of the abstract nature, etc., of the subject; see Bernhardy, *Synt.* VII. 4, p. 336, and comp. Madvig, *Synt.* § 97, note. Meyer cites 1 Cor. iii. 5, τί οὖν ἐστιν Ἀπολλώς, but the MSS. evidence [CDEFGJ opp. to AB] seems there fairly in favor of τίς.

τῶν παραβάσεων χάριν] '*on account of,*' '*because of, the transgressions,*' 'propter transgressiones,' Vulg., ܡܛܠ ܡܣܟܠܘܬܐ [propter transgressionem] Syr., Copt. *(ethbe)*, and appy. Arm. (*vasn*), — scil. to manifest, awaken a conviction of, and give as it were a distinctive existence to *the* transgressions of it (which existed but were not properly recognized as such), whether previous or subsequent to its introduction; comp. Rom. v. 13, ἄχρι γὰρ νόμου ἁμαρτία ἦν ἐν κόσμῳ, the more generic ἁμαρτία being there used, as sin is not contemplated (as here) specially in the light of a transgression of a fixed ordinance. Owing to the various shades of meaning that have been assigned to χάριν, the exact significance of these words is somewhat debatable. Of the many interpretations that have been proposed, three deserve consideration, (α) '*ad coercendas transgressiones;*' as Chrys. (ἀντὶ χαλινοῦ ὁ νόμος), Theoph. Œcum., Jerome, and most of the older expositors: (β) '*transgressionum gratiâ,*' scil. to call them forth, to multiply them, and, as it were, bring them to a head, Rom. v. 20, vii. 7; so appy. Clarom., 'factorum (?) gratiâ,' very distinctly Æth. (both), 'ut multiplicarent peccata,' and some modern expositors, Meyer, Alf., al.: (γ) '*transgressionum causâ,*' *i. e.* 'ut transgressiones palam faceret, eoque modo homines cogeret ad agnitionem sui reatus,' Calv.; Rom. iii. 20; so appy. Vulg., Syr., Copt., Arm., Aug., Beza, Winer (appy.), and also in part Hofmann (*Schriftb.* Vol. II. 2, p. 48) who objects both to (α) and the extreme view of (β). Of these interpretations we must, in spite of the authority of the Greek commentators, plainly reject (α) on lexical grounds, as no satisfactory exx. (Soph. *Œd. Col.* 443 [see Herm.] is not to the point, nor 1 John iii. 12, nor even *Clem. Hom.* XI. 16, τῶν παραπτωμάτων χάριν ἡ τιμωρία ἕπεται) have as yet been adduced of such a practically *reversed* meaning of χάριν. The second (β) is more plausible, but still open to the grave objection, that in a comparatively undogmatical passage it ascribes a purpose directly to God (contrast Rom. v. 20, νόμος παρεισῆλθεν ἵνα κ. τ. λ.), which would have certainly needed a fuller explanation. We may retain, therefore, with some confidence (γ), which is both lexically defensible (see below), and yields a good and pertinent sense. The office of the law was to make transgressions palpable, to awaken a conviction of sin in the heart (τὸ πεῖσαι εἰδέναι τὰ οἰκεῖα ἁμαρτήματα, Chrys.), and make man feel his need of a Saviour. It was thus also necessarily *temporary* (ἄχρις οὗ κ. τ. λ.), for when the Seed *did* come, higher influences began to work within.

It only remains briefly to answer the lexical objection of Meyer, by stating that χάριν (esp. in later writers) does *not* always mean 'in gratiam,' but includes all shades of meaning, from *in gratiam* to *causâ* and *propter*, just as those of ἕνεκα range from *causâ* to *quod attinet ad;* see Bernh. *Synt.* V. 16, p. 233, Ellendt, *Lex. Soph.* s.v. χάριν, and comp. exx. in Ast, *Lex. Plat.* and Rost. u. Palm, *Lex.* s. v. A discussion of this passage and the general scope of the law will be found in Petav. *de*

γελται, διαταγεὶς δι' ἀγγέλων, ἐν χειρὶ μεσίτου.

Prædest. x. 25. 1, Vol. I. p. 461; compare also Bull, *Exam. Cens.* XIX. 6, and more recently Baur, *Apost. Paul.* III. 5, p. 581 sq., but observe that all these writers adopt the negative meaning of χάριν. προσετέθη] '*was superadded*,' '*super*-addita est,' Herm.; it was, however, as Meyer observes, no ἐπιδιαθήκη, but a totally fresh institution. The reason is given by Œcum., ἵνα δείξῃ τὸν νόμον μὴ ὄντα πρωτότυπον ὥσπερ αἱ ἐπαγγελίαι εἰσίν. The present reading is supported by ABCD3 EJK; most mss.; Theod. (2), Dam., Theoph., Œcum., and is distinctly to be preferred to ἐτέθη *(Rec.)*, which has both less external authority [D[1]FG; 5 mss. (Vulg., Clarom., appy., — but in such cases Vv. can hardly be cited) Clem., Orig., Euseb.], and also seems to have been a very natural substitution for a more difficult word. ἄχρις οὗ ἔλθῃ] '*until the seed shall have come*;' 'terminus ad quem' of the duration of the newly introduced institution (Mey.), involving the obvious query, τί περαιτέρω καὶ παρὰ καιρὸν αὐτὸν ἕλκεις, Chrys. This use of the subjunct. after an aor. in temporal sentences, can be fully defended on the recognized principle, that the past is contemplated by the writer as a present, from which, as it were, he is taking his survey of what would be then future, though now past; see exx. in Winer, *Gr.* § 41. 1, p. 257 sq., comp. Schmalf, *Synt.* § 128. 2, Klotz. *Devar.* Vol. II. p. 618. It must, however, be applied with caution both in the N. T. and in later Greek, owing to the gradual disuse of the opt. and the tendency of the subj. to take its place. Meyer calls attention to the omission of ἂν as evincing the idea in St. Paul's mind of all absence of obstacles; see Herm. *de Partic.* ἄν, II. 9, p. 110, Klotz, *Devar.* Vol. II. p. 568, Schmalf. *Synt.* § 121. ᾧ ἐπήγγελται] '*to whom the promise has been made*;' περὶ Χριστοῦ λέγων, Chrys.; comp. ver. 16, ἐρρέθησαν — τῷ σπέρματι. It does not seem desirable to destroy the parallelism of these two clauses by translating ἐπήγ., sc. ὁ Θεός, actively. διαταγείς] '*ordained*;' not 'promulgated,' Ust., Winer, but simply 'ordinata,' Vulg., Copt., 'disposita,' Clarom.; see Philo, *Op. Mund.* I. 1, διατεταγμένων ὑπὸ τῶν νομοθετῶν, and comp. Hesiod, *Op.* 274, νόμον διέταξε Κρονίων, where one Scholiast (Proclus) paraphrases it by the simple verb. The participial clause serves to add accessory details and distinctions to προσετ., and is not prior to, but contemporaneous with the action described by the finite verb; comp. Col. ii. 15, and see notes *in loc.* On the union of the part. with the finite verb. see the brief but pertinent remarks of Bernhardy, *Synt.* x. 9, p. 383, and the more elaborate notice of Schmalfeld, *Synt.* § 205 sq. It would certainly seem that, esp. in later Greek writers, the part. is often associated with the finite verb, where two verbs united with a copula would have seemed more natural and even more intelligible; see the exx. in Herm. *Viger*, No. 224. On the best mode of translating these sort of participles, see notes *on Phil.* ii. 30 *(Transl.)* δι' ἀγγέλων] '*through angels*,' per angelos,' Vulg., Clarom., ܒܝܕ ܡܠܐܟ̈ܐ [in manu angelorum] Syr., scil. ἀγγέλων ὑπουργούντων, Theod.: *third* characteristic of the law (see next note) serving to show the *distinction*, in point of manner and circumstance, between its enactment and the giving of the Promise: 'per angelos, in manu mediatoris, dupliciter mediate,' Beng.; comp. Baur, *Paulus*, p. 582. There is thus no reason

20 ὁ δὲ μεσίτης ἑνὸς οὐκ ἔστιν, ὁ δὲ Θεὸς εἷς ἐστίν.

whatever for modifying this meaning of διά; it points simply and plainly to the media and intervenient actors, by whose ministry the law was enacted; see Joseph. *Antiq.* xv. 5, 3, ἡμῶν τὰ κάλλιστα τῶν δογμάτων καὶ τὰ ὁσιώτατα τῶν ἐν τοῖς νόμοις δι' ἀγγέλων παρὰ τοῦ Θεοῦ μαθόντων, Deut. xxxiii. 2 (LXX), and see Winer, *Gr.* § 47. 1, p. 339, note. ἐν χειρὶ μεσίτου] '*in the hand of a mediator,*' '*in* manu mediatoris,' Syr., Vulg., Clarom., Copt., Arm.: *fourth* and most important distinction (see below) between the law and the Promise, and to which the argument of ver. 20 specially refers. The ἐν is not instrumental '*by* the hand,' Mey. (on the ground that Moses received the law from God, and gave it to the people; comp. Baur, *Apost. Paul.* p. 583), but, as the use of the singular, and the Aramaic idiom both suggest, combines with χειρὶ as = בְּיַד, scil. 'ministerio (mediatoris);' τῇ τούτου θέσει Μωυσέως διακονοῦντος, Theodoret; see 2 Chron. xxxiii. 8, Josh. xiv. 2, Wisdom xi. 1.

That *Moses* is the mediator here referred to (Deut. v. 5), seems now so generally admitted, that we may reasonably wonder how the early expositors (Basil and Theodoret are exceptions) could have so generally coincided in the perplexing view of Origen (Vol. v. p. 273, ed. Lomm.), that the μεσίτης here mentioned was Christ. Great difference of opinion, however, exists as to St. Paul's object in recounting these details. If it was to prove the *lowliness* of the law, such a recital would in several parts rather seem to convey the contrary. If it was to show the *glorious nature* (Mey.), such an object would appear seriously at variance with the context. The more natural view is, that it was to mark the fundamental *differences* between the law and the Gospel, and *thence*, as a natural result of the contrast, the transitory and provisional nature of the former. The law was an institution (1), τῶν παραβάσεων χάριν, restricted and conditioned; (2), ἄχρις οὗ κ. τ. λ., temporary and provisional; (3), διαταγεὶς δι' ἀγγέλων mediately (not immediately) given by God; (4) ἐν χειρὶ μεσ., mediately (but not immediately) received from God: see Olsh. and Windischm. *in loc.*

20. ὁ δὲ μεσίτης] '*Now every mediator,*' or, according to our English idiom, 'a mediator;' the δὲ being *transitional* (μεταβατικόν, see notes on ch. iii. 8), and the article referring, not to the mediator previously mentioned, 'this mediator' (Brown), but to the *generic* idea of a mediator; 'articulus definit indefinita, idque duobus modis, aut designando certo de multis, aut quæ multa sunt, *cunctis in unum colligendis,*' Herm. *Iph. Aul.* p. xv. (Pref.); see Winer, *Gr.* § 18. 1, p. 97. ἑνὸς οὐκ ἔστιν] '*appertains not unto one,*' 'does not belong to any *single one*, — any one who stands isolated and by himself, but implies *two* parties;' so Copt. and Arm., both of which throw that slight emphasis on the ἕνος, which the Greek seems both to require and suggest; contrast Hofmann, *Schriftb.* Vol. II. 2, p. 48, who, appy. without any just ground, asserts the contrary. This idea of *singleness* and isolation is really our only clew. With regard to this and the remaining words it is necessary to premise that all idea of the verse being a gloss (Michaelis, Lücke, *Stud. u. Krit.* for 1828, p. 83 sq.) must be summarily dismissed, as there is no variation found in the MSS. or mss., either in the words or their order. ὁ δὲ Θεὸς εἷς ἐστίν] '*but* GOD *is one;*' 'GOD (not without slight emphasis, comp. ver. 21), the direct and personal giver of the

Promise, *does* stand single and isolated, — dealt singly with Abraham (τῷ δὲ Ἀβρ. δι' ἐπαγγελίας κεχάρισται ὁ Θεός, ver. 18), — and, by consequence, is (in the promise) *mediatorless;' prop. minor* of a syllogism, of which the conclusion, being obvious, is omitted; see below. Out of the mass of interpretations of this terse sentence (said positively to exceed 400), Schleiermacher, Winer, and Meyer best deserve attention. A brief notice of these will serve to illustrate the precise nature of the difficulties. In the first part of the verse all are agreed; 'now every mediator involves the idea of more than one:' in the concluding clause they thus differ. (1) Schleiermacher, adopted by Usteri, *Lehrb.* II. 1. 2, p. 179; 'but God is one' — in reference to His promises, free, unfettered by conditions. (2) Winer; 'but God is one'— one part *only* (compare Æth.-Pol., 'unus est duorum'); 'the people of Israel must be the other part: hence they are bound to the law.' (3) Meyer; 'but God (on the contrary) is one' — and one only (ein Einziger); there is then a fundamental difference in the *number* of parties concerned in the law and the promise. Schl. and Win. thus connect ver. 20 with ver. 19 as an epexegesis; Mey. joins it with ver. 21, making it St. Paul's own statement of a difficulty that might arise in a reader's mind. Meyer's interpretation has this advantage over Schleiermacher's, that it preserves the *numerical* idea which plainly belongs to εἷς; and this over Winer's, that ὁ Θεός, which is clearly the subject, is not practically turned into the predicate. In the under stress, however, which it places on the idea of unity as opposed to that of plurality, and more esp. in the assumption that ὁ δὲ Θεὸς κ. τ. λ. is in fact a monotheistic 'locus communis' (comp. Jowett), it cannot be pronounced wholly satisfactory. Perhaps the following simple explanation is less open to objections. The context states briefly the *four* distinctive features of the law (see above) with tacit reference to the ἐπαγγελία. Three of these are passed over; the *last* as the most important, is noticed; 'the law was *with*, the promise was *without* a mediator.' Ver. 20 thus appears a syllogism of which the conclusion is omitted: '*Now a mediator does not appertain to one* (standing or acting alone); *but* (in the promise) *God is one* (does stand and act alone): THEREFORE (in the promise) A MEDIATOR DOES NOT APPERTAIN TO GOD. *Is then the law* (a dispensation which, besides other distinctions, involved a mediator) *opposed to the promises which rested* ON GOD (and involved no mediator)? *God forbid.*' According to this view the only real difficulty is narrowed to the propositio minor. *How* was God one? And the answer seems, — not because He is essentially unity (comp. De W.), nor because he is one by Himself, and Abraham is one by himself (Baur. *Paul.* p. 583), nor yet because he is both the giver, the Father, and the receiver, the Son, united (ed. 1, Windischm.; an interpr. too devoid of simplicity and too expressly theological), but, with the aspect that the last clause of ver. 18 puts on the whole reasoning, — because He dealt with Abraham singly and directly, stood alone, and used no mediator.

The almost obvious objection to this explanation is, that it implies and involves a limitation ('in the promise') in a clause which seems a mere 'locus communis:' but the answer does not seem unreasonable, that even assuming that the minor was really suggested to the Apostle, as being a general axiomatic statement, his previous declaration of God's having dealt with Abraham with no other medium than his own gracious promise (δι' ἐπαγγελίας) showed what he really regarded as the present verifi-

21 ὁ οὖν νόμος κατὰ τῶν ἐπαγγελιῶν τοῦ Θεοῦ; μὴ γένοιτο.
εἰ γὰρ ἐδόθη νόμος ὁ δυνάμενος ζωοποιῆσαι, ὄντως ἐκ νόμου ἂν ἦν

cation of it. The reader who desires to examine some of the other interpretations may consult, for the earlier, Bonitz, *Plur. de Gal.* iii. 20 *Sentent. Examinatæ*, Lips. 1800; for the later, Winer's Excursus, and Meyer *in loc.*

21. ὁ οὖν νόμος κ. τ. λ.] *'Is the law then against the promises of God;'* the οὖν with its full *collective* force (Klotz, *Devar.* Vol. II. p. 717), gathering up the previous reasoning and immediately applying its obvious though omitted result; 'does then a confessedly distinctive, ceremonial, and *mediatorial* system stand in opposition with the promises which God gave to Abraham without a mediator and without any distinctive ceremonies?' τοῦ Θεοῦ is not without emphasis: 'the promises which rest immediately on God, and were attested by no mediator.' The plural αἱ ἐπαγγελ. is used, as in ver. 16, in ref. to different repetitions of the promise, and to hint at the various ways of fulfilment which it contemplated. *Lachm.* places τοῦ Θεοῦ in brackets, in consequence of its omission in B, Clarom. Sangerm., — but on authority almost obviously insufficient. εἰ γὰρ ἐδόθη] *'For if there had been given;'* proof of the justice of the foregoing declaration μὴ γένοιτο; πρῶτον μὲν ἀπαγορεύει εἰπών, μὴ γένοιτο· ἔπειτα καὶ κατασκευάζει, Chrys. On the use of μὴ γένοιτο see notes on ch. ii. 17. νόμος ὁ δυνάμενος] *'a law (as the principle) which could have,'* etc. This is one out of many instances, both in the N. T. and elsewhere, in which, to give prominence to the defining clause, the anarthrous noun is followed and defined by the article attached to a participle, *e. g.* Rom. ii. 14, ἔθνη τὰ μὴ νόμον ἔχοντα: see further exx. in Winer, *Gr.* § 20, 4, p. 126, Ellendt, *Lex. Soph.* s. v. ὁ, Vol. II. p. 241. ζωοποιῆσαι] *'to give life (and blessedness);'* '*vivificare*, sive vitam dare, idem est quod dare κληρονομίαν, hæreditatem vitæ cælestis atque æternæ,' Bull, *Exam. Cens.* XIX. 6; see 2 Cor. iii. 6, and comp. Ust. *Lehrb.* I. 4. § B, p. 61. So also in ver. 12, ζήσεται (= ζωὴν αἰώνιον ἕξει, Olsh. *on Rom.* i. 17) similarly involves the ideas of life and blessedness. ὄντως κ. τ. λ.] *'verily,'* etc.; 'apprime notanda est emphasis egregia in adverbio ὄντως, *vere*,' Bull, *Exam. Cens.* XIX. 6. It has been asked whether St. Paul is here reasoning (*a*) from the *effect* (ζωοπ.) to the *cause* (δικαιοσ.); or, conversely (*b*), from the *cause* (ζωοπ., assumed to mean a new moral life) to the *effect* (δικαιοσ.); compare Neander, *Plant.* Vol. I. p. 418 (Bohn). Certainly the former; δικαιοσ. is really, as Ust. properly observes, the middle member of between νόμος and ζωή, without which the law could not have given life. St. Paul, however, thus states his argument: 'lex vitam dare non potest, proinde neque veram justificationem,' Bull, *Ex. Cens. l. c.* The order adopted in *Rec.* ὄντως ἂν ἐκ νόμου ἦν, has only the support of D[3]EJK; mss.; Chrys., Theod., al., and is rejected by most critical editors. ἐκ νόμου] *'would have resulted from the law,'* 'would have come from the law as its origin,' not 'would have been suspended on law' (Peile), — a meaning which usually arises from the associated verb, δεῖν, ἀρτᾶσθαι, etc., and does not appear to be very common out of Herodot.; comp. Bernhardy, *Synt.* v. 13, p. 227. The order *in Rec.*, ἂν ἐκ νόμου ἦν, with D[3]EJK; mss.; Chrys., Theod., al.], has not sufficient authority, though,

ἡ δικαιοσύνη· 22 ἀλλὰ συνέκλεισεν ἡ γραφὴ τὰ πάντα ὑπὸ ἁμαρτίαν, ἵνα ἡ ἐπαγγελία ἐκ πίστεως Ἰησοῦ Χριστοῦ δοθῇ τοῖς

it must be admitted that, owing to the variations in the leading MSS. (B ἐν νόμῳ, D om. ἄν, FG om. ἂν ἦν), the text is not wholly free from suspicion.

22. ἀλλά] *'But on the contrary;'* not δέ, as there is a marked adversative relation between the clauses, and as a statement in ref. to the law is about to be made exactly contrary to the result of the foregoing assumption; see Klotz, *Devar.* Vol. II. p. 2, 3. In Latin, this distinction can usually be maintained by the more distinctly adversative *sed* (Vulg., Clarom.), not the more simply oppositive *autem*, in which the latter particle, 'discrimen proprie indicatur, non diversitas,' Hand, *Tursell.* Vol. I. p. 555, comp. Klotz, Vol. I. p. 361. συνέκλεισεν ἡ γραφή] *'the Scripture shut up;'* not equivalent to ὁ νόμος (Jowett, al.), but with a kind of personification, ἡ θεία γραφή (Theod.), the Scripture of the Old Test. as the representative of Him by whom it was inspired; comp. ver. 8. With regard to the meaning of συγκλείειν ('concludi sub peccato is dicitur, qui peccati reatu adhuc obstrictus tenetur,' Bull, *Ex. Cens.* XIX. 6), it may be observed (1) that the declaratory sense ('conclusos declaravit,' Bull, comp. Baur, *Paulus*, p. 581), does not lie in the verb (see Rom. xi. 32, where the act is ascribed to God), but in the *context;* and (2) that the prep. συν does not imply the similarity of situation of all (Beng.), but simply the idea of *contraction* (Mey.), 'ab omni parte clausit,' Schott 2; comp. συμπιέζειν, συμπνίγειν: see Fritz, *Rom.* xi. 32, Vol. II. p. 545, and exx. in Rost u. Palm, *Lex.* s. v. Vol. II. p. 1395, where instances are cited of συγκλ. being used in reference to a *single* person. On this text and on the general relation of the law to sin, see the weighty sermon of Usher, *Serm.* v. Vol. XIII. p. 60 sq. (ed. Elringt.). τὰ πάντα] *'all.'* The neuter cannot safely be pressed (non modo *onmes* sed *omnia* Beng.), as if it were specially chosen to include not only men, but all their actions, etc., 'humana omnia,' Jowett (comp. Alf., Windisc.); this being neither required by the context (comp. ver. 23), nor justified by St. Paul's usus loquendi: see Rom. xi. 32, where, in a passage exactly similar, the masc. is used, and comp. Theodoret *in loc.*, who divides the τὰ πάντα into τοὺς πρὸ νόμου, and τοὺς ἐν νόμῳ. The exact difference between τοὺς πάντας and τὰ πάντα is, perhaps, here no greater than between 'all men' and 'all mankind' (see Ust.): the neuter is idiomatically and instinctively chosen, as best suiting the generality of the declaration; compare Winer, *Gr.* § 27. 5, p. 160, Seidler on Eur. *Troad.* 426. ἵνα ἡ ἐπαγγ.] *'in order that the promise;'* object and *intent,* — not the mere recognized *consequence* ('quo appareat dari,' Winer) of the σύγκλεισις, on the part of ἡ γραφή and God its author. The abstract ἐπαγγελία is here, as the context suggests, practically equivalent to the concrete 'res promissa' (Schott), scil. κληρονομία; see ver. 18, Heb. x. 36, xi. 39, and comp. *Test.* XII. *Patr.* p. 725, ὁ Θεὸς εἰσάξει ὑμᾶς εἰς τὴν ἐπαγγελίαν (cited by Bretsch. *Lex.* s. v.), where this concrete notion is taken in its widest extent as = ἡ γῆ τῆς ἐπαγγελίας; so κληρονομία, 2 Macc. ii. 4. ἐκ πίστεως Ἰ. Χ.] *'by faith in Jesus Christ,'* 'resulting from faith as its *source* and *origin* (notes, ch. ii. 16); ἐκ πίστ. being in close union, — not with δοθῇ (Rück., Conyb.), but with ἐπαγγελία (compare Winer, *Gr.* § 20. 2,

πιστεύουσιν. 23 πρὸ τοῦ δὲ ἐλθεῖν τὴν πίστιν, ὑπὸ νόμον ἐφρουρούμεθα συγκεκλεισμένοι εἰς τὴν μέλλουσαν πίστιν ἀποκαλυφθῆ-

p. 123, notes *on Eph.* i. 15), and forming a retrospective antithesis to ἐκ νόμου, ver. 21. The genitive Ἰησ. Χρ. is *perhaps* here to be taken in its most comprehensive sense; not only 'faith on Christ' (gen. *objecti*), but 'faith as given by Him' (gen. *subjecti*); comp. notes on ch. ii. 16. In the N. T. especially, the connection of the nom. and gen. must often be explained solely from exegetical considerations; see Winer, *Gr.* § 30, 1, p. 168 τοῖς πιστεύουσιν] '*to them that believe;*' not 'qui erant credituri' (Grot. Peile), but 'eis qui credunt,' Clarom., al., 'credentibus,' Vulg., the apparent tautology not being intended merely as emphatic (Winer), but as suitably echoing the ἐκ πίστεως above. The Galatians were ready to admit that those who believed would be saved, but they doubted whether faith *alone* was sufficient; hence the apostle interposes the limitation in ref. to the thing promised (ἡ ἐπαγγ. ἐκ πίστ.), and virtually repeats it in ref. to the recipients. The promise was of faith not of the law; the receivers were not doers of the law, but believers; comp. Meyer *in loc.*

23. πρὸ τοῦ δὲ κ. τ. λ.] '*But before Faith (above mentioned) came;*' further account of the relation in which the law stood to faith, δὲ not being here distinctly oppositive, but with some tinge of its primary enumerative force (see Donalds. *Crat.* § 155), adding a further explanation, though in that explanation serving to introduce a contrast; see Klotz, *Devar.* Vol. II. p. 362. With regard to the position of the particle, it may be remarked that there is nothing unusual (opp. to Rück.), in δὲ thus occupying the *third* place after a prep. and its case; see exx. in Hartung, *Partik.* δέ, 1. 6, Vol. I. p. 190. The common-sense principle is, that δὲ does not necessarily occupy the *second* place, but the *first possible* place which the internal connection of the sentence will admit of; see Klotz, *Devar.* Vol. II. p. 378. ὑπὸ νόμον ἐφρουρούμεθα κ. τ. λ.] '*we were kept in ward shut up under the law;*' συγκεκλ. being joined, not with εἰς πίστιν (see following note), but, in a construction similar to that of the preceding verse, with ὑπὸ νόμον (Arm., al.); the law, in fact, is here (as ἁμαρτία in ver. 22) represented as a kind of gaoler into whose custody we were delivered; see Köster, *Stud.* u. *Krit.* 1854, p. 316. The meaning of φρουρεῖσθαι is thus not merely 'asservari' (Winer, Schott), much less 'obstringi ad obedientiam' (Bretsch.), but, as the definite expression συγκεκλ. distinctly requires, '*custodiri,*' Vulg., Clarom., Copt., Æth.), ὥσπερ ἐν τειχίῳ τινὶ κατέχεσθαι, Chrys.; compare Wisdom xvii. 15, ἐφρουρεῖτο εἰς τὴν ἀσίδηρον εἱρκτὴν κατακλεισθείς. The perf. part., it may be observed, correctly expresses the *permanent*, completed state of the captivity, and is thus not only on critical but exegetical grounds to be preferred to the pres. συγκλειόμενοι [*Lachm.* with B(Mai)D1FG; 2 mss.; Clem. (1), Cyr. (3), Dam.], which was not improbably a conformation to the imperf. ἐφρουρ.: so rightly De W., Mey., and the majority of recent critics.
εἰς τὴν μέλλουσαν κ. τ. λ.] '*for the faith about to be revealed;*' object contemplated in the action of φρούρησις, εἰς not being *temporal*, 'usque ad' (Rück., Ust., comp. Copt., Æth.), — a meaning comparatively rare in the New Test. (compare John xiii. 1), and here certainly superfluous after the predica-

ναι. [24] ὥστε ὁ νόμος παιδαγωγὸς ἡμῶν γέγονεν εἰς Χριστόν, ἵνα ἐκ πίστεως δικαιωθῶμεν·

By faith in Christ we have become freed from the pedagogy of the law, and are thus all children of God, Abraham's seed, and heirs of the promise.

[25] Ἐλθούσης δὲ τῆς πίστεως οὐκέτι ὑπὸ

tion of time in πρὸ τοῦ ἐλθεῖν, — but in its usual *ethical* meaning of 'destination for' ('in fidem,' Vulg., Clarom.); compare Winer, *Gr.* § 49. a, p. 353. The clause is thus naturally connected with the finite verb, not with συγκλ. ('conclusi, adeoque adacti ad,' Beng.), — a construction certainly *admissible* (see exx. in Schweigh. *Lex. Polyb.* s. v. συγκλ., or Raphel, *Annot.* Vol. II. p. 440 sq.), but open to this serious exegetical objection, that faith is not yet represented as existing; see Meyer *in loc.* μέλλουσαν πίστ. ἀποκ.] The unusual order seems intended to give prominence to μέλλουσαν, and to present more forcibly the contrast between former captivity and subsequent freedom; comp. Rom. viii. 18, πρὸς τὴν μέλλουσαν δόξαν ἀποκαλυφθῆναι, where the future glories are set in strong contrast to present calamities; see Fritz. *in loc.*, Vol. II. p. 148.

24. ὥστε] '*So then,*' 'itaque,' Vulg., Clarom.; consequence from the preceding statement; see notes, ch. ii. 13. παιδαγωγός] '*pedagogue;*' 'pædagogus proprie notat eum qui puerum manu prehensum ad magistrum ducit,' Schoett. (*Hor.* Vol. I. p. 741), who remarks, however, that the word was adopted by Rabbinical writers, but with some additional notions of care and *guardianship:* even among the Greek and Latin writers the idea of guardianship and also of *strictness* and *severity* is distinctly prominent; see esp. the exx. in Elsner, *Obs.* Vol. II. p. 186. The mere idea of leading to Christ ('viæ dux' [*shau-mōit*], Copt., 'ductor,' Æth.) must not, then, be retained to the exclusion of those of actual teaching (Arm., Auth.), tutelage, and disciplinary restraint. This pedagogic function of the law was displayed *positively*, in warnings and threatenings; *negatively* (the prevailing idea in this place), in awakening the conscience, and bringing a conviction of sin; compare Usteri, *Lehrb.* I. 5, p. 66. The patristic comments will be found in Suicer, *Thesaur.* s. v. νόμος, Vol. II. p. 921; see also Petav. *de Prædest.* x. 26. 1 sq. Vol. I. p. 464. εἰς Χριστόν] '*for Christ;*' not *temporal* (ἄχρις οὗ ἔλθῃ Χρ. see ver. 23), still less *local*, 'to Christ' as a διδάσκαλος (πρὸς τὸν Χρ. ἀπῆγε, Theoph., comp. Chrys.), as Christ would thus be represented under *two* offices, Teacher and (ἵνα ἐκ πίστ. δικ.) Atoner, in the same verse. If any trace of a local meaning be retained in translation, *e. g.* 'unto,' Auth. Ver., it must be understood of an *ethical* arrival (compare 2 Cor. x. 14), as εἰς with persons is not simply equivalent to πρός, but involves the idea of mingling with and association; comp. Rom. v. 12, and see Winer, *Gr.* § 49. a, p. 353. ἵνα ἐκ πίστ. δικαιωθ.] '*to the intent that we might be justified by faith;*' more distinct and specific explanation of the preceding εἰς Χριστόν, the emphatic ἐκ πίστεως serving to suggest and enhance the contrast with the non-justifying and merely pedagogic νόμος. On the proper force of the δικαιοῦν ἐκ, see notes on ch. ii. 16.

25. ἐλθούσης δέ] '*but now that (this) faith is come:*' contrast between the present freedom and the past pedagogy; ἐλθούσης, φησί, τῆς πίστεως, τῆς τέλειον ἄνδρα ποιούσης, οὐκ ἄν ἔτι εἴημεν ὑπὸ παιδαγωγόν, Theoph. The connection is so close throughout this latter

παιδαγωγόν ἐσμεν. [26] πάντες γὰρ υἱοὶ Θεοῦ ἐστὲ διὰ τῆς πίστεως ἐν Χριστῷ Ἰησοῦ· [27] ὅσοι γὰρ εἰς Χριστὸν ἐβαπτίσθητε,

portion of the chapter, that it is difficult to subdivide it into paragraphs. Meyer, Conyb., al. place a paragraph after ver. 22: it seems, however, more natural here, as ver. 23, 24, carry out the idea expressed in συνέκλεισεν, ver. 22.

ὑπὸ παιδαγωγόν] '*under a pedagogue.*' The article is not here latent after the prep. (comp. Winer, *Gr.* § 19. 2 b, p. 114), but appears studiously omitted (so rightly Copt.), the words being in fact equivalent to 'under tutelage, 'unter Pädagogengewalt,' Meyer.

26. πάντες γάρ] '*For ye all;*' confirmation, *e contrario*, of the truth of the foregoing words; they were now not παῖδες, but υἱοί ('*filii* emancipati, remoto custode,' Beng.), and that too not sons of Abraham merely (comp. ver. 7), but sons of God; πρότερον ἔδειξεν ὅτι υἱοὺς ἐποίει [ἡ πίστις τοῦ] Ἀβρ. . . . νῦν δὲ ἀποφαίνει ὅτι καὶ τοῦ Θεοῦ, Chrys. The υἱοὶ Θεοῦ, as Theod. Mops. well observes, includes the idea of τελειότης, which the preceding metaphor might serve to suggest. The reading ἅπαντες adopted by *Lachm.* is not improbable, but not supported by AB.

τῆς πίστ. ἐν Χρ. Ἰησ.] '*through the faith in Jesus Christ;*' so rightly Syr., Arm. (ed. Zohr.), Syr.-Philox., and Chrys. (ed. Field). Several commentators (Ust., al.: see Hofm. *Schriftb.* Vol. II. 2, p. 152) join ἐν Χρ. Ἰησ. with υἱοὶ Θ. ἐστέ, on the ground that the words would be a superfluous addition to πίστις, and that ver. 27 contains the amplification of the expression. But, independently of the awkwardness of adding a second modal clause to υἱοί ἐστε, the recurrence of the formula πίστις ἐν Χρ. Ἰησ. (Eph. i. 15, Col. i. 4) its grammatical accuracy (Winer, *Gr.* § 20. 2, p. 123, notes *on Eph.* i. 15), and the natural coherence of the words. all seem distinctly to suggest the simpler and less dislocated construction. If the article had been inserted, we should then have *two* ideas conveyed, the latter of which would be explanatory of the former; 'per fidem, *eamque* in Chr. Jes. collocatam,' see Fritz. *Rom.* iii. 25, Vol. I. p. 195.

27. ὅσοι γάρ] '*for as many as;*' proof and confirmatory explanation of the preceding assertion. The force of the particle is best explained by the Greek commentators, who refer it to υἱοί Θεοῦ, and base the argument on the fact that Christ was the Son of God: ἐνεδύσασθε τὸν Χρ. τὸν ἀληθῶς υἱὸν τοῦ Θεοῦ, ἐκεῖνον δὲ ἐνδεδυμένοι εἰκότως υἱοὶ Θεοῦ χρηματίζετε, Theodoret; see also Chrys. *in loc.*

εἰς Χριστόν] '*into Christ;*' not 'in Christo,' Vulg., Clarom., but 'in Christum,' Beza (compare Copt. *pichr*); scil. 'ut Christo addicti essetis,' Schott, or more strictly, into communion with Him, and incorporation in His mystical body. The meaning of εἰς with βαπτίζω appears twofold; (α) '*unto*,' object, purpose: Matth. iii. 11, Acts ii. 38, see Winer, *Gr.* § 49. a, p. 354, Bernhardy, *Synt.* v. 11. b. 3, p. 220; (β) '*into*,' union and communion with: the context always showing whether it be of the most complete and most mystical nature, as here and Rom. vi. 3 (comp. 1 Cor. xii. 13), or, as in 1 Cor. x. 2, necessarily less comprehensive and significant. We may, in conclusion, observe that the expression βαπτ. εἰς τὸ ὄνομα (Matth. xxviii. 19, Acts viii. 16, xix. 5, al.) is not identical in meaning with βαπτ. ἐν τῷ ὀνόμ. (Tholuck, *Beiträge*, No. 8, p. 49 sq.), but ever implies a spiritual and mystical union with Him in whose name the

Χριστὸν ἐνεδύσασθε. [28] οὐκ ἔνι Ἰουδαῖος οὐδὲ Ἕλλην, οὐκ ἔνι δοῦλος οὐδὲ ἐλεύθερος, οὐκ ἔνι ἄρσεν καὶ θῆλυ· πάντες γὰρ ὑμεῖς

sacrament was administered; see esp. Stier, *Reden Jesu*, Vol. VI. p. 899. The meaning of βαπτίζειν τινὰ εἴς τινα (εἴς τι) and βαπτ. εἰς τὸ ὄνομά τινος is discussed at length by Fritz. (*Rom.* vi. 3, Vol. I. p. 359 sq.), in opp. to Bindseil, *Stud. u. Krit.* 1832, p. 410 sq., — but by no means satisfactorily, as he regards εἰς as only implying ethical direction ('aliquem aquæ ita immergere ut ejus cogitationes in aliquem dirigas'), instead of that mystical incorporation which the passage seems certainly to convey. The patristic comments on this expression will be found in Suicer, *Thes.* Vol. I. p. 624 sq., but are not sufficiently exact. Χριστὸν ἐνεδύσασθε] '*ye put on Christ*,' scil. at your baptism; ὅσοι γὰρ εἰς Χριστὸν ἐβαπτίσθητε ἐκ τοῦ Θεοῦ ἐγεννήθητε, Chrys. There appears here no allusion to *Heathen* (toga virilis), *Jewish* (whether at the High Priest's inauguration, Deyling, *Obs.*, Vol. III. p. 406 sq., No. 42, or in a cabalistic sense, comp. Schoettg. *on Rom.* xiii. 14, Vol. I. p. 571), or, even, though very plausible, *Christian* customs (at baptism, Bingham, *Antiq.* Book XII. 4. 1 sq.). From the instances Wetst. has collected *on Rom.* xiii. 14, it would appear that ἐνδύεσθαί τινα is a strong expression, denoting the complete assumption of the nature, etc., of another; *e. g.* Dion. Halicar. *A. R.* XI. 15. 5 (τὸν Ταρκύνιον ἐκεῖνον ἐνδυόμ.), Tac. *Ann.* XVI. 28. Thus ἐνδ. Χριστόν implies a union with Christ of so true and so complete a nature, that we are brought εἰς μίαν συγγένειαν καὶ μίαν ἰδέαν (Chrys.) with Him, and, as it is beautifully paraphrased by Calv., 'coram Deo nomen ac personam Christi geramus, atque in Ipso magis quam nobismet Ipsis censeamur:' comp. Bp. Barlow, cited by Waterl. *Works*, Vol. IV. p. 604, and see Suicer, *Thesaur.* s. v. ἐνδ., Vol. I. p. 1112. For a good sermon on this text, see Donne, *Serm.* LXXXVII. Vol. IV. p. 102 (ed. Alf.), and for a notice of the perversion of this text by heretics, Forbes, *Instruct.* x. 111. 32 sq., p. 448.

28. οὐκ ἔνι κ.τ.λ] '*There is among (such) neither Jew nor Greek;*' digressive statement of the practical result of the Χρ. ἐνεδ.: the new and holy 'habitus' causes all other distinctions, whether of nation (compare Rom. x. 12), condition, or even sex, to be wholly lost sight of and forgotten. The form ἔνι is not *for* ἔνεστι, but according to Buttm. (see Winer, *Gr.* § 14. 2, p. 74), is the lengthened form of the adverbialized prep., to which the requisite person of the auxiliary verb must be supplied. This explanation has in its favor the similar use of πάρα, which can scarcely be called a contraction for πάρεστι; but against it those exx. where ἐν and ἔνι are used in the same sentence, *e. g.* Plat *Phæd.* 77 E, ἴσως ἔνι καὶ ἐν ὑμῖν *Theæt.* 186 D, and, according to best reading, 1 Cor. vi. 5. In such cases, however, ἔνι would seem to mean little more than ἐστί (ἔνι· ἐστίν, ὑπάρχει, Zonar. *Lex.* Vol. I. p. 748), the prepositional force being wholly lost; comp. Col. iii. 11. In either case the explanation of the present passage remains the same; ἐπὶ πλεῖον διηγεῖται τὴν ἀγαθότητα τοῦ Θεοῦ ὅπου γε πᾶσι τὴν ἴσην δέδωκε δωρεάν, Damasc. Deyling illustrates this by reference to the various personal, etc., distinctions among the Jews; *Obs. Sacr.* Vol. I p. 312 sq., No. 64; Elsner (*in loc.*) notices also the customary exclusion of slaves from certain Heathen rites and temples, *Obs.* Vol. II. p. 187. ἄρσεν καὶ θῆλυ] '*male and female;*' 'masculus et femina,' Clarom., but not

εἷς ἐστὲ ἐν Χριστῷ Ἰησοῦ. 29 εἰ δὲ ὑμεῖς Χριστοῦ, ἄρα τοῦ
Ἀβραὰμ σπέρμα ἐστέ, κατ' ἐπαγγελίαν κληρονόμοι.
IV. Λέγω δέ, ἐφ' ὅσον χρόνον ὁ κληρονό-

As every heir is under tutelage, so before Christ came we all were under bondage, but now have become free sons and inheritors.

Vulg., Goth., Copt., al., which do not preserve the slight change of particle. While the alterable political and sociable distinctions are contrasted by οὐδέ, the unalterable human one of sex is expressed by καί; Mark x. 6, ἀπὸ δὲ ἀρχῆς κτίσεως ἄρσεν καὶ θῆλυ ἐποίησεν αὐτούς, compare 1 Tim. ii. 13. This latter distinction is of course noticed not in its mere physical, but its *ethical* aspect,—the subordination of the wife to the husband (Olsh.). This, though an unchangeable law of our species when considered κατὰ σάρκα, Eph. v. 22, al., is lost sight of in this ἐγγυτέρα πρὸς τὸν Χριστὸν ἕνωσις, Chrys. πάντες γάρ] '*for ye all;*' proof of the preceding statement; τῷ ἕνα τύπον καὶ μίαν μορφὴν ἐνδεδύσθαι, τὴν τοῦ Χρ., Œcum. The reading ἅπαντ. (*Lachm.*) seems an early gloss. εἷς] '*one*;' *i. e.* one person; τὸ εἷς ἀντὶ τοῦ ἓν σῶμα, Theodoret: compare Lucian, *Toxar.* 46 (cited by Wetst.), εἷς ἄνθρωπος ὄντες οὕτω βιοῦμεν. The concluding words ἐν Χριστῷ Ἰησοῦ obviate all mistakes by defining in whom, and in whom alone, this union was fully realized.

29. εἰ δὲ ὑμεῖς] '*But if ye;*' resumption of the argument after the short digression of ver. 28, the emphasis resting slightly on ὑμεῖς: 'as ye, to whom I am speaking, and who have felt such doubts on the subject, have put on Christ, ye must be what He is (ver. 16), the seed of Abraham.'

The reading εἷς ἐστε ἐν Χ. Ἰησ. instead of Χριστοῦ, though found in D[1]EFG; Clarom. . . . . Ambrst. is clearly an exegetical gloss. τοῦ Ἀβραὰμ σπέρμα] '*Abraham's seed;*' τοῦ Ἀβρ. being put forward with a slight emphasis, and standing in correlation to Χριστοῦ to give force and perspicuity to the conclusion; εἰ δὲ ὑμεῖς ἐστὲ Χριστοῦ μορφὴ καὶ σῶμα, εἰκότως τοῦ Ἀβρ. ἐστὲ σπέρμα, Œcum.; comp. Theod. *in loc.*, and esp. Theod. Mops. (p. 126, ed. Fritz.) who has well elucidated the argument. κατ' ἐπαγγ. κληρονόμοι] '*heirs according to,* or *by way of promise;*' not by any legal observances. The κληρονομία is now stated absolutely; they were κληρονόμοι, not merely of Abraham, nor even τῆς ἐπαγγελίας (Theod. Mops.), but simply of all that which was involved in it, salvation and the kingdom of Christ; comp. Meyer *in loc.* The declaration of ver. 7 is now at length substantiated and expanded by 22 verses of the deepest, most varied, and most comprehensive reasoning that exists in the whole compass of the great Apostle's writings.

The καὶ before κατ. ἐπαγγ., adopted by *Rec.* with FGJK; mss.; Syr. (both), Goth., Æth.; Chrys., Theod., is now rightly omitted by most critical editors.

CHAPTER IV. 1. λέγω δέ] '*Now I say;*' further and more explanatory proof of the assertion that we are heirs, suggested by the term κληρονόμοι (ch. iii.29), and the comparisons it involves; comp. ch. v. 16, Rom. xv. 8, where the use of λέγω δὲ in introducing a *continued* explanatory argument rather than merely elucidating a statement or expression that had preceded (comp. ch. iii. 17, τοῦτο δὲ λέγω, 1 Cor. i. 12, λέγω δὲ τοῦτο, 1 Cor. vii. 29, τοῦτο δέ φημι), seems analogous to the present. ὁ κληρονόμος] '*the heir,*' *i. e.* '*every heir;*' compare ὁ μεσίτης, ch. iii. 20,

μος νήπιός ἐστιν, οὐδὲν διαφέρει δούλου, κύριος πάντων ὤν,
2 *ἀλλὰ ὑπὸ ἐπιτρόπους ἐστὶν καὶ οἰκονόμους ἄχρι τῆς προθεσ-*

Winer, *Gr.* § 18. 1, p. 97. There are some exegetical difficulties in this and the following verse, arising from the fact, that, while the nature of the comparison (see Brown), as well as the words ἄχρι τῆς προθεσμίας τοῦ πάτρος, would seem to imply that the father was *alive*, the expression κύριος πάντων ὤν, and the term ἐπίτροπους (but see below) might be thought to imply that he was *dead*. The latter view is taken by Theodoret and the majority of ancient (silet Chrys.), with several modern commentators; the former is ably advocated by Neubour, *Bibl. Brem. Class.* Vol. v. p. 40 (cited by Wolf), and also many recent expositors. Grotius endeavors to escape the difficulty by representing the father *absent* on travel; comp. Ælian, *Var. Hist.* III. 26, cited below in note ver. 2. The question, however, is really of little moment: St. Paul is engaged so entirely in the simple comparison of the circumstances of the nonage of the earthly κληρονόμος, with those of the nonage of believers who lived under the law (ver. 3), that the subordinate question of the life, death, or absence of the father of the κληρονόμος passes wholly out of sight; comp. Alf. *in loc.*

νήπιος] '*an infant, a minor;*' ἄνηβος, as opposed to ἔφηβος, the technical term for one who had attained his majority; see Smith, *Dict. Antiq.* s. v. ἔφηβ., and Reff. in Rost. u. Palm, *Lex.* Vol. I. p. 1282. There does not seem any sufficient reason for departing from this usual view of νήπιος (opp. to Bagge *in loc.*), or with Chrys., al., for introducing any reference to the ethical meaning of weakness of understanding.

οὐδὲν διαφέρει δούλου] '*differs in nothing from a bond-servant;*' 'imo servo [παιδαγωγῷ] subjectus est,' Erasm. The very apposite quotation from Dio Chrys., XV. p. 240, adduced by Wetst. *in loc.*, is too long for citation, but is worth referring to. κύριος πάντων ὤν] '*though he be lord of all;*' concessive use of the participle; comp. Donalds. *Gr* § 621, Krüger, *Sprachl.* § 56. 13. 1 sq. It does not seem necessary for the sake of preserving the image of a *living* father to understand these words as *prospective;* the heir was the κύριος (Grot. compares the use of 'herus minor' in Lat. comedy), in right of birth and condition.

2. ἐπιτρόπους) '*overlookers, guardians.*' The latter is the usual meaning of the word in relation to children) (comp. Isæus, *Hær. Cleonym.* § 10, p. 4 (ed. Schöm.), τὸν ἔχθιστον τῶν οἰκείων ἐπίτροπον καταλιπεῖν; ib. *Hær. Dicæ.* § 10; Plut. *Lycurg.* § 3, τοὺς τῶν ὀρφανῶν βασιλέων ἐπιτρόπους), and that in which it appears to have been adopted by Hebrew writers; compare Schoettg. *Hor. Hebr. in loc.*, Selden, *de Success.* ch. 9, Vol. II. p. 25. It seems here, however, better to adopt the more general meaning '*overlooker, one entrusted with the charge of anything*' (comp. Aristoph. *Eccl.* 212, ἐπιτρόποις καὶ ταμίαισι, Xen. *Œcon.* XII. 2, ὁ ἐν τοῖς ἀγροῖς ἐπίτροπος), and not to embarrass the passage with terms which might bring in irrelevant considerations (the father's being alive or dead) into the present simple comparison. We may, however, not unsuitably comp. Ælian, *Var. Hist.* III. 16, ἐπίτρ. καὶ τοῦ παιδός, καὶ τῶν χρημάτων, where the context distinctly shows that the father was *alive*, though absent.

οἰκονόμους] '*stewards,*' ܕܡܪ̈ܝ ܒܝܬܐ [dominos domus] Syr., 'acto-

μίας τοῦ πατρός. [3] οὕτως καὶ ἡμεῖς, ὅτε ἦμεν νήπιοι, ὑπὸ τὰ

res,' Vulg., Clarom. [compare Plin. *Ep.* III. 19], less accurately, Goth. *fauragaggam* [Vorsteher]; managers of the property of the κληρονόμος, and standing in the same relation to his *estate* as the ἐπίτροποι did to his *education* and general bringing up; comp. Plutarch, *Educ.* § 7, δούλων . . . τοὺς δὲ οἰκονόμους, τοὺς δὲ δανειστάς. Most commentators not inaptly cite the case of Eliezer, Gen. xv. 2, comp. xxiv. 2; illustrations from Roman law (Bagge, al.) do not seem here in point, as the comparison is simple and general. τῆς προθεσμίας] '*the time appointed (beforehand),*' 'præfinitum tempus,' Vulg. The term προθεσμία, scil. ὥρα or ἡμέρα (for the distinction between these, see Bagge *in loc.*), is properly the term limited for bringing actions or prosecutions, the time fixed by the statute of limitations, 'Tag der Verjährung:' see Smith, *Dict. of Antiq.* s. v., and exx. in Rost. u. Palm, *Lex.* s. v.; — thence, any *pre-appointed time* or *day;* see the numerous exx. in Wetst. *in loc.*, Kypke, *Obs.* Vol. II. p. 279, Krebs. *Obs.* p. 322. In eccles. writers, προθεσμ. is sometimes used for the time assigned for repentance before excommunication; see Bingham, *Antiq.* XVI. 2. 7. It may be observed that as the termination of nonage was *fixed* in Hebrew (13 years and a day for males; 12 years and a day for females, Selden, *de Success.* ch. 9, Vol. II. p. 25), as well as Greek and Roman law, the dependence of the ἡ προθεσμία *on the father,* must be explained, — either (*a*) by the very reasonable assumption that St. Paul is here speaking theologically rather than juridically, — or (*b*) less probably, by the supposition that he was here referring, with technical exactness, to an extended parental authority which the Galatians appear to have possessed; see Göttl. *Gesch. d. Rom. Staatsverf.* p. 109, 517 (cited by B. Crus.), and comp. Cæsar, *Bell. Gall.* VI. 19.

3. οὕτως καὶ ἡμεῖς] '*So we also;*' application of the preceding statements; καί, as usual in comparative sentences, bringing into prominence and throwing a slight emphasis on the contrasted member of the comparison; see notes *on Eph.* v. 23. It has been doubted whether the ἡμεῖς are Jews (Chrys., Theod.), Gentiles (Aug.), or both equally (Win., Mey.). The most natural reference seems to be (*a*) to Jews, primarily and principally, as the nature of the *preceding* argument seems distinctly to require; but also (*b*) secondarily, Gentiles, in accordance with the nature of the *succeeding* argument. τὰ στοιχεῖα τοῦ κόσμου] '*the rudiments of the world.*' It is very difficult to decide on the exact meaning of these words. Taken separately, στοιχεῖον is used in the N. T., both in a physical (2 Pet. iii. 10, 12) and an ethical sense (Heb. v. 12). Κόσμος, again, has, practically at least, three meanings; *physical* (Matth. xxv. 34), *collective* (mankind, Joh. iii. 16), and *ethical* (1 Cor. ii. 12). From the combination of both words, a great variety of interpretations have arisen, all, however, separable into two general classes, (1) Physical; *elementa mundi,* either, (*a*) festivals of Judaism, Chrysost.; (*b*) Zabianism, August.; or (*c*) abstractedly, religion in sensible forms, Neand. *Planting,* Vol. I. p. 465, Bohn. (2) Ethical; *rudimenta mundi,* first, but not necessarily erroneous (comp. Æth.), principles of religious knowledge among men, whether (*a*) Jews (De W.); or (*b*) Jews and heathens (Meyer). Grammatical considerations seem in favor of (1); for στοικεῖα, in a sense *rudimenta,* would

στοιχεῖα τοῦ κόσμου ἤμεν δεδουλωμένοι· 4 ὅτε δὲ ἦλθεν τὸ πλήρωμα τοῦ χρόνου, ἐξαπέστειλεν ὁ Θεὸς τὸν υἱὸν αὐτοῦ, γενόμενον

appear to require, as in Heb. v. 12, a *gen. objecti*, and not as here a *gen. subjecti* (see Neander *l. c.*); still κόσμου need not be considered a pure *gen. subj.*, the connection between the nom. and gen. being often somewhat lax; see Winer, *Gr.* § 30. 2, p. 214 sq. Exegetical considerations must be also extended to ver. 9, and to Col. ii. 8, 20, where the same words occur. These we can only briefly notice. In Col. ii. 8, the parallelism with παράδοσις τῶν ἀνθρώπων, seems so distinct, and so palpably in favor of (2), as to outweigh the argument drawn by Schneckenb. from the supposed physical use of κόσμος in ver. 20. The use of the term φιλοσοφία seems also there to point slightly more to *heathen* rudiments (see notes *in loc.*), while on the contrary in Col. ii. 20, and below, ver. 9, the reference seems mainly to *Jewish* rudiments. All these conflicting views being considered, we seem here justified in deciding in favor of (2) *generally;* assigning, however, to the words (as both ἡμεῖς and the nature of the argument require) a primary, but by no means exclusive reference to the Jews. For further notices of this doubtful expression, see Baur, *Paulus*, p. 594 sq., and for a defence of the physical meaning, Schneckenburg. in *Theol. Jahrb.* 1848, p. 444 sq., and Hilgenf. *Galat.* p. 68 sq. The application to the ceremonial law will be found, Petav. *de Prædest.* x. 23. 12, Vol. I. p. 456. δεδουλωμένοι] *'in a state of slavery;'* the perf. pass. part. marking the permanent nature and continuance of the δουλεία; comp. Winer, *Gr.* § 45. 1, p. 305. The verb ἦμεν may be regarded either as in union with δεδουλ. and as forming a compound tense, or as in more immediate connection with ὑπὸ τὰ στ.: the latter is most probable, as forming the best parallel to ὑπὸ ἐπιτρόπους ἐστίν; so distinctly Copt., and *perhaps* Vulg., Clarom., 'sub elementa eramus servientes;' see Meyer *in loc.*

4. τὸ πλήρωμα τοῦ χρόνου] *'the fulness of the time,' i. e.* the moment which makes the time complete, answering to the ἄχρι τῆς προθεσμίας τοῦ πατρός, ver. 2; see Stier, *Ephes.* Vol. I. p. 203, and compare Usteri, *Lehrb.* II. 1, p. 83. These words have been the subject of considerable discussion. Taken in its most general view πλήρωμα has two meanings; (1) Active; τὸ πλήρη ποιεῖν, *implendi actio*, not *id quod implet*, as Fritz. (*on Rom.* xi. 12) has satisfactorily proved against Storr, *Opusc.* I. p. 144. (2) Passive; either in the less usual sense (α) *id quod impletum est*, or the more common and regular sense (β), *id quo res impletur;* compare 1 Cor. x. 26, Mark viii. 20. Hence τὸ πλήρωμα τοῦ χρ. will seem to be *'id quo temporis spatium impletur*, sc. *expletur;'* the idea being rather that of a temporal space (so to speak) filled up, as it were, by the flowing in of time; see Olsh. *in loc.*, and comp. Herod. III. 22, ὀγδώκοντα δ' ἔτεα ζόης πλήρωμα ἀνδρὶ μακρότατον. Fritz., on the contrary, but with less probability, regards πλήρωμα as the abstract notion of the concrete idea πλήρης, 'temporis plenitas,' i. q. 'plenum tempus;' see, however, his very valuable note, *Rom. l. c.* Vol. II. p. 469 sq. The doctrinal meaning of this term is investigated at length in Hall, *Bampt. Lect.* for 1797, esp. Serm. VIII. p. 211 sq.; see also the good sermons on this text by Andrewes, Serm. VI. Vol. I. p. 49, and Donne, *Serm.* III. Vol. I. p. 39 (ed. Alf.). ἐξαπέστειλεν]

ἐκ γυναικός, γενόμενον ὑπὸ νόμον, [5] ἵνα τοὺς ὑπὸ νόμον ἐξαγο-

'*sent forth*,' '*emisit*, *ex* cœlo *a* sese,' Beng.; comp. Acts vii. 12, xi. 22, xvii. 14. On the doctrinal questions connected with this word, see Petav. *Trin.* VIII. 1. 10. γενόμ. ἐκ γυναικός] '*born of a woman;*' defining participial clause added to attest the pure manhood of Christ, and to obviate any misconception of the meaning of the clause that follows; comp. Usteri, *Lehrb.* II. 2. 4, p. 311 sq. No doctrinal stress is thus to be laid either on γυναικός ('absque virili semine,' Est.), or on the prep. (τὸ δὲ ἐκ ἔμελλε . . . παραδηλοῦν τὴν κοινωνίαν τῆς φύσεως τοῦ τικτομένου πρὸς τὴν γεννήσασαν, Basil, *de Sp. Sanct.* v. 12; compare Theophyl. Œcum.); γυναικός being only used to mark our Lord's true humanity, and ἐκ having only its usual and natural ref. to the circumstances of birth; compare Matth. i. 16, John iii. 6, and see Rost. u. Palm. *Lex.* s. v. III. 2, Vol. I, p. 818, Winer, *Gr.* § 47. b, p. 327, 328. For a sound and striking sermon on this verse, and on the general relation of woman to man, see Jackson, *Creed*, Vol. VI. p. 226 (Oxf. 1844). The reading γεννώμενον, (found in some cursive mss., Ath., Theod., al.), has every appearance of being an explanatory gloss.

γενόμενον ὑπὸ νόμον] '*born under the law*,' 'natum inter Judæos legi Mos. obnoxios,' Schott; second defining clause added to show that not only was Christ truly man (γεν. ἐκ γυν.), but also a true member of the Jewish nation (γεν. ὑπὸ νόμ.), and standing in the same religious relations as all other Israelites; see Olshaus. and Turner *in loc.*, and comp. Andrewes, *Serm.* I. Vol. I. p. 13 (A.C.L.). On the most suitable rendering of γενόμενον, see notes to *Transl.*

5. ἵνα τοὺς ὑπὸ νόμον ἐξαγ.] '*in order that He might ransom those under the law;*' *first* gracious purpose of God's having sent forth his Son thus γενόμ. ἐκ γυναικ. and thus γενόμ. ὑπὸ νόμον,—the ransom of those who were under the same religious obligations as those under which our Lord vouchsafed to be born. The redemption was, as De W. (after Beng.) rightly maintains, not merely from the curse, but from the *bondage* of the law; comp. ver. 3. On the meaning of ἐξαγορ. see notes on ch. iii. 13. ἵνα τὴν υἱοθεσ. ἀπολ.] '*in order that we might receive the adoption of sons;*' *second* gracious purpose of God, resulting from the first,—the adoption of sons not only of Jews, but of all men (ἡμεῖς), of all those whose nature our Lord vouchsafed to assume. The first ἵνα thus, by a kind of χιασμὸς (Jelf, *Gr.* § 904. 3) found occasionally elsewhere in the Apostle's writings (comp. Philem. 6), refers to the second participial member γενόμ. ὑπὸ νόμον, while the second ἵνα refers to the first and less circumscribed γενόμ. ἐκ γυναικός. For examples of a double ἵνα thus appended to a single finite verb, comp. ch. iii. 14, Eph. v. 25. τὴν υἱοθεσίαν] '*the adoption of sons;*' comp. Rom. viii. 15, 23, ix. 4, Eph. i. 5. The interpretation, '*conditio filiorum*,' '*sonship*,' adopted by several commentators (see Ust. *in loc.* and *Lehrb.* II. 1. 2, p. 186, note), both here and Rom viii. 15, has been convincingly refuted by Fritz. *Rom. l. c.*, Vol. II. p. 137 sq. We were formerly in the light of servants, but now have been adopted and are free sons. Neander traces a threefold gradation in this adoption; (*a*) as existing but not appropriated; (*b*) as appropriated through faith in Christ; (*c*) as perfected by a full communion in his blessedness and glory; *Planting*,

ράσῃ, ἵνα τὴν υἱοθεσίαν ἀπολάβωμεν. 6 ὅτι δέ ἐστε υἱοί, ἐξαπέστειλεν ὁ Θεὸς τὸ Πνεῦμα τοῦ υἱοῦ αὐτοῦ εἰς τὰς καρδίας

Vol. I. p. 477 (Bohn). ἀπολάβωμεν] '*might receive.*' The special force of the prep. has been somewhat differently explained. Of the two more ancient interpretations (*a*), that of Chrys., καλῶς εἶπεν ἀπολ. δεικνὺς ὀφειλομένην, though lexically admissible (see Win., *de Verb. Comp.* Fasc. IV. p. 13), does not harmonize with the context, as the υἱοθεσία is not *here* alluded to as the subject of promise; again (*b*), that of Aug., 'non dixit *accipiamus* sed *recipiamus*,' though equally admissible on lexical grounds (opp. to Meyer; comp. Herod. I. 61. and see Rost u. Palm, *Lex.* s. v. ἀπό, E, and ib. s. v. ἀπολαμβ. 2. a.) is more than doubtful in point of doctrine, as the correct dogmatical statement, 'ut quod perdideramus in Adam . . . hoc in Christo reciperemus' (Iren.; see Bull, *State of Man*, p. 492, Oxf. 1844) can only be applied to what Adam had before his fall, and not to a gracious gift which was not bestowed on him. It seems best then to fall back on the general local meaning of ἀπό, and to regard the verb as hinting at receiving *from* an imaginary place where the things given might be conceived as having been laid up in store; 'ἀπολαμβ. dicuntur imprimis illi, qui, quæ ipsis destinata et quasi reposita sunt, accipiunt, Col. iii. 24, 2 Joh. 8,' Winer, *l. c.*; add Luke xvi. 25, ἀπέλαβες τὰ ἀγαθά σου, which the context shows could scarcely receive any other interpretation.

6. ὅτι δὲ κ. τ. λ.] '*and as a proof that ye are sons,*' 'quemadmodum autem' [*kamasa*], Æth., the δὲ introducing with a faintly oppositive force the demonstration of the assertion. It is difficult to decide whether ὅτι is here *causal* ('quoniam,' Vulg., Clarom., Syr.-Philox.) or, more probably, *demonstrative* (πόθεν δῆλον ὅτι, Chrys., Theoph., Œcum., and by obvious inference Theod. and Theod. Mops.). Independently of the authority of the Greek commentators, which in such cases is very great, we seem justified by the context in adopting the *latter* view, as, on the one hand, the causal interpretation seems to interfere with the easy transition from the declaration of ver. 4, 5, to the consequence in ver. 7; and, on the other hand, the demonstrative ὅτι seems to accord better with the emphatic position and the tense of ἐστέ. The sentence is thus what is called brachylogical, 'and as a proof that ye really are sons,'— a construction to which De W. and Alf. object, but which still seems perfectly correct and admissible; see Winer, *Gr.* § 66. 1, p. 546, Fritz. *Rom.* ii. 14, Vol. I. p. 117, Lücke *on* 1 *John* v. 9. The insertion of τοῦ Θεοῦ after υἱοί, in DEFG; Clarom., Demid., Tol., Goth., and Lat. Ff., seems an obvious explanatory addition.

τὸ Πνεῦμα τοῦ υἱοῦ αὐτοῦ] '*the Spirit of His Son,*' scil. the Holy Spirit ('Spiritus Christi quia per Christum obtinetur, Joh. xiv. 16,' Grot.), here suitably thus designated in harmony with the preceding mention of our relation to God as *sons* (Ust.); compare Rom. viii. 9, where Πν. Θεοῦ and Πν. Χριστοῦ appear interchangeable. On the doctrinal significance of this passage — that it is the 'substantia' and 'persona' of the Spirit which dwells in the hearts of believers (1 Cor. vi. 19), comp. Petav. *Trin.* VIII. 4. 6, Vol. II. p. 459, and on the *heart* as the seat of the in-working power of God, Beck, *Seelenl.* § 27, p. 107. In the following words *Rec.* reads ὑμῶν with BD³EJK; mss.; several Vv. and Ff., but with slightly less probability than ἡμῶν, which

ἡμῶν, κρᾶζον Ἀββᾶ ὁ πατήρ. 7 ὥστε οὐκέτι εἶ δοῦλος ἀλλὰ υἱός·
εἰ δὲ υἱός, καὶ κληρονόμος διὰ Θεοῦ.

7. διὰ Θεοῦ] This reading, which *Tisch.* has adopted with ABC[1](FG διὰ Θεόν); 17; Boern., Vulg., Copt.; Clem., Bas., Cyr., Did.; Ambr., Aug., Pel., Bed., Ambrst. (*Lachm.*, *Mey.*), appears, on the whole, the most satisfactory. Fritz. (*Opusc.* p. 148) supports the *Rec.* on paradiplomatic considerations (Χρ. and Θε. being confused with one another, hence omission of διὰ Χριστοῦ; then διὰ Θε. by omission of Χρ.), which seem somewhat precarious. In answer to the internal objection of Usteri that the inheritance is never represented by St. Paul as coming διὰ Θεοῦ (compare, however, ver. 5), it may be remarked, that Θεοῦ may fairly be taken in its widest sense, as including the three Persons of the blessed Trinity, just separately mentioned; see Windischm. *in loc.*

is found in ACD[1]EG; many mss; Amit. (Flor.), Clarom., Ath. (2), and many Ff. and is adopted by the best recent editors. Ἀββᾶ ὁ πατήρ] '*Abba father;*' Mark xiv. 36, Rom. viii. 15. In this solemn expression ὁ πατὴρ (nom. for vocat., Winer, *Gr.* § 29. 2, p. 164) does not seem appended to the Aramaic Ἀββᾶ as a mere explanation of it, 'Abba, id est, Pater' (Beza), nor yet united with it to indicate the union of Jews and Gentiles (Hebræum verbum ad Judæos, Græcum ad Gentes . . . pertinet,' Aug.; comp. Andrewes, *Serm.* IV. Vol. I. p. 60), but is appy. blended with it as making up the 'solemnis formula' of the early Christian prayers. The Aramaic title under which our Lord addressed his Heavenly Father was, probably, at a very early period (hence Mark *l. c.*) united to the Greek synonym in reverent and affectionate remembrance of Him who had taught and enabled us truly to call God Our Father, and thence used as a single form in all *more fervent* addresses to God; compare Schoettg. *Hor.* Vol. I. p. 252, where instances are given of addresses to God in which Hebrew and Greek words are somewhat similarly united. Whether there is any allusion to the fact that, among the Jews, a *freedman* might, by addressing any one with the title Abba, prepare the way for adoption by him (Selden, *de Success.* ch. 4. Vol. II. p. 15), seems *very* doubtful.

7. ὥστε κ. τ. λ.] '*So then,*' '*Consequently;* conclusion from the statements in the two preceding verses, ὥστε with its usual and proper force denoting the '*consecutionem* alicujus rei ex antecedentibus,' Klotz, *Devar.* Vol. II. p. 771. On the force of this particle with the indic. and infin., see notes on ch. ii. 13, and for its use with the imperative, notes on *Phil.* ii. 12. οὐκέτι εἶ] '*thou art no more,* as thou wert when in bondage under rudiments of the world.' Meyer finds a climax of person in ἀπολάβωμεν, ver. 6, ἐστέ, ver. 6, εἶ, ver. 7, the mode of address becoming more and more personal and individualizing; for further exx. of this use the second person in more cogent addresses, see Rom. xi. 17, xii. 20, xiii. 4, xiv. 4, 1 Cor. iv. 7, al., and comp. notes, ch. ii. 18. εἰ δὲ υἱός, καὶ κληρονόμος] '*but if a son* (not a slave) *then also an heir;*' comp. Rom. viii. 17, εἰ δὲ τέκνα, καὶ κληρονόμοι. Both these passages must appy. be explained on the principles of the Roman, and not of the Hebrew law. According to the latter, only *sons* (legitimate, 'ex concubinis,' or 'ex incestu,' but not 'ex ancillis et Gentilibus,' Seld. *de Succ.* ch. 3) succeeded to the inheritance; the first-born

How then can ye now turn back again to the bondage of rudiments as, alas! ye are doing?

8 Ἀλλὰ τότε μὲν οὐκ εἰδότες Θεὸν ἐδουλεύ-

having double; according to the former *all children*, male or female; 'nec interest utrum naturales sint an *adoptivi*,' Gajus, *Com. Inst.* III. § 2 (cited by Fritz.). It is scarcely necessary to observe that υἱὸς is not to be pressed, being simply, as Fritz. observes, in antithesis to δοῦλος: women are distinctly included in ch. iii. 28. The whole subject is ably investigated by Fritzsche, *Fritzsch. Opusc.* p. 143—149.

8. ἀλλά] '*Howbeit*;' appeal based on the preceding statements, and involving a strong *contrast* between their past and present states. The adversative ἀλλὰ has thus here no species of affirmative force (Ust.), — a meaning which, however, may be justified, see Klotz, *Devar.* Vol. II. p. 14, — but introduces an explanation of the words οὐκέτι εἶ κ. τ. λ., by the very contrast which it states; '*now* ye are free children of God, — *then* (before the time of your υἱοθεσία) ye knew Him not, and were the bondservants of demons.' It need scarcely be added that τότε does not refer to ver. 3 (Winer, Schott.), still less is to be regarded equivalent to πάλαι (Koppe), but merely marks the period when they were not, as they now are, sons; 'quasi digito intento designat omne tempus quod ante vocationem Galatarum exierat,' Grot. οὐκ εἰδότες] '*ignorantes*,' — an historic fact; contrast 1 Thess. iv. 5, τὰ μὴ εἰδότα τὸν Θεόν, where they are only so characterized by the writer, and see Winer, *Gr.* § 55. 5, p. 428 sq. It may be observed that with certain participles οὐ regularly and formally coälesces, so as to express one single idea; see Gayler, *Part. Neg.* p. 287. ἐδουλεύσατε] '*were slaves*;' emphatic, and, as in ver. 9, in a *bad* sense. The proper force of the aorist, as marking an action that took place in and belongs wholly to the past, is here distinctly apparent; comp. the exx. in Krüger, *Sprachl.* § 53. 5. 1, Scheuerl. *Synt.* § 32. 2, p. 331 sq., and for some excellent remarks on the use of the tense, Schmalf. *Synt. d. Gr. Verb.* § 60 sq., and esp. Fritz. *de Aor. Vi*, Frankf. 1837. This passage has been pressed into the controversy respecting δουλεία and λατρεία, and is noticed in Forbes, *Instruct.* VII. 1, p. 331 sq. τοῖς φύσει μὴ οὖσιν θεοῖς] '*which by nature are not gods*;' φύσει being emphatic, and serving to convey an unconditioned denial of their being gods *at all*; comp. 1 Cor. x. 20. The order in *Rec.* τοῖς μὴ φύσει οὖσι θεοῖς [D[3]FGJK; mss.; Syr.-Phil.; Chrys., Theod., al.] is much less expressive, as implying that the false gods were thought to be true gods, though not naturally so, and is decidedly inferior in external authority to that adopted in the text, which has the support of ABCD[1]E; 6 mss.; Syr. (plural), Vulg., Goth., Copt.; Athan. (4), Nyss. (4), al., and is adopted by the best recent editors. On the meaning of φύσει 'substantially,' 'essentially,' and the connection of the verse with the argument for the divinity of Christ, see Waterl. *Second Def.* Qu. 24, Vol. II. p. 722. μὴ οὖσι is a subjective negation, and states the view in which they were regarded by the writer; see above, and comp. the numerous exx. cited by Winer, *Gr.* § 55. 5, p. 428. The student must be reminded that μὴ with participles is the prevailing usage in the N. T., so that while οὐ with participles may be pressed, it is well to be cautious with regard to μή; see notes on 1 *Thess.* ii. 15.

σατε τοῖς φύσει μὴ οὖσιν θεοῖς· [9] νῦν δὲ γνόντες Θεόν, μᾶλλον δὲ γνωσθέντες ὑπὸ Θεοῦ, πῶς ἐπιστρέφετε πάλιν ἐπὶ τὰ ἀσθενῆ καὶ πτωχὰ στοιχεῖα, οἷς πάλιν ἄνωθεν δουλεύειν θέλετε; [10] ἡμέρας

9. γνόντες Θεόν] '*after having known God;*' temporal participle here expressing an action preceding that specified by the finite verb; see Winer, *Gr.* § 45. 1, p. 306, and notes *on Eph.* ii. 8, but transpose the accidentally interchanged words 'subsequent to' and 'preceding.' Olsh. finds a climax in εἰδότες, γνόντες, and γνωσθέντες; the first, merely outward knowledge that God is; the second, the inner essential knowledge in activity; the third, the passive knowledge of God in love. The distinction between the two latter (see below) *seems* correct, but that between εἰδ. and γν. very doubtful, especially after the instances cited by Meyer, viz. John vii. 27, viii. 55, 2 Cor. v. 16.

μᾶλλον δέ] '*imo vero,*' '*vel potius,*' Rom. viii. 34; 'corrigentis est ut sæpissime,' Stalb. Plat. *Symp.* 173 E: see exx. collected by Raphel, *in loc.*

γνωσθέντες] '*being known;*' 'cogniti,' Vulg., Clarom. [cognoti]; not 'approbati' (Grot.), nor even acknowledged as His own' (Ust., compare Ewald), still less 'scire facti' (Beza), — but simply, in the usual and regular meaning of the word in the N. T., 'known,' recognized;' see 1 Cor. viii. 3, xiii. 12, and comp. Winer, *Gr.* § 39. 3, p. 235. Before the time of their conversion, the Galatians were not known by God, — had not become the objects of His divine knowledge; now they were known by Him and endowed with spiritual gifts; αὐτὸς ὑμᾶς ἐπεσπάσατό, Chrys. The distinction drawn by Olsh. (above) between γνόντες, *cognitio activa*, knowledge, which must be, if genuine, preceded by γνωσθ., *cognitio passiva*, love, — hence the corrective μᾶλλον δέ, — seems borne out by 1 Cor. *l. c.* (on which see Beng.); comp. Neand. *Plant.* Vol. I. p. 157, note (Bohn.).

πῶς] '*qui fit ut,*' '*how cometh it that;*' see ch. ii. 14. ἐπιστρέφετε πάλιν] '*turn back again;*' 'convertimini iterum' Vulg., Clarom., ܬܘܒ ܗܦܟܬܘܢ [iterum conversiestis] Syr.; πάλιν not being the Homeric and Hesiodic 'retro' (an idea involved in ἐπιστρέφετε, Matth. xii. 44, 2 Pet. ii. 22), but *denuo*, *iterum*, the more common meaning in the N. T.; see exx. in Bretsch. *Lex.* s. v. The lapse of the Galatians into Judaism is thus represented as a *re*lapse into those στοιχεῖα among which Judaism was included: 'πάλιν non rem eandem respicit sed similem,' Glass. ap. Pol. *Syn. in loc.*

τὰ ἀσθενῆ κ. τ. λ.] '*the weak and beggarly elements;*' ἀσθενῆ as having no power to justify or promote salvation, πτωχὰ as having no rich dowry of spiritual gifts and blessings; compare Heb. vii. 18, and see Grot. *in loc.*

πάλιν ἄνωθεν] '*again anew,*' 'aftra ïupana,' Goth.; not pleonastic like πάλιν ἐκ δευτέρου (Matth. xxvi. 42), ἔπειτα μετὰ τοῦτο (John xi. 7), but expressive of two distinct ideas, *relapse to* bondage and *recommencement of* its principles. The Galatians had been slaves to the στοιχεῖα in the form of heathenism; now they were desiring to enslave themselves *again* to the στοιχεῖα, and to *commence* them *anew* in the form of Judaism; comp. 'rursum denuo,' Plaut. *Cas.* Prol. 33 (Wetst.), and see Hand. *Tursell.* Vol. II. p. 279.

10. ἡμέρας] '*days,*' scil. *Jewish* Sabbaths, fasts, etc. (compare Rom. xiv. 5, 6, Col. ii. 16); appy. emphatic, and not

παρατηρεῖσθε καὶ μῆνας καὶ καιροὺς καὶ ἐνιαυτούς. 11 φοβοῦμαι
ὑμᾶς, μήπως εἰκῇ κεκοπίακα εἰς ὑμᾶς.

improbably placed forward as marking what they observed with most scrupulosity; see Alf. *in loc.* It, however, can scarcely be considered exegetically exact to urge this verse against 'any theory of a *Christian Sabbath*' (Alf.), when the Apostle is only speaking of legal and Judaizing observances; see *on Col.* ii. 16. παρατηρεῖσθε] '*Ye are studiously observing*,' compare Æth. *tetāqabu* [where the Conjug. (III. 1, Dillm.) does not seem without its force]; the force of the compound being appy. '*sedulo*' (Meyer), not '*superstitiose* observatis' (Bretsch.) — a meaning which the passages adduced, *e. g.* Joseph. *Ant.* III. 5. 5, παρατηρεῖν τὰς ἑβδομάδας, Cod. A. *Relat. Tilat.* (Thilo, *Cod. Ap.* p. 806), τὸ σάββατον παρατηρεῖσθαι, do not substantiate. It may be observed that the primary use of παρὰ in this verb is appy. *local*, and by implication *intensive*, scil. — 'standing close beside for the purpose of more *effectually* observing' (compare Acts ix. 24, and see Rost u. Palm, *Lex.* s. v. Vol. II. p. 720): the secondary force is more distinctly *ethical*, but appy. restricted to the idea of *hostile* observation (Mark iii. 2, Luke vi. 7, xiv. 1); compare Polyb. *Hist.* XVII. 3. 2, ἐνεδρεύειν καὶ παρατηρεῖν, and see exx. in Schweigh. *Lex. Polyb.* s. v., and in Steph. *Thes.* s. v. Vol. VI. p. 410. The punctuation of this verse is doubtful. *Tisch.* Mey., Alf., al., place a mark of interrogation after ἐνιαυτούς, but appy. with somewhat less contextual probability than the simple period *(Lachm.)*; as in this latter case the verse supplies a natural verification of the statement implied in the preceding question, explaining τίς τῆς δουλείας τρόπος (Theod.), and forming a natural transition to the sadder tone of ver. 11. To derive a hint merely from the use of the pres. tense that the Galatians were then celebrating a Sabbatical year (Wieseler, *Chron. Apost.* p. 286, note) seems very precarious.

καιρούς] '*seasons*,' *i. e.* of the festivals; comp. Chron. viii. 13, τοῦ ἀναφέρειν κατὰ τὰς ἐντολὰς Μωϋσῇ ἐν τοῖς σαββάτοις, καὶ ἐν τοῖς μησί, καὶ ἐν ταῖς ἑορταῖς, τρεῖς καιροὺς τοῦ ἐνιαυτοῦ, and Lev. xxiii. 4. ἐνιαυτούς] '*years*,' — the sabbatical years, *and* (according to the usual explanation) the years of Jubilee. These latter, Meyer asserts on the authority of Kranold (*de Anno Jubil.* p. 79), were never really celebrated; contrast, however, the direct command in Lev. xxv. 5, and compare the distinct allusions to it in other places (*e. g.* Isaiah, lxi. 1, 2). Whether the year of Jubilee is *here* alluded to may be a matter of opinion; but that both *before* (opp. to Winer, *RWB.*, Art. 'Jubeljahr,' Vol. I. p. 626) and *after* the captivity it was fully observed, there seems no sufficient reason to doubt; see Kitto, *Bibl. Cyclop.* Art. 'Jubilee,' Vol. II. p. 162.

11. φοβοῦμαι ὑμᾶς] '*I am apprehensive of you*,' 'res vestræ mihi timorem incutiunt,' Grot.; definite and independent statement receiving its further explanation from what follows; comp. Col. iv. 17, βλέπε τὴν διακονίαν . . . . ἵνα αὐτὴν πληροῖς, and see notes *in loc.* To regard this verse as an example of that kind of attraction, where a word, really belonging to the subordinate clause, is made the object of, and assimilated by the principal clause (Ust., Winer, *Gr.* § 66. 5, p. 552), does not seem grammatically exact, as in such cases the *object* of the former clause is nearly always the *subject* of the latter

Treat me now with reciprocity: you once despised me not even in my infirmity, but evinced towards me the deepest reverence and warmest love.

12 Γίνεσθε ὡς ἐγώ, ὅτι κἀγὼ ὡς ὑμεῖς,

(Scheuerl. *Synt.* § 49. 2, p. 507) *e. g.* Acts xv. 36, ἐπισκεψώμεθα τοὺς ἀδελφοὺς . . . . πῶς ἔχουσι: see exx. in Winer, *l. c.* and Kypke, *Obs.* Vol. I. p. 375. It will be best then, with *Lachm.*, *Buttm.*, al. to place a comma after ὑμᾶς, and to regard μήπως κ. τ. λ. as a separate, explanatory clause. μήπως—κεκοπίακα] '*lest haply I have (actually) labored in vain:*' 'μὴ etiam indicativum adjunctum habet, ubi rem a nobis *pro verâ haberi* indicare volumus,' Herm. *Viger*, No. 270; see also Winer, *Gr.* § 56. 2, p. 446, Klotz, *Devar.* Vol. I. p. 129, and notes on ch. ii. 2. Chrysost., not having appy. observed this idiom, has unduly pressed φοβοῦμαι and μήπως, and implied nearly a contrary sense; οὐδέπω, φησίν, ἐξέβη τὸ ναυάγιον, ἀλλ' ἔτι τὸν χειμῶνα τοῦτο ὠδίνοντα βλέπω; contrast Theod., μεμνημένος μὲν τῶν πόνων, τὸν δὲ καρπὸν οὐχ ὁρῶν. εἰς ὑμᾶς] '*upon you;*' not 'in vobis,' Vulg., Clarom., Arm., but 'propter vos,' Æth., or more exactly, '*in vos*, emphatica locutio,' Beng.; compare Rom. xvi. 6, ἐκοπίασεν εἰς ἡμᾶς. The meaning of εἰς ('looking towards,' Donalds. *Crat.* § 170) is thus not so much simply ethical, 'in reference to,' and hence '*for* you' (De W.),—this being more naturally expressed by a dat. *commodi* (Ecclus. xxiv. 34),—as ethically-*local*, 'upon you,' Auth.; comp. Bernhardy, *Synt.* v. 10, p. 217: the Apostle's labor was directed *to* the Galatians, actually reached them, and so had passed *on* to them.

12. γίνεσθε ὡς ἐγώ] '*Become as I am;*' affectionate appeal calling on them to treat their Apostle with reciprocity (see below), and reminding them of their former love and reverence for him. ὅτι κἀγὼ ὡς ὑμεῖς] '*since I have become as ye are;*' dissuasive from Judaism urged on the ground of his own dereliction of it; comp. 1 Cor. ix. 20, 21. The exact sentiment conveyed by these words has received several different explanations. Of these (*a*) that of the Greek expositors—'I was once a zealot for Judaism, as ye now are' (ταῦτα πρὸς τοὺς ἐξ Ἰουδαίων, Chrys.)—is open to the objection that ἤμην ('*fui*, nec amplius sum') would have thus seemed almost a necessary insertion (Mey.); comp. Just. *ad Græc.* 5 (Wetst.), γίνεσθε ὡς ἐγώ, ὅτι κἀγὼ ἤμην ὡς ὑμεῖς. Again (*b*) that of Bengel, Fell, al., that it is only a scriptural mode of expressing warm affection (1 Kings xxii. 4), *i. e.* 'love me as I love you,' is certainly not in harmony with the use of γίνεσθε, and still less with the context, where *apprehension* (φοβοῦμαι ὑμᾶς) rather than *love* is what is at present uppermost in the Apostle's thoughts. It seems best then, (*c*) with Fritz., De W., and most modern expositors, to regard the clause as urging a course of reciprocity on the part of the Galatians corresponding to that which had been pursued by the Apostle; 'become free from Judaism like me, for I, though a native Jew, have become (and am) a Gentile like you,' 'I am τοῖς ἀνόμοις ὡς ἄνομος (1 Cor. ix. 21) *now*, though περισσοτέρως ζηλωτὴς κ. τ. λ. (ch. i. 14) *then;*' see Neand. *Planting*, Vol. I. p. 223 (Bohn), and *Fritzsch. Opusc.* p. 232 sq., where the passage is fully discussed. ἀδελφοί δέομαι ὑμῶν] '*brethren, I beseech you;*' earnest entreaty ('verba περιπαθῆ,' Grot.) belonging not to what follows,—though so taken by Chrys., al., and all the ancient Vv.,—but with what *precedes*, as the δέησις is in the first and not in the last portion. This passage is curious as one in which the best ancient, and the

ἀδελφοί, δέομαι ὑμῶν· οὐδέν με ἠδικήσατε· 13 οἴδατε δὲ ὅτι δι' ἀσθένειαν τῆς σαρκὸς εὐηγγελισάμην ὑμῖν τὸ πρότερον,

best modern interpreters, are, as happens but very rarely, in direct opposition to each other. οὐδέν με ἠδικήσατε] '*ye injured me in nothing;*' allusion to their past behavior as a reason and motive why they should now accede to the entreaty just urged; 'ye did not injure me formerly, do not injure me now by refusing to act as I beseech you to act.' The connection is thus, as the parallel aorists ἠδικήσατε, ἐξουθενήσατε, ἐξεπτύσατε, seem distinctly to suggest, very close with what follows, ver. 13 and 14 (which really make up a single period) forming a sort of antithetical member (see below) to the present clause, and the aor. referring to the Apostle's first visit. The usual interpretation 'there is nothing personal between us' (δηλῶν ὅτι οὐ μίσους οὐδὲ ἔχθρας ἦν τὰ εἰρημένα, Chrys.) is both exegetically untenable (there was no ἔχθρα in what he had said but the reverse), and grammatically precarious as implying in ἠδικήσατε either the force of a present or perfect. The interpr. reproduced by Rettig, *Stud. u. Krit.* 1830, p. 109, 'ye have not injured *me*, but Christ' ('nihil me privatim læsistis,' Grot.), implies an emphasis on με which does not seem to exist (οὐδὲν is surely the emphatic word), and equally tends to infringe on the force of the aorist.

13. οἴδατε δέ] '*but ye know,*' 'scitis potius;' opposition, not so much of clauses (this would be οὐκ — ἀλλά, compare Chrys.), as of the sentiments conveyed in the preceding clause and in the two verses which here follow: 'when I first came among you, and that under trying circumstances to you, far from wronging me, ye received me as an angel of God.' δι' ἀσθένειαν τῆς σαρκός] '*on account of weakness of the flesh; i. e.* on account of some sickness or bodily weakness, which caused the Apostle to stay longer with the Galatians than he had originally intended, and of which we know nothing beyond the present allusion: see, as to lexical usage, Winer, *Gr.* § 49. c, p. 356, Fritz. *Rom.* iii. 25, Vol. I. p. 197, and, as to the historical probability, Wieseler, *Chron. Apost.* p. 30, and Conyb. and Hows. *St. Paul*, Vol. I. p. 294 (ed. 1). Though, on the one hand, it may admitted, that the line of demarcation between διὰ with the gen. and with the accus. is occasionally so faint that, in some few passages (esp. with *persons*), an interchange seems really to have taken place (see exx. in Steph. *Thes.* s. v., collected by Dindorf, and in Bretsch. *Lex.* s. v., — but except Heb. v. 13, Rev. iv. 11, and appy. Rev. xii. 11), still in the present case there seems nothing so irreconcilable with the context (Peile, Bagge), or so improbable in itself as to lead us to adopt either of the two only possible (?) alternatives, (*a*) an enallage of case (Ust., al.), or (*b*) a temporal use of διά, scil. 'during a period of sickness.' To the first of these there is the great objection that no certain instance has yet been adduced from the N. T., — neither John vi. 57 (see Lücke *in loc.*) nor Phil. i. 15 (see notes *in loc.*) being exx. in point; and to (*b*) the equally valid objection that this species of temporal, or, more correctly speaking, local meaning, *e. g.* διὰ νύκτα, comp. διὰ πόντον, διὰ στόμα, etc., is only found in poetry, and that rarely Attic; compare Bernhardy, *Synt.* v. 18, p. 236, Madvig, *Gr.* § 69. We seem bound then to maintain the simple meaning of the words, and to refer to our ignorance of the circum-

14 καὶ τὸν πειρασμὸν ὑμῶν ἐν τῇ σαρκί μου οὐκ ἐξουθενήσατε
οὐδὲ ἐξεπτύσατε, ἀλλὰ ὡς ἄγγελον Θεοῦ ἐδέξασθέ με, ὡς Χρισ-

14. ὑμῶν] So *Lachm.* and *Tisch.* (ed. 2) with AB(C^2 adds τὸν)D^1FG; 17. 89. 67** .... Vulg., Clarom., Copt.; Cyr., Hieron., Aug., Ambrst., Sedul. *(Meyer, Bagge). Tischendorf* (ed. 2) reads μου τὸν with D^3EJK; appy. great majority of mss.; Syr.-Phil. (appy. Syr., Goth.), Arm.; Chrys., Thdrt., Dam., Œcum. *(Rec., Scholz, Fritz.* om. μου, *Alf.).* Independently of the preponderance of external authority, the change from the easier to the more difficult reading seems so *very* probable, that, in spite of the internal objections of Fritz. (*Opusc.* p. 245 sq.), we can here scarcely hesitate to adopt the reading, though not the punctuation (see note), of *Lachmann. Mill* (*Append.* p. 51) retracts his former opinion, and distinctly advocates ὑμῶν.

stances (Green, *Gr.* p. 300) any difficulties the expression may *appear* to involve. τὸ πρότερον may be translated either '*formerly*' (Deut. ii. 12, Josh. xi. 10, Joh. vi. 61, ix. 8), or '*the first time*' (πρότερον, Heb. iv. 6, vii. 27). The latter is preferable; for, as Meyer observes, the words would be surperfluous if St. Paul had been only *once*. Still no historical conclusions can safely be drawn from this expression alone; see Wieseler, *Chron. Apost.* p. 30, 277.

14. τὸν πειρασμὸν ὑμῶν] '*your temptation*,' scil. 'your trial, which arose, or might reasonably have arisen, from the bodily infirmity on account of which I ministered among you;' ἐν τῇ σαρκί μου coalescing with, and forming an explanatory addition to the otherwise seemingly ambiguous τὸν πειρασμ. ὑμῶν; comp. 2 Cor. x. 10, ἡ δὲ παρουσία τοῦ σώματος, ἀσθενής, καὶ ὁ λόγος ἐξουθενημένος, and see *Mill (Append. to N. T.)*, p. 51. The objection to this interpretation, founded on the absence of the art. before ἐν τῇ σαρκί μου (Rück.), is here not valid, as πειράζειν ἔν τινι (compare Ecclus. xxvii. 5) is appy. an admissible construction; see Winer, *Gr.* § 20. 2, p. 123, and notes *on Eph.* i. 15. *Lachmann* places a period after μοῦ, and connects τὸν πειρασμ. ὑμ. with ver. 13; but this does very little to remove the difficulty in the former part of this verse, and makes the latter part intolerably harsh and abrupt. ἐξεπτύσατε] '*loathed*,' 'respuistis,' Vulg., Clarom., ܢܕܬܘܢ [abominati estis] Syr.: 'plus est ἐκπτύειν quam ἐξουθενεῖν, hoc enim contemptum, illud et abominationem significat,' Grot.; see Kypke, *Observ.* Vol. II. p. 280. Of the compounds of πτύω, those ἐν and ἐκ are only used in the *natural*, and not, as καταπτ., διαπτ., ἀποπτ., in the *metaphorical* sense; see Lobeck, *Phryn.* p. 15 sq. Probably, as Fritz. suggests, ἐκπτ. was here used rather than the more common ἀποπτ. by a kind of alliteration after ἐξουθενήσατε, 'non *re*probastis aut *re*spuistis,' more esp. as a repetition of the same prep. in composition appears to be an occasional characteristic of the Apostle's style; compare Rom. ii. 17, xi. 7. De Wette feels a difficulty in ἐξουθ. and ἐξεπτ. being applied to πειρασμὸς on the part of the Galatians. Yet surely, whether referred to St. Paul or to the Galat., the expression is equally elliptical, and must in either case imply despising that which formed or suggested the πειρασμός. ὡς Χριστὸν Ἰησοῦν] '*(yea) as Christ Jesus*;' climactic, denoting the deep affection and veneration with which he was received; comp. 2 Cor. v. 20; the Galatians received the Apos-

τὸν Ἰησοῦν. [15] τίς οὖν ὁ μακαρισμὸς ὑμῶν; μαρτυρῶ γὰρ ὑμῖν

tle not only as an angel, but as One higher and more glorious (Heb. i. 4), even as Him who was the Lord of angels.

15. τίς οὖν] '*Of what kind then,*' scil. ἦν [inserted in DEK(ηFG): mss.; Chrys.]; '*qualis* (not *quanta*), h. e. quam levis, quam inconstans, *igitur erat,*' Fritz.; sorrowful enquiry, expressive of the Apostle's real estimate of the nature of their μακαρισμός; οἴχεται, ἀπώλετο· καλῶς οὐκ ἀποφηνάμενος, ἀλλὰ δι' ἐρωτήσεως ἐνδειξάμενος, Theod. Mops. If ποῦ be adopted, for which there is greater external authority [ABCFG; 6 mss.; Boern., Syr. Vulg., Copt., Arm. al.; Dam., Hier. al.], but which seems to bear every appearance of having been a correction (τὸ τίς ἀντὶ τοῦ ποῦ τέθεικεν, Theod.), then ἐστὶν must be supplied, and οὖν taken in its 'vis *collectiva*,' whereas in the present case, what has been called the vis *reflexiva* ('takes up what has been said and continues it,' Donalds. *Crat.* § 192) is more apparent; see Klotz, *Devar.* Vol. II. p. 719, and notes *on Phil.* ii. 1. μακαρισμὸς ὑμῶν] '*the boasting of your blessedness,*' 'beatitatis vestræ prædicatio,' Beza; the Galatians themselves being obviously both the μακαρίζοντες (not St. Paul and others, Œcum., comp. Theoph.) and the μακαριζόμενοι: see Rom. iv. 6 (where λέγει τὸν μακαρισμὸν = μακαρίζει), and compare Fritz. *in loc.* The word is occasionally found in earlier writers (*e. g.* Plato, *Rep.* IX. 59 D, Aristot. *Rhet.* I. 9. 4) and is of common occurrence in the Greek liturgies; see Suicer, *Thesaur.* s. v. Vol. II. p. 290 sq. τοὺς ὀφθαλμοὺς ὑμῶν) '*your eyes,*' 'oculos vestros,' Vulg., Clarom.; not 'your own eyes,' Auth. (τοὺς ἰδίους ὀφθαλμούς), as the article and pronoun are found in the N. T. constantly associated with ὀφθ., where no emphasis is intended; compare Joh. iv. 35, and see the numerous exx. in Bruder, *Concord.* s. v. p. 667. All inferences then from this passage that the ἀσθένεια of the Apostle was a disease of the eyes, are in the highest degree precarious; see Alf. *in loc.* ἐξορύξαντες] '*having plucked out,*' 'eruissetis et dedissetis,' Vulg., Clarom.; participle expressive of an act *immediately* prior to, and all but synchronous with that of the finite verb; comp. Hermann, *Viger,* No. 224. That the verb ἐξορύττειν ('usgraban,' Goth.) is a 'verbum solemne' (Mey.) for the extirpation of the eye (1 Sam. xi. 2, Herod. VIII. 116, etc.) may perhaps be doubted, as ἐκκόπτειν ὀφθαλμὸν is used in cases apparently similar (Judges xvi. 21, comp. Lucian, *Toxaris,* 40), though more generally applicable to the simple destruction of the organ; see Demosth. 247. 11, Aristoph. *Nub.* 24 (λίθῳ), Plutarch, *Lycurg.* 11 (βακτηρίᾳ). The Greek vocabulary on this subject is very varied; see the numerous synonymns in Steph. *Thes.* s. v. ὀφθαλμός. ἐδώκατε] '*ye would have given;*' the ἂν [*Rec.* with D³EJK; mss.] being rightly omitted with great preponderating evidence [AB CD¹FG; 2 mss.]; comp. John xv. 22, xix. 11. This omission of the article has a 'rhetorical' force (Herm)., and differs from the past tense *with* ἂν, as marking more definitely the *certainty* that the event mentioned in the apodosis would have taken place, if the restriction expressed or implied in the protasis had not existed; see Herm. *de Partic.* ἄν, p. 58 sq., Schmalfeld, *Synt.* § 79, p. 185. Whether this distinction can always be maintained in the N. T. is perhaps doubtful, as the tendency to omit ἂν in the apodosis (especially with the imperf.) is certainly a distinct feature of later Greek; see Winer, *Gr.* §

ὅτι εἰ δυνατὸν τοὺς ὀφθαλμοὺς ὑμῶν ἐξορύξαντες ἂν ἐδώκατέ μοι.
16 ὥστε ἐχθρὸς ὑμῶν γέγονα ἀληθεύων ὑμῖν;
17 Ζηλοῦσιν ὑμᾶς οὐ καλῶς, ἀλλὰ

Your false teachers only court you for selfish ends: and ye are fickle. Would that I were with you, and could alter my tone.

42. 2, p. 273, and comp. Ellendt, *Lex. Soph.* s. v. x. 1, Vol. I. p. 125.

16. ὥστε] 'So then?' 'Ergo?' Vulg., Clarom., consequence (expressed interrogatively) from the present state of things as contrasted with the past, — 'so then, as things now stand, am I become your enemy?' οὐχ ὑμεῖς ἐστε οἱ περιέποντες καὶ θεραπεύοντες, καὶ τῶν ὀφθαλμῶν τιμιώτερον ἄγοντες; Τί τοίνυν γέγονε; πόθεν ἡ ἔχθρα, Chrys. The consecutive force of ὥστε is more strongly pressed by Meyer, who accordingly connects the particle with the interrogation τίς οὖν μακαρ., of which it is to be conceived as expressing the special consequence, 'is it in consequence of the unstable nature of your μακαρ., that,' etc., — but this seems to involve the necessity of regarding μαρτυρῶ γὰρ κ. τ. λ. as parenthetical, and seems less in accordance with the context than the general and more abrupt reference to present circumstances; see De Wette *in loc.* The use of ὥστε with interrog. sentences is briefly noticed by Klotz, *Devar.* Vol. II. p. 776. ἐχθρὸς ὑμῶν γέγονα] '*am I become your enemy,*' *i. e.* '*hostile to you,*' ܒܥܠܕܒܒܐ [dominus inimicitiæ] Syr. (both), 'inimicus vobis,' Vulg., Clarom., 'fijands' [Feind], Goth., Copt., Æth., Arm., — nearly all regarding ἐχθρὸς as used substantively, and *appy.* actively, as in most of the languages above cited there are forms which would have distinctly conveyed the passive meaning. This latter meaning is adopted by Mey., Alf., al., and is not only grammatically admissible (ἐχθρος, as the gen. shows, acting here as a substantive), but even contextually plausible, as the opposition between the former love of the Galatians and their present aversion would thus seem more fully displayed. Still as the active meaning yields a good sense, and is adopted by most of the ancient Vv., and as there is also some ground for believing that ὁ ἐχθρὸς ἄνθρωπος (*Clem. Recogn.* I. 70, 71, 'ille inimicus homo') was actually a name by which the Judaists designated the Apostle, the active meaning is to be preferred; see Hilgenf. *Clem. Recogn.*, p. 78, note, Wieseler, *Chronol.* p. 277. ἀληθεύων] '*by speaking the truth,*' scil. 'because I speak the truth;' οὐκ οἶδα ἄλλην αἰτίαν, Chrys. To what period does the participle refer? Certainly not (*a*) to the present Epistle, as the Apostle could not now know what the effect would be (Schott); nor (*b*) to the *first* visit, when the state of feeling (ver. 15) was so very different, but (*c*) to the *second* (Acts xviii. 23), when Judaism had probably made rapid advances; see Wieseler, *Chronol.* p. 277. No objection can be urged against this from the use of the present (imperf.) participle, as the action was still lasting; see Winer, *Gr.* § 45. 1, p. 304, Schmalfeld, *Synt.* § 202, p. 406.

17. ζηλοῦσιν ὑμ.] '*they are paying you court,*' scil. they are showing an anxious zeal in winning you over to their own party and opinions; contrast between the honest truthfulness of the Apostle towards his converts, and the interested and self-seeking court paid to them by the Judaizing teachers. For an example of a similar use of ζηλοῦν ('sich eifrig um Jem. kümmern, Rost. u. Palm, *Lex.* s. v.), — here

ἐκκλεῖσαι ὑμᾶς θέλουσιν, ἵνα αὐτοὺς ζηλοῦτε.

neither exclusively in its better sense (2 Cor. xi. 2) nor yet in its worse (Acts vii. 9; compare Chrys.), but in the neutral meaning of 'paying court to' ('studiose ambire,' Fritz.), — see Plut. VII. 762 (cited by Fritz.), ὑπὸ χρείας τὸ πρῶτον ἕπονται καὶ ζηλοῦσιν, ὕστερον δὲ καὶ φιλοῦσιν.

ἀλλὰ ἐκκλεῖσαι κ. τ. λ.] '*nay, they desire to exclude you;*' they not merely follow the positive and less dishonorable course of *in*cluding you among themselves [Syr. reads ἐγκλ., but appy. only from mistake] but the baser and more negative one of *ex*cluding you from others to make you thus court them. The omission of a gen. after ἐκκλ. (see Kypke, *Obs.* II. 181) makes it difficult to determine the objects *from which* the false teachers sought to exclude those whom they affected, and has caused the ellipsis to be supplied in various ways; *e. g.* τῆς τελείας γνώσεως (Chrys.), 'a Christo et fiduciâ ejus' (Luther), 'ab aliis omnibus' (Schott), 'e circulis suis,' *i. e.* 'by affecting exclusiveness to make you court them' (Koppe, comp. Brown), — the last ingenious, but all more or less arbitrary. The only clue afforded by the context is the position of αὐτοὺς, which suggests a marked *personal* antithesis, and the use of ἐκκλεῖσαι, which seems more naturally to refer to numbers or a community (Mey.) than to anything abstract or individual. Combining these two observations, we may perhaps with probability extend the reference from St. Paul (ed. 1, Fritz.) to that of the sounder portion of the Church with which he in thought associates himself, and from which he reverts back again to himself in ver. 18. The moment of thought, however, rests really on the *verb*, not on the objects to which it may be thought to refer. The Galatians were courted, and that οὐ καλῶς, in every way; direct proselytizing on the part of these teachers (if they had been sincere in their convictions) might have worn a semblance of being καλόν; their course, however, was rather (ἀλλὰ) indirect, it was to *isolate* their victims, that in their isolation they might be forced to affect those who thus dishonestly affected them. 'Αλλὰ thus preserves its proper force, and becomes practically *corrective;* see Klotz, *Devar.* Vol. II. p. 2, 3, Hartung, *Partik.* Vol. II. p. 35. The reading ὑμᾶς which has still some few defenders (Scholef. *Hints*, p. 96, comp. De W.) appears to have been a conjecture of Beza. Though *said* to have been since found in a few mss., the assertion of Scholz, 'ἡμᾶς e codd. recent. *fere omnibus*' is a complete mis-statement.

ζηλοῦτε] '*in order that ye may zealously affect them;*' purpose of the ζηλοῦσιν οὐ καλῶς, ἵνα not being adverbial ('ubi, quo in statu,' Fritz., Mey.), but the simple conjunction, here as also in 1 Cor. iv. 6, associated with the indic., *per solœcismum;* see Winer, *Gr.* § 41. 5. p. 259, and Green, *Gr.* p. 73, who calls attention to the fact that both solœcisms appear in a contracted verb, where they might certainly have more easily occurred. Hilgenfeld cites as a parallel Clem. *Hom.* XI. 16 (read 6), ἵνα ὑπῆρχεν, but the preceding clause, εἰ θέλετε αὐτὸν ποιῆσαι, seems, structurally considered, in effect equivalent to εἰ ἐποίησεν, and ὑπῆρχεν only the imperf. 'in re irritâ vel infectâ,' — a usage appy. not familiar to this expositor (see p. 131, and comp. notes on ch. ii. 2), but perfectly regular and idiomatic; see Madvig, *Synt.* § 131, Schmalfeld, *Synt.* § 143, p. 294. It may be remarked that the

18 καλὸν δὲ τὸ ζηλοῦσθαι ἐν καλῷ πάντοτε, καὶ μὴ μόνον ἐν τῷ
παρεῖναί με πρὸς ὑμᾶς. 19 τεκνία μου οὓς πάλιν ὠδίνω ἄχρις

Mss. and mss. (219** [ζηλῶτε], only excepted) are unanimous in the indic., and that all the ancient Vv. appear to have regarded ἵνα as a conjunction.

18. καλὸν δὲ τὸ ζηλοῦσθαι κ. τ. λ.] '*But it is good to be courted in a good way at all times;*' contrasted statement of what it is to be courted in a good and lasting manner. There is some little obscurity in this verse owing to the studied and characteristic παρονομασία (compare Winer, *Gr.* § 68. 1, p. 560) which marks the terms in which it is expressed. As the explanations of the verse are somewhat varied, we may perhaps advantageously premise the following limitations:—(1) All interpretations which do not preserve one uniform meaning of ζηλόω in both verses (*e. g.* Rück., and even De W. and Fritz.) may be rejected: from which it would seem to follow that ἐν καλῷ does not point to the sphere of the ζηλοῦσθαι, in the sense of the virtues which called out the feeling (ἐπὶ τῇ τελειότητι, Theoph., compare De W.),—as this would practically cause ζηλοῦν to pass from its neutral meaning 'ambire,' to the more restricted 'admirari,'—but is to be regarded as simply adverbial (compare Bernhardy, *Synt.* v. 8. b, p. 211), and perhaps as varied only from the preceding καλῶς to harmonize structurally with the following ἐν τῷ παρεῖναί. (2) ζηλοῦσθαι must be regarded as pass. (comp. Syr.), not as a middle, equiv. in sense to active (Vulg., Clarom., Goth.), as no evidence of such a use of ζηλοῦσθαι has yet been found. (3) The object of ζηλοῦσθαι must be *the Galatians*, as in ver. 17, and not (Ust.) St. Paul. (4) ἐν τῷ παρεῖναι is not to be translated *prospectively* (Peile), but must mean simply 'when I am with you.' Thus narrowed, then, the meaning would seem to be, 'But it is a good thing to be courted,—to be the object of ζῆλος, in an honest way (as you are by me, though not by them) *at all times*, and not merely just when I happen to be with you.' Thus ζηλοῦσθαι ἐν καλῷ forms, as it were, a compound idea = ζηλοῦσθαι καλῶς (Peile), and is in strict antithesis to the act. ζηλ. οὐ καλῶς in the preceding verse; see Wieseler, *Chron. Apost.* p. 278. πρὸς ὑμᾶς] '*with you;*' the primary idea of direction is frequently lost sight of, especially with persons; compare John i. 1, 1 Thess. iii. 4, 2 Thess. ii. 5, and see notes on ch. i. 18.

19. τεκνία μου] '*my little children;*' appropriate introduction to the tender and affectionate address which follows. Usteri, *Scholz*, *Lachmann*, and other expositors and editors connect these two words with ver. 18, putting a comma only after ὑμᾶς. By such a punctuation (suggested probably by a difficulty felt in the idiomatic δέ, ver. 20) the whole effect of the present address is lost, and the calm and semiproverbial comment of ver. 18, to which it now forms such a sudden and tender contrast, weakened by the addition of an incongruous appeal. The appropriate and affectionate τέκνια (only here in St. Paul, but often in St. John) is changed by *Lachm.* into τέκνα [only with BFG], but rightly retained by the majority of recent editors. ὠδίνω] '*I am in travail;*' not 'in utero gesto' (Heinsius, *Exerc.* p. 424, compare Alf.),—a meaning for which there is no satisfactory authority in the N. T. or the LXX, but simply 'parturio,' Vulg. Clarom., ܡܚܒܠ [sum

οὗ μορφωθῇ Χριστὸς ἐν ὑμῖν, 20 *ἤθελον δὲ παρεῖναι πρὸς ὑμᾶς*
ἄρτι καὶ ἀλλάξαι τὴν φωνήν μου, ὅτι ἀποροῦμαι ἐν ὑμῖν.

parturiens] Syr., with the idea, not so much of the pain, as of the long and continuous effort of travail; see exx. in Loesner, *Obs.* p. 333, and observe the tender touch in the πάλιν, scil. ὥστε τῶν παλαίων ὠδίνων ἀγαγεῖν εἰς μνήμην. The use of ὠδίνω in eccl. writers is illustrated by Suicer, *Thes.* II. p. 1595.

ἄχρις οὗ μορφωθῇ] '*until Christ be formed,*' 'until the new man, Christ in us (ch. ii. 20, compare Eph. iii. 17) receive, as I doubt not he will (ἂν perhaps designedly omitted; see iii. 19, and Herm. *de Partic.* ἄν, p. 40), his completed and proper form;' the obvious meaning of this word (ἐξεικονίζεσθαι, εἰδοποιεῖσθαι, see Heinsius, *Exerc.* p. 424) seeming to show that the metaphor is continued, though in a changed application. The doctrinal meaning of μορφ. is alluded to by Ust. *Lehrb.* II. 1. 3, p. 225 sq., but see esp. Waterland, *on Regen.* Vol. IV. 445, who satisfactorily shows that this passage cannot be urged in favor of a *second* regeneration. On the meaning of ἄχρι and its distinction from μεχρί, see notes *on* 2 *Tim.* ii. 9.

20. ἤθελον δὲ] '*I could indeed wish;*' imperf. without ἄν; comp. Rom. ix. 3, Acts xxv. 22. In all such cases the simple imperf., which here appears in the true distinctive character of the tense (Bernh. *Synt.* x. 3, 373), must be referred to a suppressed conditional clause, *vellem* sc. *si possem, si liceret* (Fritz. *Rom.* IX. 3, Vol. II. p. 245), but must be distinguished from the imperf. with ἄν, which involves a thought ('but I will not') which is here not intended; see Herm. *de Partic.* ἄν, p. 56, Winer, *Gr.* § 41. 2, p. 253. The distinction drawn by Schömann (*Isæus* x. 1, p. 435, cited by Win.) between ἤθελον or ἐβουλόμην *with* ἄν ('significat voluntatem a conditione suspensam sc. *vellem, si liceret*') and *without* ἄν ('vere nos illud voluisse, etiam si omittenda fueret voluntas, scilicet, quod frustra nos velle cognovimus,' — in such cases often with a preparatory μὲν) is subtle, but appy. of limited application, even in earlier Greek; in later Greek it is still more precarious; see notes on ver. 15. The omission of ἂν in cases of 'objective necessity' is well treated by Stalbaum on Plato, *Sympos.* 190 c, p. 130.

δὲ has caused some difficulty to be felt in this connection. Scholef. (*Hints*, p. 77) proposes to regard δὲ as redundant; Hilgenfeld commences with ἤθελον δὲ a new clause, leaving ver. 20 an unfinished address. This is not necessary; the present use of δὲ is analogous to its use with personal pronouns after vocatives or in answers (Bernhardy, *Synt.* III. 5, p. 73, Pors. *Orest.* 614), the principle of explanation being the same, 'adseveratio non sine oppositione;' see Klotz, *Devar.* Vol. II. p. 365 sq. This 'opposition' Meyer traces in the tacit contrast between the subject of his wish, to be present with them, and his actual absence and separation. ἄρτι] '*now;*' see notes on ch. i. 9.

ἀλλάξαι τὴν φωνήν μου] '*to change my voice,*' scil. to a milder, not necessarily to a more mournful (Chrys.), still less to a more severe tone (Michael.), which would be wholly at variance with the preceding affectionate address. There does not, however, appear any historical allusion to the tone which the Apostle used at his last visit (Wieseler, *Chron. Apost.* p. 280, note), but only to the severity of tone adopted generally in this epistle. The peculiar meanings of ἀλλάξαι adopted by Theodoret (τῶν μὲν τὴν ἐκτροπὴν

Ye understand not the deeper meanings of the law, as the allegory of Abraham's two sons, the one typical of the earthly, the other of the heavenly Jerusalem, will fully prove.

21 Λέγετέ μοι, οἱ ὑπὸ νόμον θέλοντες εἶναι,
τὸν νόμον οὐκ ἀκούετε; 22 γέγραπται γὰρ ὅτι
Ἀβραὰμ δύο υἱοὺς ἔσχεν, ἕνα ἐκ τῆς παιδίσκης

θρηνῆσαι τῶν δὲ τὸ βέβαιον θαυμάσαι; comp. also Theod. Mops.), Greg. Nyss. (μέλλων μετατιθέναι τὴν ἱστορίαν εἰς τροπικὴν θεωρίαν), Grotius ('modo asperius modo lenius loqui'), Whitby ('temper my voice'), al., — seem all artificial, and are certainly not confirmed by the two exx. cited by Wetst., viz. Artemidor. II. 20, Dio Chrys. 59, p. 575, in both of which there are qualifications, which render the meaning more apparent. The change of tense παρεῖναι, ἀλλάξαι, must not be overpressed (Peile), such a change being only due to the essential difference of meaning between the two verbs, and even in the case of other verbs being far from common; see Jelf, *Gr.* § 401. 5, Winer, *Gr.* § 40. 2, p. 238. ἀποροῦμαι] '*I am perplexed*,' Arm., ܡܬܡܗ ܐܢܐ [obstupesco] Syr., ἀπορ. being a pass. in a *deponent* sense; compare John xiii. 22, Acts xxv. 20, 2 Cor. iv. 8. Fritz. (*Opusc.* p. 257) still adopts the pure pass. sense, 'nam in vestro cœtu de me trepidatur, *i. e.* sum vobis suspectus' (comp. Vulg., Clarom., 'confundor'), but this is at variance with the regular use of the verb in the N. T., and ill harmonizes with the wish which the Apostle has just expressed. He feels *perplexed* as to how he shall bring back the Galatians to the true faith; by ἀληθεύων he had called out their aversion, perhaps a change of tone might work some good. ἐν ὑμῖν] '*in you*,' scil. '*about you*;' ἐν, as usual, marking as it were the sphere in which, or substratum on which the action takes place; see Winer, *Gr.* § 48. a, p. 345, and comp. 2 Cor. vii. 16, θαῤῥῶ ἐν ὑμῖν. Other constructions of ἀπορ. are found in the N. T., *e. g.* with περί, John xiii. 22, and with εἰς, Acts xxv. 20.

21. λέγετέ μοι κ. τ. λ.] Illustration of the real difference between the law and the promise as typified in the history of the two sons of Abraham; see notes on ver. 24. θέλοντες] '*are willing, desirous*;' not without emphasis and significance; οὐ γὰρ τῆς τῶν πραγμάτων ἀκολουθίας, ἀλλὰ τῆς ἐκείνων ἐκαίρου φιλονεικίας τὸ πρᾶγμα ἦν. τὸν νόμον οὐκ ἀκ.] '*do ye not hear the law*;' 'do ye not give ear to what it really says.' Various shades of meaning have been given to this verb. Usteri and Meyer retain the simplest meaning with ref. to the custom of reading in the synagogues (Luke iv. 16), — an interp. to a certain degree countenanced by the ancient gloss ἀναγινώσκετε [DEFG; 3 mss.; Vulg., Clarom., al.]. As however (1) it is fairly probable that *the law* was not *as commonly* read in Christian communities as in the Jewish [Justin Mart. *Apol.* I. p. 83, *only* mentions τὰ ἀπομνημονεύματα τῶν ἀποστόλων, ἢ τὰ συγγράμματα τῶν προφητῶν; but this must not be *pressed*, as the earliest congregations, probably to some extent, adopted the practice of the synagogue; see Bingham, *Antiq.* XIII. 4], and (2) as οἱ θέλοντες refers rather to persons Judaically inclined than to confirmed Judaists, the meaning '*give ear to*' (*scarcely* so much as 'attento animo percipere,' Schott), seems most suitable in the present case; comp. Matth. x. 14, Luke xvi. 29, 31.

22. γέγραπται γάρ] '*For it is written*;' explanatory proof from the law of the justice of the negation involved in the foregoing question. The

καὶ ἕνα ἐκ τῆς ἐλευθέρας. 23 ἀλλὰ ὁ μὲν ἐκ τῆς παιδίσκης
κατὰ σάρκα γεγέννηται, ὁ δὲ ἐκ τῆς ἐλευθέρας, διὰ τῆς ἐπαγγελίας. 24 ἅτινά ἐστιν ἀλληγορούμενα· αὗται γάρ εἰσιν δύο διαθῆ-

particle γὰρ has here the mixed argumentative and explicative force in which it is so often found in these Epp., and approaches somewhat in meaning to the more definite *profecto;* see Hartung, *Partik.* γάρ, 2. 2, Vol. I. p. 464 sq., Klotz, *Devar.* Vol. II. p. 234 sq., and comp. Hand, *Tursell.* Vol. II. p. 376. The Apostle *explains* by the citation the meaning of his question, while at the same time he slightly *proves* the justice of putting it; see notes *on* 1 *Thess.* ii. 1. τῆς παιδίσκης] '*the bond-maid;*' the well-known one, Hagar. The word, though here, is not always so restricted; see Lobeck, *Phryn.* p. 239.

23. ἀλλὰ] '*Howbeit.*' The full force of this particle may be felt in the statement of the complete opposition of character and nature between the two sons, which it introduces; 'Abraham had two sons; though sprung from a common father, they were *notwithstanding* of essentially different characters.' On the force of this particle, see the good article by Klotz, *Devar.* Vol. II. p. 1 sq. κατὰ σάρκα] '*according to the flesh,*' scil. 'after the regular course of nature,' Bloomf. κατὰ φύσεως ἀκολουθίαν, Chrys.; not perhaps without some idea of imperfection, weakness, etc., and, as the next clause seems to hint, some degree of latent opposition to πνεῦμα; see Müller, *Doctr. of Sin*, Vol. I. p. 355 (Clark), Tholuck, *Stud. u. Krit.* for 1855, p. 487, and comp. notes on ch. iii. 3. διὰ τῆς ἐπαγγελίας] '*by means of, by virtue of* (Hamm.) *the promise,*' not 'under the promise' (Peile); the prep. here marking not merely the 'condition,' 'circumstances' (δι' ὑπομονῆς, Rom. viii. 25), but, as Usteri justly remarks, denoting the *causa medians* of the birth of Isaac. Through the might and by virtue of the promise (see Gen. xviii. 10), Sarah conceived Isaac, even as the virgin conceived our Lord through the divine influence imparted at the Annunciation; see Chrys. *in loc.*, who, however, reads κατ' ἐπαγγελίαν.

24. ἅτινά] '*All which things* viewed in their most general light;' (Col. ii. 23, ἅτινά ἐστι λόγον μὲν ἔχοντα. It is very doubtful whether Usteri is correct in maintaining that ἅτινά is here simply equivalent to ἅ. The difference between ὃς and ὅστις may not be always *very* distinctly marked in the N. T., but there are certainly grounds for asserting that in very many of the cases where ὅστις appears used for ὃς it will be found to be used either,—(1) *Indefinitely;* *i. e.* where the antecedent is more or less indefinite, either (*a*) in its own nature, from involving some general notion (Pape, *Lex.* s. v. ὅστις, 2), or (*b*) from the way the subject is presented to the reader; *e. g.* Phil. i. 28 (where the subj. is really a portion of a sentence) Col. ii. 23, al.; in such cases the relative frequently agrees with the consequent, see exx. in Winer, *Gr.* § 24. 3, p. 150. The present passage appears to fall under this head, as the subject is not merely the facts of the birth of the two sons, but all the circumstances viewed generally:—(2) *Classifically, i. e.* where the subject is represented as one of a class or category; *e. g.* ch. ii. 4, 1 Cor. iii. 17 (see Mey. *in loc.*); comp. Matth. *Gr.* § 483, Jelf, *Gr.* § 816. 4:—(3) *Explicatively, e. g.* Eph. i. 23 (see Harless *in loc.*); not merely in a causal sense, as is commonly asserted; see

και, μία μὲν ἀπὸ ὄρους Σινᾶ, εἰς δουλείαν γεννῶσα, ἥτις ἐστὶν

Ellendt, *Lex. Soph.* s. v. 3, Vol. II. p. 385, comp. Herm. *Œd. Rex.* 688 : — or lastly (4) *Differentially, i. e.* where it denotes an attribute which essentially belongs to the nature of the antecedent; see Jelf, *Gr.* § 816. 5, Krüger, *Sprachl.* § 51. 8. 1 sq. Great difference of opinion, however, still exists among scholars upon this subject. After the instances cited by Struve (who has said all that can be said in favor of an occasional equivalence), *Quæst. Herod.* I. p. 2 sq., it seems best to adopt the opinion of Ellendt, *l. c.*, that though the equivalence of ὅστις and ὃς has been far too generally applied, there are still a *few* instances even in classical Greek. In later Greek this permutation took place more often, see Rost. u. Palm, *Lex.* s. v. II. Bb. 2, Vol. II. p. 547; still it must never be admitted unless none of the above distinctions can fairly be applied.

ἐστιν ἀλληγορούμενα] '*are allegorized*,' '*are allegorical*,' 'by the which things another is meant,' Genev. Transl., ἑτέρως μὲν λεγόμενα, ἑτέρως δὲ νοούμενα, Schol. ap. Matth.; ἀλληλορίαν ἐκάλεσε τὴν ἐκ παραθέσεως τῶν ἤδη γεγονότων πρὸς τὰ παρόντα σύγκρισιν, Theod. Mops. As the simple meaning of the word in this passage has been somewhat obscured by exegetical glosses, it may be observed the ἀλληγορεῖν properly means to '*express or explain one thing under the image of another*' (comp. Plutarch, *de Isid. et Osir.* § 32, p. 363. Ἕλληνες Κρόνον ἀλληγοροῦσι τὸν χρόνον), and hence in the pass., '*to be so expressed or explained*;' comp. Clem. Alex. *Strom.* v. 11, p. 687, ἀλληγορεῖσθαί τινα ἐκ τῶν ὀνομάτων ὁσιώτερον, ib. *Protrept.* 11, p. 86, ὄφις ἀλληγορεῖται ἡδονὴ ἐπὶ γαστέρα ἕρπουσα; Porphyr. *Vit. Pythag.* p. 185 (Cantabr. 1655), where ἀλληλορεῖσθαι is in antithesis to κοινολογεῖσθαι; see exx. Wetst. *in loc.*, and in Kypke, *Obs.* Vol. II. p. 282. The explanation of Chrys. is thus perfectly clear and satisfactory; οὐ τοῦτο δὲ μόνον (ἡ ἱστορία) πραδηλοῖ ὅπερ φαίνεται, ἀλλὰ καὶ ἄλλα τινα ἀναγορεύει. The remarks made above, ch. iii. 16, apply here with equal force to the late attempts of several modern expositors (*e. g.* Meyer, De Wette, Jowett) to represent this as a *subjective, i. e.* to speak plainly, — an erroneous interpretation of St. Paul arising from his Rabbinical education. It would be well for such writers to remember that St. Paul is here declaring, under the influence of the Holy Spirit, that the passage he has cited has a second and a deeper meaning than it appears to have: that it has that meaning, then, is a positive, objective, and indisputable truth; see Olshausen's note *in loc.*, Hofmann, *Schriftb.* Vol. II. 2, p. 59, and the sound remarks of Waterland (*Pref. to Script.* Vol. IV. p. 159) on the general nature of an allegory.

αὗται] '*these women*;' τῶν παιδίων ἐκείνων αἱ μητέρες ἡ Σάῤῥα καὶ ἡ Ἄγαρ, Chrys. The insertion of the art. before δύο (*Rec.*) is opposed to the authority of all the uncial MSS., and is rejected by nearly all modern editors.

μία μὲν κ. τ. λ.] '*one indeed from Mount Sinai*,' scil. originating from, taking its rise from, ἀπό, with its usual force, marking the place or centre (Alf.) whence the διαθήκη emanated; compare Krüger, *Sprachl.* § 68. 16. 5. The μὲν has here no strictly correlative δέ, as that in ver. 26 refers to τῇ νῦν Ἱερουσ. in the verse immediately preceding; comp. Winer, *Gr.* § 63. 2. e, p. 507.

εἰς δουλείαν γεννῶσα] '*bearing children unto bondage*,' *i. e.* to pass under and to inherit the lot of bondage; δούλη ἦν [Ἄγαρ] καὶ εἰς δουλείαν ἐγέννα, Theoph.

ἥτις ἐστὶν Ἄγαρ] '*and this is Hagar*.' The use of ὅστις

Ἄγαρ. [25] τὸ γὰρ Ἄγαρ Σινᾶ ὄρος ἐστὶν ἐν τῇ Ἀραβίᾳ·

25. τὸ γὰρ Ἄγαρ Σινᾶ ὄρος] The reading adopted by *Lachm.* viz. τὸ γὰρ Σινᾶ with CFG; 17; Boern., Vulg., Æth., Arm.; Cyr., Epiph., Dam.; Orig. (interpr.) Hieron., al. (*Ust.*, *De W.*, *Griesb.* 'forsitan;' see Hofm. *Schriftb.* Vol. II. 2. p. 62) is plausible and gives a very satisfactory sense. Still *Tisch.* ed. 2 (see *Mill*, *Mey.*, *Scholz*,) appears to have rightly returned to the *Text. Rec.*, as the juxtaposition of γὰρ and Ἄγαρ would render (on paradiplomatic considerations, Pref. p. xvi.) the omission of the latter word very probable. The conversion of the former into δὲ [*Tisch.* ed. 1 with ADE; 37. 73. 80, Copt. (Wilk., not Bött.), Cyr. 1.] was perhaps suggested by the μὲν in ver. 24.

here seems to fall under (4): it is this covenant peculiarly, this one of which the *differentia* is, that it originates from Sinai, which is allegorically identical with Hagar; see above, and esp. Jelf, *Gr.* § 816. 4.

25. τὸ γὰρ Ἄγαρ κ. τ. λ.] '*For the word Hagar is Mount Sinai in Arabia,*' *i. e.* among the Arabians; τὸ δὲ Σινᾶ ὄρος οὕτω μεθερμηνεύεται τῇ ἐπιχωρίῳ αὐτῶν γλώττῃ, Chrys.: etymological reason, added almost parenthetically, for the foregoing statement of the allegorical identity of Mount Sinai and Hagar, τὸ not agreeing with Ἄγαρ but referring to it in its abstract form (Jelf, *Gr.* § 457. 1), and ἐν τῇ Ἀραβίᾳ not supplying a mere topographical statement (comp. Syr., Copt.), but serving to define the people by whom Sinai was so called; τοῦτο τῇ τῶν Ἀράβων γλώσσῃ Ἄγαρ καλεῖται, Schol. ap. Matth.
It is thus obvious that this interpretation presupposes that Ἄγαρ was a provincial name of the mountain. Nor does this seem at all improbable, though we are bound to say that the corroborative evidence from the modern appellations of the mountain, is less strong than the appeals to it (Bloomf. Forster, *Geogr. of Arabia*, Vol. I. p. 182) would seem to imply. The best authority for the assertion seems to be the careful and diligent Büsching (*Erdbeschr.* Vol. V. p. 535), who adduces the statement of Harant, that Sinai was still called 'Hadschar' in his time ('Hadsch heisst bekanntlich auch Fels,' Ritter, *Erdkunde*, Vol. XVI. Part. I. p. 1086), though now it is *commonly* called either 'Dschebel Musa' (in a more limited reference), or 'Dschebel et Tûr;' see Ritter, *Erdk.* Vol. XIV. Part I. p. 535, Martiniere, *Dict. Geogr. et Crit.* s. v. 'Sinai.' It must also be said that the evidence from etymology is also not *very* strong, as the Arabian word 'Hadjar' (comp. Chald. יְגַר Gen. xxxi. 47), appears certainly only to mean 'a stone' (see Freytag, *Lex. Arab.* s. v. Vol. I. p. 346), still, — even if we leave unnoticed the fact of there having been a town called Ἄγαρ in the vicinity (Ewald; compare Assemann, *Bibl. Orient.* Vol. III. 2, p. 753), there are so many analogous instances of mountains bearing names in which the word 'stone' is incorporated (*e. g.* 'Weissestein' al.), that there seems nothing unnatural in supposing that Ἄγαρ actually was, and possibly *may* be now, the strictly *provincial* name of the portion of the mountain now commonly called 'Dschebel Musa.' This St. Paul might have learnt during his stay in that country.
It must be admitted that we escape all this if we adopt the reading of *Lachmann*: τὸ γὰρ Σινᾶ . . . Ἀραβίᾳ will then form a parenthesis, and the emphasis will rest on ἐν τῇ Ἀραβίᾳ; 'For Mount Sinai is *in Arabia*,' — Arabia, the home of the bond-maid's children, the υἱοὶ

συστοιχεῖ δὲ τῇ νῦν Ἱερουσαλήμ, δουλεύει γὰρ μετὰ τῶν τέκνων αὐτῆς. 26 ἡ δὲ ἄνω Ἱερουσαλὴμ ἐλευθέρα ἐστιν, ἥτις ἐστὶν

Ἄγαρ, Baruch iii. 23; comp. Hofmann, *Schriftb.* Vol. II. 2. p. 62. In this case also διαθήκη is the subject of συστοιχεῖ (opp. to Hofm.), without the grammatical distortion in making Hagar the subject. Still there is a difficulty in the covenant being said συστοιχεῖν; as δουλεία (δουλεύει γάρ) is plainly the *tertium comparationis* between Hagar and Jerusalem, and the assertion ἥτις ἐστὶν Ἄγαρ is really not so much supported by the sentence which follows, as by the emphasis which is assumed to rest on ἐν τῇ Ἀραβ., the last words of it. We have, therefore, nothing better to offer than the former interpretation. συστοιχεῖ δέ] '*she stands too in the same file* or *rank with*,' 'is conformable with,' Arm., the nominative obviously being Ἄγαρ ('*quæ* consonat,' Clarom.) not Σινᾶ ὄρος (Vulg.), nor even μία διαθήκη (De W.), as there would thus be no point of comparison (δουλεία) between the subject of συστοιχεῖ and ἡ νῦν Ἱερουσ. (Mey.); see above. The δὲ ('und zwar,' Hilgenf.) appears to add a fresh explanatory characteristic, and retains its proper force in the latent contrast that the addition of a new fact brings with it; see Klotz, *Devar.* Vol. II. p. 362. Συστοιχεῖν is best illustrated by Polyb. *Hist.* x. 21 (cited by Wetst.), συζυγοῦντας καὶ συστοιχοῦντας διαμένειν: where συζυγ. evidently refers to soldiers in the same *rank*, συστοιχ. to soldiers in the same *file*: see Fell *in loc.*, where the two lists are drawn out; each name in which συστοιχεῖ with those in the same list, but ἀντιστοιχεῖ with those in the opposite list. The geographical gloss of Chrys. γειτνιάζει, ἅπτεται ('qui conjunctus est,' Vulg., 'gamarko' [comp. 'marge'] Goth.), due probably to the assumption that Σινᾶ ὄρος is the nom. to συστοιχεῖ, is not exegetically tenable, and has been rejected by nearly all modern expositors. τῇ νῦν Ἱερ.] '*the present Jerusalem*,' scil. τῇ ἐνταῦθα, τῇ ἐπὶ γῆς, Schol. ap. Matth.: 'antitheton *supernæ*; *nunc* temporis est, *supra* loci,' Bengel. δουλεύει γάρ] '*for she is in bondage*,' scil. ταῖς νομικαῖς παρατηρήσεσιν, Schol. ap. Matth., comp. Hofmann, *Schriftb.* Vol. II. 2, p. 61; the nom. being ἡ νῦν Ἱερ., and the γὰρ serving to confirm the justice of the assertion of συστοιχία. The reading δὲ [*Rec.* with D3EJK; al.; Syr.-Phil. (marg.), al.; Ff.] is rightly rejected by most recent editors with preponderant external evidence, viz. ABCD1FG; many mss. and Vv.

26. ἡ δὲ ἄνω Ἱερουσαλήμ] '*But the Jerusalem above*;' contrast to the ἡ νῦν Ἱερ. of the preceding verse: the correspondence of Sarah, *i. e.* the other covenant, with the heavenly Jerusalem is assumed as sufficiently obvious from the context. The meaning of ἄνω can scarcely be considered doubtful. It cannot be *local* (Mount Sion, ἡ ἄνω πόλις, Elsner, al.) as this is inconsistent with the foregoing νῦν, nor yet *temporal* ('the ancient Jerus., the Salem of Melchizedek,' Michael. al.), as such a ref. is inconsistent with a context which only points to later periods, — but has simply its usual *ethical* reference, 'above,' 'heavenly,' 'quæ sursum est,' Vulg., Clarom., ܕܠܥܠ, Syr.-Phil.; compare Ἱερουσαλὴμ ἐπουράνιος, Heb. xii. 22, Ἱερουσ. καινή, Rev. iii. 12, xxi. 2; see the rabbinical quotations in Wetst., and comp. Ust. *Lehrb.* II. 1. 2, p. 182. As Jerusalem ἡ νῦν was the centre of Judaism and the ancient theocratic kingdom, so Jerusalem ἡ ἄνω is the typical

μήτηρ ἡμῶν· 27 γέγραπται γάρ, Εὐφράνθητι στεῖρα ἡ οὐ τίκτουσα, ῥῆξον καὶ βόησον ἡ οὐκ ὠδίνουσα, ὅτι πολλὰ τὰ τέκνα τῆς ἐρήμου μᾶλλον ἢ τῆς ἐχούσης τὸν ἄνδρα. 28 ὑμεῖς δέ, ἀδελφοί,

representation of Christianity, and the Messianic kingdom. On the threefold meaning of Ἱερουσ. in the N. T. (scil. the heavenly community of the righteous, the Church on earth, the new Jerus. on the glorified earth), and the distinction observed by St. John between Ἱερουσαλήμ (the sacred name) and Ἱεροσόλυμα, see Hengstengb. *on Apocal.* Vol. II. p. 319 (Clark); and on the general use and meaning of the expression, the learned treatise of Schoettgen, *Horæ Hebr.* Vol. I. p. 1205—1248.

ἥτις κ. τ. λ.] '*and this one* (this ἄνω Ἱερουσ.) *is our mother*;' ἥτις being used appy., as in ver. 25, in its 'differential' sense (see notes on ver. 24) and retaining the emphasis, which, as the order of the words seems to imply, does not rest on ἡμῶν (Winer). The addition of πάντων before ἡμῶν (*Rec.* [*Lachm.*], with AJK; mss.; Arab.-Pol., al.) is rightly rejected by *Tisch.* al., with BCDEFG; 5. 6, and majority of Vv. and Ff.

27. γέγραπται γάρ] '*for it is written*,' proof of the clause immediately preceding, ἥτις κ. τ. λ., from the prophetic consolation of Isaiah (ch. liv. 1), which though esp. addressed primarily to Israel and Jerusalem (Knobel, *Jes.* p. 380), was directed with a further and fuller reference to the Church of which they were the types.

ῥῆξον] '*break forth (into a cry)*.' The ellipsis is usually supplied by φωνήν; see Rost u. Palm, s. v. ῥηγν., and the numerous examples of ῥῆξον φωνήν cited by Wetst. *in loc.* The critical accuracy of Schott leads him to supply εὐφροσύνην (Isaiah xlix. 13, lii. 9), reverting to εὐφράνθητι, on the principle that the ellipsis is always to be supplied from the context; compare 'erumpere gaudium,' Terent. *Eun.* III. 5. 2. It is perhaps more simple to supply βοήν, derived from βόησον with which ῥῆξον is so closely joined, or still more probably, to regard ῥῆξον as understood from long usage to be simply equivalent to κράξον; ῥήξατο· κραξάτω, Hesych. ὅτι πολλὰ μᾶλλον κ. τ. λ.] '*for many are the children of the desolate more than of her that hath the husband*,' 'multi filii desertæ magis quam,' etc. Vulg., Clarom., Goth.; πολλὰ μᾶλλον being not simply equivalent to πλείονα ἤ, but implying that both should have *many*, but the desolate one *more* than the other (Mey.). The compound expression τῆς ἐχούσης τὸν ἄνδρα answers to the simpler בְּעוּלָה (ܒܥܝܠܬܐ, Syr.; sim. Æth., Arm.) in the original, and is thus little more than 'the married one,' the force of the art. (τὸν ἄνδρα) being perhaps, as Alf. observes, too delicate to be expressed in English. This prophecy is somewhat differently applied by Clem. *ad Cor.* II. 2, and Orig. *in Rom.* vi. Vol. II. p. 33 (ed. Lomm.), ἡ στεῖρα being referred more peculiarly to the Gentile church as opposed to the Jewish church (τῶν δοκούντων ἔχειν Θεόν); whereas St. Paul understands under the image of Sarah (μήτηρ ἡμῶν) the church, as composed both of Jews *and* Gentiles, and thus as in contradistinction to the children of the law, the bond-children of the ancient theocracy.

28. ὑμεῖς δέ] '*But ye*;' application of the foregoing allegory to the case of those whom the Apostle is now addressing, the δὲ being here μεταβατικόν (Hartung, *Partik.* δέ, 2. 3. Vol. I. p. 165, see notes on ch. i. 11, and marking a *tran-*

κατὰ Ἰσαὰκ ἐπαγγελίας τέκνα ἐστέ. [29] ἀλλ' ὥσπερ τότε ὁ κατὰ σάρκα γεννηθεὶς ἐδίωκεν τὸν κατὰ Πνεῦμα, οὕτως καὶ νῦν.

sition to the readers while also hinting at their contrast to the children of τῆς ἐχούσης τὸν ἄνδρα. If the reading of *Rec.* ἡμ.-ἐσμέν be adopted, which, however, though well supported [AC D[3]E(?)JK; mss.; Syr., Vulg., Copt., Goth., Æth.-Platt, Arm.; Chrys., Theod., Theodrt., al.], is opposed to good external evidence [BD[1]E(?)FG; Clarom., Sah., mss.; Æth--Pol.; Orig., Iren.; Ambr., Ambrst., al.], and is suspicious as appy. being a confirmation to ver. 31, then δὲ must be considered as indicating a *resumption* of ver. 26, after the parenthetical quotation in ver. 27; see Klotz, *Devar.* Vol. II. p. 377, Hartung, *Partik.* δέ, 3. 1, Vol. I. p. 173. κατὰ Ἰσαάκ] '*after the example of Isaac;*' κατὰ pointing to the 'norma' or example which was furnished by Isaac; so 1 Pet. i. 15, κατὰ τὸν καλέσαντα, Eph. iv. 24, Col. iii. 10: see Winer, *Gr.* § 49. d, p. 358. Several exx. of this usage are cited by Kypke, *Obs.* Vol. II. 284, and Wetst. *in loc.* ἐπαγγελίας τέκνα] '*children of promise.*' These words admit of three interpretations; — (*a*) 'children who have God's promise;' or (*b*) 'children promised by God,' *i. e.* the seed promised by God to Abraham; or (*c*) 'children of, *i. e.* by virtue of, promise.' Both the emphasis, which appears from the order to rest on ἐπαγγ., and the words διὰ τῆς ἐπαγγ., ver. 23, seem decisively in favor of the last interpretation; compare Rom. ix. 8, and see Fritz. *in loc.*

29. ἀλλ' ὥσπερ] '*Howbeit as;*' special notice of an instructive and suggestive comparison between the circumstances of the types and of the antitypes, ἀλλὰ with its usual adversative force directing the reader's attention to a fresh statement, which involves a species of contrast to the former; 'ye are children of promise it is true, *howbeit* ye must expect persecution;' see esp. Chrys. *in loc.*, and comp. Klotz. *Devar.* Vol. II. p. 29. ἐδίωκεν] '*persecuted,*' 'persequebatur,' Vulg., Clarom., al.; imperf., as designating an action which still spiritually continues; see Winer, *Gr.* § 40. 3, p. 240. Whether the reference is to be regarded as (*a*) exclusively to Genesis xxi. 9, וַתֵּרֶא שָׂרָה אֶת־בֶּן־הָגָר · · · · מְצַחֵק (Alf., Ewald, al.), or (*b*) to an ancient, and therefore, as cited by St. Paul, *true* tradition of the Jewish Church (see below) will somewhat depend on the meaning assigned to צָחַק in Gen. *l. c.* That it *may* mean 'mocked' (opp. to Knobel *in loc.*) seems certain from Gen. xxxix. 14, 17, and indeed from the command in Gen. xxi. 10. As however it *does* appear to mean no more than 'playing like a child,' παίζοντα, LXX., 'ludentem,' Vulg. (see Tisch. *in loc.*, and Gesen. *Lex.* s. v.), and as Joseph. (*Antiq.* I. 12, 3), says only κακουργεῖν αὐτὸν δυνάμενων, it seems on the whole best to adopt (*b*); see *Beresch.* LIII. 15 (Wetst.), 'Ismael tulit arcum et sagittas et jaculatus est Isaacum, et præ se tulit ac si luderet,' and Studer (in Ust.), who alludes to a similar rabbinical interpretation founded on the cabalistic equivalence in numbers of the letters in צַחֵק and the explicit הָגַ־; comp. Hackspan, *Notes on Script.* Vol. I. 220. τὸν κατὰ Πνεῦμα] '*him that was according to the Spirit,*' scil. γεννηθέντα, supplied from the preceding clause. The prep. it need scarcely be said does not here point to the cause or medium, 'Dei opera' (Vatabl.), but simply 'according to,' *i. e.* in accordance with the

[30] ἀλλὰ τί λέγει ἡ γραφή; Ἔκβαλε τὴν παιδίσκην καὶ τὸν υἱὸν
αὐτῆς· οὐ γὰρ μὴ κληρονομήσῃ ὁ υἱὸς τῆς παιδίσκης μετὰ τοῦ
As ye are free, stand fast in your freedom. υἱοῦ τῆς ἐλευθέρας. [31] Διό,

working by promise of the Holy Spirit; compare Rom. iv. 19, 20. Κατὰ σάρκα refers to the *natural* laws according to which Ishmael was born; κατὰ Πνεῦμα, the *supernatural* laws according to which Isaac was conceived and born.

οὕτως καὶ νῦν] '*so also is it now;*' scil. those descended from Abraham κατὰ σάρκα (the Jews) still persecute the free children of promise (the Christians). The sentiment is expressed in general terms, but perhaps may here be conceived as pointed at the pernicious efforts of the Judaizers, which probably involved persecution both spiritual and material; comp. Meyer *in loc.* A good sermon on this text, though with a somewhat special application, will be found in Farindon, *Serm.* XI. Vol. I. p. 287 sq. (ed. 1849.)

30. ἀλλά] '*Nevertheless;*' strongly consolatory declaration (παραμυθία ἱκανή, Chrys.) introducing a distinct contrast with the preceding declaration of the persecution, and calling away the thought of the reader to a totally fresh aspect; 'avocat mentem ab illis tristibus ad illam rem, quam jam opponit,' Klotz, *Devar.* Vol. II. p. 6.

ἡ γραφή] '*the Scripture.*' The following words are really the words of Sarah to Abraham, but confirmed, ver. 12, by God Himself; 'ejecta est Agar Sarâ postulante et Deo annuente,' Est. The interrogative form which introduces the citation gives it force and vigor; comp. Rom. iv. 3, x. 8, xi. 4.

οὐ κληρονομήσῃ] '*shall in no wise be heir;*' emphatic: 'liberi autem ex concubinâ *conditionis servilis* aut extraneâ seu gentili a successione plane apud Ebræos excludebantur,' Selden, *de Success.* cap. 3, Vol. II. p. 11. Hammond cites the instance of Jephthah, who was thrust out by his brethren, under the second condition of the law, as the son of a strange woman; Judges xi. 2. With regard to the use of οὐ μὴ with the subj. [κληρονομήσει BDE; mss.; Theoph.], it may be observed that the distinction drawn by Hermann (*Œd. Col.* 853) between οὐ μὴ with future indic. (duration or futurity) and with aor. subj. (speedy occurrence) is not applicable to the N. T., on accouut of (1) the varyings (as here; (2) the decided violations of the rule where the MSS. are unanimous, *e. g.* 1 Thess. iv. 15: and (3) the obvious prevalence of the subjunctive over the future, both in the N. T. and 'fatiscens Græcitas;' see Lobeck, *Phryn.* p. 722, Thiersch, *Pentat.* II. 15, p. 190, and exx. in Gayler, p. 433. On the general use of the united particles see Winer, *Gr.* § 56. 3, p. 450, and esp. Donalds. *Crat.* § 394, Gayler, *Partic. Neg.* p. 405, exx. p. 430, and on the best mode of translation, notes *on* 1 *Thess.* iv. 15 (*Transl.*)

31. διό] '*Wherefore;*' commencement of a short semi-paragraph stating the consolatory application of what has preceded ('*quamobrem;* aptius duas res conjungit,' Klotz. *Devar.* Vol. II. p. 173), and passing into an exhortation in the following verse. It is *very* difficult to decide on the exact connection, as St. Paul's use of διό does not appear to have been very fixed. Sometimes, as Rom. ii. 1, Eph. ii. 11, iii. 13, iv. 25, it begins a paragraph; sometimes (especially with καί) it *closely* connects clauses, as Rom. i. 24, iv. 22, 2 Cor. iv. 13, v. 9, Phil. ii. 9; while in 2 Cor. xii. 10, 1 Thess. v. 11 (imperat.), it closes a paragraph, though not in a way

ἀδελφοί, οὐκ ἐσμὲν παιδίσκης τέκνα ἀλλὰ τῆς ἐλευθέρας. V. 1 τῇ

1. τῇ ἐλευθερίᾳ κ. τ. λ.] The difficulty of deciding on the true reading of this passage, owing to the great variation of MSS., is *very* great. The reading of *Lachm.*, τῇ ἐλευθερίᾳ ἡμᾶς Χριστὸς ἠλευθέρωσεν στήκετε οὖν, is plausible, and well supported, as ᾗ is omitted by ABCD[1]; mss.; Copt., Damasc., al.; still the doubtful meaning of the dat. ἐλευθερ. (not the article, at which *Rück.* stumbles), and the abrupt character of the whole, make it, on internal grounds, very difficult to admit. *Tisch.* (so *Matth.*, *Scholz*, *Rinck*, *Rück.*, *Olsh.*, al., though differing in other points) seems rightly to have retained ᾗ with D[3]EJK (FG ᾗ ἐλευθ. ἡμ.; compare Vulg., Clarom.); mss. Syr.; Chrys., Theod. (2), al., as the H is less likely to have arisen from a repetition of the first letter of HMAΣ (*Mey.*), than to have

strictly similar to the present. On the whole, it seems most probable that St. Paul was about to pass on to an application of, not a deduction from, the previous remarks and citation. He commences with διό, but the word ἐλευθέρας suggesting a digression (see Davidson, *Introd.* Vol. II. p. 148), he turns the application by means of τῇ ἐλευθερίᾳ, into an inferential exhortation (Æth. erroneously makes the first clause a reason 'quia Christus'), ver. 1, and recommences a new parallel train of thought with ἴδε ἐγώ. We thus put a slight pause after iv. 30, and a fuller one after v. 1. If ἡμεῖς δὲ be adopted [AC; mss.; Copt.; Cyr. (1), Damasc., al.] the connection will be more easy. Ver. 30 describes the fate of the bond-children; ver. 31 will then form a sort of consolatory conclusion, deriving some force from the emphatic κληρον.; 'but *we* shall have a different fate; we shall be inheritors, for we are children, not of a bond-maid, but of a free-woman.' This reading is, however, more than doubtful, as appearing to be only a repetition from ver. 28. For ἄρα (*Rec.*), which would perhaps imply a little more decidedly than διὸ a continuance of what was said (Donalds. *Crat.* § 192), the external evidence [JK (ἄρα οὖν FG, Theodrt.] is very weak, and the probability of correction not inconsiderable. παιδίσκης] '*of a bond-maid*,' scil. 'of any bond-maid.' The omission of the article *may* be accounted for, — not by the negative form of the proposition (Middleton *in loc.*), but by the principle of correlation, whereby when the governing article is anarthrous (here *possibly* so after the predicative ἐσμέν, Middl. p. 43) the governed becomes anarthrous also; see Middl. *Gr. Art.* III. 3. 7, p. 50 (ed. Rose), comp. Winer, *Gr.* § 19. 2. b, p. 113 sq. As, however, παιδίσκη appears in every other place with the art. (even after the prep. in ver. 23), the present omission is perhaps more probably regarded as intentional, and as designed to give a general character to the Apostle's conclusion; see Peile *in loc.* Τῆς ἐλευθέρας cannot, however, be translated 'of *a* free woman.'

CHAPTER V. 1. τῇ ἐλευθερίᾳ κ. τ. λ.] '*Stand firm, then, in the freedom for which*,' etc.; inferential exhortation from the declaration immediately preceding. Of the many explanations which the expression τῇ ἐλευθερίᾳ στήκειν has received, the two following appear to be the most probable; (α) '*libertati stare*, quam deserere est nefas,' Fritz. *Rom.* xii. 12, Vol. III. p. 80, Winer, *Gr.* § 31. 3. obs. p. 244 (ed. 5; less distinctly p. 188, ed. 6); (β) '*quod attinet ad libertatem, stare*,' Bretschn., Meyer *on* 2 Cor. i. 24. The objection to (α) is, that such expressions as τῇ

ἐλευθερίᾳ ᾗ ἡμᾶς Χριστὸς ἠλευθέρωσεν στήκετε οὖν, καὶ μὴ πάλιν ζυγῷ δουλείας ἐνέχεσθε.

been omitted from having been accidentally merged in it. His omission of οὖν, however, with DE; Vulg., Clarom., Syr. (Philox.); Theodrt. (2) against ABC[1] FG; 10. 17. 31. 37, al.; Boern., Augiens., Goth., Copt., al.; Cyr., Aug., al.—does not seem tenable. The order Χριστὸς ἡμᾶς (*Rec.*) has but weak external support [CJK; mss.; *appy.* some Vv.; Chrys., Theod.], and is reversed by most recent editors.

θλίψει ὑπομένειν are not strictly similar, as the idea of a hostile attitude (dat. incommodi) is involved in the dative, 'calamitatem non subterfugientes,' etc., so ὑποστῆναί τινι, μένειν τινι (Bernh. *Synt.* III. 13. b, p. 98), and Hom. *Il.* XXI. 600, στῆναί τινι. The latter interpretation seems thus the most correct; the dative, however, must not be translated too laxly ('as regards the freedom'), as it serves to call attention to the exact sphere in which, and to which, the action is limited, *e. g.* ἕστη τῇ διανοίᾳ, Polyb. XXI. 9. 8; see Scheuerl. *Synt.* § 22. 2, p. 179, and notes on ch. i. 22. It may be remarked that we sometimes find an inserted ἐν (1 Cor. xvi. 13, compare Rück.) without much apparent difference of meaning, still it does not seem hypercritical to say that in this latter case the idea of the 'sphere or element in which' was designed by the writer to come more distinctly into view; compare Winer, *Gr.* § 31. 8, p. 194. On the meaning of στήκειν, which *per se* is only 'stare' (Vulg., Clarom.), but which derives its fuller meaning from the context; comp. Chrys., στήκετε εἰπών, τὸν σάλον ἔδειξε, and see notes *on Phil.* i. 27. ᾗ] '*for which;*' dat. commodi. The usual *ablatival* explanation 'quâ nos liberavit' (Vulg.), scil. ἣν ἡμῖν ἔδωκεν (so expressly Conyb.), may perhaps be justified by the common constructions χαίρειν χαρᾷ, etc., but as it is very doubtful whether this construct. occurs in St. Paul's Epp. (1 Thess. iii. 9 seems an instance of *attraction;* see notes *in loc.*), it seems safer to adhere to the former explanation; see Meyer *in loc.* (obs.) For a good sermon on the notion of Christian liberty, see Bp. Hall, *Serm.* XXVI. Vol. v. p. 339 sq. (Talboys).

πάλιν refers to the previous subservience of the Galatians to heathenism; see notes on ch. iv. 9. ζυγῷ δουλείας] '*the yoke of bondage,*' not '*a* yoke,' etc., Copt., Ewald, al.; the anarthrous δουλεία (comp. Winer, *Gr.* §19. 1, p. 109) being appy. used somewhat indefinitely to mark the general character of the ζυγόν, and by the principle of correlation causing the governing noun to lose its article; see Middleton, *Gr. Art.* III. 3. 6, and compare notes on ch. v. 31. It will be observed that πάλιν is more easily explained on the hypothesis of ζυγῷ being taken indefinitely; the present view, however, seems most in accordance with the definite statement in ver. 2; ζυγὸν δὲ δουλείας τὴν κατὰ νόμου ζωήν, Theod. On the use of the gen. as denoting the *predominant nature* or *quality* inherent in the governing noun, see Scheuerl. *Synt.* § 16. 3, p. 115, and compare Soph. *Aj.* 944, οἷα δουλείας ζυγά, Æsch. *Agam.* 365, δουλείας γάγγαμον. ἐνέχεσθε] '*be held fast;*' not exactly ܬܬܥܒܕܘܢ [mancipemini, subjiciatis vos], but simply 'implicamini,' Beza, with ref. perhaps to the tenacity of the hold, and the difficulty to shake it off; comp. Beng. For exx. of the use of

If ye submit to circumcision, ye are bound to the whole law, and your union with Christ is wholly void.

2 Ἴδε ἐγὼ Παῦλος λέγω ὑμῖν ὅτι ἐὰν πε-
ριτέμνησθε Χριστὸς ὑμᾶς οὐδὲν ὠφελήσει·
3 μαρτύρομαι δὲ πάλιν παντὶ ἀνθρώπῳ περιτεμνομένῳ ὅτι ὀφει-

the verb both in a physical (Herod. II. 121, ἐνέχομαι τῇ παγῇ), and in an ethical sense (Plutarch *Symp.* II. qu. 3. 1, ἐνέχεσθαι δόγμασιν Πυθαγαρικοῖς), see Kypke, *Obs.* Vol. II. p. 285, and Wetst. *in loc.*

2. ἴδε ἐγὼ Παῦλος] '*Behold I Paul;*' emphatic and warning declaration (τόση ἀπειλή, Chrys.) of the dangerous consequences, and worse than uselessness of undergoing circumcision. The Apostle's introduction of his own name (compare 2 Cor. x. 1, Eph. iii. 1), prefaced by the arresting ἴδε ('attentionem excitantis est,' Grot.), has been differently explained. The most natural view seems to be that it was to increase conviction (θαῤῥοῦντος ἦν οἷς λέγει, Chrys., comp. Theod.) and to add to the assertion the weight of his Apostolic dignity; τῆς τοῦ προσώπου ἀξιοπιστίας ἀρκούσης ἀντὶ πάσης ἀποδείξεως, Chrys. On the accentuation of ἴδε, which, according to the grammarians, is oxytone in Attic and paroxytone in non-Attic Greek, see Winer, *Gr.* § 6. 1, p. 47. ἐὰν περιτεμν.] '*if ye be circumcised;*' *i. e.* 'if you continue to follow that rite,' the present marking the action as one still going on. On the use of ἐὰν with pres. subj., compare notes on ch. i. 8, 9. οὐδὲν ὠφελήσει] '*shall profit you nothing;*' the fut., having no ref. whatever to the nearness of the Lord's παρουσία (Mey.), but simply marking the certain *result* of such a course of practice; 'Christ (as you will find) will never profit you anything;' see Winer, *Gr.* § 40. 6, p. 250, and compare Schmalf. *Synt.* § 57, p. 116 sq.

3. μαρτύρομαι δέ] '*yea I bear witness,*' testificor *autem,*' Vulg., Clarom., not 'enim,' Beza; further and slightly contrasted statement; the δὲ not being merely connective, but as usual implying a certain degree of opposition between the clause it introduces and the preceding declaration; 'not only will Christ prove no benefit to you, *but* you will in addition become debtors to the law;' see Klotz, *Devar.* Vol. II. p. 362, Hermann, *Viger*, No. 343. b, and for a notice of the similar use of 'autem,' Hand. *Tursell.* Vol. I. p. 562. The verb μαρτύρομαι, a δὶς λεγόμ., in St. Paul's Epp. (Eph. iv. 24, compare Acts xx. 26), is here used in the sense of μαρτυροῦμαι, appy. involving the idea of a solemn declaration, as if before witnesses; comp. notes *on Eph.* iv. 24. That there is no ellipsis of Θεὸν (Hilgenf., Bretschn.) appears plainly from Eph. *l. c.*, and from the similar usage of the word in classical Greek, *e. g.* Plato, *Phileb.* 47 D, ταῦτα δὲ τότε μὲν οὐκ ἐμαρτυράμεθα, νῦν δὲ λεγόμεν. Dindorf in Steph. *Thess.* s. v. cites Eustath. *Il.* p. 1221. 33, ὡς αἱ ἱστορίαι μαρτύρονται. πάλιν may refer to the preceding verse, or to a previous declaration of the same kind made by word of mouth. The former is more probable, as παντὶ ἀνθρώπῳ appears a more expanded application of ὑμῖν, ver. 2; οὐχ ὑμῖν λέγω μόνον, φησίν, ἀλλὰ καὶ παντὶ ἀνθρώπῳ περιτεμν., Chrys.; see Neander, *Planting*, Vol. I. p. 214 note (Bohn). περιτεμνομένῳ] '*submitting to be circumcised,*' '*undergoing circumcision,*' 'circumcidente se,' Vulg., Clarom., or, more idiomatically '*qui* curat se circumcidi,' Beza, — but less accurately, as the participle is anarthrous, and what is called a tertiary predicate; see Donalds. *Crat.* § 306, ib. *Gr.* § 495.

λέτης ἐστὶν ὅλον τὸν νόμον ποιῆσαι. 4 κατηργήθητε ἀπὸ τοῦ
Χριστοῦ οἵτινες ἐν νόμῳ δικαιοῦσθε, τῆς χάριτος ἐξεπέσατε.
5 ἡμεῖς γὰρ Πνεύματι ἐκ πίστεως ἐλπίδα δικαιοσύνης ἀπεκδεχόμεθα.

The tense περιτεμν., not περιτμηθέντι or περιτετμημένῳ, must not be overlooked: it was not the circumcised, *as such*, that had become in this strict sense ὀφειλέται ὅλον τὸν νόμον ποιῆσαι, but he who was designedly undergoing the rite. Ὅλον, as its position shows, is emphatic; ὅλην ἐφειλκύσω τὴν δεσποτείαν, Chrys.

4. κατηργήθητε ἀπὸ τοῦ Χρ.] '*Ye were done away from Christ*,' '*Your union with Christ became void*,' scil. 'when you entered upon the course which now ye are pursuing;' further and forcible explanation of Χριστὸς ὑμᾶς οὐδὲν ὠφελήσει (ver. 2), the absence of all connecting particles serving to give the statement both vigor and emphasis. The construction is what is called 'prægnans' (Rom. vii. 2, 6, see Winer, *Gr.* § 66. 2, p. 547); ἀπό, *strictly* considered, not belonging to κατηργέθητε in the sense of ἠλευθερώθητε ἀπό, but to some word which can easily be supplied, *e. g.* κατηργήθητε καὶ ἐχωρίσθητε ἀπὸ Χρ., 'nulli estis redditi et a Christo avulsi;' comp. 2 Cor. xi. 3, φθείρεσθαι ἀπό, and Fritz. *Rom. l. c.* Vol. II. p. 8, 9. The verb καταργέω is a favorite word with St. Paul, being used in his Epp. (the Ep. to the Hebrews not being included) twenty-five times. In the rest of the N. T. it is used only twice, Luke xiii. 7, Heb. ii. 14, and in the whole LXX. only four times, all in Esdras. It is rare in ordinary Greek; see Eurip. *Phœniss.* 753, and Polyb. *Frag. Hist.* 69. The τοῦ is omitted by *Lachm.* with BCD[1]FG; 2 mss.; Theoph.,— but, as being less usual, esp. when preceded by a prep., is more probably retained, with AD[3]EJK; nearly all mss.; Chrys., Theod., Dam., al. (*Tisch.*). ἐν νόμῳ δικαιοῦσθε] '*are being justified in the law*,' 'in lege,' Vulg., Clarom.; ἐν not being instrumental (Ewald), but pointing to the sphere of the action; compare notes on ch. iii. 11. The pres. δικαιοῦσθε is correctly referred by the principal ancient and modern commentators to the feelings of the subject (ὡς ὑπολαμβάνετε, Theophyl., 'ut vobis videtur,' Fritz. *Opusc.* p. 156); compare Goth. 'garaihtans qiþiþ ïzvis' [justos dicitis vos]. On this use of the *subjective* present (commonly employed to indicate certainty, prophetic confidence, expectation of speedy issue, etc.), see Bernh. *Synt.* x. 2, p. 371, Schmalfeld, *Synt.* § 54. 2, p. 91. τῆς χάριτος ἐξεπέσατε] '*ye fell away from grace*;' the aor., as in the first clause, referring to the time when legal justification was admitted and put forward; see, however, notes to *Transl.* On the meaning of ἐκπίπτειν τινος ('aliquâ re excidere, scil. ejus jacturam facere') see Winer, *de Verb. Comp.* Fasc. II. p. 11, and comp. Plato, *Rep.* VI. 496, ἐκπεσεῖν φιλοσοφίας, Polyb. XII. 14, 7, ἐκπίπτειν τοῦ καθήκοντος. The Alexandrian form of aor. ἐξεπέσατε is noticed and illustrated by exx. in Winer, *Gr.* § 13. 1, p. 68 sq.; compare Lobeck, *Phryn.* p. 724.

5. ἡμεῖς γάρ] '*For we*;' proof of the preceding assertion by a declaration *e contrario* of the attitude of hope and expectancy, not of legal reliance and self-confidence, which was the characteristic of the Apostle and of all true Christians. If δὲ had been used, the opposition between ἡμεῖς and οἵτινες (ἡμεῖς) would have been more prominent than would seem in harmony with the context and with the conciliatory character of the present address.

Πνεύματι] '*by the Spirit*,' 'Spiritu,' Vulg., Clarom., with an implied contrast to the σὰρξ which was the active principle of all legal righteousness; comp. ch. iii. 3, and notes *in loc.* The dative is not equivalent to ἐν Πνεύματι (Copt.), still less to be explained as merely adverbial, 'spiritually' (Middl. *in loc.*), but, as the context suggests, has its definite ablatival force and distinct personal reference; our hope flows from faith, and that faith is imparted and quickened by the Holy Spirit. No objection can be urged against this interpr. founded on the absence of the article, as neither the canon of Middleton (*Gr. Art.* p. 126, ed. Rose), nor the similar one suggested by Harless (*Ephes.* ii. 22.), — that τὸ Πνεῦμα is the personal Holy Spirit, πνεῦμα the indwelling influence of the Spirit (Rom. viii. 5), can at all be considered of universal application; see ver. 16. It is much more natural to regard Πνεῦμα, Πνεῦμα ἅγιον, and Πνεῦμα Θεοῦ as proper names, and to extend to them the same latitude in connection with the article; see Fritz. *Rom.* viii. 4, Vol. II. p. 105. ἐκ πίστεως] '*from faith*,' as the origin and source (comp. notes on ch. iii. 22), — in opposition to the ἐν νόμῳ of the preceding clause, which practically includes the more regular antithesis ἐξ ἔργων. ἐλπίδα δικαιοσύνης] '*the hope of righteousness*.' This is one of those many passages in the N. T. (see Winer, *Gr.* § 30. 1, p. 168) in which it is difficult to decide whether the genitive is *subjecti* or *objecti*; the ἓν διὰ δυοῖν, 'spem et justitiam (æternam),' suggested by Aquinas, being clearly inadmissible. If (α) the gen. be *subjecti*, ἐλπίδα δικαιοσ. must be 'ipsum præmium quod speratur, sc. vitam æternam' (Grot.), 'coronam gloriæ quæ justificatos manet' (Beza), ἐλπὶς being used μετωνυμικῶς for the thing hoped for: if (β) *objecti*, then simply 'speratam justitiam,' the hope which turns on δικαιοσύνη as its object, — fairly paraphrased by Æth., 'we hope we may be justified;' sim. Tynd., Cran. Of these (β) seems clearly most in accordance with the context, as this turns not so much upon any adjunct to δικαιοσύνη as upon δικαιοσύνη itself; 'Ye,' says St. Paul, in ver. 4, 'think that ye are *already* in possession of δικαιοσ. (δικαιοῦσθε), we on the contrary *hope for it*.' There is no difficulty in δικαιοσύνη thus being represented *future*. For in the first place this view necessarily results from the contrast between Judaism and Christianity. The Jew regarded δικαιοσ. as something outward, present, realizable; the Christian as something inward, future, and, save through faith in Christ, unattainable. And in the second place, δικαιοσύνη is one of those divine results which, as Neander beautifully expresses it, 'stretch into eternity:' it conveys with it and involves the idea of future blessedness and glorification; οὓς ἐδικαίωσεν τούτους καὶ ἐδόξασεν, Rom. viii. 30; see Neand. *Planting*, Vol. I. p. 478 note (Bohn). ἐλπίδα ἀπεκδεχόμεθα] '*tarry for*,' '*patiently wait for*.' This expressive compound has two meanings (*a*) *local*, with reference either to the place *from which* the expectation is directed to its object ('in quo locatus aliquem expectes,' Fritz.), or, more usually, the place *whence* the object is expected to come ('unde quid expectaretur,' Winer), — a decided trace of which meaning may be observed in Phil. iii. 20: (*b*) *ethical*, with ref. to the assiduity of the expectation, 'studiose constanter expectare,' — the meaning in the present case and appy. in all the remaining passages in the N. T.; comp. viii. 19, 23, 25, 1 Cor. i. 7, Heb. ix. 28, 1 Pet. iii. 20 (*Lachm.*, *Tisch.*), and see Tittmann, *Synon.* p. 106, Fritz.

6 ἐν γὰρ Χριστῷ Ἰησοῦ οὔτε περιτομή τι ἰσχύει οὔτε ἀκροβυστία, ἀλλὰ πίστις δι' ἀγάπης ἐνεργουμένη.

Opusc. p. 156, Winer, *Verb. Comp.* Fasc. IV. p. 14. It may be added that the expression ἐλπίδ. ἀπεκδ. is not pleonastic for ἐλπ. δικ. ἔχομεν (Ust., comp. Æth.), but, as Fritz. observes, forcible and almost poetical (Eur. *Alcest.* 130, ἐλπίδα προσδέχωμαι), ἐλπίδα being the cognate accus.; comp. Acts. xxiv. 15, ἐλπίδα . . . ἣν καὶ αὐτοὶ οὗτοι προσδέχονται, Tit. ii. 13, προσδεχόμενοι τὴν μακαρίαν ἐλπίδα. The whole clause may be thus paraphrased: 'by the assistance of the Holy Spirit we are enabled to cherish the hope of being justified, and the source out of which that hope springs is faith;' comp. Ust. *Lehrb.* II. 1, p. 90 sq., and for a fuller explanation of the verse, Chillingworth, *Works*, p. 402 sq. (Lond. 1704), Manton, *Serm.*, Vol. IV. p. 927 sq. (Lond. 1698).

6. ἐν γὰρ Χριστῷ Ἰησ.] '*For in Christ Jesus;*' confirmation of the preceding statement that the ἀπεκδοχὴ was ἐκ πίστεως; when there is a union with Christ, neither circumcision or uncircumcision avails anything, but faith only; it is clear, then, why we entertain the hope of righteousness *from faith.* The solemn formula ἐν Χρ. Ἰησ. is not to be explained away, as 'in Christi regno, ecclesiâ' (Paræus), 'Christi religione' (Est.), 'Christi lege' (Grot.), — all of which fall utterly short of the true meaning, — but, as the regular use of ἐν Χρ. and the addition of Ἰησοῦ distinctly suggest, conveys the deeper idea of 'union, fellowship, and incorporation' in Christ crucified: comp. notes on ch. ii. 17. For an elaborate but wholly insufficient explanation of the vital expression ἐν Χρ., comp. Fritz. *Rom.* viii. 1, Vol. II. p. 82, and contrast with it the deep and spiritual illustrations of Bp. Hall, *Christ Mystical*, ch. 2, 3.

δι' ἀγάπης ἐνεργουμένη] '*energizing, displaying its activity through love,*' ζῶσα δείκνυται Theoph., 'efficax est,' Bull, Andrewes (*Serm.* v. Vol. III. p. 193); comp. 1 Thess. i. 3, τοῦ κόπου τῆς ἀγάπης, Polyc. *ad Phil.* § 3, πίστιν . . . . ἐπακολουθούσης τῆς ἐλπίδος προαγούσης τῆς ἀγάπης, and see esp. Ust. *Lehrb.* II. 1. 4, p. 236 sq., and reff. in notes *on* 1 *Thess. l. c.* The verb ἐνεργεῖσθαι *may* have two meanings, (*a*) passive, '*is made perfect,*' ܕܡܫܬܡܠܝܐ [quæ perficitur, Schaaf, but see Capell. *in loc.*] Syr., '*adschueghyal,*' Arm., — maintained by the older Romanist divines, Bellarm. al. (see Petav. *de Incarn.* VIII. 12. 15, Vol. v. p. 407), as well as several Protestant interpreters, Hammond, al., and even the recent editors of Steph. *Thesaur.* s. v.; or (*b*) active, '*is operative,*' Vulg., Clarom., Goth., Copt., — as maintained by nearly all recent commentators. Of these (*a*) is perfectly lexically tenable (Polyb. *Hist.* I. 13, 5, ἐνεργεῖται πόλεμος), but distinctly at variance with the usage of the word in the N. T. (see Meyer, 2 *Cor.* i. 6, Bretsch. *Lex.* s. v.), while (*b*) harmonizes with the prevailing usage, and can be correctly distinguished from the active; ἐνεργεῖν being '*vim exercere,*' and commonly applied to *persons*, ἐνεργεῖσθαι '*ex se* (aut suam) *vim exercere,*' a species of what has been called the 'dynamic' middle (Krüger, *Sprachl.* § 52. 8), and commonly applied to *things*, see Fritz. *Rom.* Vol. II. p. 17, Winer, *Gr.* § 38. 6, p. 231. Although the pass. meaning is not now maintained by the best critical scholars of the Church of Rome, the passage is no less strongly claimed as a testimony to the truth of the Tridentine doctrine (Sess. VI. c. 7) of *fides formata;* see

Who perverted you? Whosoever they are they shall be punished, for their doctrine is not mine. Yea, I wish they would cease from all communion with you.

7 Ἐτρέχετε καλῶς· τίς ὑμᾶς ἐνέκοψεν τῇ ἀληθείᾳ μὴ πείθεσθαι; 8 ἡ πεισμονὴ οὐκ ἐκ

Windischm. *in loc.*, and comp. Möhler, *Symbolik*, § 16, p. 131 note, § 17, p. 137.

7. ἐτρέχετε καλῶς] '*Ye were running well;*' forcible and yet natural transition from the brief statement of the characterizing principle of Christian life, once exemplified in the Galatians, but now lost sight of and perverted; ἐπαινεῖ τὸν δρόμον καὶ θρηνεῖ τοῦ δρόμου τὴν παῦλαν, Theod. τίς ὑμᾶς ἐνέκοψεν] '*who did hinder you;*' not without some expression of surprise, πῶς ὁ τοσοῦτος ἐνεκόπη δρόμος; τίς ὁ τοσοῦτον ἰσχύσας, Chrys.; comp. ch. iii. 1. The primary meaning of the verb ἐγκόπτειν (Hesych. ἐνεκοπτόμην· ἐνεποδιζόμην, Suid. ἀναχαιτίζει· ἀναποδίζει· ἐγκόπται) appears to be that of *hindering* by *breaking up a road* (*e. g.* Greg. Nazianz. *Or.* XVI. p. 260, ἢ κακίας ἐγκοπτομένης δυσπαθείᾳ τῶν πονημῶν, ἢ ἀρετῆς ὁδοποιουμένης εὐπαθείᾳ τῶν βελτιόνων; comp. 'intercidere,' *e. g.* Cæs. *Bell. Gall.* II. 9, pontem, etc.); while that of ἀνακόπτειν (*Rec.*) is rather that of *hindrance* with the further idea of *thrusting back;* compare Hom. *Odyss.* XXI. 47, θυρέων ἀνέκοπτεν ὀχῆσας. The reading of *Rec.* (ἀνέκοψεν) is, however, opposed to all the uncial MSS., and appy. to nearly all mss. and Ff., and neither on internal (opp. to Bloomf.) nor external grounds has any claim on attention. The accus. is similarly found with ἐγκόπτειν, Acts xxiv. 4, 1 Thess. ii. 18; see also Themist. *Or.* XIV. p. 181 C. τῇ ἀληθ. μὴ πείθεσθαι] '*that ye should not obey the truth;*' infin. expressive of the *result* or effect, with some trace of the *purpose* or end contemplated, this being one of those forms of the 'consecutive' sentence, which may be regarded as partly *objective* and as partly *final;* see Donalds. *Gr.* § 602. The popular explanation that μὴ with the infin., after certain negative and prohibitive verbs, is pleonastic (Meyer compare Herm. *Viger,* No. 271), is now justly called in question (see esp. Klotz, *Devar.* Vol. II. p. 668), the true explanation being that the μὴ is prefixed to the infinitive, whether in its more simply objective form (Donalds. *Gr.* § 584 sq.), or its more lax and general ref. to result (Bernh., *Synt.* IX. 6. b, p. 364, Madvig, *Synt.* § 156. 4), to indicate the further idea of some latent purpose involved in the action which specially contemplated or tended to the effect expressed by the infinitive; see esp. Schmalfeld, *Synt.* § 181. 2, p. 359, and for an illustrative example compare Aristoph. *Pax,* 315, ἐμποδὼν ἡμῖν γένηται τὴν θεὸν μὴ ἐξελκύσαι; see Madvig, *Synt.* § 210. The elliptical mode of explanation adopted by Gayler (*de Partic. Neg.* p. 359) in the parallel expressions ἀρνοῦμαι μὴ δρᾶσαι, sc. 'nego, *et dico* me non fecisse' is appy. doubtful in principle, and certainly is not here applicable. *Lachm.* omits the article before ἀληθ. but only with AB, and appy. a few mss.

8. ἡ πεισμονή] '*the persuasion,*' 'suasio,' Clarom., scil. 'servandi legalia,' Lyra; the subst. being regarded as active, and the article (not 'this pers.' Arm., Auth., — a *most* doubtful usage in the N. T., see Winer, *Gr.* § 18. 1, p. 97 sq.) marking the particular (counter-) persuading of the false teachers implied in the τίς ὑμᾶς ἐνέκοψεν. Owing to the apparent paronomasia, and the nature of the termination (compare Donalds. *Cratyl.* § 255) the meaning of

τοῦ καλοῦντος ὑμᾶς. 9 μικρὰ ζύμη ὅλον τὸ φύραμα ζυμοῖ.

πεισμονὴ is slightly doubtful. As the similar form πλησμονὴ means both *satietas* (the state) and *expletio* (the act), Col. ii. 23, Plato, *Symp.* 186 c, πλ. καὶ κένωσις, — so πεισμονὴ may mean (*a*) the state of being persuaded, *i. e.* 'conviction' (Θεος τὰ καλεῖν τὸ δὲ πείθεσθαι τῶν ὑπακουόντων, Theod.), or (*b*) the act of persuading 'persuadendi sollertia,' Schott.; comp. Chrys. *on* 1 *Thess.* i. 4, οὐ πεισμονὴ ἀνθρωπίνη . . . ἦν ἡ . . . πείθουσα. Of these (*a*) has here the support of the Greek expositors τὸ πεισθῆναι τοῖς λέγουσιν, Œcum., compare Chrys., Theoph.), and certainly on that account deserves consideration; (*b*) however, is to be preferred, as lexically defensible (see below), as in harmony with the active τοῦ καλοῦντος; ἡ πεισμ. pointing to a gracious act in which the human will is regarded more as subjected to the divine influence (John vi. 44), τοῦ καλ. to one in which it is regarded more as free; comp. Meyer *in loc.* In three out of the four instances cited by Wetst. from Eustath. (*ad Il.* α, p. 21. 46; 99. 45, *Il.* ι, p. 637. 5), the prevailing meaning appears to be 'pervicacia;' but in Justin Mart. *Apol.* I, 53, αὐταρκεῖς εἰς πεισμονήν, Epiphan. *Hares*, XXX. 21, εἰς πεισμονὴν τῆς ἑαυτῶν πληροφορίας, Apollon. *de Synt.* p. 195. 10, τὴν ἐξ ἀλλήλων πρὸς ἀλλήλους πεισμονήν, the active meaning is sufficiently distinct. Ignat. *Rom.* 3, is commonly adduced, but here Cod. Colb. reads σιωπῆς. οὐκ ἐκ τοῦ καλοῦντος] '*is not from him who calleth you,*' *i. e.* does not emanate, does not result from, see note, ch. ii. 16; not an answer to the preceding question, which is rather an expression of surprise than a mere interrogation, — but a warning declaration. The ὁ καλῶν is obviously not St. Paul (Locke), not even Christ (Theoph.), but as usual, God; the act of *calling* in St. Paul's Epp. (*e. g.* Rom. ix. 11, 24; 1 Cor. i. 9, vii. 15, al.) being regularly ascribed to the Father; see notes and reff. on ch. 1. 6. The tense of the participle need not be pressed either as a definite pres. ('non desinit etiam nunc vocare,' Beza), or, still less probably as an imperf. ('qui vos vocabat,' Beng.), — ὁ καλῶν, as Chrys. appears to have felt (οὐκ ἐκάλεσεν ὑμᾶς ὁ καλῶν), being only the common substantival participle; see the numerous exx. collected by Winer, *Gr.* § 45. 7, p. 316, comp. Bernhardy, *Synt.* VI. 23, p. 318, Madvig, *Syntax*, § 180. b, and notes *on* 1 *Thess.* v. 24.

9. μικρὰ ζύμη κ. τ. λ.] '*a little leaven leaveneth the whole lump;*' proverbially expressed warning (compare 1 Cor. v. 7), forming a sort of antithetical continuation of what has preceded. It is somewhat doubtful whether ζύμη is to be considered as (*a*) having an *abstract* reference to the false teaching (τὸ μαιρὸν τοῦτο κακόν, Chrys.; compare Theoph.), or as (*b*) pointing in the *concrete* ('hi pauci,' Paræus; compare Aug., Jerome) to those who disseminated it; see Clem. *Hom.* VIII. 17 (cited by Hilgenf.), where the race of men living before the flood are characterized as a κακὴ ζύμη. On the one hand, (*a*) yields a pertinent sense, and is appy. confirmed by Matth. xvi. 11, and by 1 Cor. *l. c.* (where ver. 8 seems distinctly to show that ζύμη does not mean the individual so much as his sin): on the other, the active meaning assigned to πεισμονή, and still more the *seeming* quantitative limitation *hinted* at in the use of the individualizing singular in ver. 10 (compare Beng.) appears to preponderate in favor of (*b*). We adopt, therefore, the concrete reference, and necessarily continue it to the following φύραμα; 'vel pauci homines

10 ἐγὼ πέποιθα εἰς ὑμᾶς ἐν Κυρίῳ ὅτι οὐδὲν ἄλλο φρονήσετε· ὁ δὲ
ταράσσων ὑμᾶς βαστάσει τὸ κρῖμα, ὅστις ἂν ᾖ. 11 ἐγὼ δέ, ἀδελ-

perperam docentes possent *omnen* [*totum*] *cœtum* corrumpere,' Winer *in loc.*

10. ἐγώ] '*I for my part;*' emphatic, and not without a reassuring contrast. The insertion of δὲ [C¹FG; a few mss.; Demid., Aug., Syr.-Phil., al.] is due to the desire to make this contrast still more apparent. εἰς ὑμᾶς] '*with regard to you;*' this more lax use of εἰς is noticed by Winer, *Gr.* § 53, p. 473, and Bernh. *Synt.* v. 11. p. 220. The addition of the words ἐν Κυρίῳ (sc. Ἰησοῦ, Rom. xiv. 14, compare Winer, *Gr.* § 19. 1, p. 113) serves to designate the ground of the hope, and to show that it was not an earthly and doubtful, but a heavenly (Phil. ii. 24) and certain assurance which St. Paul entertained; compare 2 Thess. iii. 4, πεποίθαμεν δὲ ἐν Κυρίῳ ἐφ' ὑμᾶς, where ἐπὶ is used in a sense little different from the present εἰς, to denote the objects about whom the hope was felt, ἐν Κυρ. the nature of that hope; see notes on 2 *Thess. l. c.*, where distinctions are drawn between the ethical uses of εἰς, ἐπί, and πρός. οὐδὲν ἄλλο] '*nothing else,*' — than what? Either *specially*, — than the subject and purport of the words immediately preceding; or, *generally*, — than the doctrines which St. Paul had propounded. The latter accords best with the future φρονήσετε, which seems more naturally used in reference to the general issue (ὅτι διορθώσεσθε, Chrys.), than merely to the time when the words would be read. Alf. refers to Phil. iii. 15 (compare Usteri, 'no novel sentiments'), but there the word is ἑτέρως; see notes *in loc.* ὁ δὲ ταράσσων] '*but he that disturbeth you;*' contrast, not with the preceding ἐγώ (Rück.), but generally with the expression of confidence which has just preceded; ὁ ταράσσ. not being used on the one hand, for οἱ ταράσσοντες (Brown), nor on the other, in ref. to some *one particular* false teacher (Olsh.; contrast Davids. *Introd.* Vol. II. p. 315), but in accordance with the exact selective and definitive force of the article, to the one who, for the time being, comes under observation. Οἱ ταράσσοντες ὑμᾶς (ch. i. 7) are the class generally, ὁ ταράσσων is the individual of the class who may happen to call forth the Apostle's censure; ἐπῆρε τὸν λόγον, Chrys.; compare Madvig, *Synt.* § 14. βαστάσει τὸ κρῖμα] '*shall bear*' ('ut grave onus,' Beng.), *the judgment (he deserves);*' κρῖμα not being equivalent to κατάκριμα, nor used as cause for effect, sc. 'punishment' (Schott, Olsh.), but retaining its proper meaning both here and Rom. ii. 3, al. and with app. ref. to the judgment which he will receive *from God;* δίκας ὀφείλουσι τῷ Θεῷ, Theod. The idea of 'punishment,' or 'condemnation,' is conveyed by, and to be deduced from the *context;* see Fritz. *Rom. l. c.* Vol. I. p. 94. ὅστις ἂν ᾖ] '*whoever he may be;*' not with any reference to the dignity of the momentarily-selected individual (κἂν μεγάλοι τινες δοκῶσι καὶ ἀξιόπιστοι, Theoph.), but simply with the *inclusive* reference of the formula; comp. Acts. iii. 23.

11. ἐγώ δέ ἀδελφοί] '*But I, brethren,*' — with abrupt reference to what might have been said of himself. The connection between this and the preceding verse is not perfectly clear. The use of the expression ὁ ταράσσων appears to have suggested the remembrance that he himself was open to the charge of being a subverter, inasmuch as he had circumcised Timothy. The

φοί, εἰ περιτομὴν ἔτι κηρύσσω, τί ἔτι διώκομαι; ἄρα κατήργηται

replication is final and decisive; 'But if it be a fact that I really do still preach *circumcision*, what further ground is there for persecuting me?' *i. e.* 'the very fact of my persecution is a proof that I am not a preacher of circumcision;' see esp. Theoph. *in loc.*

εἰ περιτ. ἔτι κηρύσσω] '*If I preach circumcision*,' 'if, as is assumed to be a matter of fact (compare notes on ch. i. 9), *circumcision* is still what I preach;' the emphasis resting not on κηρύσσω (τουτέστιν οὐκ οὕτο κελεύω πιστεύειν . . περιέτεμον μὴν γὰρ [τὸν Τιμόθεον], οὐκ ἐκήρυξα δὲ περιτομήν, Chrys.), but on the prominently placed περιτομήν. The ἔτι does not suggest any contrasted reference to the period before the coming of Christ ('still — as in the ante-Christian times,' Olsh.), — a reference which would here be very pointless, nor again to any special change in the Apostle's teaching since he had become a Christian, — for which there is not the *slightest* grounds, but simply to the period prior to his conversion, '*still*, in contrast to my former Judaism;' comp. Wieseler, *Chronol.* p. 206 note. The Apostle might not have 'preached' circumcision before his conversion, but he strenuously advocated (περισσοτέρως ζηλωτὴς ὑπάρχων τῶν πατρικῶν μου παραδόσεων, ch. i. 14) all the principles of Judaism; comp. Neander, *Planting*, p. 304, note. The present tense is probably used, as Schott observes, from his having the present accusation of his adversaries in his mind.

τί ἔτι διώκομαι] '*why am I still persecuted*,' almost 'why am I to be,' etc.; this second ἔτι being, as De Wette observes, *logical;* see Rom. iii. 7, τί ἔτι κἀγὼ ὡς ἁμαρτωλὸς κρίνομαι, 'what further ground is there for,' etc., Rom. ix. 19, al.

ἄρα] '*then after all*,' 'ergo,' Vulg., Clarom. (see Hand, *Tursell.* Vol. II. p. 450 sq.); inference from what has preceded, not perhaps here without *some* tinge of ironical reference to a conclusion that could not have been expected. The fundamental idea of ἄρα is 'distance or progression (to another step in the argument)'; from which the *derivative* meaning, — that at the advanced point at which we have arrived, our present view is different to our antecedent one, can easily be deduced;' see esp. Donalds. *Crat.* § 192. That this, however, is the normal and *primary* idea of the particle (see Hartung, *Partik.* ἄρα, I. 3, Vol. I. p. 422) cannot now be maintained; see Klotz, *Devar.* Vol. II. p. 160 sq., where the whole question is discussed at great length. According to this writer, ἄρα involves 'significationem levioris cujusdam ratiocinationis, quæ indicat *rebus ita comparatis*, aliquid ita aut esse aut fieri,' *in Devar.* p. 167. The interrogatory form (ἆρα), as adopted by Syr., Ust., al., seems here less forcible and appropriate.

τὸ σκάνδαλον τοῦ σταυροῦ] '*the offence of the cross*,' 'offendiculum crucis,' Beza; the offence which the Jews took at Christianity, because faith in a crucified Saviour, — faith without legal observances, was *alone* offered as the means of salvation; οὐδὲ γὰρ οὕτως ὁ σταυρὸς ἦν σκανδαλίζων τοὺς Ἰουδαίους ὡς τὸ μὴ δεῖν πείθεσθαι τοῖς πατρῴοις νόμοις, Chrys.; compare 1 Cor. i. 18, etc., see Brown, *Galat.* p. 278, Usteri, *Lehrb.* II. 2. 1, p. 253. Σκάνδαλον, though occurring (quotations included) 15 times in the N. T. and 25 times in the LXX and Apocrypha, is scarcely ever found 'apud profanos.' Σκανδάληθρον τὸ ἐνιστάμενον ταῖς μυάγραις, Poll. *Onomast.* x. 34, occasionally occurs; *e. g.* in a metaphorical sense, Aristoph. *Acharn.* 687.

τὸ σκάνδαλον τοῦ σταυροῦ. 12 ὄφελον καὶ ἀποκόψονται οἱ ἀνασ-
τατοῦντες ὑμᾶς.

12. ὄφελον] '*I would that;*' indignant wish called forth by the last deduction, and by the thought of the antagonism of circumcision to the cross of Christ; see Ewald *in loc.*, and compare ch. ii. 21. This word is used *purely* as a particle, both in the N. T. (see 1 Cor. iv. 8, 2 Cor. xi. 1), and in the LXX, *e. g.* Exod. xvi. 3, Numb. xiv. 2, xx. 3, Psalm cxviii. 5; see Winer, *Gr.* § 41. 5. 2, p. 270, Sturz, *de Dialect. Maced.* s. v. § 12. Its construction, therefore, here with a future, though unusual and (appy. according to Lucian, *Solœc.* 1) solœcistic, need not have caused Bengel to alter the punctuation (τὸ σκάνδαλον τοῦ σταυροῦ· ὄφελον.), and to connect ὄφελον as a kind of exclamation ('velim ita sit!') with what precedes. On the similar use of ὤφελον and ὤφελε in later writers, comp. Matth. *Gr.* § 513. obs. 3, and on the correct and classical use ('ὤφελον non nisi tum adhiberi, quum quis optat, ut fuerit aliquid, vel sit, vel futurum sit, quod non fuit, aut est, aut futurum est'), see Herm. *Viger*, No. 190. καὶ ἀποκόψονται] '*they would even cut themselves off (from you).*' The exact meaning of these words has been much discussed. The usual passive translation ('abscindantur,' Vulg., Goth., appy. Syr. [Schaaf], Æth.-Platt, Arm.), cannot be defended, as the N. T. furnishes no certain instance of a similar enallage. The most plausible is 1 Cor. x. 2, καὶ πάντες ἐβαπτίσαντο, but even here the middle voice (sc. 'baptismum susceperunt,' Beng.) may be correctly maintained; see Winer, *Gr.* § 38. 4, p. 228, and exx. in Jelf, *Gr.* § 364. 4. a. We have thus only two possible translations, (α) '*I would that they would even cut themselves off* (plane discedant) from communion with you,' Bretschn.; or (β) '*I would that they would* (not only circumcise, but) *even castrate themselves;*' μὴ περιτεμνέσθωσαν μόμον, ἀλλὰ καὶ ἀποκοπτέσθωσαν, Chrys., ἀποκόπους ἑαυτοὺς ἐποίησαν, Œcum.: see exx. in Wetst. *in loc.* This latter reference to bodily mutilation is adopted by the principal patristic expositors, as well as by most modern writers; and it must be admitted that thus not only καὶ is more readily explained, and the expression of the *wish* (ὄφελον) more easily accounted for, but that there is also a species of parallelism in the use of κατατομήν, Phil. iii. 2. Still as there seems no certain trace of this *corporeal* reference in any of the ancient Vv., — as in some (Æth.-Platt, and perhaps Arm.) the reference seems plainly *ethical*, — as there is a *seeming* contrast in the καλεῖν ἐπὶ of the confirmatory clause which follows, and as this seems alone suited to the earnest gravity with which St. Paul is here addressing his converts, we adopt somewhat unhesitatingly the *former* interpretation. The Apostle's deep insight into the exact spiritual state of the Galatians, and the true affection that throughout the Epistle tempers even his necessary severity, leads him here to express as a *wish*, what he might have (as in 1 Cor. v. 11) urged as a command: comp. Waterl., *Works*, Vol. III. p. 458. οἱ ἀναστατ. ὑμᾶς] '*they who are unsettling you,*' Hamm., sc. 'your subverters;' the participle with its case becoming by means of the article a kind of substantive; see notes and reff. on ch. i. 23. The verb ἀναστατοῦν (Hesych. ἀνατρέπειν) occurs three times in the N. T. (Acts xvii. 6, xxi. 38) as an equivalent of the more usual ἀνάστατον ποιεῖν, but is of rare occurrence

Do not misuse your freedom, but love one another. Love is the fulfilment of the law; hatred brings destruction.

13 Ὑμεῖς γὰρ ἐπ ἐλευθερίᾳ ἐκλήθητε, ἀδελ-
φοί· μόνον μὴ τὴν ἐλευθερίαν εἰς ἀφορμὴν τῇ
σαρκί, ἀλλὰ διὰ τῆς ἀγάπης δουλεύετε ἀλλήλοις. 14 ὁ γὰρ πᾶς νόμος ἐν ἑνὶ λόγῳ πεπλήρωται, ἐν τῷ

(Wetst. *on Acts* xvii. 6), and is said to belong to that somewhat numerous class of words (Tittm. *Synon.* p. 266) which are referred to the Macedonian dialect; see Sturz, *de Dial. Maced.* § 9, p. 146. It has a stronger meaning than ταράσσω, and is admirably paraphrased by Chrys., ἀπὸ τῆς ἄνω Ἱερουσαλὴμ καὶ τῆς ἐλευθέρας ἐκβαλόντες, βιαζόμενοι δὲ καθάπερ αἰχμαλώτους καὶ μετανάστας πλανᾶσθαι.

13. ὑμεῖς γάρ] '*For ye;*' commencement of a new paragraph, and according to Olsh., De W., al., of a new portion (the hortatory) of the Epistle; ἐνταῦθα λοιπὸν δοκεῖ μὲν εἰς τὸν ἠθικὸν ἐμβαίνειν λόγον, Chrys. St. Paul knew so well the human heart, its tendencies and temptations, and saw so clearly how his own doctrine of Christian liberty might be perverted and adulterated, that he at once hastens, with more than usual earnestness, to trace out the ineffaceable distinction between true spiritual freedom, and a carnal and antinomian license. There is, however, no marked or abrupt division, but one portion of the epistle passes insensibly into the other. γάρ is thus not illative (Turner), nor a mere particle of transition (Brown), but stands in immediate connection with the preceding words, which it serves to confirm and justify; 'and I may well wish that they would cut themselves off from your communion, for ye were called to a state with which they have nothing in common.' The reading δέ, found in FG; 80; Chrys., Aug., al., seems a very palpable correction. ἐπ' ἐλευθερίᾳ] '*for freedom;*' ἐπί here denoting the *purpose* or *object* for which they were called; compare 1 Thess. iv. 7, οὐ γὰρ ἐκάλεσεν ὑμᾶς ὁ Θεὸς ἐπὶ ἀκαθαρσίᾳ, where see notes *in loc.* Further exx. will be found in Winer, *Gr.* § 48. c, p. 351, and in Rost. u. Palm, *Lex.* s. v. II. 2. f, Vol. I. p. 1040. μὴ τὴν ἐλευθερίαν] '*make not your liberty;*' scil. ποιεῖτε, τρέπετε [not, however, used in N. T.], δῶτε (FG; Boern., al), or some similar verb. Instances of this very intelligible and idiomatic omission of the verb after μή are cited by Hartung, *Partik.* μή, 6. b. 4, Vol. II. p. 153, Klotz. *Devar.* Vol. II. p. 669, Winer, *Gr.* § 66. I. 5, p. 663: compare Hor. *Epist.* I. 5. 12, 'Quo mihi fortunas, si non conceditur uti.' Such ellipses must of course be common in every cultivated language. διὰ τῆς ἀγάπης] '*by the love* ye evince,' '*by your love;*' not 'in your love' (Peile), with any reference to state or condition (compare Rom. iv. 11, δι' ἀκροβυστίας, viii. 25, δι' ὑπομονῆς, al.; Winer, *Gr.* § 47. i, p. 339), but simply 'per caritatem,' Vulg., Armen. [instrumental case], Copt.; love was to be the means by which their reciprocal δουλεία was to be shown. The reading τῇ ἀγάπῃ τοῦ Πνεύματος, found in DEFG; 81; Clarom., Goth., Copt. [Wilk., but not Böttich.]; Bas., al., is in addition suggested by the preceding σαρκός. δουλεύετε] '*be in bondage,*' 'servite,' Vulg., Clarom.; in antithesis to the preceding ἐλευθερίαν: οὐκ εἶπεν ἀγαπᾶτε ἀλλήλους, ἁπλῶς, ἀλλὰ δουλεύετε, τὴν ἐπιτεταμένην δηλῶν φιλίαν, Chrys.

14. ὁ γὰρ πᾶς νόμος] '*For the whole law;*' confirmation from Scripture of the command immediately preceding, διὰ τῆς ἀγάπης κ. τ. λ. A few instances of this order occur in the N. T.; see

'Αγαπήσεις τὸν πλησίον σου ὡς σεαυτόν. 15 εἰ δὲ ἀλλήλους δάκνετε καὶ κατεσθίετε, βλέπετε μὴ ὑπὸ ἀλλήλων ἀναλωθῆτε.

14. σεαυτόν] *Tisch.* (ed. 2) here adopts the more difficult, though not wholly unusual reading ἑαυτὸν (see Winer, *Gr.* § 22. 5) too much in defiance of external authority. Σεαυτὸν is supported by ABCDEK; very many mss.; Marc. ap. Epiph., Theodoret, Dam. (*Rec.*, *Griesb.*, *Scholz*, *Tisch.* ed. *Lachm.*). 'Εαυτὸν appears only in FGJ; appy. the majority of mss.; Theophyl., Œcum., (*Mey.*, *Tisch.*). Usteri very plausibly suggests the falling away of one of the contiguous sigmas in the course of transcription.

Middl. *Greek Art.* ch. VII. p. 104, note where Rose cites Acts xx. 18, 1 Tim. i. 16 (sing.), Acts xix. 7 (plural); add xxvii. 37. ἐν ἑνὶ λόγῳ] '*in one word*,' scil. in one declaration or commandment: comp. Rom. xiii. 9. πεπλήρωται] '*hath been (and is) fulfilled*.' This reading is supported no less by external evidence [ABC; 6 mss.; Marc. in Epiph., Damasc. (2), Aug.] than by internal probability. While πληροῦται (*Rec.*) would imply that the process of fulfilment was still going on, the perfect πεπλήρωται suitably points to the completed and *permanent* act; comp. Rom. xiii. 8, ὁ ἀγαπῶν τὸν ἕτερον νόμον πεπλήρωκεν, — a meaning of the perf. which Marcion (according to Tertull. *adv. Marc.* v. 4) appears, either ignorantly or wilfully, to have misunderstood, 'adimpleta est, quasi jam non adimplenda.' It may be observed that there is no discrepancy between this passage and Matth. xxii. 38, Mark xii. 29; for, as Meyer observes, St. Paul here takes a lofty spiritual eminence, from which, as it were, he sees all other commands so subordinated to the law of love, that he cannot consider the man who has fulfilled this in any other light than as having fulfilled the whole law: comp. Usteri, *Lehrb.* II. 1. 4, p. 242, Reuss, *Théol. Chrét.* IV. 19. Vol. II. p. 204 sq. The explanation of Vorstius and others πληροῦσθαι = ἀνακεφαλαιοῦσθαι, Rom. xiii. 9, here falls far short of the full spiritual meaning of the passage, and also is at variance with the regular meaning of πληρ. in the N. T.; see Matth. iii. 15, Rom. viii. 4, xiii. 8, Col. iv. 17. ἀγαπήσεις] '*Thou shalt love*.' The use of the imperatival future appears in the N. T. under three forms; (*a*) as a mild imperative, in simple prohibition; compare Matth. vi. 5, οὐκ ἔσῃ ὡς οἱ ὑποκριταί; (*b*) as a strong imperative, including prohibition and reproof; compare Acts xiii. 10, οὐ παύσῃ διαστρέφων τὰς ὁδοὺς Κυρίου; (*c*) as a *legislative* imperative, — both negatively (Matth. v. 21, Rom. vii. 7, al), and positively, as here, and Rom. xiii. 9. The two former usages (which in fact may be considered as one, varied only by the tone of the speaker) are common in classical Greek, see Jelf, *Gr.* § 413. 1, 2, Bernh. *Synt.* x. 5, p. 378: the latter seems distinctly Hebraistic; comp. Gayler, *Part. Neg.* II. 3. 3, p. 75, Winer, *Gr.* § 43. 5, p. 282. The uses of the future in the LXX appear to be very varied, and serve to express, negatively, *quod non convenit* (Gen. xx. 9), *quod non potest* (Gen. xxxii. 12: comp. Matth. iv. 4, al.), and positively, *quod licet* (Numb. xxxii. 24), *quod solet* (Deut. ii. 11). These are almost purely Hebraistic; see esp. Thiersch, *de Pentat.* III. § 11 sq.

15. δάκνετε καὶ κατεσθίετε] '*bite and devour*;' οὐκ εἶπε, δάκνετε, μόνον ὅπερ ἐστὶ θυμουμένου, ἀλλὰ καί, κατεσθίετε, ὅπερ ἐστὶν ἐμμένοντος τῇ πονηρίᾳ. ὁ μὲν γὰρ δάκνων ὀργῆς ἐπλήρωσε

Walk according to the Spirit, whose fruits no law condemns; and not according to the flesh, the works of which exclude from the kingdom of God.

16 Λέγω δέ, Πνεύματι περιπατεῖτε καὶ ἐπι-

πάθος· ὁ δὲ κατεσθίων θηριωδίας ἐσχάτης παρέσχεν ἀπόδειξιν, Chrys. Instances of a similar use of δάκνετε are cited by Kypke, *Obs.* Vol. II. p. 287, Wetst. *in loc.* ἀναλωθῆτε] '*be consumed,*' 'consumamini,' Vulg., Clarom.; continuation of the metaphor, there being appy. a species of climax in the three verbs δάκνετε, κατεσθίετε, and ἀναλωθῆτε. The meaning is sufficiently explained by Chrys., ἡ γὰρ διάστασις καὶ ἡ μάχη φθοροποιὸν καὶ ἀναλωτικὸν καὶ τῶν δεχομένων αὐτήν, καὶ εἰσαγόντων.

16. λέγω δέ] '*Now I say.*' The Apostle now reverts to the first portion of the command in ver. 13, μὴ τὴν ἐλευθερίαν εἰς ἀφορμὴν τῇ σαρκί. Πνεύματι] '*by the Spirit;*' not exactly 'in (*khen*) the Spirit,' Copt., still less 'Spiritui vitam consecrate' (dat. commodi; Fritz. *Rom.* Vol. I. p. 225), but simply 'Spiritu,' Vulg., Clarom., — the dative being here what is called the dat. *normæ*, and indicating the metaphorical path, manner, or rule of the action; compare ch. vi. 16, Acts xv. 1, Phil. iii. 16, and see Hartung, *Casus*, p. 79, Winer, *Gr.* § 31. 6. b, p. 193, Bernh. *Synt.* III. 14, p. 102, and exx. collected by Fritz. *Rom.* xiii. 13, Vol. III. p. 142. It is necessary to observe that Πνεύματι is not 'after a heavenly or spiritual manner,' Peile (κατὰ τὰς πνευματικὰς ἐντολάς, Schol. ap. Matth.), — a very insufficient paraphrase, nor even, 'in accordance with indwelling grace' (πνεῦμα δὲ τὴν ἐνοικοῦσαν χάριν, αὕτη γὰρ ἐπὶ τὰ κρείττω ποδηγεῖ τὴν ψυχήν, Theod.), as all such cases tend to obscure the true nature of the contrast between Πνεῦμα and σάρξ. Whenever these two words stand thus opposed, it has been satisfactorily shown by Müller (*On Sin*, Vol. I. p. 354 sq., Clark,) that the Πνεῦμα is not either the spiritual part of man (das Geistige), or the human spirit, if even always strengthened by the Holy Spirit, — the 'divinized spiritual' (das Geistliche; comp. Reuss, *Théol. Chrét.* Vol. II. p. 54), but the Holy Spirit itself, in so far as it is conceived the governing principle in man, the active and animating principle of Christian life, the Πνεῦμα τῆς ζωῆς ἐν Χρ. Ἰησ. Rom. viii. 2, the Πν. Χριστοῦ, Πν. Θεοῦ, *ib.* ver. 9; see also Neander, *Planting*, Vol. I. p. 467 (Bohn), and esp. Hofmann, *Schriftb.* Vol. I. p. 254 sq. On the omission of the article, see notes on ver. 5, and on the meaning of περιπατεῖν as implying life in its regular and practical manifestations, see notes *on Phil.* iii. 12, and *on 1 Thess.* iv. 12.

ἐπιθυμίαν σαρκός] '*the desire of the flesh;*' scil. all the motions and desires of the merely natural man, all that tends to earth and earthliness. The meaning of σάρξ in this important and deeply suggestive passage deserves the reader's careful consideration. The context seems clearly to show that here, as in many other passages in the N. T., σάρξ is not *merely* the carnal as opposed to the spiritual, — the purely sensational part of man, but comprehends in a more general notion the whole 'life and movement of man in the world of sense' (Müller), or perhaps, to speak a little more precisely, the 'whole principle and realm of earthliness and earthly relations' (σάρκα ἐνταῦθα τὸν λογισμὸν καλεῖ τὸν γεώδη, Chrys.); selfishness, as Müller has well observed, ever appearing in the background. The transition from this to the more definitely ethical notions of weakness, sin, and sensationalism, which Müller has too much lost sight of (see notes *on Col.* ii. 11), is thus easy and natural; see esp. the good article of Tholuck, *Stud. u. Krit.* for 1855, p.

θυμίαν σαρκὸς οὐ μὴ τελέσητε. 17 ἡ γὰρ σὰρξ ἐπιθυμεῖ κατὰ

17. ταῦτα γάρ] So *Lachm.* and *Tisch.* (ed. 1), with BD[1]EFG; 17; Vulg., Clarom., Copt., Arm.; Latin Ff. (*Mey.*, *Alf.*, *Bagge*), — and appy. correctly, as δέ, though strongly supported, viz., by ACD[3]JK; nearly all mss.; Syr. (both), Æth. (both); Chrys., Theodoret, Dam., al. (*Rec.*, *Griesb.*, *Scholz*) is much more likely to have been a change from γὰρ (to avoid the seeming awkwardness of a repetition of the particle) than vicè versâ. There is also some weight in the internal evidence; the repetition of γὰρ being so well-known a characteristic of the Apostle's style.

485—488, Müller, *On Sin*, Vol. I. p. 350 sq. (Clark), and compare Beck, *Seelenl.* II. 18, p. 53, Delitzsch, *Bibl. Psychol.* V. 6, p. 325 sq. οὐ μὴ τελέσητε] '*ye shall not accomplish;*' 'non perficietis,' Vulg., Clarom.; comp. Matth. x. 23, οὐ μὴ τελέσητε τὰς πόλεις. This clause may be translated either (*a*) *imperatively;* καὶ being the simple copula joining two imperatival clauses, the first expressed affirmatively, the second negatively (Copt., Arm., Æth., and more recently Hamm., Mey., al.), or (*b*) as a *future*, in which case καὶ will be *consecutive*, and nearly equiv. to 'ita fiet ut;' compare notes *on Phil.* iv. 42. Of these (*a*) is perfectly admissible on grammatical grounds; for the general principle — that οὐ μὴ with the 2nd pers. fut. is *prohibitive*, and that, with the other persons of the future and all persons of the subj., it enounces a *negation*, and not a prohibition (Hermann *on Elmsl. Med.* 1120, p. 391) — includes so many scarcely doubtful exceptions even in classical Greek (see exx. in Gayler, *Partic. Neg.* p. 435), that it may be sometimes doubted whether the first negative both in οὐ μὴ and μὴ οὐ may not really be 'oratorium magis quam logicum' (Gayler). Be this as it may, it seems certain that in the later Greek and esp. in the LXX, this use of οὐ μὴ in nearly all combinations, but esp. with subj., is so very abundant (see exx. in Gayler, p. 440), that no grammatical objections (opp. to Bloomf.) can be urged against the *prohibitive* usage. As, however, there is no *distinct* instance of such a construction in the N. T., and still more as the next verses seem more naturally to supply the reasons for the assertion than for the command, it seems best with Vulg., Clarom., Syr., and appy. Goth. (see De Gabel. *Gr. Goth.* § 182. 1. b. 3) to adopt the *future* translation. On the use of the subj. aor. for the future in negative enunciations, see notes and reff. on ch. iv. 30; and on the subject of the verse as limited to religious contentions, see 2 sermons by Howe, *Works*, Vol. III. p. 123 sq. (ed. Hewlett).

17. ἡ γὰρ σὰρξ κ. τ. λ.] '*for the flesh lusteth against the Spirit;*' reason for the foregoing declaration that walking after the Spirit will preclude the fulfilling the lusts of the flesh; 'merito hoc addit cum in uno et eodem homine regenerato sit caro et Spiritus: cujus certamen copiosissime explicatur, Rom. VII. [15—20],' Beza. In the following words the order ἀντίκ. ἀλλήλοις [*Rec.* with JK; mss.; Ff.] is rightly reversed with greatly preponderating authority. ἵνα μὴ] '*to the end that ye may not;*' not 'so that ye cannot do,' Auth. (οὐκ ἐπὶ αἰτίας εἶπεν, ἀλλ' ὡς ἀκόλουθον κατὰ τὸ οἰκεῖον ἰδίωμα, Theod.), but with the usual and proper (telic) force of ἵνα 'ut non quæcunque vultis illa (ista, Cl.) faciatis,' Vulg., Clarom., compare Goth., Æth.; the object and end of the τὸ ἀντικεῖσθαι on the part of each Principle

τοῦ Πνεύματος, τὸ δὲ Πνεῦμα κατὰ τῆς σαρκός· ταῦτα γὰρ ἀλλήλοις ἀντίκειται, ἵνα μὴ ἃ ἂν θέλητε ταῦτα ποιῆτε. 18 εἰ δὲ Πνεύ-

is to prevent man doing what the other Principle would lead him to; 'τὸ Πνεῦμα impedit vos, quo minus perficiatis τὰ τῆς σαρκός, contra ἡ σάρξ adversatur vobis ubi τὰ τοῦ Πνεύματος peragere studetis,' Winer; see Fritz. *Excurs. in Matth.* p. 838, Baur, *Paulus*, p. 533 sq., and compare the very good remarks of Hammond, *Serm.* VII. Part I. p. 123 (Angl. Cath., Libr.) where, although he quotes the eventual (ecbatic) sense of ἵνα in translation he almost appears to adopt the final sense in his remarks and deductions. On the use of ἵνα in the N. T., see notes *on Eph.* i. 17, Fritz. *Excurs. l. c.*, and Winer, *Gr.* § 53. 6, p. 406, and for a notice and example of its secondary-telic, or sub-final use, notes *on* 1 *Thess.* v. 4. Neither this derivative sense, however, nor any assumed eventual force (opp. to Ust. and De W.) is here to be ascribed to the particle, both being appy. inconsistent with the probable meaning of θέλητε; see next note. ἃ ἂν θέλητε] '*whatsoever ye may wish.*' This latter clause will admit of *three* different explanations, according as θέλητε is referred to (*a*) the carnal will; John. viii. 44, 1 Tim. v. 11; (*b*) the moral or better will, or (*c*) the free-will in its ordinary acceptation. Of these explanations, the first (*a*), though supported both by Chrys., Theod., and several distinguished modern expositors (Bull, *Harm. Ap.* II. 9. 25 sq., Neander, *Planting*, Vol. I. p. 468, ed. Bohn), must still be pronounced logically inconsistent with ταῦτα γὰρ ἀλλ. ἀντίκ., which seems rather to point to the *opposition* incurred than the victory gained by the Spirit. The second (*b*), though perhaps in a less degree, is open to the same objection, notwithstanding the support it may be thought to receive from Rom. vii. 15 sq., where θέλειν seems to point to the imperfect though better will; see Calv., Schott, De W., who conceive that St. Paul is here expressing briefly what in Rom. *l. c.* he is stating more at length. The simple and logical connection of the words is, however, much better supported by (*c*), subject only to this necessary and obvious limitation, that this ἰσόῤῥοπος μάχη must be only predicated, in its full extent, of the *earlier* and *more imperfect* stages of a Christian course; see Olsh. *in loc.* The state of the true believer is conflict, but *with final victory*,— a truth that was felt even by the Jews, among whom Abraham, Isaac, Jacob, and more especially Joseph, were ever cited as instances of a victorious issue: Schoettg. *de Luctâ Carnis et Spiritus*, III. 10, 11 (Vol. I. p. 1204.)

18. εἰ δὲ κ. τ. λ.] '*But if ye be led by the Spirit;*' contrasted state to the struggle described in the preceding verse; 'ubi *vero* Sp. vincit, acie res decernitur,' Beng. When the Spirit becomes truly the leading and guiding principle, then, indeed, the doubtful struggle has ceased; there would be no fulfilling of the works of the flesh, and by consequence no longer any bondage to the law; compare Maurice, *Unity of N. T.*, p. 510, and Baur, *Paulus*, p. 534, note.

Πνεύματι ἄγεσθε] '*by the Spirit;*' instrumental dative; comp. 2 Tim. iii. 6, ἀγόμενα ἐπιθυμίαις ποικίλαις, and see Winer, *Gr.* § 31. 7, p. 194, and exx. collected by Kypke, *Obs.* Vol. II. p. 172. Who can doubt, says Müller (*Doctr. Sin*, Vol. I. p. 355, Clark), that Πν. ἄγεσθ. here entirely corresponds in the mind of the Apostle with Rom. viii. 14, Πνεύματι Θεοῦ ἄγονται; and that thus the fuller and deeper meaning of Πνεῦμα

ματι ἄγεσθε, οὐκ ἐστὲ ὑπὸ νόμον. 19 φανερὰ δέ ἐστιν τὰ
ἔργα τῆς σαρκός, ἅτινά ἐστιν πορνεία, ἀκαθαρσία, ἀσέλγεια,

must be maintained throughout this paragraph. οὐκ ἐστὲ ὑπὸ νόμον] '*ye are not under the law;*' — not, on the one hand, because there is now no need of its beneficial influences (οὐ δεῖται τῆς ἀπὸ τοῦ νόμου βοηθείας, Chrys., al.), nor on the other, because it is now become an alien principle (Usteri, *Lehrb.* I. 4. A, p. 57), but simply — 'because it finds nothing in you to forbid or to condemn;' see ver. 23. The more obvious conclusion might have seemed, 'ye are not under the influences of the flesh;' but as the law was confessedly the principle which was ordained against the influences and ἔργα τῆς σαρκός (Rom. vii. 7 sq.), the Apostle (in accordance with the general direction of his argument) draws his conclusion relatively rather to the principle, than to the mere state and influences against which that principle was ordained.

19. φανερὰ δέ] '*But*, to explain and substantiate more fully the last assertion (οὐκ ἐστὲ ὑπὸ νόμον), the *open* difference between the works of the flesh (against which the law is ordained) and the fruit of the Spirit (against which there is no law) shall now be manifested by special examples.' ἅτινά ἐστι] '*of which class are;*' not quite so much as 'quippe quæ,' De Wette, 'quæ quidem,' Schott., — but merely 'such for instance as,' ὅστις having appy. here its *classifying* force; see notes on ch. iv. 24. πορνεία] '*fornication.*' Observe the prominence always given to condemnations of this deadly sin, it being one of the things which the old pagan world deemed as merely ἀδιάφορα; see Meyer *on Acts* xv. 20. The insertion of μοιχεία [*Rec.* with DE (FG ειαι) JK; Clarom., Goth., Syr.-Phil.; Gr. and Lát. Ff.] and the change to plurals [FG; Orig., al.] are rightly rejected by the best recent editors with ABC; 3 mss., Vulg., Syr., Copt., Æth. (both); Clem., Marc. in Epiph.; Cyr., al. ἀκαθαρσία, ἀσέλγεια] '*uncleanness, wantonness;*' comp. Rom. xiii. 13, 2 Cor. xii. 21 (where the same three words are in connection), Eph. iv. 19. The distinction between these words is thus drawn by Tittmann, *Synonym.* p. 151, — ἀκαθ. (more generic) 'quælibet vitæ animique impuritas;' ἀσέλγ., 'protervitas et impudens petulantia hominis ἀσελγοῦς (qui nullam verecundiæ pudorisque rationem habet), — non obscœnitas aut fœditas lubidinis;' comp. *Etym. Mag.* ἀσέλγεια· ἑτοιμότης πρὸς πᾶσαν ἡδονήν, and Trench, *Synon.* § XVI. where this latter word is defined as 'petulance or wanton insolence,' and as somewhat stronger than 'protervitas,' and more nearly approaching 'petulantia.' The derivation is very doubtful; it does not seem from θέλγειν (Trench), but perhaps from ἀσ. (satiety) and ἐλγ. connected with ἀλγ. (Benfey, *Wurzellex.* Vol. II. p. 15), or more probably (Donalds.) from ἀ priv. and σαλαγ-[σαλαγέω, σέλας], the primary idea being 'dirtiness,' 'foulness.' Winer observes that the vices here enumerated may be grouped into four classes, — (1) *sensuality;* (2) *idolatry*, not merely spiritual, but actual, — amalgamation of Christianity and heathenism (1 Cor. viii. 7); comp. Neander, *Planting*, Vol. I. p. 243 note (Bohn); (3) *malice;* (4) *excesses.* Beng. similarly divides them as 'peccata commissa cum proximo, adversus Deum, adversus proximum, et circa se ipsum, cui ordini respondet enumeratio fructus Spiritus.' There does not, however, appear any studied precision in the classification; St. Paul, as Aquinas re-

20 εἰδωλολατρεία, φαρμακεία, ἔχθραι, ἔρις, ζῆλος, θυμοί, ἐριθεῖαι,

marks, 'non intendit enumerare omnia vitia ordinate et secundum artem, sed illa tantum in quibus abundant, et in quibus excedunt illi ad quos scribit.'

20. φαρμακεία] 'sorcery,' ܚܪܫܘܬܐ [magia] Syr. This word, like the Lat. 'veneficium' (Vulg., Clarom.), may either imply (α) *poisoning*, as Æth., perhaps Goth., 'lubjaleisei' [compare Angl.-Sax. *lib.*], al., or (β) *sorcery*, as Syr. (both), Copt. (appy.), Arm., al. The former is not improbable on account of its juxtaposition to ἔχθραι (see exx. in Schleusn. *Lex. in LXX.* s. v., Exod. vii. 11, al.); the latter, however, seems here more probable, sorcery, as Meyer notices, being especially prevalent in Asia; see Acts xix. 19. On the subject generally, see Delitzsch, *Bibl. Psychol.* IV. 17, p. 262, sq. Both in this and the following words there is much variation between the sing. and plural forms. *Rec.* commences the list of plurals with ἔχθραι; the singulars ἔρις [ABD[1]; mss.] and ζῆλος [A? BD[1]E (FG ζῆλους); 17. Goth.] seem, however, to have the critical preponderance and are adopted by *Lachm. Tisch.*, and most modern editors. θυμοί] '*displays of wrath;*' both this and the associated plurals serving to denote the various concrete forms of the abstract sins here specified; see exx. of θυμοὶ noticed by Lobeck, *Ajax*, 716, Bernhardy, *Synt.* II. 6, p. 62, and esp. the good note of Heinichen on Euseb. *Eccl. Hist.* VIII. 6, Vol. III. p. 18 sq. The meaning of θυμός, as its derivation implies [θύω, *perhaps* connected with Sanscr. *dhu*, 'agitare,' Pott, *Etym. Forsch.* Vol. I. p. 211], is not so much '*inimicitia* hominis acerbi et iracundi' (Tittm. *Synon.* p. 133), as *iracundia*, or rather *excandescentia*, the principal idea being that of 'eager motion towards,' 'impulse;' see esp. Donalds. *Crat.* § 473, — where, however, the derivation of θύω is plausibly referred to ΘΕ-, on the principle of 'suggestion by contrast.' It thus differs from ὀργή, both in its *rise*, as more sudden (Luke iv. 28, Acts xix. 28), and its *nature*, as less lasting (compare Ecclus. xlviii. 10, κοπάσαι ὀργὴν πρὸ θυμοῦ); see Trench, *Synon.* § XXXVII., Fritz. *Rom.* Vol. I. p. 105, and notes *on Eph.* iv. 31.

ἐριθεῖαι] '*caballings;*' compare Syr. ܚܪܝܢܐ [rebellio, calumnia]. The accurate meaning of the word ἐριθεία appears to have been missed by most of the older, and indeed most of the modern expositors, by whom it is commonly connected with ἔρις (compare Œcum.), and understood to mean 'contention;' comp. 'rixa,' Vulg. 'inritationes,' Clarom. Its true etymological connection, is, however, with the Homeric word ἔριθος, 'a day-laborer,' and thence either with ἔριον (τὴν ἐργαζομένην τὰ ἔρια, Phavor. *Eclog.* p. 201, ed. Dind.), or more probably with ἘΡΩ, ἔρδω, ἐρέθω; compare Lobeck, *Patholog.* p. 365. Its meaning, then, is (α) *Labor for hire;* compare Suidas, s. v. δεκάζεσθαι; (β) *Scheming* or *intriguing for office*, 'ambitus:' compare Aristot. *Pol.* v. 2. 3, p. 1302, (ed. Bekk.); (γ) *Party-spirit*, a contentious spirit of faction; compare Schol. ap. Matth. ἐριθ. ἐμφιλόνεικοι πράξεις, and Steph. *Thes.* s. v. where there are also traces of a right perception of the true meaning. Of these (γ) seems to be the prevailing meaning in the N. T., where ἐριθ. occurs no less than 7 times, and in the following combinations; in Rom. ii. 8, οἱ ἐξ ἐριθ. are coupled with οἱ ἀπειθοῦντες τῇ ἀληθείᾳ, and in antithesis to οἱ καθ' ὑπομονὴν ἔργου ἀγαθοῦ; in 2 Cor. xii. 20, ἐριθεῖαι are enumerated between θυμοὶ and καταλαλίαι; in Phil. i. 16, ἐριθ. is in antithesis

διχοστασίαι, αἱρέσεις, [21] φθόνοι, φόνοι, μέθαι, κῶμοι, καὶ τὰ ὅμοια
τούτοις· ἃ προλέγω ὑμῖν, καθὼς καὶ προεῖπον, ὅτι οἱ τὰ τοιαῦτα

21. φόνοι] Omitted by *Tisch.* with B; 17. 33. 35. 57. 73; Demid. Aug.*; Clem., Marcion ap Epiph., Iren.; Cypr., Hieron. (distinctly), Ambrst., Aug. ([*Lachm.*], approved by *Mill*). The authorities for the text are ACDEFGJK; great majority of mss.; Clarom., Boern., Vulg., Syr. (both), Copt., al.; Chrys., Theod., al. (*Rec.*, *Griesb.*, *Scholz*, *Mey.*, *Alf.*, *Bagge*). These so decidedly preponderate, the characteristic paronomasia is so probable, and the omission in transcription, owing to the similarity in words, so very likely, that we do not hesitate to restore φόνοι.

to ἀγάπῃ; ib. ii. 3, it is connected with κενοδοξία, and in James iii. 14. 16, with ζῆλος. In Ignat. *Phuad.* 8, ἐριθ. is opposed to χριστομάθεια. It would thus seem that in all these passages, with the exception perhaps of Rom. *l. c.*, and Phil. *l. c.*, — where the *context* points less to party-spirit than to the *contentiousness* it gives rise to (see notes *on Phil.* i. 17, *Transl.*) — the meaning of ἐριθ. is fairly covered by the definition of Fritz. as 'summa invidia pectore inclusa proclivitasque ad machinationes;' see Rückert *on Rom.* ii. 8, and esp. Fritz. Excursus on ἔριθος, ἐριθεία, ἐριθεύομαι, *Comm. on Rom.* Vol. I. p. 143 sq. διχοστασίαι, αἱρέσεις] '*divisions, parties;*' the 'standing apart' (comp. 'tvisstasseis,' Goth.) and divisions (Rom. xvi. 17) implied in the former word, leading naturally to the more determinate choice ('electio præsertim disciplinæ cujusdam' Schott) exercised in the formation of the latter; comp. Theoph. and Bagge *in loc.*

21. μέθαι, κῶμοι] '*drunkenness, revellings,*' 'ebrietates, comessationes,' Vulg., Clarom.; the latter being the more generic and inclusive, to which the former was the usual accompaniment. On the nocturnal κῶμοι (τὰ ἀσελγῆ καὶ πορνικὰ ᾄσματα, συμπόσια, Hesych.) of the ancients see Schwarz. *de Comiss. Vet.*, Altdorf, 1744, Welcker in Jacobs, *Philostr.* I. 2, p. 202 sq. and on the derivation of the word [appy. connected with κοιμάω, and from a root κι-] Benfey, *Wurzellex.* Vol. II. p. 150. ἃ προλέγω ὑμῖν] '*about which I tell you beforehand;*' either 'præmoneo, priusquam veniat dies retributionis, sive judicii, quem hic respicit,' Est., or more simply, '*prædico*, ante eventum,' Beng.; comp. 1 Thess. iii. 4. It is not necessary to refer ἃ to πράσσοντες, as an accus. derived by attraction from the accus. *objecti* after that word (Schott, Olsh.); the ordinary explanation, 'quod attinet ad ea quæ,' (Camerar.), being perfectly satisfactory. In such cases, the relative is really governed by the finite verb as a species of 'quantitative' accus.; its prominence in the sentence, and *appy.* absolute use being designed to call attention to that on which the thought or action principally turns; comp. John. viii. 54, and see Scheuerl. *Synt.* § 8. 4, p. 55. Such sentences often involve a slight, but perfectly intelligible, anacoluthon; see Fritz. *Rom.* vi. 10, Vol. I. p. 393, and compare notes on ch. ii. 20.
καθὼς καὶ προεῖπον] '*as I also told you beforehand,*' sc. when I was with you; the καὶ appy. reminding them that these were warnings not new to them. The particle is omitted in BFG; Amit., Demid.; Chrys. (1), al., and bracketed by *Lachm.*, but rightly retained as part of the text by most recent editors, the external evidence in its favor [ACDEJK; nearly all mss., and

πράσσοντες βασιλείαν Θεοῦ οὐ κληρονομήσουσιν. 22 ὁ δὲ καρπὸς τοῦ Πνεύματός ἐστιν ἀγάπη, χαρά, εἰρήνη, μακροθυμία, χρηστό-

most Vv.; Clem., Chrys., Theod.] being so greatly preponderant. τὰ τοιαῦτα] '*such things as these*,' '*all such things*.' The article with τοιοῦτος denotes a known person or thing, or the whole class of such, but not an undefined individual out of the class; as in that case τοιοῦτος is anarthrous; see Kühner on Xenoph. *Mem.* I. 5. 2, and Krüger, *Sprachl.* § 50. 4. 6.

βασιλ. Θεοῦ οὐ κληρον.] '*shall not inherit the kingdom of God*;' comp. Eph. v. 5, where with equal pertinence the declaration is made of present time. On the meaning of the inclusive term βασιλείαν Θεοῦ,—that kingdom which was completely established at the ascension (see Jackson, *Creed*, x. 45. 2), of which Christ is the founder, and Christ (and God, Rev. xi. 15, xii. 10) the King, and of which the true Christian, even while here on earth, is a subject, see esp. Tholuck, *Bergpred.* p. 72 sq., Bauer, *Comment. Theol.* II. p. 107 sq., Heemskerk, *Notio* τῆς βασ. κ. τ. λ. (Amst. 1839), and the comments of Reuss, *Théol. Chrét.* II. 4, Vol. I. p. 180 sq. On its distinction (whether 'in sensu *initiali* or *finali*') from the more collective and, so to say, localized ἐκκλησία, see Stier, *Ephes.*, Vol. II. p. 252 sq.

22. καρπός] '*fruit*;' used appy. with a significant reference to the *organic development* from their root, the Spirit (Olsh., Bloomf.); διὰ τί δὲ καρπὸν καλεῖ τοῦ Πν.; ὅτι τὰ μὲν πονηρὰ ἔργα ἐξ ἡμῶν γίγνεται μόνον· διὸ καὶ ἔργα καλεῖ· τὰ δὲ καλὰ οὐ τῆς ἡμετέρας ἐπιμελείας δεῖται μόνον, ἀλλὰ καὶ τῆς τοῦ Θεοῦ φιλανθρωπίας, Chrys. It is possible that no marked distinction may be intended (Mey.), still, as καρπὸς is nearly always used by St. Paul 'in *bonam* partem' (Rom. i. 13, vi. 22, xv. 28, Eph. v. 9, Phil. i. 11, 22, iv. 17), and as even in Rom. vi. 21, where it is used in ref. to *evil* works, the same meaning ('what fruit,' *i. e.* 'what really beneficial result had ye,' etc.) appears to be preserved, we may safely press the peculiar meaning and significance of the term; see an excellent sermon on this text by Sanderson, *Serm.* XVII. (ad Aul.), p. 594 sq. (Lond. 1689). ἀγάπη, χαρά] '*love, joy*;' ἀγάπη, as Mey. observes, standing at the head, as the moving principle of all the rest (compare 1 Cor. xiii. 1 sq.), and χαρὰ following, as that special gift of the Spirit (comp. 1 Thess. i. 6), which ought to be the pervading principle of Christian life (Phil. iv. 4); comp. Reuss. *Théol. Chrét.* IV. 18, Vol. II. p. 202. εἰρήνη] '*peace*;' not so much *here* in ref. to peace with God (Phil. iv. 7, see notes *in loc.*) as, in accordance with the associated and partially contrasted terms ἔχθραι κ. τ. λ. (ver. 20),—peace with one another; compare 1 Thess. v. 15. On the meaning of μακροθυμία (*clementia*, quâ iræ temperans delictum non statim vindices,' Fritz. *Rom.* Vol. I. p 98), see notes *on Eph.* iv. 2, and for its distinction from ὑπομονή, notes *on Col.* i. 11.

χρηστότης, ἀγαθωσύνη] '*benevolence, goodness*.' These words are nearly synonymous. The former (defined in [Plato] *Def.* 412 E, as ἤθους ἀπλαστία μετ' εὐλογιστίας) may perhaps denote that benevolence and sweetness of disposition ('benignity,' Wicl., Rhem.) which finds its sphere and exercise in our intercourse with one another; comp. Tit. iii. 4, where it is joined with φιλανθρωπία, and see Tittm. *Synon.* p. 140, Planck, *Comment. Theol.* Part I. p. 197, and the citation from

της, ἀγαθωσύνη, πίστις, 23 πραΰτης, ἐγκράτεια· κατὰ τῶν τοιού-

Jerome in Trench, *Synon.* Append. p. 198 (ed. 1). The latter (ἀγαθ.), a somewhat rare word (though occurring in three other places in St. Paul's Epp. Rom. xv. 14, Eph. v. 9, 2 Thess. i. 11), seems more than ἡ ἀπηρτισμένη ἀρετή (Phavorinus, Zonaras) or even, 'animi ad optima quæque propensio' (Gom. *on Rom.* xv. 14), and may not improbably be extended to that 'propensio' as exhibited in *action*, the propension *both to will and do* what is good; see Stier, *Ephes.* Vol. II. p. 265, and compare Suicer, *Thes.* Vol. I. p. 16. The idea of 'bountifulness,' Nehem. ix. 25, is necessarily included. It may thus be distinguished from the somewhat late word ἀγαθότης (Lob. *Phryn.* p. 350), which rather denotes 'goodness in its *essence*,' and is thus commonly used in reference to God. πίστις] '*faith*;' not merely 'fidelitas, veracitas in promissis' (Men. ap. Pol. *Syn.*), *i. e.*, 'good faith' (Matth. xxiii. 23; Tit. ii. 10, πίστις ἀγαθή), but *trustfulness* (Conyb.), faith in God's promises and mercies and loving trust towards men; compare 1 Cor. xiii. 7, πάντα πιστεύει, where, like μακροθυμία and χρηστότης (ver. 4), it stands as one of the characteristics of ἀγάπη.

23. πραΰτης] '*meekness*,' 'modestia,' Vulg. The πραΰς is defined by Tittmann, *Synon.* p. 140, as 'mansuetus, qui æquo animo omnia fert *(sanftmüthig)*,' compare Aristot. *Eth.* IV. 11. This, however, seems wholly insufficient; the *Christian* grace of πραΰτης is not mere gentleness or ἀταραξία, (τὸ δυσκίνητον εἶναι πρὸς τὰς ὀργάς, Stob. *Floril.* I. 18), but appy. denotes a submissiveness to God *as well as* man, and may be distinguished from ἐπιείκεια as having its seat in the inner spirit, while the latter seeks to embody itself in acts; see Trench, *Synon.* § XLIII. 16, and notes *on Col.* iii. 12. On the orthography πραότης (*appy.* the more Attic form, Phot. *Lex.* p. 386) or πραΰτης, compare Lobeck, *Phryn.* p. 403. ἐγκράτεια] '*temperance*,' the exercise of control over passions and desires; compare Acts xxiv. 25, 2 Pet. i. 6; ἐγκρ. δέ ἐστιν ἀρετὴ τοῦ ἐπιθυμητικοῦ καθ' ἣν κατέχουσι τῷ λογισμῷ τὰς ἐπιθυμίας ὁρμώσας ἐπὶ τὰς φαύλας ἡδονάς, Stob. *Floril.* I. 18. It is distinguished by Diog. Laert. from σωφροσύνη as implying a control over the *stronger* passions, whereas the latter implies a self-restraint in what is less vehement; ἡ σωφροσύνη ἠρεμαίας ἔχει τὰς ἐπιθυμίας, ἡ δὲ ἐγκράτεια σφοδράς, Suid. *Lex.* s. v. Vol. I. p. 1138 (ed. Gaisf.). The addition of ἁγνεία (D^1EFG); Clarom. Vulg. [not Amit.; Bas., al.] is rightly rejected by appy. all recent editors. τῶν τοιούτων) '*all such things*;' not masc. (Theod.), but as seems much more natural, and is *perhaps* suggested by the art. (Olsh.) *neut.* in reference to the preceding virtues; compare the somewhat parallel passage, Stobæus, *Floril.* 18, fin., ἀκολουθεῖ δὲ τῇ ἀρετῇ χρηστότης, ἐπιείκεια, εὐγνωμοσύνη, ἐλπὶς ἀγαθή, ἔτι δὲ καὶ τὰ τοιαῦτα. Brown's argument (p. 307) is certainly not convincing, 'τοιούτων and τοιαύτων,' — a curious oversight. οὐκ ἔστι νόμος] '*there is no* (condemnatory) *law*.' The explanation *per meiosin*, 'tantum abest ut iis legis Mosaicæ terrores sint metuendi, ut potius Deo sint grati,' Rosenm. (cited by Brown), is not satisfactory. St. Paul draws a contrast between the legal judgment under which the former class lay, and the freedom from it which those who are led by the Spirit enjoy;

των οὐκ ἔστιν νόμος. [24] οἱ δὲ τοῦ Χριστοῦ τὴν σάρκα ἐσταύρωσαν
σὺν τοῖς παθήμασιν καὶ ταῖς ἐπιθυμίαις. [25] εἰ ζῶμεν Πνεύματι,

24. τοῦ Χριστοῦ] *Tisch.* adds Ἰησοῦ with ABC; mss.; Copt., Sahid., Æth. (both); Cyr. (often), Doroth., Bas., Procop., Dam., al.; Aug. [*Lachm.*]. The external authorities for the omission are DEFGJK (FG add εντες, scil. οντες); Vulg., Clarom., Syr. (both), Goth., Arm.; Chrys., Theodoret, Pseud-Ath., al.; very many Lat. Ff. (*Rec., Griesb., Scholz, Alf.*). Owing to the importance of ABC, the external evidence may perhaps be considered slightly in favor of the addition; the order, however, is so unusual (Eph. iii. 1, Col. ii. 6, but in both with var. readings), and external evidence for and against so nearly balanced, that we decide in favor of the shorter reading.

compare Bull, *Exam. Censuræ*, xvii. 16, where, however, the masc. interpr. of τοιούτων is adopted.

24. οἱ δέ] '*Now they*;' slightly contrasted application of the whole foregoing particulars to the special case of Christians, δὲ not being simply continuative (Auth.), nor yet resumptive, in ref. to ver. 16 (De W.), or to ver. 18 (Beng.), but almost syllogistic, the application to Christians forming a sort of practical 'propositio minor' to the foregoing group of verses. The connection of the whole paragraph, then, from ver. 16 appears to be as follows: — 'The Spirit and the flesh are contrary to each other; if the flesh prevail, man is given over to all sin, and excluded from the kingdom of God: if the Spirit be the leading principle, man brings forth good fruits, and is free from the curse of the law. *Now* the distinguishing feature of the true Christian is the crucifixion of the flesh; consequently, as must be obvious from what has been said, the living in and being led by the Spirit;' see Rückert *in loc.* ἐσταύρωσαν] '*crucified*,' scil. when they became Christians, and by baptism were united with Christ in His death; compare Rom. vi. 3. Though this ethical crucifixion is here designated as an act *past* (compare Rom. vi. 6, ὁ παλαιὸς ἡμῶν ἄνθρωπος συνεσταυρώθη), it really is and must be a continuing act as well; compare Rom. viii. 13. This however the aor., with its usual and proper force, leaves unnoticed; it simply specifies, in the form of a general truth, the act as belonging to the past, without affirming or denying any reference to the present; see Fritz. *de Aor. Vi*, p. 17, notes *on* 1 *Thess.* ii. 16, and compare Soph. *Antig.* 1318 (last line) ἐδίδαξαν, on which Wex remarks, 'unum exemplum, quod aliquando evenerit, tanquam norma proponitur:' see also Schmalfeld, *Synt.* § 60. 2, p. 128. In all such cases the regular reference of the tense to the past may be *felt* in the kind of summary way in which the action is stated, — the sort of implied dismissal of the subject, and procedure to something fresh; compare Donalds. *Gr.* § 433. On the vital truth, that our crucifixion of the flesh is included and involved in that of Him with whom we are united, comp. Usteri, *Lehrb.* ii. 1. 3, p. 202 sq.; and on the whole verse read the good sermon of South, *Serm.* xxiii. Vol. iv. p. 338 sq. (Lond. 1843).

25. εἰ ζῶμεν Πνεύματι] '*If we live by the Spirit*;' — 'if, as a matter of fact (see notes on ch. i. 9), we *live* (emphatic) by the efficacy and operation of the Spirit; assumption naturally arising from the preceding declaration of crucifixion of the opposing principle, the flesh; 'enecatâ in hominibus Christianis τῇ σαρκί, necesse est in iisdem vivat suamque vim libere exserat τὸ Πνεῦμα,'

Πνεύματι καὶ στοιχῶμεν. 26 *μὴ γινώμεθα κενόδοξοι, ἀλλήλους προκαλούμενοι, ἀλλήλοις φθονοῦντες.*

Schott. The omission here of all illative particles makes the exhortation more forcible and emphatic; comp. 1 Cor. iii. 17. There is some little difficulty in the explanation of the dative Πνεύματι. It is certainly not (*a*) a dative of *manner*, scil. 'spiritually' Middl.; as thus not only the force of the verse, but the connection with what precedes, arising from the opposition of the Πνεῦμα and the σάρξ, is completely lost. Nor again (*b*) is it a dative of *relation*, — 'si vitam nostram ad Spiritum referimus, ad Spiritum etiam dirigamus vitam,' Fritz. (*Rom.* xiii. 13, Vol. III., p. 142); for though Rom. xiv. 6—8 supplies a somewhat parallel sentiment, the antithesis between the two clauses is thus obviously deprived of all force and pertinence. On the whole, then, the ordinary explanation (*c*) would seem to be most satisfactory, according to which Πνεύματι is to be regarded as a form of the *instrumental* or *ablatival* dative (Winer, *Gr.* § 31. 7, p. 194), and as here adopted rather than διὰ with the accus. (John vi. 57, compare Winer p. 356), as thus forming a sharper antithesis to the dative which follows, — 'if we live by the Spirit (if the Spirit is our principle of life) by the Spirit let us also walk;' compare 2 Cor. iii. 6, τὸ δὲ Πνεῦμα ζωοποιεῖ, and see Neand. *Planting*, Vol. I. p. 469 sq. (Bohn). The second Πνεύματι is obviously the dat. *normæ*, scil. κατὰ τοὺς ἐκείνου νόμους πολιτευόμενοι, Chrys., see notes on ver. 16. Fritz (*Rom.* iv. 22, Vol. I. p. 225) explains it as a dat. *commodi*, 'Spiritui vitam consecrate;' but this, *on Rom.* xiii. 13, he appears to have retracted. στοιχῶμεν] '*let us walk.*' The hortatory imperative is not without some doctrinal significance (Ust.); the Apostle evidently assuming the union and coëxistence of the Divine and human powers in the heart of the true Christian; compare Beck, *Seelenl.* I. 8, p. 29, II. 13, p. 32 sq., Usteri, *Lehrb.* II. 1. 3, p. 218 note. The command is substantially the same as that in ver. 16, except perhaps that στοιχεῖν [στιχ-] may imply a more *studied* following of a prescribed course, than the more general περιπατέω (notes *on Phil.* iii. 18); compare Polyb. *Hist.* XXVIII. 5. 6, στοιχεῖν τῇ τῆς συγκλήτου προθέσει, Dion. Hal. *Antiq.* VI. 65, στοιχεῖν ταῖς πλείοσι γνώμοις, and the somewhat unusual expression στοιχεῖν μιᾷ γυναικί, Schol. Arist. *Plut.* 773.

26. μὴ γινώμεθα κ. τ. λ.] '*Let us not become;*' not 'let us not be,' Auth. (comp. Syr.), but 'ne efficiamur' Vulg., Clarom., 'vairþamma,' Goth., there being appy. no less in the verb than in the person an intentional *mildness*, which seems to imply that the sin of κενοδοξία had not yet taken root, though the very warning suggests that it was to be expected. The verse thus forms a suitably concluding warning against those particular sins of the Galatians to which the Apostle alluded in ver. 13—15 and at the close of ver. 20, and belongs to Chap. v., though it also serves very naturally to connect the doctrinal with the more directly admonitory portion of the Epistle, which begins with the next chapter. A *close* connection with Ch. vi. (Mey., al.) seems clearly at variance with the introductory ἀδελφοί (compare ch. iv. 12), and the change of person.

ἀλλήλ. προκαλούμενοι] '*provoking each other;*' scil. εἰς φιλονεικίας καὶ ἔρεις, Chrys. 'calling one another out to the field of controversy,' Brown; see Herodian, *Hist.* VI. 9 (Oxon., 1704), προκαλεῖται ἡμᾶς εἰς μάχην, and simply,

Ye who are spiritual should bear and forbear; examine yourselves before ye judge others.

VI. Ἀδελφοί, ἐὰν καὶ προλεμφθῇ ἄνθρωπος ἔν τινι παραπτώματι, ὑμεῖς οἱ πνευματικοὶ

Polyb. *Hist.* I. 46. 11, προκαλούμενος τοὺς πολεμίους. The meaning of φθονοῦντες has been modified by some commentators, 'withholding out of envy' (Olsh.), 'hating' (Brown). This is not necessary; φθονεῖν is the correlative act on the part of the weak, to the προκαλεῖσθαι on the part of the strong. The strong, vauntingly challenged their weaker brethren: the weak could only retaliate with *envy.* It may be remarked that φθονεῖν does not occur elsewhere in N. T.; in James iv. 2, the correct reading is φονεύετε.

CHAPTER VI. 1. ἀδελφοί] '*Brethren;*' conciliatory mode of address introducing the more directly admonitory portion; 'latet in hoc etiam uno verbo argumentum,' Beza. ἐὰν καὶ προληφθῇ] '*if a man be even surprised* or *caught;*' præoccupatus fuerit,' Vulg., Clarom., Syr., 'gafauhaidan,' Goth. The verb προλημφθῇ has received several different interpretations, in accordance with the different meanings assigned to πρό. The more strict *temporal* meaning, 'antea,' whether referred to the arrival of the Epistle (Grot.), to a recurrence of the offence (Winer), or to the attempt at restoration, — the λαμβάνεσθαι taking place before the καταρτ. (Olsh.), — is unsatisfactory, as the emphatic position of προλημφθῇ and the force of καὶ are thus both obscured. The common reference to the *unexpectedness* of the sin ('notat improvisam occupationem,' Vorst., ἐὰν συναρπαγῇ, Chrys.), is also inconsistent with καί, as this meaning of πρὸ would tend to excuse and qualify, whereas καὶ seems to point out an aggravation of the offence. If, however, πρὸ be referred to *the power of escape,* — 'be caught before he could escape,' 'flagrante delicto,' — not only the intensive force of καί, but the emphatic position of προλημφθῇ and the general tenor of the exhortation is fully preserved. This meaning of προλαμβ., it must be admitted, is rare, but see exx. in Kypke, *Obs.* Vol. II. p. 289, and esp. Wisdom, xvii. 17, προληφθεὶς, τὴν δυσάλυκτον ἔμενεν ἀνάγκην. On the Alexandrian form προλημφθῇ, see Winer, *Gr.* § 5, 4, *Tisch. Prolegom.* p. xx., and on the difference between ἐὰν καὶ and καὶ ἐάν, see note, ch. i. 8, Herm. *Viger*, No. 307, Klotz, *Devar.* Vol. II. p. 519. ἐν τινὶ παραπτώματι] '*in any transgression,*' in any particular act of sin, esp. on the side of error, stumbling, or transgression of a command. On the distinction between παράπτωμα (more particular), and ἁμαρτία (more general), see notes *on Eph.* ii. 1. ὑμεῖς οἱ πνευματικοί] '*ye the spiritual ones,*' '*ye that are spiritual.*' The tenor of the exhortation, coupled with the similar distinctions which St. Paul seems elsewhere to have recognized in his converts (e. g., 1 Cor. iii. 1), appears in favor of the opinion that the Apostle is here designating not merely those who were *subjectively* πνευματικοί, *i. e.*, who thought themselves so (comp. Windischm.), but those who were *objectively* πνευματ., those who had remained true to him and his doctrines; see Olsh. *in loc.* That the teachers are mainly addressed in ver. 1—6, and the hearers and laity in ver. 6—10, is also probable. καταρτίζετε] '*restore.*' The technical meaning ἀπὸ τῶν ἐξαρθρημάτων 'reponere in artu luxata membra,' Steph. (*Thes.* Vol. IV. p. 1213), adopted by Beza, Blooomf., Brown, al., does not appear here alluded to, as examples of the sim-

καταρτίζετε τὸν τοιοῦτον ἐν πνεύματι πραΰτητος, σκοπῶν σεαυτόν μὴ καὶ σὺ πειρασθῇς. [2] *ἀλλήλων τὰ βάρη βαστάζετε, καὶ οὕτως*

2. ἀναπληρώσετε] *Tisch.* (ed. 2) reads ἀναπληρώσατε with ACDEJK; appy. nearly all mss.; Syr.-Philox., perhaps Goth. [but conjunct. acts both for fut. and imper.; De Gabel. *Gr.* § 182, 186]; Clem., Ath., Chrys., Theodoret, Dam., al. (*Rec., Griesb., Scholz*). The authorities for text are BFG; 2 mss.;. Vulg., Clarom., Syr., Arm., Copt., Sahid., Æth. (both); Theodoret (mss.) Aster. Procl.,

ple ethical sense (διορθοῦτε. Chrys.) are sufficiently common; comp. Herodot. v. 28, καταρτίζειν (Μίλητον,) Stob. *Floril.* I. 85, καταρτ. φίλους διαφερομένους, Greg. Nazianz. *Orat.* XXVI. Vol. I. p. 443 B, πόθεν οὖν ἄρξομαι καταρτίζειν ὑμᾶς ἀδελφοί (cited by Dindorf). πνεύματι πραΰτητος] '*the spirit of meekness;*' not merely 'a meek spirit,' — a wholly inadmissible dilution of the true meaning of the words, — but a spirit of which the principal constituent (comp. Bernhardy, *Synt.* III. 44, p. 161) or *characterizing quality* (Scheurl. *Synt.* § 16. 3, p. 115) is πραΰτης, compare Winer, *Gr.* § 34. 2. b, p. 212. The anarthrous πνεῦμα (but after a prep.) refers *ultimately*, as Chrysostom felt, to the Holy Spirit, one of whose especial charisms is 'gentleness;' see ch. v. 23. This reference, however, must not be overstated, or expressed by the use of a capital letter; for, as in 1 Cor. iv. 21 (where πν. πραΰτητος is joined with ἀγάπῃ), so here πν. seems *immediately* to refer to the state of the inward spirit as wrought upon by the Holy Spirit, and *ultimately* to the Holy Spirit as the inworking power; compare Rom. i. 4, πν. ἁγιωσύνης, viii. 15, πν. υἱοθεσίας, 2 Cor. iv. 13, πν. τῆς πίστεως, Eph. i. 17, πν. σοφίας, in all which cases πν. seems to indicate the Holy Spirit, and the abstract gen. the specific χάρισμα; see Hamm. *in loc.*, and notes *on* 2 *Tim.* i. 7. σκοπῶν σεαυτόν] '*looking to thyself;*' temporal clause stating the (proper) concomitants of the action ('considering all the time thy own case'), or perhaps with a secondary-causal force hinting at the reasons for it; see Krüger, *Sprachl.* § 56. 12. 1, Schmalfeld, *Synt.* § 207, and compare Donalds. *Gr.* § 615. For instances of the emphatic and individualizing enallage of number, see Bernhardy, *Synt.* XII. 5, p. 421. *Lachm.* connects this clause with ver. 2, putting a full stop after πνεύμ. πραΰτητος, and a comma after πειρασθῇς, but thereby obviously weakens the whole force and point of the address. The πνευματικοὶ were reminded of their own liability to fall into temptation: why? Surely not to urge them merely *generally* to bear one another's burdens, but *particularly* to evince their Christian spirit, by restoring one who had fallen, only after all, as they themselves might. μὴ κ. τ. λ.] '*lest thou also shouldst be tempted,*' scil. in a like case; subjunctive ('verentis,' est ne quid nunc sit, simulque nescire se utrum sit necne significantis,' Herm. Soph. *Ajax*, 272), and in the *aor.*, in reference to an event still impending; see Winer, *Gr.* § 46. 2, p. 447, and the copious list of exx. of this and similar constructions in Gayler, *Part. Neg.* p. 325.

2. ἀλλήλων τὰ βάρη] '*the burdens of* ONE ANOTHER;' the ἀλλήλ., as Meyer rightly observes, being emphatic, not however, with any oblique reference to the burden of the Law (Alf.), but simply in opposition to that selfish feeling which would leave each one to bear

ἀναπληρώσετε τὸν νομον τοῦ Χριστοῦ. [3] εἰ γὰρ δοκεῖ τις εἶναί τι

Marc. erem.; Tert., Cypr., al. (*Lachm.*, *Tisch.*, ed 1, *Meyer*, *De Wette*, approved by *Mill*, Prolegom., p. 123). The preponderance of *MSS.* evidence is thus plainly in favor of the imper.; still the testimony of the *Vv.* joined with the extreme probability of a change from the future to the imperfect (see *Mill*, *l. c.*) seems sufficient to authorize the rejection of a reading, which on strict grammatical principles may be pronounced *somewhat* suspicious.

his own; contrast the Apostle's own example, 2 Cor. xi. 29. The meaning of this expressive word must not be too much circumscribed. It seems chosen, with inclusive ref. to all forms of weaknesses (ἀσθενήματα, Rom. xv. 1), sufferings, and, perhaps more especially, *sins;* the purport of the command being φέρειν τὰ τῶν πλησίον ἐλαττώματα, Chrys., or, with more exactness, ἐπικουφίζειν τὴν ψυχὴν ὑπὸ τῆς τοῦ ἁμαρτήματος συνειδήσεως βεβαρημένην, Theod. Mops. p. 129. βαστάζετε] '*bear*,' *i. e.* sustain as a superimposed burden. On the particular use and meaning of βαστάζειν in the important doctrinal statement, Matth. viii. 17, — as exemplified by this passage, see Magee, *Atonement*, No. XLII. Vol. I. 415 sq. καὶ οὕτως ἀναπληρώσετε] '*and thus shall ye fulfil*,' — *thus*, in this way, and no other, viz., by following the exhortation just given. Future after imperat., as in ch. v. 16. On the whole (see crit. note), the future seems the more probable, as well as perhaps the more strictly grammatical reading; for though no opposing argument can be founded on the use of the imperfect aor. combined with the imperfect present (the former often stating the *general* command, the latter some of the *details;* comp. Schömann, *Isæus*, p. 235), still in the case of this particular verb the use of the present (compare Barnab. *Ep.* ch. 21, ἀναπληροῦτε πᾶσαν ἐντολήν), is much more natural. The compound ἀναπληροῦν is not simply synonymous with πληροῦν (Rück., al.), but appears in all cases to denote a *complete* filling up, and to point to a *partial* rather than an entire vacuum; 'hæc demum erit perfecta legis impletio,' Winer, *Verb. Comp.* Fasc. III. p. 11; compare Plut. *Poplic.* § 11, ἀνεπλήρωσε τὴν βουλὴν ὀλιγανδροῦσαν ('made up the full number of'), and see notes *on Phil.* iii. 30. The explanation of Chrys., κοινῇ πάντες πληρώσατε, is not satisfactory. τὸν νόμον τοῦ Χρ.] '*the law of Christ;*' not generally 'le mobile des actes du Chretien' (Reuss, *Théol. Chr.* IV. 16, Vol. II. p. 168), but definitely 'the law of love' (τὴν ἀγάπην φησίν, Theod. Mops.), which he gave (John xiii. 34, ἐντολὴν καινὴν δίδωμι ὑμῖν, ἵνα ἀγαπᾶτε ἀλλήλους; 1 John iii. 23, ἀγαπῶμεν ἀλλήλους καθὼς ἔδωκεν ἐντολὴν ἡμῖν), and which He so graciously exemplified, αὐτὸς γὰρ τὰς ἁμαρτίας ἡμῶν ἀνέλαβε καὶ τὰς νόσους ἐβάστασεν, Schol. ap. Matth. The peculiar term νόμος is *perhaps* here chosen with some reference to the case of the Galatians: they affected an observance of the law of Moses, here was a law of Christ in which was included the fulfilment of the whole law; comp. ch. v. 14. This '*novum* præceptum Christi' is illustrated and explained by Knapp, *Script. Var. Arg.* No. x. p. 369 sq.

3. εἰ γὰρ κ. τ. λ.] '*For if any one thinks*,' etc.; confirmation of the foregoing exhortation to gentleness and humility, by showing the evils of the opposite course. 'The best motive to indulgence towards others is, as Olsh. remarks, the sense of our own weakness.

μηδὲν ὤν, φρεναπατᾷ ἑαυτόν. 4 τὸ δὲ ἔργον ἑαυτοῦ δοκιμαζέτω

μηδὲν ὤν] '*when he is nothing,*' 'being all the time nothing;' temporal, or in the more accurate language of Schmalfeld, 'temporal-concessive' participle, stating what the man after all is, in spite of his opinion of himself; see the exx. in Schmalfeld, *Synt.* § 207. 2, p. 415. Alford finds in this use of the subjective μηδὲν rather than οὐδὲν (absolute) a fine irony, — 'being if he would come to himself, and look on the real fact.' This, however, is somewhat precarious, as the use of the subjective negation with participles is the prevailing usage in the N. T.; see Green, *Gr.* p. 122. While, then, we may press οὐ when so connected, we must be careful in overpressing μή; see notes *on* 1 *Thess.* ii. 15, iii. 1. For illustrative exx. of the general form of expression, see Wetst. *in loc.*, and Kypke *Obs.* Vol. II. p. 291; one of the most apposite is, Plato, *Apol.* p. 41 E, ἐὰν δοκῶσί τι εἶναι, μηδὲν ὄντες. φρεναπατᾷ] '*deceiveth his own mind,*' '*inwardly deceiveth himself;*' comp. Goth., 'fraþjamarzeins ïst,' [intellectus deceptio est]. The verb is an ἅπαξ. λεγ. in the N. T.; comp., however, φρεναπάτης, Tit. i. 10, and James i. 26, ἀπατῶν καρδίαν αὐτοῦ. This last passage may perhaps enable us to draw a distinction between ἀπατᾷ ἑαυτὸν and φρεναπατᾷ ἑαυτόν. The former may imply a deception which had something objective to rest upon; the latter a more studied inward-working, and purely subjective deception; comp. notes *on Tit.* i. 10. Hence the force of the command which follows, τὸ ἔργον δοκιμαζέτω, put to the proof his *outward* acts, and form his judgment upon *them.* The gloss of Hesych. (χλευάζει), or even of Zonaras (διαπαίζει) does not, consequently, seem quite sufficient.

The order ἑαυτὸν φρεναπ. [*Rec.* with DEFGJK; al.] is well supported, but inferior in point of critical authority to that of the text (*Lachm.*, *Tisch.*, with ABC; 80, al.), and not improbably a correction to give ἑαυτόν studied prominence.

4. τὸ ἔργον ἑαυτοῦ δοκιμ.] '*prove his own work;*' put to the test all that he is particularly engaged on; '*rem* non opinionem de se,' Beng. The singular with the article is appy. here used collectively (De W., Mey.), scil. τὰς ἑαυτοῦ πράξεις, Theophyl., τὰ βεβιωμένα αὐτῷ, Œcum.; 'universam agendi rationem complectitur,' Schott: comp. Rom. ii. 15, 1 Pet. i. 17, and see Winer, *Gr.* § 27. 1, p. 157. On the meaning of δοκιμάζειν μετ' ἀκριβείας ἐξετάζειν, Theoph.), see notes *on Phil.* i. 10, Suicer, *Thesaur.* s. v. Vol. I. p. 936, and for a good practical sermon on this and the preceding verse, see Usher, *Serm.* III. Vol. XIII. p. 31 sq. (ed. Elrington). τὸ καύχημα κ. τ. λ.] '*his ground of boasting.*' The true meaning of this passage has been somewhat obscured by a neglect of the exact meaning and force of the different words. (1) The concrete καύχημα, *gloriandi materies* (Rom. iv. 2, 1 Cor. ix. 15, 16, al.), must not be confounded with καύχησις, *gloriatio* (Rom. iii. 27, al.), the distinction between these words being appy. always observed in the N. T., — even in 2 Cor. v. 12, ix. 3, al. (2) The article is not used κατ' ἐξοχήν, but pronominally (Middleton, ch. v. 3), '*his* ground of boasting,' the καύχημα which properly belongs to him; compare 1 Cor. iv. 5, τότε ὁ ἔπαινος γενήσεται ἑκάστῳ. (3) The prep. εἰς must in each clause bear the same meaning (opp. to De Wette); the most simple and suitable appearing to be, 'with regard to,' 'in relation to,' not 'contra,' Schott (which can be justified,

ἕκαστος, καὶ τότε εἰς ἑαυτὸν μόνον τὸ καύχημα ἕξει, καὶ οὐκ εἰς
τὸν ἕτερον. 5 ἕκαστος γὰρ τὸ ἴδιον φορτίον βαστάσει.

e. g. Luke xii. 10, but connected with ἑαυτ. would involve an artificial explanation); comp. 2 Cor. xi. 10, ἡ καύχησις αὕτη οὐ σφραγίσεται εἰς ἐμέ, Eph. iii. 16, κραταιωθῆναι . . . . εἰς τὸν ἔσω ἄνθρωπον; comp. Winer, *Gr.* § 49. a, p. 354, Bernh. *Synt.* v. 11, p. 220. (4) The force of τὸν ἕτερον (not ἕτερον, as implied by Auth.) must not be overlooked, scil. '*the* one with whom he is contrasting himself;' 'his neighbor,' Copt., Arm. The meaning of the whole clause then will be, 'If any one wishes to find matter for boasting, let it be truly searched for in his own actions, and not derived from a contrast of his own fancied virtues with the faults of others;' compare Hammond *in loc.* True Christian καύχημα, like St. Paul's, must be found either in a deep and thankful acknowledgment of blessings and successes (ἐν Κυρίῳ καυχάσθω, 2 Cor. x. 17), or in afflictions and weakness (2 Cor. xi. 30, xii. 5), which still more show forth both the mercy and the mighty power of the Lord; comp. 2 Cor. xii. 9.

5. ἕκαστος γάρ] '*For each man;*' confirmatory clause standing in close connection with the last words of ver. 4, and assigning a reason why a man would have little real ground or justice for claiming spiritual superiority over his neighbor; he had only to look at himself, to see that he had his own burden to bear; καὶ σὺ κἀκεῖνος τὸ ἴδιον φορτίον βαστάσετε, Œcum. φορτίον] '*load;*' not identical with the preceding βάρος, ver. 2 (Vulg., Clarom., Arm.,— but not any of the other Vv.), which perhaps is used as a more general term in reference to the community at large, while φορτ. has a more *individualizing* reference to the particular *load* of sins and infirmities which each one, like a wayfarer (comp. Wisdom xxi. 6, Xenoph. *Mem.* III. 13. 6), had to carry: 'alia sunt onera participandæ infirmitatis, alia reddendæ rationis Deo de actibus nostris: illa cum fratribus sustentanda communicantur, hæc propria ab unoquoque portantur,' August. *de Consens. Evang.* II. 30. 72. The qualitative and humbling distinction of Chrys. (τοῖς ὀνόμασι τοῦ φορτίου καὶ τῆς ἀχθοφορίας πιέζων αὐτῶν τὸ συνειδός), and the quantitative of Beng. ('φορτίον, par ferentis viribus; βάρη quæ excedunt') do not appear so natural or probable. The allusion which Conyb. here finds to Æsop's well-known fable (the Πῆραι δύο ? p. 165, ed. De Furia) is not very plausible, as the point of the fable and the tenor of this verse are far from being identical.

βαστάσει] '*shall bear,*' scil. '*has to bear,*' '*must bear.*' The future does not here refer to the day of judgment (Theod., al.; see ch. v. 10), nor even (like ἕξει) to the future period when the conviction is arrived at, 'will find he has to bear' (Windischm., al.), but is appy. used *ethically*, in ref. to what according to the nature of things *must* be the case; compare notes *on Eph.* v. 31, Thiersch, *de Pent.* III. 11, p. 158, sq., and see exx. in Jelf, *Gr.* § 406. 3, and Bernhardy, *Synt.* x. 5, p. 377. It was not so much from a sense of future responsibility, as from a consciousness of present *unavoidable* ἀχθοφορία, that a man would be led to think humbly of himself and kindly of his neighbor. The observation of Fritzsche on the use of the future is worthy of citation; 'Futurum in sententiâ generali recte ponitur, quandoquidem rei quæ in nullum tempus non convenire

Be liberal to your teachers; as ye sow now, whether it be to the flesh or to the Spirit, so shall ye reap.

6 Κοινωνείτω δὲ ὁ κατηχούμενος τὸν λόγον

videatur, etiam futuro tempore locum futurum esse jure sumitur,' *on Rom.* vii. 3, Vol. II. p. 9.

6. κοινωνείτω δὲ κ. τ. λ.] '*but let him that is instructed share with,*' etc.; exhortation to the duty of sharing temporal blessings with others, placed in contrast (δὲ) to the foregoing declaration of individual responsibility in spiritual matters. With regard to the construction there is some little doubt whether κοινωνεῖν is here transitive ('sit benignus in magistrum in omni bonorum genere' Fritz. *Rom. l. c.*; compare Chrys., πᾶσαν ἐπιδεικνύσθω περὶ αὐτὸν δαψίλειαν) or intransitive. The verb has three constructions in the N. T.; (*a*) with gen. of the *thing;* only Heb. ii. 14; (*b*) with dat. of *thing,* the common construction, Rom. xii. 13, xv. 27, 1 Tim. v. 22, 1 Pet. iv. 13, 2 John 11; (*c*) dat. of *person,* the *thing* under the regimen of a prep., Phil. iv. 15. In all these instances (even in Rom. xii. 13) the meaning seems clearly *intransitive.* The same appears to be the meaning in the present case: for though the transitive constr. is lexically admissible (Thom. Mag. κοινωνῶ σοι ὧν ἔχω, ἀντί τοῦ μεταδίδωμι), and yields a perfectly good sense, still the prevailing use of κοινωνεῖν in the N. T., the analogy of construction between this passage and Phil. iv. 15, οὐδεμία μοι ἐκκλησία ἐκοινώνησεν εἰς λόγον δόσεως καὶ λήμψεως, and the general context supply arguments in favor of the *intransitive* meaning, which seem distinctly to preponderate.

ὁ κατηχούμ. τὸν λόγον] '*he that is instructed in* THE *word,*' scil. in the Gospel (see Acts xv. 7, τὸν λόγον τοῦ εὐαγγελίου, and compare Luke i. 2), τὸν λόγον being the accus. of reference, or what is termed the 'qualitative object' (Hartung, *Casus,* p. 55, 61) after the pass. part. κατηχούμενος (Acts xviii. 25); see Winer, *Gr.* § 32. 5, p. 104, and esp. Schmalfeld, *Synt.* § 25, compared with § 16, and fin. With regard to the meaning of κατηχέω which has here been somewhat unduly pressed, we may observe that the word appears to have four meanings; (α) *sono;* ἀντὶ τοῦ ἠχῶ, Suidas; (β) *sono impleo;* compare Lucian, *Jup. Trag.* 39, κατᾴδουσι καὶ κατηχοῦσι; (γ) *vivâ voce erudio,* προτρέπομαι καὶ παραινῶ, Suid.; compare Syr. ܕܫܡܥ [qui audit], Æth., and see Joseph. *Vit.* § 69, where this meaning seems confirmed by the context ἀλήθειαν ἐμαρτύρει; and lastly (δ), with a more general and unrestricted reference, *edoceo* (διδάσκω, Hesych., Zonaras), — *appy.* the meaning in the present case ('sa laisida,' Goth., ܕܡܠܦܢܐ [qui instituit] Syr.-Phil.), and in the majority of the passages in the N. T. (Luke i. 4, Acts xviii. 25, Rom. ii. 18, — perhaps even 1 Cor. xiv. 20, Acts xxi. 21, 24), in which it occurs; the idea of *oral* teaching being merged in that of general instruction however communicated. On the use of the word, esp. in Eccl. writers, see Suicer, *Thesaur.* s. v. Vol. I. p. 69 sq., where this word is fully explained.

ἐν πᾶσιν ἀγαθοῖς] '*in* (sphere of the action of κοινωνεῖν) *all good things,*' *i. e.* 'all temporal blessings;' compare 1 Cor. ix. 11. There does not seem sufficient reason for leaving the ancient interpretation, κελεύει τοῖς πνευματικῶν ἀπολαύουσι μεταδιδόναι τῶν σαρκικῶν, Œcum.: see Neand. *Planting,* Vol. I. p. 152 note (Bohn). The usual objections are based on the isolation of the verse from ver. 5 and ver. 7, which this interpretation is thought to cause. This, however, does not appear to be the case.

τῷ κατηχοῦντι ἐν πᾶσιν ἀγαθοῖς. 7 μὴ πλανᾶσθε, Θεὸς οὐ μυκτηρίζεται. ὃ γὰρ ἐὰν σπείρῃ ἄνθρωπος, τοῦτο καὶ θερίσει· 8 ὅτι

The concluding words of ver. 5, if left without any further addition, might have been misconstrued into an implied declaration, that it was not right to be chargeable on anybody. This the Apostle specially, but almost parenthetically, obviates, indicating with δὲ (see above) the contrast between the spiritual and the temporal application.

7. μὴ πλανᾶσθε] *'Be not deceived;'* continuation of the subject in a more general and extended way, though still not without reference to the subject of the special command. This solemn and emphatic mode of admonition is used by St. Paul in two other passages, 1 Cor. vi. 9, and xv. 33; in the former with reference to an evil act, in the latter to an evil conclusion, just mentioned. In the present case the reference appears rather to what *follows;* though a reference to what precedes ('præstringit tenaces,' Paræus) need not be excluded. Ignatius uses the same form, *Eph.* 5, 10, *Philad.* 3, *Smyrn.* 5. οὐ μυκτηρίζεται] *'is not* (actually or with impunity) *mocked;'* 'non irridetur,' Vulg. This emphatic word is used several times in the LXX, and occasionally in later classical writers: μυκτηρίζειν λέγομεν τοὺς ἐν τῷ διαπαίζειν τινὰς τοῦτό πως τὸ μέρος (μυκτῆρα) ἐπισπῶντας, *Etym. M.* s. v. μυκτήρ, p. 594 ed. Gaisf.). Elsner (*Obs.* Vol. II. p. 199) has illustrated this meaning by a few examples, e. g. Quintil. *Inst.* VIII. 6. 59, Sueton. *August.* 4, Cicero, *Epist. Fam.* xv. 19. In Hippoc. p. 1240 D, it occurs in the sense of 'bleeding at the nose.' ὃ γὰρ ἐὰν κ. τ. λ.] *'for whatsoever a man soweth;'* confirmation of the truth of the preceding assertion by means of a significant image (compare Matth. xiii. 39) derived from the natural world. τοῦτο καὶ θερίσει] *'this*—and nothing else than this—*shall he also reap;'* the καὶ with its ascensive force pointing to the regularly developed issues. Wetst. *in loc.* aptly cites Cic. *de Orat.* II. 65, 'ut sementem feceris ita metes.' On this text see two sermons by Farindon, *Serm.* LXI., LXII. Vol. I. p. 52 sq. (Lond. 1849.)

8. ὅτι ὁ σπείρων] *'because he that is sowing;'* reason for the concluding τοῦτο καὶ θερίσει, and exemplification, of it in spiritual things; he that is sowing one kind of seed (the Spirit) will reap the regular products and developments of that seed; he that is sowing another (the flesh), those of that other: ὥσπερ γὰρ ἐπὶ τῶν σπερμάτων οὐκ ἔνι σπείροντα ὀρόβους (vetches) σῖτον ἀμῆσαι· δεῖ γὰρ τοῦ αὐτοῦ γένους καὶ τὸν σπόρον εἶναι καὶ τὸν ἀμητόν, Chrys. εἰς τὴν σάρκα ἑαυτοῦ] *'unto, or for, his own flesh,'* not '*in* carne suâ,' Vulg., Clarom.; for though the flesh and the Spirit are represented under the image of two corn-fields, in which seed is sown, and from which the harvest is gathered, the meaning of εἰς is still not *local* ('*in*, tanquam in agrum,' Beng.), but, in accordance with its more usual meaning, *ethical* ('carni suæ,' Beza, compare Copt.); the prepp. used in the N. T. in a *strictly local* sense being appy. ἐν and ἐπί,—the former in reference to the inclosure *in* which the seed is sown (Matth. xiii. 24, 27, ib. 19, and metaphorically, Mark iv. 15),—the latter to the spot *on* which it is cast (Matth. xiii. 20, 23, Mark iv. 16, 20, 31). In the expression εἰς τὰς ἀκάνθας (Matth. xiii. 22, Mark iv. 18) εἰς rather means 'among;' comp. Plato, *Leg.* VIII. 839 A. The force of the pronoun ἑαυτοῦ must

*ὁ σπείρων εἰς τὴν σάρκα ἑαυτοῦ ἐκ τῆς σαρκὸς θερίσει φθοράν, ὁ
δὲ σπείρων εἰς τὸ Πνεῦμα ἐκ τοῦ Πνεύματος θερίσει ζωὴν αἰώνιον.
9 τὸ δὲ καλὸν ποιοῦντες μὴ ἐγκακῶμεν· καιρῷ γὰρ ἰδίῳ θερίσομεν*

not be overlooked, *selfishness* being implied as well as carnality; 'caro *suitati* dedita est,' Beng.: compare Aquinas (cited by Windisch.), 'sed nota quod cum agit de seminatione carnis dicit, *in carne suâ*, quia caro est nobis, de naturâ nostrâ; sed cum loquitur de semine Spiritus non dicit *suo*, quia Spiritus non est nobis a nobis, sed a Deo.'

φθοράν] '*corruption*,' — of the whole man, both body and soul; not merely in the narrower physical sense of 'decay' (καὶ γὰρ αὐτὰ φθείρονται καὶ συμφθείρει τὸ σῶμα, Chrys.); but also in the fuller ethical sense of 'corruption of soul,' in which of course eternal death and 'destruction' (Hesych. φθορά· ὄλεθρος) are involved and implied: see 2 Pet. i. 4, ii. 12, 19, and compare Rom. vi. 21, 22. The use, however, of φθορὰ rather than ἀπωλεία (Phil. iii. 19), — though it *possibly* may be introduced as more applicable to σάρξ (Schott), — seems to preclude our adopting 'destruction' as the *primary* meaning; see Stier, *Ephes.* Vol. II. p. 180.

ζωὴν αἰώνιον] '*eternal life*;' ζωήν, in contrast to the preceding φθοράν (comp. Psalm ciii. 4, Jonah ii. 6), and that too, as the nature of the principle to which the sowing is made distinctly suggests, — αἰώνιον. On the meaning of the term αἰώνιος, comp. notes *on* 2 *Thess.* i. 9.

9. τὸ δὲ καλὸν ποιοῦντες] '*But in well-doing let us*,' etc.; exhortation to perseverance in the form of sowing just mentioned, the δὲ idiomatically introducing an address after foregoing details (compare Eurip. *Rhes.* 165, ναί, καὶ δίκαια ταῦτα τάξαι δὲ μισθὸν κ. τ. λ.), and, though practically approaching in meaning to οὖν ('so let us not'), still preserving its proper force in the contrast between the corrupted class just prominently mentioned, and the better class which is now addressed: see exx. in Hartung, *Partic.* δέ, 2. *n*, Vol. I. p. 166. On the general and inclusive meaning of τὸ καλόν, see notes on ver. 10.

μὴ ἐγκακῶμεν] '*let us not lose heart*.' Both here and in the other passages where the word occurs (Luke xviii. 1. 2 Cor. iv. 1, 16, Eph. iii. 13, 2 Thess. iii. 13) *Lachm.* and *Tisch.* read ἐγκακ. instead of ἐκκακ. (*Rec.*, al.), and rightly; as it seems very doubtful whether ἐκκακ. is a genuine word at all, and whether its occurrence in lexicons and use in later writers (see exx. collected by L. Dind. in Steph. *Thes.* s. v. Vol. v. p. 430) is not, as Usteri thinks, entirely due to these doubtful readings. At any rate, if ἐκκακ. exist, the difference will be very slight; ἐκκακεῖν may perhaps mean, 'to retire from fear *out* of any course of action,' (nearly ἀποκακεῖν); ἐγκακεῖν, 'to behave cowardly,' 'to lose heart,' when *in* it. In Rost u. Palm, *Lex.* (Vol. I. p. 833), Polyb. *Hist.* IV, 19. 10 is cited in favor of ἐκκακεῖν. This is an oversight; the reading is ἐνεκάκησεν, and is actually so cited by Rost u. Palm under ἐγκακέω; see p. 762.

καιρῷ ἰδίῳ] *in due, proper time*; 'tempore præstituto' (Beza), the time appointed by God for the reward to be given; compare καιροῖς ἰδίοις, 1 Tim. ii. 6, vi. 15. On the present use of the dative to denote the space of time *within which* the action takes place, — more correctly expressed with an inserted ἐν (Rom. iii. 26, 2 Thess. ii. 6, al.), see notes *on* 1 *Tim.* ii. 16, and *comp. Eph.* ii. 12.

μὴ ἐκλυόμενοι] '*if (now) we faint not (in our well-doing')*,

μὴ ἐκλυόμενοι. 10 ἄρα οὖν, ὡς καιρὸν ἔχομεν, ἐργαζώμεθα τὸ

'provided that we do not;' hypothetical use of the temporal participle, the present tense pointing to the state in which they must now be if they would reap hereafter: see Krüger, *Sprachl.* § 56. 11, and exx. in Schmalfeld, *Synt.* § 207. 5, p. 415. The simple predicative connection with θερίσομεν ܘܠܐ ܢܠܐܐ ܠܢ [et non erit molestum nobis] Syr., or the more practically adverbial, 'without fainting' (surely not 'unweigerlich,' Ewald), scil. πόνου δίχα θερίσομεν (Theod., Theoph. al., who thus draw a contrast between the toilsome nature of the earthly, and the unwearying nature of the heavenly harvest) does not seem satisfactory. For though this interpretation cannot be pronounced *grammatically* incorrect, on account of the use of the μὴ rather that οὐ (Rück., Schott), — the connection of μὴ with participles being so distinctly the prevailing usage in the N. T. and later writers (see notes on ver. 3, and comp. exx. in Winer, *Gr.* § 55, 5, p. 428 sq., and in Gayler, *Partic. Neg.* p. 36), — it still must be rejected on *exegetical* grounds, as adding no particular force to the general exhortation; whereas the conditional meaning serves fully to bring out the mingled warning and encouragement (προτρέπει καὶ ἐφέλκεται, Chrys.), which seems to pervade the verse. The distinction drawn by Beng. between ἐκκακεῖν (in *velle*) and ἐκλύεσθαι (in *posse*), the former referring to the faintness of heart, the latter to the *unstrung* state, and the '(interna) virium remissio' seems fairly tenable: see exx. in Steph. *Thesaur.* s. v., from which we may select (though with a more simply physical ref.), Plutarch, *Moral.* VI. 613, ἐκλελυμένος καὶ κεκμηκώς. A sensible sermon on this verse will be found in Sherlock, *Serm.* XXXIX. Vol. II. p. 275 sq. (ed. Hughes).

10. ἄρα οὖν] '*Accordingly then,*' '*So then;*' collective and inferential exhortation arising immediately out of the preceding statements, and bringing to a natural close the group of verses beginning with ver. 6, and the more directly hortatory portion of the epistle. The proper meaning of ἄρω, *rebus ita comparatis*, and its primary reference to simple 'progression to another step in the argument' (Donalds. *Crat.* § 192), is here distinctly apparent; its weaker ratiocinative force being supported by the collective power of οὖν: 'as things are so, let us in consequence of their being so,' etc. In Attic Greek this combination is only found in the case of the interrogative ἆρα; see Herm. *Viger*, No. 292, and on the general distinction between ἄρα and οὖν, see Klotz, *Devar.* Vol. II. p. 717, — but compare Donalds. *Gr.* § 604, and notes on ch. iii. 5. ὡς καιρὸν ἔχομεν] '*as we have opportunity,*' *i. e.* 'an appointed season for so doing;' not merely 'prout,' *i. e.* quandocunque et quotiescunque occasio nascatur' (Wolf), but, 'as, in accordance with the circumstances;' see Meyer *in loc.* The particle ὡς is thus rather *causal*, 'quoniam' (Ust., al.), nor *temporal* 'dum' (Vulg., Clarom., Syr.-Phil.), as appy. Ign. *Smyrn.* 9, ὡς ἔτι καιρὸν ἔχομεν (both, esp. the latter, very doubtful meanings in St. Paul's Epp., though not uncommon in classical writers; see Klotz, *Devar.* Vol. II. p. 759), but has only its simple relative force; the true link between this and the preceding verse being supplied by καιρός (Brown, p. 348); 'as there is a καιρὸς for τὸ θερίζειν, so is there one for τὸ σπείρειν. As we have it then, let us act accordingly and make

ἀγαθὸν πρὸς πάντας, μάλιστα δὲ πρὸς τοὺς οἰκείους τῆς πίστεως.

Recapitulation. Your false teachers seek to have you circumcised to avoid persecution and to boast of your submission. All true boasting, however, must be in Christ and His Cross.

11 Ἴδετε πηλίκοις ὑμῖν γράμμασιν ἔγραψα

the most of it;' κατεπείγει καὶ συνωθεῖ, Chrys. Hammond (*on Phil.* iv. 10) translates καιρὸν 'ability,' but the exx. cited by Wetst. *in loc.* will show this modification to be quite unnecessary.

τὸ ἀγαθόν] '*that which is good;*' 'the thing which in each case is good,' whether considered in a spiritual or temporal sense. The distinction between τὸ καλόν, as implying *good* in its highest sense, and τὸ ἀγαθόν, as referring more particularly to *kindness*, etc. (Baum.-Crus.), does not seem tenable in the N. T.: as τὸ καλὸν includes what is beneficent (Matth. xii. 12), as well as what is morally good (1 Thess. v. 21), so τὸ ἀγαθὸν includes what is morally and essentially good (Rom. ii. 10), as well as what is merciful (Philem. 14, compare Eph. iv. 28), — ἀγαθωσύνην as well as εὐποιΐαν, Heb. xiii. 16; compare notes *on* 1 *Thess.* v. 21. The reading ἐργαζόμεθα adopted by *Lachm.* ed. sterest. (but retracted in larger ed.) with AB²J and some mss., is rightly rejected by recent editors on decidedly preponderant external evidence [B¹CDE FGK (-σωμεθα), and a great majority of mss. Vv. and Ff.] and not without some probability of the interchange of the ο and ω (though rare in such MSS. as B) being here accidental; comp. Scrivener, *Collat.* p. LXIX. sq.

πρὸς τοὺς οἰκείους τῆς πίστ.] '*unto them who belong unto the faith.*' The meaning of πρὸς is here not merely the general ethical one, *with regard to*, but the particular one, *erga;* comp. Eph. vi. 9, 1 Thess. v. 14 (notes), and exx. in Winer, *Gr.* § 49. h, p. 361. The meaning *erga*, or *contra* (this latter rare if a hostile notion is not implied in the verb, Joseph. *Apion.* I. 31) will result from the context. With regard to the peculiar phrase οἰκεῖοι τῆς πίστεως, it may be observed that it does not appear to involve any allusion to οἶκος in the peculiar sense of 'the *house* of God' (Schott), or to any especial idea of composing a single *family* (Reuss, *Théol. Chrét.* IV. p. 124), as the numerous exx. from latter writers of this use of οἰκεῖος with an abstract subst. (*e. g.* οἰκεῖοι φιλοσοφίας, ὀλιγαρχίας, γεωγραφίας, τρυφῆς) all seem to show that the adjective has lost its meaning of peculiar, and only retains that of *general* though *close* connection; see Schweighæus. *Lex. Polyb.* s. v., and Wetst. *in loc.* A sermon on this and the preceding verse, but of no particular character, will be found in Tillotson, *Serm.* LXXXIX. Vol. II. p. 592 (Lond. 1752).

11. πηλίκοις ὑμῖν γράμμασιν ἔγραψα] '*in what large letters I have written to you.*' The only possible way of arriving, even approximately, at the meaning of this much debated clause, is to adhere closely to the simple lexical meanings of the words. These it will be best to notice separately.

πηλίκος strictly denotes *geometrical* magnitude, 'how large' (comp. Plato, *Meno*, 82, πολίκη τις ἔσται ἐπείνου ἡ γραμμή; so too Zachar. ii. 2. πηλίκον τὸ πλάτος . . . πηλίκον τὸ μῆκος) in contradistinction to *arithmetical* magnitude, expressed by πόσος, 'how many.' This meaning and distinction appear to have been observed in the N. T., as in the only other passage in which πηλίκος occurs, Heb. vii. 4, πηλίκος οὗτος, the same primary idea of *magnitude* (though in an ethical sense) is distinctly recognizable. To assume then in the present case (*a*) any confusion of πηλίκος with πόσος (Schott, Neander, *Planting*, Vol. I. p. 221, Bohn), when there is no trace of such a usage either in the N. T. or LXX, seems distinctly *uncritical;* nor can (*b*) any assumed equivalence with ποῖος ('qualibus literis,' Vulg., Clarom., Arm., 'wileikaim,' Goth., compare Hesych. πηλίκον, οἷον, ὁποῖον, and see Tholuck, *Anzeig.* 1834, No. 32), and any reference to the ἀμορφία of the letters (Chrys., Theoph., Œcum., Theod. 2; comp. Zonar. *Lex.* s. v. πηλίκον· τὸ ἐν ἀμορφίᾳ ὄν. ὡς παρὰ τῷ 'Αποστόλῳ· ἴδετε κ. τ. λ., Vol. II. p. 1547) be pronounced otherwise than purely *arbitrary;* for magnitude does not mean shapelessness. We can have then no other correct translation than simply, '*how large;*' ἄγαν μίζοσιν ἐχρήσατο γράμμασιν, Theod.,— who, however, appears to limit the autographic portion to what follows.

γράμματο *may* be interpreted 'an epistle;' see Acts xxviii. 21, compare 1 Macc. v. 10, Ignat. *Rom.* 8: but (*a*) St. Paul in no other passage so uses it, though he has occasion to use a word denoting a letter (ἐπιστολή) seventeen times; and (*b*) this species of cognate dative γράψαι γράμμασιν (compare εἰπὲ λόγῳ, Matth. viii. 8) is not found in St. Paul's Epp., nor has here any of the additional force which the usage implies (Bernh. *Synt.* III. 16, p. 107), and which alone could account for the introduction of a *third* dative (instead of the natural accus.) in a sentence of eight words. We seem, therefore, forced to adhere to the simple meaning, '*letters, characters,*' as in Luke xxiii. 38, 2 Cor. iii. 7 *(Rec.):* so Copt. *han-skhai*, and appy. Arm.; the other Vv. are ambiguous.

ἔγραψα] '*I wrote,*' or in idiomatic English, —'*I have written,*' in ref. to the whole foregoing epistle; not 'I write' (Scholef. *Hints* p. 197, Conyb., al.), epistolary aorist. The real difficulty lies in this word, owing to the different conclusions to which historical and grammatical considerations appear respectively to lead us. On the one hand it appears distinctly (Rom. xvi. 22, 24, 1 Cor. xvi. 21, Col. iv. 18, 2 Thess. iii. 17), that St. Paul was in the habit of using an amanuensis, and of adding only the concluding words. From ver. 11 to end would seem, then, very probably such addition. But, on the other hand, it is very doubtful whether St. Paul or any of the writers of the N. T. ever use the epistolary aor. ἔγραψα exclusively in reference *to what follows.* The aorist in all cases appears to have its proper force, either (*a*) in reference to a former letter (1 Cor. v. 9, 2 Cor. ii. 3, iv. 9, vii. 12, 3 John 9 [see Lücke *in loc.*]), or (*b*) in reference to an epistle now brought to its conclusion (Rom. xv. 15, 1 Pet. v. 12), or (*c*) to a foregoing portion of the epistle (1 Cor. ix. 15, 1 John ii. 21 [see Lücke and Huther *in loc.*]; compare Philem. 19), and even stands in a species of antithesis to γράψω in reference to what has already been written (1 John ii. 14, where see Huth.); see Winer, *Gr.* § 40. 5. 2, p. 249, and notes *on Philem.* 19. With this partially conflicting evidence it seems impossible to decide positively whether St. Paul wrote the *whole* epistle or only the *concluding portion.* On the whole, however, the use of ἔγραψα, especially when contrasted with γράφω (2 Thess. iii. 17), inclines us to the former supposition, and we thus conclude, that to prevent any possible mistake as to the authorship of the epistle (Chrys.; compare 2 Thess. ii. 2), — especially as this was an encyclical missive (ch. i. 2, where see Olsh.), — St. Paul here deviated from his usual custom, and wrote the *whole* letter with his own hand (Chrysostom, Theod., Theoph., Œcum.), and in characters, whether from design or inexpertness,

τῇ ἐμῇ χειρί. 12 *ὅσοι θέλουσιν εὐπροσωπῆσαι ἐν σαρκὶ οὗτοι*
ἀναγκάζουσιν ὑμᾶς περιτέμνεσθαι, μόνον ἵνα τῷ σταυρῷ τοῦ Χρισ-
τοῦ μὴ διώκωνται. 13 *οὐδὲ γὰρ οἱ περιτεμνόμενοι αὐτοὶ νόμον*

2. διώκωνται] *Tisch.* διώκονται, with ACFGJK: many mss.; few, however, will hesitate to consider this an improbable solœcism. The text is rightly adopted by *Griesb.*, *Scholz*, *Lachm.*, *Alf.*, with B (Mai) DE, and appy. many mss. The transposition ἵνα μὴ (*Rec.* with FGJK; mss.) is rightly rejected by nearly all recent editors.

larger than those of the ordinary amanuensis.

12. ὅσοι θέλουσιν] '*as many as wish;*' concluding warning against the false Teachers whose true motives are here exposed, and contrasted with those which influenced the Apostle (ver. 14). εὐπροσωπῆσαι ἐν σαρκί] '*to make a fair show in the flesh,*' not so little as 'placere,' Vulg., Clarom., or even ܢܫܬܒܗܪܘܢ (ut glorientur] Syr., but rather 'pulchram faciem assumere' [*shi skenho*] Copt., scil. 'to wear a specious exterior in the earthly unspiritual element in which they move. The verb εὐπροσωπέω is not used by any earlier writer: but from the use of the adj. εὐπρόσωπος 'fair and specious' (Herod. VII. 168, Demosth. *Coron.* p. 277; see Elsner, *Obs.* Vol. II. p. 200), and the similar compounds, σεμνοπροσωπέω (Aristoph. *Nub.* 363), and φαινοπροσωπέω (Cic. *Att.* VII. 21), cited by the commentators on this verse, the meaning would appear correctly stated by Chrys. as εὐδοκιμῶ, though not necessarily παρὰ ἀνθρώποις; see below. The appended words ἐν σαρκὶ are commonly explained, either (*a*) 'in observatione rerum carnalium,' with *physical* reference to circumcision; or (*b*) 'apud homines,' with reference to *judgment* and opinions of others, — ἵνα ἀνθρώποις ἀρέσωσι, Chrys. τὴν παρὰ ἀνθρώπων θηρώμενοι δόξαν, Theod. Both interpretations, however, seem distinctly insufficient, as they put out of sight that more profound and far-reaching meaning of σάρξ, 'the earthly existence and conditions of man,' 'notio universa rerum externarum' (Schott), which pervades this whole epistle; see notes ch. v. 16, and Müller, *on Sin*, ch. II. ad fin., Vol. I. p. 353 (Clark). οὗτοι] '*these;*' it is this class and this preëminently, that are engaged in constraining you, etc.; see notes ch. iii. 7. τῷ σταυρῷ] '*on account of the cross;*' not exactly 'in cruce' (Copt.), but 'ob crucem' (Beza), scil. 'for preaching the doctrine of the cross of Christ.' The dative points out the *ground* or *cause* of the persecution; compare Rom. xi. 20, ἐξεκλάσθησαν τῇ ἀπιστίᾳ, and see Winer, *Gr.* § 31. 6, p. 193, Bernhardy, *Synt.* III. 14, p. 102. The ablatival explanation, that they may be persecuted *with* the cross of Christ ('perpessiones Christi,' 2 Cor. i. 5, Grot., comp. Vulg. 'crusis Christi persecutionem'), either, on the one hand, involves an unsatisfactory explanation of ὁ σταυρός, — which, as Brown (p. 359) rightly observes, in such expressions as the present always implies the fact of the *atoning* death of Christ, — or, on the other, causes a still more untenable meaning to be assigned to διώκωνται, viz. 'lest the doctrine of Christ wear a hostile aspect to them,' as Neand. *Planting*, Vol. I. p. 226 (Bohn). The meaning, 'that they may not follow after,' Arm. (comp. Æth. 'ut non adhæreatis'), is wholly untenable.

13. οὐδὲ γὰρ . . . αὐτοί] '*For not*

φυλάσσουσιν, ἀλλὰ θέλουσιν ὑμᾶς περιτέμνεσθαι ἵνα ἐν τῇ ὑμετέρᾳ σαρκὶ καυχήσωνται.
14 ἐμοὶ δὲ μὴ γένοιτο καυχᾶσθαι εἰ μὴ

even they,' 'nam ne ipsi quidem,' Beza, —*they* of whom it might reasonably have been expected; confirmation of the preceding by a statement of the openly lax conduct of the Judaizers, and of the true motives by which they were influenced; tantum abest, ut illorum intersit, a vobis legem observari,' Beng. On the force of οὐδὲ—ἀλλά, see on ch. i. 17.

οἱ περιτεμνόμενοι] '*those who are having themselves circumcised*,' 'qui circumciduntur,' Vulg.; pres. part., with reference to the prevailing practice of the false teachers either in respect of themselves or others. The explanation of Peile, Hilgenfeld, al., according to which the pres. part. περιτεμν. loses its precise temporal reference (Winer, *Gr.* § 45. 7, p. 316) and combines with the article to form a kind of subst., 'the party or advocates of the circumcision' (comp. οὗτοι οἱ περιτεμνόμενοι, *Acta Pet. et Paul.* § 63, cited by Hilgenfeld), is plausible, but perhaps not necessary; as the use of the pres. may be fairly explained on the ground that St. Paul includes in the idea not merely their conformity to the rite (which strictly becomes a past act), but their endeavor thereby to draw others into the same state, which is a *present* and continuing act. It must be admitted that the reading, περιτετμημένοι [*Lachm.*, *Scholz*, *Rinck*, *Mey.*, with BJ; 40 mss.; Clarom., al.; Lat. Ff.] would give a more appropriate sense; the external authorities, however [ACDEK; Vulg., Syr. (both), al.; Marcion, ap. Epiph., Chrys., Theodoret, al.], are distinctly in favor of the more *difficult* reading, περιτεμνόμενοι.

νόμον] '*the law*.' Middleton here explains the anarthrous νόμος as 'moral obedience' ('the principle of Law,' Peile), adducing the parallel passage, Rom. ii. 25; but there also, as here, νόμος is the Mosaic law: see Alford *on Rom. l. c.* The reason why these Judaizers did not keep the law is not to be referred to their distance from Jerusalem (Theod.), nor to any similarly extenuating circumstances, but, as the context seems to show, is to be attributed simply to their consummate hypocrisy; see Meyer *in loc.* ἐν, τῇ ὑμετέρᾳ σαρκί] '*in* YOUR *flesh*,'—'*your* bodily and ritualistic mutilation;' *i. e.* ἐν τῷ κατακόπτειν τὴν ὑμετέραν σάρκα, Theoph., — not *their own* observances of that law for which they are affecting so zealously to contend. There is no contradiction between the two motives assigned for their enforcement of the circumcision. The second, as Usteri observes, states positively what the first did negatively. They boasted that they had not only made Christian, but Jewish converts ('quod vos Judaismo implicuerint,' Beza), and thus sought to escape persecution at the hands of the more bigoted Jews.

14. ἐμοὶ δὲ μὴ γέν. καυχ.] '*But from me far be it that I boast;*' contrasted statement (δὲ) of the feelings of the Apostle and the substratum on which his καύχησις alone rested. For exx. of this use of γένοιτο with an infin., see Gen. xliv. 7, 17, Josh. xxii. 29, al., and Polyb. *Hist.* xv. 10. 4, μηδενὶ γένοιτο πεῖραν ὑμῶν λαβεῖν. ἐν τῷ σταυρῷ] '*in the cross*:' *i. e.* in the principle of the sufferings and death of Christ being the only means whereby we are justified and reconciled unto God (Rom. v. 9, 10); καὶ τί ἐστι τὸ καύχημα τοῦ σταυροῦ; Ὅτι ὁ Χριστὸς δι' ἐμὲ τὸν δοῦλον, τὸν ἐχθρόν, τὸν ἀγνώμονα· ἀλλ' οὕτω με ἠγάπησεν ὡς καὶ ἑαυτὸν ἐκδοῦναι ἀρᾷ, Chrys. See a sound sermon on this

ἐν τῷ σταυρῷ τοῦ Κυρίου ἡμῶν Ἰησοῦ Χριστοῦ, δι' οὗ ἐμοὶ κόσμος ἐσταύρωται κἀγὼ τῷ κόσμῳ·
15 οὔτε γὰρ περιτομή τι ἔστιν

15. οὔτε γάρ] So *Tisch.* with B; 17; Syr. (both), Goth., Sah., Æth., Arm.; Chrys., Syncell.; Hieron., Aug. *(De. W., Mey., Bagge, Alf.)* much commended by *Griesb.;* approved by *Mill* (Prolegom. p. 85). The longer reading, ἐν γὰρ Χριστῷ Ἰησοῦ is found in ACDEFGJK; Vulg., Clarom., Copt., Æth.-Platt, Syr.-text by Beveridge, *Serm.* XXI. Vol. I. p. 396 sq. A. C. Libr.). δι' οὗ] '*by whom;*' scil. by whose crucifixion.' The relative may refer either to σταυρός (Theodoret), or to Ἰησ. Χριστός. It is curious that Baumg. Crus. in adopting the latter reference, and Windischm. the former, should both urge that, on the contrary supposition, St. Paul would have writien ἐν ᾧ instead of δι' οὗ. As far as this argument goes, both are right (see Winer, *Gr.* § 48. a, p. 346, 347), though probably the frequent use of ἐν in the N. T. with reference to Christ is slightly in favor of Windischm. comp. Eph. i. 7. The context, however, is a far surer guide, and here, as the important and indeed emphasized subject τοῦ Κυρ. ἡμ. Ἰησ. Χρ. immediately precedes, the relative will more naturally seem to refer to those words. κόσμος] '*the world;*' τὰ βιωτικὰ πράγματα, Chrys.; not 'res et religio Judaica,' Schoettg. The full meaning has been well expressed by Calvin, 'mundus procul dubio opponitur novæ creaturæ; quicquid ergo contrarium est spirituali Christi regno mundus est, quia ad veterem hominem pertinet. Mundus est quasi objectum et scopus veteris hominis' (cited by Peile). The present omission of the article with κόσμος is very unusual, and only to be accounted for by the supposition that κόσμος was sometimes practically regarded in the light of a proper name: in all other places in the N. T., except the present, 2 Cor. v. 9, and, somewhat differently, 2 Pet. ii. 5, the omission is only found after a preposition (1 Cor. viii. 4, Phil. ii. 15, Col. ii. 20), or when the noun is under the regimen of a preceding substantive (John xvii. 24, Rom. i. 28, iv. 13, xi. 12, 15, Eph. i. 4, al.); see Middl., *Gr. Art.* p. 350 (ed. Rose), Winer, *Gr.* 19. p. 112. Whether in the concluding member the article is to be retained or rejected *(Lachm.)* is very doubtful. The external authority (ABC[1]D[1]FG; 17, Orig. (3), Ath., al.] for κόσμῳ is very strong; still as an omission to conform with the preceding member seems highly probable, and the external authority [C[3]C[3]E JK; nearly all mss.; Clem., Orig. (7), and many Ff.] of considerable weight, we retain with *Tisch., Mey.,* al., the longer reading τῷ κόσμῳ. ἐμοί] '*to me;*' dative of what is termed 'ethical relation,' — a usage of this case which is more fully developed in the dat. *commodi* or *incom.;* see Winer, *Gr.* § 31. 4, p. 190, Bernhardy, *Synt.* III. 9, p. 85, Krüger, *Sprachl.* § 48. 5. This reciprocal crucifixion is a forcible mode of expressing the utter cessation of all communion between the Apostle and world: as Schott well observes, 'alter pro mortuo habet alterum;' compare John vi. 56, 2 Thess. i. 12, 1 Cor. vi. 13. On the profound significance of these expressions of union with Christ, comp. Reuss, *Théol. Chrét.* IV. 16, Vol. II. p. 164.

15. οὔτε γάρ] '*For neither;*' explanatory confirmation of the preceding words δι' οὗ κ. τ. λ., εἶδες σταυροῦ δύναμιν. . . . . οὐ γὰρ δὴ μόνον τὰ τοῦ κόσμου πράγματα ἐνέκρωσεν αὐτῷ πάντα, ἀλλὰ τὰ

οὔτε ἀκροβυστία, ἀλλὰ καινὴ κτίσις. 16 καὶ ὅσοι τῷ κανόνι τούτῳ

Phil. with asterisk; Theod., Dam.; Ambrst., al. *(Rec., Scholz, Lachm.)*. The external evidence is thus *very* strong; still, the probability that the longer reading is a gloss from ch. v. 6, seems so great that, supported as we are by ancient Vv., we do not hesitate in adhering to the shorter reading. The reading ἰσχύει *(Rec.* with D3JK; mss.; al.), has less claim on attention.

τῆς πολιτείας τῆς παλαιᾶς ἀνώτερον πολλῷ κατέστησε, Chrys. On the reading, see critical note. καινὴ κτίσις] '*a new creature.*' Κτίσις has two meanings in the N. T.; *active*, 'the act of creation' (Rom. i. 20) *passive*, 'the thing created,'—whether personal and individual (2 Cor. v. 17), or impersonal and collective (Rom. viii. 19). Either meaning will suit the present passage; the latter, perhaps (comp. 2 Cor. v. 17, εἴ τις ἐν Χριστῷ, καινὴ κτίσις is most probable. The form of expression may possibly have originated from the use of the similar term בְּרִיָּה חֲדָשָׁה, to denote proselytes (Schoettg. *Hor. Hebr.* Vol. I. p. 328); the meaning, however, and application, is here, of course, purely Christian. On these words see an admirable sermon by Hammond, *Serm.* XXVII. Part. II. p. 380 sq. (A. C. Libr.), comp. also Beveridge, *Serm.* XIX. Vol. I. p. 342 sq. (A. C. Libr.), and five sermons by Tillotson, *Serm.* Vol. III. p. 324 sq. (Lond. 1752).

16. καὶ ὅσοι] '*and as many as walk;*' prominent specification of the personal subjects in regard of whom the prayer is offered, the nominatival clause standing isolated, and passing κατ' ἀνακολουθίαν into another structure; see Jelf. *Gr.* § 477. 1. The reading is doubtful. On the one hand, the fut. στοιχήσουσιν is fairly supported [B (Mai.) C2JK; mss.; Vulg.; Chrys., Theod.], and perhaps not quite so likely to have been changed from the pres. as *vice versâ*. Still, on the other, as the external evidence [AC1DEFG; mss.; Clarom.; Syr. (both), Goth., Copt. (appy.), Arm.; Chrys., Jerome, Aug., al.] is *very strong*, and a change to a future, as pointing out the course the Galatians were to follow, not wholly improbable, we adopt with *Tisch.*, *De W.*, al. the present στοιχοῦσιν. τῷ κανόνι τούτῳ] '*according to this rule,*' scil. of faith; κανόνα ἐκάλεσε τὴν προκειμένην διδασκαλίαν, Theod. It is perhaps slightly doubtful whether we are here to adopt the more literal meaning of κανών, 'directing line' (Mey.), ܫܒܝܠܐ [Semitam] Syr.) or the more derivative meaning 'maxim,' 'norma vivendi' (garaideinai, Goth., *heg* [lex] Æth.); the former seems, at first sight, in better accordance with στοιχοῦσιν, but as this verb is used above (ch. v. 16), with but little tinge of its physical meaning (contrast Rom. iv. 12), and as κανὼν may very naturally be referred to the principle stated in ver. 15, the latter and metaphorical meaning (τῷ κανόνι καὶ τῇ διδαχῇ ταύτῃ, Œcum.) is here to be preferred. On the derivative meaning of κανών, see an article by Planck, in *Comment. Theol.* Vol. I. 1, p. 209 sq. and for exx. Elsner, *Obs.* Vol. II. p. 201. The dat. is obviously the dativus *normæ;* see notes on ch. v. 16, Winer, *Gr.* § 31. 6, p. 193, Fritz. *Rom.* xiii. 13, Vol. III. p. 142. εἰρήνη ἐπ' αὐτούς] '*peace be upon them,*' 'super illos,' Vulg., Clarom., not perhaps without some idea of peace and mercy coming down *upon them* from heaven *(Mey.)*; comp. Acts xix. 6, 2 Cor. xii. 9. It has

στοιχοῦσιν, εἰρήνη ἐπ' αὐτοὺς καὶ ἔλεος, καὶ ἐπὶ τὸν Ἰσραὴλ τοῦ
Θεοῦ.

Trouble me not: I am Christ's accredited servant.

17 τοῦ λοιποῦ κόπους μοι μηδεὶς παρεχέτω·
ἐγὼ γὰρ τὰ στίγματα τοῦ Ἰησοῦ ἐν τῷ σώματί
μου βαστάζω.

been urged (De W.) that ἐστὶν or ἔσται (Syr. ܢܗܘܐ comp. Chrys.) is here to be supplied rather than εἴη, and that the verse is to be regarded as declaratory, and not benedictory. Both the position of the verse, however, and the significant union of εἰρήνη and ἔλεος (1 Tim. i. 2, 2 Tim. i. 2, 2 John 3, Jude 2) seem in favor of the ordinary construction; ἐπηύξατο τὸν ἔλεον καὶ τὴν εἰρήνην, Theod. The order (contrast 1 Tim. i. 2, 2 Tim. i. 2, Jude 2) *may* be due to the fact that the Apostle desires to put the effect before the 'causa efficiens' (Mey.) as more in harmony with the reässuring character of the benediction, or arises merely from the feeling that in the absence of χάρις, εἰρήνη formed the more natural commencement. Jude 2 is rather different, owing to the addition of ἀγάπη. On the meaning of ἔλεος, as involving not only 'misericordia' (οἰκτιρμός), but 'ipsum miseris succurrendi studium,' see Tittmann, *Synon.* p. 69, sq. καὶ ἐπὶ τὸν Ἰσραὴλ τοῦ Θεοῦ] '*and upon the Israel of God.*' It is doubtful whether καὶ is explicative, '*namely*, upon the Israel of God,' or simply copulative. The explanatory καί, though needlessly obtruded on several passages of the N. T., is still distinctly found in St. Paul's Epp. (contr. De Wette), see Fritz. *Rom.* ix. 23, Vol. II. p. 339, Winer, *Gr.* § 53. 3, p. 388. Still, as it is doubtful whether καὶ is ever used by St. Paul in so *marked* an explicative force as must here be assigned (the exx. cited by Meyer, 1 Cor. iii. 5, viii. 11, xv. 38, do not seem conclusive), and as it seems still more doubtful whether Christians generally could be called 'the *Israel* of God' (contrast Brown, p. 382), the simple copulative meaning seems most probable (Ps. Ambr., Grot., Est.). St. Paul includes all in his blessing, of whatever stock and kindred; and then, with his thoughts turning (as they ever did) to his own brethren after the flesh (Rom. ix. 3), he pauses to specify those who were once Israelites according to the flesh (1 Cor. x. 18), but now are the Israel of God ('τοῦ Θεοῦ auctorem innuit, quem Deus veluti peculium suum reddidit,' Schott), — true spiritual children of Abraham.

17. τοῦ λοιποῦ] '*Henceforth;*' not for ἀπὸ τοῦ λοιποῦ (Bos, *Ellips.* p. 461, Brown), or for λοιπόν (Bloomf.), though commonly used both for it and τὸ λοιπὸν in later writers (Bernh. *Synt.* III. 36, p. 145), but the correct temporal genitive, denoting 'the time within which,' or at some epoch of which the action is represented as taking place; compare Madvig, *Synt.* § 66. a. Thus, taken *strictly*, τοῦ λοιποῦ κ. τ. λ. is, 'let no one *at any time in* the future,' etc., τὸ λοιπὸν κ. τ. λ., 'let no one *during* the future,' etc.; comp. Herm. *ad Vig.* No. 26, 'τὸ λοιπὸν dicitur et τοῦ λοιποῦ, hoc discrimine, quod τὸ λοιπὸν continuum et perpetuum tempus significat; τοῦ λοιποῦ autem repetitionem ejusdem facti reliquo tempore indicat.' The general temporal genitive, it may be remarked, appears to be more correctly referred to the *partitive* force of that case, than to ideas either of origination or antecedence (Hartung, *Casus*, p. 34, Jelf, *Gr.* § 523), or of possession (Alf.);

Benediction.

18 Ἡ χάρις τοῦ Κυρίου ἡμῶν Ἰησοῦ Χριστοῦ μετὰ τοῦ πνεύματος ὑμῶν, ἀδελφοί· ἀμήν.

see Scheuerl. *Synt.* § 15, p. 100, Donalds. *Gr.* § 451. κόπους παρεχέτω] '*cause trouble*;' surely not by obliging the Apostle to send further letters, but by troubling his spirit by their inability (σαλευόμενοι, Œcum.), and still more, as the next clause shows, by thwarting his apostolic authority. ἐγὼ γάρ] '*for I*;' reason for the command; the ἐγὼ being emphatic and in opposition to the false teachers, — not to μηδεὶς (De W.), unless considered as one of them, — and the γὰρ introducing the fact that he was a fully accredited servant of Christ: εἰς φόβον πλειόνα ἐμβάλλων καὶ πηγνὺς τοὺς παρ' αὐτοῦ τεθέντας νόμους, Chrys. τὰ στίγματα] '*the marks*;' the local addition ἐν τῷ σώματί μου necessarily referring the term to the wounds and scars and outward tokens of the persecutions and sufferings which the Apostle had undergone in the service of Christ; comp. 2 Cor. xi. 23 sq. There is appy. further a distinct allusion to the marks burnt on slaves to denote whom they *belonged to*; compare Herod. VII. 233, ἔστιζον στίγμ. βασιλήϊα, Martial, *Epigr.* XII. 61, 'stigmate non meo,' and especially Deyling, *Observ. Sacr.* Vol. III. No. 43, p. 423 sq., where the various classes of στιγματοφόροι are enumerated, and the whole subject copiously illustrated. The gen. Ἰησοῦ thus indicates, neither *origin* ('auctore Christo,' Gom.), nor remote *reference to* ('propter Christum,' Pisc.; compare Olsh., — a most doubtful translation both here and 2 Cor. i. 5), but simply *the owner*; the marks attested who the Apostle's Master was; and were the 'signa militiæ Christi quæ me comprobant ejus esse,' *Gloss. Interl.* (cited by Bagge). The insertion of Κυρίου before Ἰησοῦ (*Rec.*) is fairly supported [C³D³EJK; mss. Vulg., Clarom., Syr. (both), Goth., Æth.-Platt), but owing to the variations (D¹FG, ἡμῶν Ἰ. Χ.; Copt., Æth.-Pol., al., τοῦ Χρ.; al. aliter) rightly rejected by *Lachm.*, *Tisch.* [ABC¹; mss.; Amit., — but not Æth., Arm., as *Tisch.*, *Alf.*] in favor of the text. βαστάζω] '*I bear*;' either in the 'sensus molestus' of ch. v. 10, vi. 5, or perhaps, with some solemnity, in ref. to the dignifying nature of his Master's marks: οὐκ εἶπεν, ἔχω, ἀλλά, βαστάζω, ὥσπερ τις ἐπὶ τροπαίοις μέγα φρονῶν ἢ σημείοις βασιλικοῖς, Chrys.; compare Acts ix. 15, βαστάσαι τὸ ὄνομά μου, and Clem. *Hom.* ap. Coteler, Vol. I. p. 692, εἰκόνα Θεοῦ βαστάζειν.

18. ἡ χάρις κ. τ. λ.] On the varied nature of the Apostle's concluding benedictions, see the exx. and illustrations in notes *on* 1 *Thess.* v. 28. μετὰ τοῦ πνεύματος ὑμῶν] '*be with your spirit*;' not appy. with any allusion to the σάρξ (ἀπάγων αὐτοὺς τῶν σαρκικῶν, Chrys.), but simply with reference to the πνεῦμα as the 'potior pars' of man ('hominem a potior; parte sic antiquis dici Theologis, nec novum nec inusitatum est,' Heinsius, *Exerc.* p. 429), and not improbably to the fact that it is in the spirit of man that the operations of grace make themselves felt; τῇ ψυχῇ τὴν χάριν ἐπεύχεται γενέσθαι, Œcum.; compare Philem. 25, 2 Tim. iv. 22, and notes *in loc.* ἀδελφοί] Here the unusual position of the word *seems* to be intentional: they were indeed brethren, and though for a while severed from the Apostle, and the subjects of his censure, still *brethren* in their common Lord.

TRANSLATION.

NOTICE.

The general principles on which this translation has been drawn up are explained in the Preface. I will here only again remind the reader that, as a general rule, I have not departed from the Authorized Version, unless it appears to be either *incorrect*, *inexact*, *insufficient*, *obscure*, or (see notice to Transl. of *Past. Epp.*) noticeably *inconsistent* in its translations of more important expressions. These deviations are all stated in the notes, and if not there specially alluded to, or self-evident, will be found to depend on reasons assigned in the Commentary. I have also subjoined, in all the more important cases, citations from eight of the older versions, viz., those of Wiclif, Tyndale, Coverdale, (Bible), Coverdale (Testament), Cranmer, Geneva, Bishops', and Rheims. For the citations from five of these (Wiclif's, Tyndale's, Cranmer's, the Genevan and Rhemish Versions), I am indebted to THE ENGLISH HEXAPLA, of Messrs. Bagster. Those from Coverdale have been taken respectively from the first edition of his Bible in 1535 (now made accessible to the general reader by the reprint of the same publishers), and from the same venerable translator's Duglott Testament of 1538, which, though expressly taken from the Latin, still contains some interesting and suggestive translations. The citations from the Bishops' Bible are derived from the second and slightly amended edition of 1572, a copy of the N. T. portion of which, in small portable quarto, appy. differing only from the folio edition in the modes of spelling, has been sometimes used for the sake of convenience. All these extracts, though but of doubtful authority in disputed texts, will still be found frequently to suggest useful alternative renderings, and will also give the reader such a practical acquaintance with the principles on which the Authorized Version was drawn up, as will tend to make him thankfully acknowledge, that it is truly, what Selden termed it, "the best translation in the world."

The abbreviations in the notes will, I think, easily explain themselves. It may be only necessary to remark, that where an asterisk is affixed to a citation from the Authorized Version, the deviation in the text has arisen from a different reading. In the text, the *italics* (which slightly differ from those in the first edition of the Auth. Vers.) denote, as usual, words *not in the original;* the small capitals mark words which are *emphatic* in the original, but which could not occupy an emphatic position in the translation, without harsh inversions.

In the present edition, a few emendations (especially in reference to the aorist) have been introduced into the translation, and a few additional comments, either on the reasons for the changes, or on general principles of translation, inserted in the notes: see Notice to Translation of the *Epp. to the Thessalonians.* p. 132.*

As the subject of a revision of the Authorized Version is now becoming more and more one of the questions of the day, I again desire to remind the reader that the Revised Version which follows is only one designed for the *closet* (see Pref. to *Pastoral Epp.* p. xvi.), and that it is in no way to be considered as a specimen of what might be thought a desirable form of an authoritative Revision. The more experience I gain in the difficult task of revising, the more convinced am I of the utter insufficiency and hopelessness of any single translator's efforts to produce a Version for general purposes. The individual may sometimes suggest something more or less worthy of passing consideration, but it is from the collective wisdom of the many that we must alone look for any hopeful specimen of a revision of the noble Version at present in use.

* English Edition.

THE EPISTLE TO THE GALATIANS.

CHAPTER I.

PAUL, an apostle, not from men, neither by man, but by Jesus
Christ, and God the Father who raised Him from the dead,
— 2 and ALL the brethren which are with me, unto the churches of
Galatia. 3 Grace *be* to you and peace from God the Father, and
our Lord Jesus Christ, 4 who gave Himself for our sins, that He
might deliver us out of the present evil world, according to the will

CHAPTER I. 1. *From*] '*Of,*' *Auth.* and the other Vv. Though it does not seem desirable in every case to change the familiar 'of,' of *Auth.* into the now more usual 'from,' it is perhaps better to do so in most of the cases where it is used as a translation of ἀπό: where, on the other hand, ἐκ is used, 'of' ('out of') will often be found a very convenient translation; see notes on chap. iii. 16. With regard to διά, it is nearly impossible to lay down any fixed principles of translation: where the idea of *medium* is designed to be expressed with especial distinctness, we may adopt 'through,' but where this is not the case, the inclusive 'by' ('agent, instrument, cause, *means*,' Johnson) will be found sufficiently exact, and commonly much more idiomatic.

2. *Which*] It may be here observed that archaisms, as such, are not removed from the Authorized Version except where a positive error is involved. Here there is none; 'which' is not merely the neuter of 'who,' but is a compound word; Latham, *Engl. Lang.* § 305. 4 (ed. 3).

3. *And our*] 'And *from* our,' *Auth.* and the other Vv. except *Wicl.*, 'of.' It seems desirable to leave out the preposition in the second member, as more true to the original; see notes *on Phil.* i. 2 (*Transl.*).

4. *Out of*] So *Coverd.* (Test.): '*from,*' *Auth.* and the remaining Vv. In the next words it seems better to retain *Auth.* (changing 'this,' into 'the'), as the transl. 'world of evil' (ed. 1), though better preserving the unusual order of the Greek, might be thought to imply in the original the existence of a gen. of quality. Neither of the usual translations, 'world,' or 'age' (though the former perhaps more nearly) give the *exact* meaning of αἰών; the best *paraphrase* seems, 'spirit of the age;' see notes *on*

of God and our Father: [5] to whom *be* the glory for ever and ever.
Amen.

[6] I marvel that ye are so soon changed over from Him that
called you in the grace of Christ, unto a different gospel: [7] which
is NOT another; save that there are some who trouble you, and
desire to pervert the Gospel of Christ. [8] Howbeit even if we, or
an angel from heaven, should preach any gospel unto you contrary
to that which we preached unto you, let him be accursed. [9] As
we have said before, so say I now again, If any *man* preacheth any
gospel unto you contrary to that which ye received, let him be
accursed. [10] For NOW am I making men my friends, or God? or

Eph. ii. 2. *God and our Father*] Scholefield (*Hints on* 1 *Cor.* xv. 24), while fully admitting the reference of the gen. only to the latter noun, suggests the omission of the copula in translation (so Syr., Æth.) as more conformable to the idiom of our language. As, however, there are several cases where the copula is omitted in the Greek, and others, as here, where it is inserted, it seems best, in so solemn a designation, to preserve the distinction by a special and even peculiar translation: so Vulg., Clarom., Copt., Arm., and Syr.-Philox.

5. *The glory*] 'Glory,' *Auth.* As the art. is appy. here used κατ' ἐξοχὴν (see notes), and may be inserted in this passage without seriously violating English idiom, it seems best to follow here the usage of *Auth.* in Matth. vi. 13 (*Rec.*).

6. *Changing over*] 'Removed,' *Auth.;* 'moved,' *Wicl.;* 'turned,' *Tynd., Cov.* (both), *Cran., Gen., Bish.;* 'transferred,' *Rhem.* *By*] So *Cran.:* 'into,' *Auth., Wicl., Rhem.;* 'in,' *Tynd., Cov., Bish.;* 'unto,' *Cov.* (Test.) *Gen.:* see notes. *A different*] 'Another,' *Auth.* and all the other Vv.

7. *Save that*] So *Cov.* (Test.): 'but there be some that,' *Auth.;* 'but that there be some,' *Wicl., Tynd., Cov., Cranmer, Gen., Bish.;* 'unless,' *Rhem.* The present participle might at first sight seem to suggest the use of the auxiliary '*are* troubling;' as, however, οἱ ταράσσοντες is equivalent to a kind of substantive, and serves to mark the characteristic of the false teachers, the (iterative) present is more appropriate; comp. Latham, *Engl. Lang.*, § 573 (ed. 3.).

8. *Howbeit*] Similarly *Cov., Bish.*, 'neuerthelesse:' 'but,' *Auth.* and the remaining Vv. *Even if*] 'Though,' *Auth.* and the other Vv. except *Rhem.*, 'although.' *Should preach*] 'Preach,' *Auth.* and all the other Vv. The idea of future contingency involved in the use of ἐὰν with subj. (Herm. *Viger*, No. 312), may here be suitably expressed by inserting *should*. *Any gospel, etc.*] 'Any other gospel unto you than,' *Auth., Tynd., Cov., Cran., Bish.;* 'otherwaies than,' *Gen.;* 'beside that,' *Wicl., Rhem.* *Preached*] 'Have preached,' *Auth.* and the other Vv.

9. *Have said*] So *Cov.* (both), *Rhem:* 'said,' *Auth.* and the remaining Vv. *Preacheth*] 'Preach,' *Auth.;* change to the indicative to preserve the opposition of moods in original; see notes on 2 *Thess.* iii. 14. (*Transl.*). *Any gospel, etc.*] 'Other gospel unto you than that,' *Auth.* *Received*] 'Have received,' *Auth.* and the other Vv. except *Wicl.*, 'han undirfongen.'

10. *Now am I making, etc.*] 'Do I now

am I seeking to please men? if I were STILL pleasing men, I
should not be a servant of Christ.
11 Now I certify you, brethren, touching the gospel which was
preached by me that it is not after man. 12 For neither did I receive it from man, neither was I taught *it*, but through revelation
from Jesus Christ. 13 For ye heard of my conversation in time
past in Judaism, how that beyond measure I persecuted the church
of God, and was destroying it; 14 and made advance in Judaism
beyond many my equals in mine own nation, being more exceedingly zealous for the traditions of my fathers. 15 But when it

persuade men,' *Auth.*, *Bish.*; *Rhem.*: 'counceil,' *Wicl.*; 'preach man's doctrine,' *Tynd.*, *Gen.*; 'preach I men,' *Cov.*; 'speak fayre,' *Cov.* (Test.); 'speak unto,' *Cran.*; 'use persuasion,' *Rhem.* The change to the more definitely present, 'am I making,' seems required by the emphasis which evidently rests on ἄρτι. On the nature of the English present, comp. Latham, *Engl. Lang.* § 573, 579 (ed. 3). *If*] So *Wicl.*, *Tynd.*, *Rhem.*: 'for if,' *Auth*, *Cran.*, *Gen.* *Am I seeking*] 'Do I seek,' *Auth.*, *Wicl.*, *Coverd.* (Test.), *Rhem.*; 'go I about,' *Tynd.*, and the remaining Vv. *Were still pleasing*] 'Yet pleased,' *Auth.* *A*] 'The,' *Auth.* and the other Vv. except *Wicl.*, 'Christis servant.'

11. *Now*] 'But,' *Auth.*, *Cov.*; omitted in *Tynd.*, *Cran.*, *Gen.*, *Bish.* *Touching the Gospel, etc.*] 'That the Gospel which was, etc. . . . . is not,' *Auth.* Perhaps the text, which is more exactly in accordance with the order of the Greek, makes the denial a little more emphatic. *By*] 'Of,' *Auth.* and all the other Vv.

12. *Did I receive*] So *Rhem.*: 'I neither received it,' *Auth.*, *Cov.*, *Cran.*; 'ne I took it of man, ne lerned,' *Wicl.*; 'nether received I it,' *Tynd.*, *Gen.*; 'I did not receive it nor learned it,' *Cov.* (Test.). There is here some little difficulty in both preserving the emphasis on 'I,' and also indicating that the first negative is not strictly correlative to the second. The insertion of the auxiliary *perhaps* partially effects this, as it places the 'neither' a little further from the verb, and still leaves it in that prominence which it seems most naturally to occupy. In ed. 1 ('for I indeed received it not'), this latter point was perhaps too much sacrificed. *From man*] 'Of man,' *Auth.* and the other Vv. except *Wicl.*, 'bi man.' *Through rev. from*] 'By the rev. of,' *Auth.* and the other Vv. except *Wicl.*, 'bi reuelacioun.'

13. *Ye heard*] 'Ye have heard,' *Auth.* and the other Vv. *Judaism*] So *Rhem.*: 'the Jews' religion,' *Auth.*, *Gen.* ('the Jewishe rel.'), *Bish.*; 'the Jurie,' *Wicl.*; 'the Jews' wayes,' *Tynd.*; 'the Jewshippe,' *Cov.* *Was destroying it*] 'Wasted it,' *Auth.*; 'faughte agen it,' *Wicl.*; 'spoyled it,' *Tynd.*, *Cov.*, *Cran.*, *Gen.*, *Bish.*; 'drove them out,' *Cov.* (Test.); 'expugned it,' *Rhem.* This change is in consequence of the strong meaning of πορθέω, which it seems desirable to maintain. To resolve also the other imperfects would make the sentence heavy and cumbrous, and add but little to the sense.

14. *Made advance, etc.*] 'Profited in (*Wicl.*, *Gen.*, *Bish.*, *Rhem.*) the Jews' religion above,' *Auth.*; 'prevayled in,' *Tynd.*, *Coverd.*, *Cranmer.* *For*] 'Of,' *Auth.*

15. *Set me apart*] 'Separated me,'

pleased God, who set me apart from my mother's womb, and called
me through His grace, [16] to reveal His Son within me, that I
might preach Him among the Gentiles; immediately I conferred
not with flesh and blood: [17] neither went I away to Jerusalem to
them which were apostles before me; but I went away into Arabia,
and returned again unto Damascus. [18] Then after three years, I
went up to Jerusalem to visit Cephas, and I tarried with him fifteen
days. [19] But other of the apostles saw I none, save James the
brother of the Lord. [20] Now the things which I write unto you,
behold, before God, I lie not. [21] Afterwards I came into the regions
of Syria and Cilicia; [22] and remained unknown by face unto the
churches of Judæa which were in Christ: [23] but they were hearing
only That he who was our persecutor in times past is now preach-

Auth. and the other Vv. except *Wicl.*, 'departid me,' and *Cov.* (Test.), 'sundered me.' The change is made to prevent 'from' being understood as local: see notes. *Through*] 'By,' *Auth.* and the other Vv. In this passage, it seems desirable to adopt the more rigorous translation of διά, as suggesting more distinctly the fact that χάρις was not the *instrument*, but the '*causa medians*;' see notes.

16. *Within*] 'In,' *Auth.*, *Wicl.*, *Cov.*, *Bish.*, *Rhem.*; 'by,' *Tynd.*, *Cov.* (Test.), *Cran.*; 'to,' *Gen.*, *Rhem.*: 'heathen,' *Auth.* and the remaining Vv. *Conferred*] So *Auth.* This translation is not wholly adequate, but it is not easy to fix upon a more exact one. The original word seems to involve two ideas, *addressing one's self to* (πρός, direction), and *taking counsel with.* Most of the older translations give prominence to the latter and more important idea, *e. g.* 'I commened not of the matter,' *Tynd.*, *Cov.*, *Cran.*, *Genev.*; some of the moderns, *e. g.* Meyer, Lewin, express more distinctly the former. It seems difficult to combine both without paraphrasing. The singular translation in *Cov.* (Test.), 'I did not graunt' (comp. *Rhem*, 'I condescended not,'), results from the Vulg. 'acquievi.'

17. *Away* (bis)]* 'Up,' *Auth.* In the concluding clause it seems better to maintain the order of *Auth.* 'returned again,' not as the Greek order might seem to suggest, 'again returned'; for the πάλιν is only idiomatically added to the verb, and is appy. without any special emphasis; comp. Acts xviii. 21, and see exx. in Kühner on Xenoph. *Mem.* II. 4. 4.

18. *Visit Cephas*] 'See *Peter,' *Auth.* and all the other Vv. *I tarried*] Sim. *Rhem.*: 'abode,' *Auth.*, *Tynd.*, *Cov.* (both), *Cran.*, *Gen.*, *Bish.*; 'dwellid,' *Wicl.*

19. *The brother of the Lord*] Sim. *Rhem.*, 'the brother of our Lord:' 'the Lord's brother,' *Auth.* and other Vv. This latter mode of translation is perhaps more appropriate when neither substantive has the article.

22. *Remained*] 'Was unknown,' *Auth.* and all the other Vv.

23. *Were hearing*] 'Had heard,' *Auth.*, *Cov.*, *Rhem.*, *Bish.*; 'hadden oonli an hearynge,' *Wicl.*; 'heard,' *Tynd.*, *Cran.*, *Gen.* Conybeare and Howson have given a good paraphrase: 'tidings only were brought them from time to time;' comp. Erasm., 'rumor apud illos erat.' *Who was our persecutor*] 'Which persecuted us,' *Auth.*, *Tynd.*, *Cran.*, *Gen.*,

ing the faith which once he destroyed. 24 And they glorified God
in me.

CHAPTER II.

THEN after fourteen years I went up again to Jerusalem with
Barnabas, and took Titus also with *me*. 2 And I went up by revelation, and communicated unto them the gospel which I preach
among the Gentiles, but privately to them which were of reputation, lest by any means I might be running, or have run, in vain.
3 Howbeit not even TITUS, who was with me, though he was a
Greek, was compelled to be circumcised: 4 and that, because of
the false brethren craftily brought in, men who came in stealthily
to spy out our liberty which we have in Christ Jesus, that they
might bring us into bondage: 5 to whom we gave place by our submission, no, not for an hour; that the truth of the gospel might

Bish., *Rhem.*; 'that pursued us,' *Wicl.*; 'that persecuted us,' *Cov.*; 'that did persecute us,' *Cov.* (Test.).

Is now preaching] 'Now preacheth,' *Auth.* *Tynd.*, *Cov.* ('pr. now'), *Cran.*, *Gen.*, *Bish.*; 'doth now preach,' *Cov.* (Test.); 'doth now evangelize,' *Rhem.* The change is made to mark more definitely the *present act*; comp. notes and ref. on ch. i. 10.

CHAPTER II. 1. *After fourteen years*] So *Rhem.*: 'fourteen years after,' *Auth.* and the other Vv. (*Tynd.*, *Cov.*, 'after that;' *Cran.*, 'thereafter'). The change is perhaps desirable as it slightly tends to prevent the last-mentioned events being considered as the *terminus a quo* of the fourteen years. *Titus also*] So *Rhem.*: 'Titus with me also,' *Auth.*, *Tynd.*, *Cov.*, *Gen.*; 'Titus also beynge taken with me,' *Cov.* (Test.); the rest omit καὶ in translation.

2. *The Gospel*] So all Vv. except *Auth.*, 'that Gospel.' *Might be running, etc.*] 'Should (om. *Wicl.*) run or had run,' *Auth.* and all Vv. The text seems to preserve more exactly, and perhaps also more grammatically, the contrast between the pres. (subj.) and past tense. It may be observed that *should* 'simpliciter futuritionem indicat:' *might* 'de rei possibilitate dicitur;' Wallis, *Gram. Angl.* p. 107.

3. *Howbeit not even*] Sim. *Cov.* (Test.), 'neuerthelesse nother:' 'but neither,' *Auth.*, *Rhem.*: 'and neither,' *Wicl.*; 'also,' Titus . . . yet, etc.' *Tynd.*, *Cran.*, *Gen.* *Though he was*] 'Being,' *Auth.*

4. *The false, etc.*] Similarly *Rhem.*: 'false brethren unawares brought in, who,' *Auth.*; 'and that because of ('certayne,' *Cov.*) incommers beynge falce br.,' *Tynd.*, *Cran.*, *Bish.* *Stealthily*] 'Privily,' *Auth.*, *Cov.* (Test.) *Cran.*, *Gen.*, *Bish*; *Wicl.* omits; 'amonge other,' *Tynd.*, *Cov.*; 'craftily,' *Rhem.* Perhaps the change is desirable as avoiding repetition, and as harmonizing slightly better with the action described by the verb.

5. *By our submission*] 'By subjection,' *Auth.*, *Bish*; 'to subjeccioun;' 'as concerning to be brought into subjection,' *Tynd.*, *Cov.*, *Cran.*, *Gen.*; 'yelded not subjection,' *Rhem.*; *Cov.* (Test.) omits.

continue with you. 6 But from those who were high in reputation,
— whatsoever they were, it maketh no matter to me; God accepteth no man's person, — to me certainly they who were of reputation communicated nothing; 7 but contrariwise, when they saw that
I was entrusted with the gospel of the uncircumcision, even as
Peter was with that of the circumcision, 8 (for He that wrought
for Peter towards the apostleship of the circumcision, the same
wrought for me also towards the Gentiles), 9 and became aware
of the grace that was given unto me, James, and Cephas, and John,
who are accounted as pillars, gave to me and Barnabas right hands
of fellowship; that we *should be apostles* unto the Gentiles, and

6. *From*] 'Of,' *Auth.* and the other Vv. except *Cov.*, 'as to them;' *Cov.* (Test.), 'as for them.' The change here seems necessary to prevent 'of' being considered a mere sign of the gen. case. *Were high, etc.*] 'Seemed to be somewhat,' *Auth.*, *Cran.*, and sim. *Cov.* (Test.); 'that seemed to be great,' *Cov.*, and sim. *Tynd.*, *Gen.* The very slight distinction between δοκοῦντες and δοκ. εἶναί τι, and the apparent ref. to the judgment of others (see notes) are appy. both conveyed more nearly by this translation than by the more literal rendering of *Auth.*
To me certainly, etc.] 'For they who seemed *to be somewhat* in conference added nothing to me,' *Auth.*; 'added nothynge,' *Tynd.*, *Cran.*, *Bish.*, *Rhem.*; 'taught me nothing,' *Cov.*; 'avayled me nothing,' *Cov.* (Test.); 'dyd communicate nothing with me,' *Gen.*

7. *I was entrusted, etc.*] 'The gospel . . . was committed unto me as *the Gospel* of the circumcision *was* unto Peter,' *Auth.*, and sim. the other Vv. The change of order is made, for the sake of keeping the emphasis on πεπίστευμαι: see Meyer. *Even as*] 'As,' *Auth.* and all the other Vv. On the translation of καθώς, see notes *on* 1 *Thess.* i. 5.

8. *Wrought*] So *Wicl.*, *Cov.* (Test.), *Rhem.*: 'wrought effectually,' *Auth.*; 'was mighty,' *Tynd.*, *Cov.*, *Cran.*, *Gen.*, *Bish.* The idea of *effectual* working, though to a considerable extent involved in ἐνεργεῖν, is perhaps scarcely sufficiently prominent to be expressed definitely; see, however, notes *on* 1 *Thess.* ii. 13.
For] Similarly *Wicl.*, 'to Peter:' 'in,' *Auth.*, *Tynd.*, *Cran.*, *Bish.*, *Rhem.*; 'with,' *Cov.*; 'by,' *Cov.* (Test.), *Gen.*
Towards] 'To,' *Auth.*, *Wicl.*, *Cov.*, *Bish.*, *Rhem.*; 'in,' *Tynd.* and the remaining Vv.
Wrought] 'Was mighty in me toward,' *Auth.* All the other Vv. give the same translation to ἐνεργέω in the second clause that they adopt in the first.

9. *And became aware, etc.*] Similarly, as to order, *Wicl.*, *Tynd.*, *Cran.*, *Bish.*, *Rhem.*, except that they repeat the idiomatic 'when' in the translation of the temporal participle γνόντες, but thus slightly impair the natural sequence of the ἰδόντες . . . καὶ γνόντες. *Auth.* inverts, 'and when James, Cephas, and John, who seemed to be,' etc.; *Cov.* turns into a finite verb, 'they perceived.'
And Cephas] Sim. *Wicl.*, *Rhem.*: *Auth.* and the remaining Vv. omit 'and.'
Are accounted as] 'Seemed to be,' *Auth.* and all the Vv. except *Wicl.*, 'weren seyn to be;' *Gen.*, 'are taken to be.'
Right hands] 'The right hands,' *Auth.* and the other Vv. except *Wicl.*, 'right hond.' *Be apostles*] So *Cran.*, *Bish.*: 'should go,' *Auth.*; 'that we among

they unto the circumcision. [10] Only *they would* that we should
remember THE POOR; which very thing I also was forward to do.
[11] But when Cephas came to Antioch, I withstood him to the face,
because he had been condemned. [12] For before that certain *men*
came from James, he was eating with the Gentiles; but when they
came, he began to withdraw and separate himself, fearing them
which were of the circumcision. [13] And the rest of the Jews also
dissembled with him; insomuch that even Barnabas was carried
away with by their dissimulation. [14] Howbeit when I saw that they
were not walking uprightly according to the truth of the gospel, I
said unto Cephas before all, If thou, being a Jew, livest after the
manner of Gentiles, and not as do the Jews, how *is it that* thou
constrainest the Gentiles to keep the customs of the Jews? [15] WE
truly are by nature Jews, and not sinners of the Gentiles;

the hethen,' *Wicl.;* 'shuld preach,' *Tynd., Cov.* (both), *Gen.;* 'that we unto,' *Rhem.* *Gentiles*] So *Gen., Rhem.:* 'heathen,' *Auth.* and the remaining Vv.

10. *Which very thing*] 'The same which,' *Auth.;* 'the whiche thing,' *Wicl., Cov.* Test. ('thing also'); 'whiche thing also,' *Tynd., Cov., Gen.;* 'wher in also,' *Cran., Bish.;* 'the which same thing also,' *Rhem.*

11. *Cephas*] * 'Peter,' *Auth.* *Came*] So *Cov.* (Test.): 'was come,' *Auth.* and the remaining Vv. *Had been condemned*] 'Was to be blamed,' *Auth., Bish.;* 'was worthy to be blamed,' *Tynd., Cov., Cran., Gen.,* and similarly *Wicl.,* 'to be undirnomen;' 'was blameable,' *Cov.* (Test.); 'was reprehensible,' *Rhem.*

12. *Certain men came*] 'Certain were come,' *Auth.* *Was eating*] 'Did eat,' *Auth., Cov.* (both), *Cran., Bish., Rhem.;* 'ete,' *Wicl., Tynd., Gen.* *Began to, etc.*] 'Withdrew and separated,' *Auth.* and all Vv. The imperf. denotes the commencement and continuance of the act, or as Bengel, '*subducebat* paullatim.'

13. *The rest of the*] So *Cov.* (Test.), *Rhem.:* 'the other,' *Auth* and the remaining Vv. *Also dissembled*] 'Dissembled likewise,' *Auth., Tynd., Cran., Bish.:* the other Vv. omit the καὶ in translation. *Even Barnabas*] 'Barnabas also,' *Auth.* *By their*] *Auth.* omits 'by;' 'into,' *Wicl.* and the remaining Vv.

14. *Howbeit*] 'But,' *Auth.* and all the other Vv. *Were not walking*] 'Walked not,' *Auth.* *Cephas*] 'Peter,' *Auth.* *All*] So *Cov.* (both), and sim. *Wicl., Tynd., Gen.,* 'all men:' 'them all,' *Auth.,* and the remaining Vv. *How cometh it, etc.*] * 'Why compellest thou,' *Auth.,* and sim. *Rhem.,* 'dost thou compel;' 'hou constreynest thou,' *Wicl.;* 'why causest thou,' *Tynd., Cov., Cran., Gen., Bish.* *Keep the customs, etc.*] 'To live as do the Jews,' *Auth.,* and sim. the other Vv. except *Rhem.,* 'Judaize.'

15. *We (truly) are, etc.*] Similarly *Rhem.:* 'we who are Jews by nature,' *Auth., Tynd, Cran., Gen.;* 'though we be, etc.' *Cov.;* 'we which are . . . know,' *Bish.* This address of St. Paul to St. Peter involves so many difficulties both in meaning and connection, that it will be perhaps best to subjoin a free para-

16 but as we know that a man is not justified by the works of the
law, save *only* through faith in Jesus Christ, — we too believed in
Christ Jesus, that we might be justified by faith in Christ, and not
by the works of the law; since by the works of the law shall no
flesh be justified. 17 But if, while we seek to be justified in Christ,
we are found ourselves also to be sinners, *is* Christ therefore a

phrase of the whole. 'We, I concede, are by birth Jews, not Gentiles, and consequently, from our point of view, sinners; but as we know that a man is not justified by the works of the law, in fact is not justified at all, except through faith in Christ; — even we, with all our privileges, believed in and into Christ, that we might be justified, etc. But what, if, while we are seeking to be justified in Christ, the result show that we, with all our privileges, are sinners like the Gentiles; is Christ the minister of a dispensation that after all only leads to sin? God forbid! For if I (or you) build up again the system I pulled down, and set up nothing better in its place, it is thus, and not in seeking to be justified in Christ, that I show myself (vox horrenda!) *a transgressor* of the law; yes, a violator of its deeper principles. For I (to adduce a proof from my own spiritual experience) through the medium of the law, and in accordance with its higher principles, died unto it in regard to its claims and its curse: I have been and am crucified with Christ. Though I live then, it is no longer as my old self, but as reänimated by Christ; yes, the life which now I live, this earthly, mundane life, I live in the element of faith in Christ, who so loved me that He gave His own life for me. Thus I do not, like these Judaists, regard the grace of God as a principle that could be dispensed with; for if, as they pretend, the law is sufficient to make men righteous, the obvious inference is, there was no object in the death of Christ.

16. *But as we know*] 'Knowing,' *Auth.*, *Wicl.*, *Cov.* (Test.), *Rhem.*; 'we which . . . knowe,' *Tynd.*, *Cran.*, *Gen.*, *Bish.*; 'yet insomuche as we knowe,' *Cov.* *Save only through, etc.*] 'But by the faith of Jesus Christ,' *Auth.* and the other Vv. except *Cov.*, 'on J. C.;' *Cov.* (Test.), 'save by the faith by J. C.' *We too believed*] 'Even we have believed in J. C.,' *Auth.*; 'and we bileuen,' *Wicl.*; 'we have believed also,' *Cov.*; 'we also beleue,' *Cov.* (Test.), *Rhem.*; 'and we have bel. on,' *Cran.*, *Bish.*, *Tynd.*; ('and therfor') 'even we I *say* have bel. in,' *Gen.* *Faith in*] 'The faith of,' *Auth.* and all Vv. *Since*] 'For,' *Auth.*; 'because that,' *Tynd.*, *Cov.* (both), *Cran.*, *Gen.*; 'wherfor,' *Wicl.*; 'because,' *Bish.*; 'for the which cause,' *Rhem.*

17. *In Christ*] So *Wicl.*, *Cov.* (Test.), *Rhem.*: 'by Christ,' *Auth.* and remaining Vv. *We are found, etc.*] 'We ourselves also are found sinners,' *Auth.* English idiom here, in consequence of the union with the pres. part., seems to require the pres. 'are found" as the translation of εὑρέθημεν. The aorist in the original has an idiomatic reference to a discovery past and done with, and about which no more need be said, which cannot be expressed without paraphrase; comp. Donalds. *Gr.* § 433. *Is Christ, etc.*] 'Is therefore Christ the,' *Auth.* *God forbid*] *Auth.* and all Vv. except *Cov.* (Test.), 'that be farre.' On reconsideration it would seem best, and even practically most exact, that in a passage of the present nature, where the revulsion of feeling and thought is very decided, to retain the familiar and idiomatic translation of *Auth.*

minister of sin? God forbid! 18 For if the things that I destroyed
THESE again I build up, I prove myself a transgressor. 19 For I
through the law died to the law, that I might live unto God. 20 I
have been crucified with Christ: it is, however, no longer I that
live, but Christ liveth in me; yea the life which NOW I live in the
flesh I live in faith,—*faith* in the Son of God, who loved me, and
gave Himself for me. 21 I do not make void the grace of God; for
if righteousness *come* THROUGH THE LAW, then for nought did Christ
die.

CHAPTER III.

O foolish Galatians, who did bewitch you, before whose eyes
Jesus Christ was evidently set forth among you, CRUCIFIED. 2 This
only would I learn of you, Was it by the works of the law that ye

18. *The things that I destroyed*] 'I build again the things which I destroyed,' *Auth.*, *Cran.*, *Bish.*; 'that which,' *Tynd.*, *Cov.*, *Gen.*; 'the same things againe which,' *Rhem.* The inversion, though involving a slight irregularity in structure, seems here needed, as serving both to keep the emphasis on the right words, and to exhibit the true point of the argument. *Prove myself*] 'Make myself,' *Auth.* and all the other Vv.

19. *Died*] 'Am dead,' *Auth.* and the other Vv. except *Cran.*, 'haue bene deed.'

20. *Have been crucified*] 'Am crucified,' *Auth.*, and sim., as to the auxiliary, all the other Vv. Of the two modes of expressing the Greek perfect ('am' and 'have been'), the latter seems here most appropriate, as the associated aor. renders the ref. to past time more prominent than one to present effects; see notes on *Col.* i. 16 (*Transl.*). *It is, however, etc.*] 'Nevertheless I live; yet not I,' *Auth.*, sim. *Cov.*, *Cran.*; 'I live verely, yet now not I,' *Tynd.*, *Gen.* *Yea*] 'And,' *Auth.*, *Gen.*, *Cran.*, *Bish.*, *Rhem.*; 'for,' *Tynd.*, *Cov.*; 'but,' *Wicl.*, *Cov.* (Test.). *Now I*] 'I now,' *Auth.* *In faith, etc.*] 'By ('in,' *Wicl.*, *Cov.* (both), *Rhem.*), the faith of,' *Auth.*, *Tynd.*, *Cran.*, *Gen.*, *Bish.*

21. *Make void*] 'Frustrate,' *Auth.*; 'cast not awei,' *Wicl.*, *Cov.* (both), *Rhem.*; 'despyse not,' *Tynd.*, *Cran.*; 'do not abrogate,' *Gen.*; 'reject not,' *Bish.* *Through*] So *Wicl.*: 'by,' *Auth.*, *Cov.* (both), *Rhem.*; 'of,' *Tynd.*, *Gen.*, *Cran.*, *Bish.* *For nought*] 'In vain,' *Auth.*, *Tynd.*, *Cov.*, *Cran.*, *Bish.*, *Rhem*; 'without cause,' *Wicl.*, *Gen.* ('a cause.') *Did Christ die*] 'Christ is dead,' *Auth.*, *Bish.*; 'died,' *Wicl.*, and the remaining Vv. The slight change in the text seems to give the due prominence to δωρεάν, and also to preserve a better rhythm than the unresolved 'died.'

CHAPTER III. 1. *Did bewitch*] 'Hath bewitched,' *Auth.* and the other Vv. **Auth.* inserts after 'you,' 'that ye should not obey the truth.'

2. *Was it, etc.*] Similarly *Rhem.*, 'by the workes of the law did you receiue:' 'received ye the Spirit by the,' etc. *Auth.*, and sim. as to order all the remaining Vv.

received the Spirit, or by the hearing of faith? 3 Are ye so very
foolish? having begun with the Spirit are ye now being made perfect with the flesh? 4 Did ye suffer so many things in vain, if
indeed it really be in vain. 5 He then, *I say*, that ministereth to
you the Spirit and worketh mighty powers within you, *doeth he it*
by the works of the law or by the hearing of faith?

6 Even as Abraham believed God, and it was accounted to him
for righteousness. 7 Know ye then that THEY WHICH ARE OF
FAITH, the same are the sons of Abraham. 8 Moreover the Scripture, foreseeing that God justifieth the Gentiles by FAITH, proclaimed beforehand the glad tidings unto Abraham, *saying*, In thee
shall all the nations BE BLESSED. 9 So then they which be of faith
are blessed together with the faithful Abraham.

10 For as many as are of the works of the law are under curse:

3. *So very*] 'So,' *Auth.* and the other Vv. except *Cov.*, 'such fooles.' *Begun with*] So *Rhem.*: 'begun in' *Auth.* and the other Vv. except *Cov.*, 'by.' *Being made perfect with*] 'Made perfect by,' *Auth.*, *Genev.* ('in'); 'ben ended,' *Wicl.*; 'nowe ende,' *Tynd.*, *Cov.* (Test.); 'ende now then,' *Cov.*; 'ende in,' *Tynd.*, *Cran.*; 'be consummate with,' *Rhem.*

4. *Did ye suffer*] 'Have ye suffered,' *Auth.*, *Cov.* (both), *Bish.*, *Rhem.*, and sim. the other Vv., except that they do not adopt the interrogative form. *Indeed it really be*] 'It be yet,' *Auth.*, *Bish.*; 'if that be vayne,' *Tynd.*, *Gen.*; 'yf it be also in vayne,' *Cran.*; 'if yet without cause,' *Rhem.*

5. *He then, etc.*] 'He therefore,' *Auth.*, *Cov.* (Test.), *Gen.*, *Bish.*, *Rhem.*; 'moreover, he, etc.,' *Cran.*; *Wicl.*, *Tynd.*, *Cov.* omit οὖν in translation. *Mighty powers, etc.*] 'Miracles among you,' *Auth.* and the other Vv. except *Wicl.*, 'vertues in you;' *Cov.*, 'great actes.'

7. *Then*] 'Therefore,' *Auth.* and the other Vv. except *Cov.*, 'thus I know,' and *Gen.*, 'so ye know.' The only other version that takes γινώσκετε indicatively is that of *Cranmer*. *Sons*] So *Wicl.*: 'children,' *Auth.* and the remaining Vv.

8. *Moreover*] 'And,' *Auth.*, *Wicl.*, *Cov.* (Test.), *Rhem.*; 'for,' *Tynd.* and remaining Vv. (*Cov.* omits). *Justifieth*] So *Wicl.*, *Cov.* (Test.), *Rhem.*: 'would justify,' *Auth.*, *Tynd.*, *Cran.*, *Gen.*; 'justifyed,' *Cov.* *The Gentiles*] So *Gen.*, *Rhem.*: 'the heathen,' *Auth.* and the remaining Vv. *By faith*] So *Cov.* (Test.), *Rhem.*, and sim. *Wicl.*, 'of faith:' 'through faith,' *Auth.* and the remaining Vv. *Proclaimed beforehand, etc.*] Sim. *Tynd.*, *Cov.*, *Cran.*: 'preached before the Gospel,' *Auth.*, *Gen.* ('before hand'); 'told to for,' *Wicl.*; 'told,' *Cov.* (Test.); 'shewed . . . before,' *Rhem.* *All the nations*] Sim. *Wicl.*, *Cov.*, 'alle the hethen:' 'all nations,' *Auth.* and the remaining Vv. except *Gen.*, 'all the Gentiles.' The change in the translation of τὰ ἔθνη in the same verse seems required by a kind of chronological propriety.

9. *Together with*] 'With,' *Auth.* and all the other Vv. *The faithful*] So *Bish.*, *Rhem.*: 'faithful,' *Auth.* and all the remaining Vv.

10. *Curse*] So *Wicl.*, *Rhem.*, and sim-

for it is written, Cursed *is* every one that continueth not in all
things which are written in the book of the law to do them. 11 But
further, that in the law no man is justified in the sight of God, *it is*
evident; because, The just shall live by FAITH. 12 Now the law is
not of faith; but, He that doeth them shall live in them. . . . .
13 Christ redeemed us from the curse of the law, having become A
CURSE for us, — because it is written, Cursed *is* every one that
hangeth on a tree, — 14 that unto the Gentiles the blessing of Abraham might come in Christ Jesus; that we might receive the promise of the Spirit THROUGH FAITH.

15 Brethren, I speak after the manner of men; though it be but
a MAN'S covenant, yet when it hath been confirmed, no man annulleth it, or addeth new conditions. 16 Now to Abraham were the
promises made, AND TO HIS SEED. He saith not, And to seeds,
as of many; but as of one, And to thy seed, which is Christ.
17 Now this I say, A covenant, that hath been before confirmed by

ilarly *Tynd.*, 'under malediccion:' 'the curse,' *Auth.*, *Cov.* (both), *Cran.*, *Gen.*, *Bish.*

11. *But further, etc.*] 'But that no man is justified by the law,' *Auth.* *Because*] So *Rhem.*: 'for,' *Auth.* and the remaining Vv.

12. *Now*] 'And,' *Auth.*, *Cov.* (Test.), *Gen.*, *Bish.*; *Tynd.*, *Cov.*, *Cran.*, omit; 'but,' *Wicl.*, *Rhem.* *He*] * 'The man,' *Auth.*

13. *Redeemed*] Similarly *Wicl.*, 'agenbought:' 'hath redeemed,' *Auth.* and the remaining Vv. except *Cov.*, 'hath delyuered.' *Having become*] 'Being made,' *Auth.*, *Bish.*, *Rhem.*; 'and was made,' *Wicl.*, *Tynd.*; 'when he became,' *Cov.*; 'beynge become,' *Cov.* (Test.); 'inasmoch as he was made,' *Cran.*; 'when he was made,' *Gen.* *Because*] So *Rhem*: 'for,' *Auth.* and the remaining Vv.

14. *Unto the Gentiles*] 'Come on the Gentiles,' *Auth.* *In Christ J.*] 'Through *J. C.,' *Auth.*, *Tynd.*, *Cran.*, *Gen.*, *Bish.*; 'in,' *Wicl.*, *Cov.* (both), *Rhem.*

15. *Yet when it hath been*] 'Yet if it be,' *Auth.* The *temporal* translation in the text is adopted by *Tynd.*, *Cov.*; the hypothetical by *Auth.* with *Cran.*, *Bish.*: the remaining Vv. adopt purely participial translations. *Annulleth it, etc.*] 'Disannulleth or addeth thereto,' *Auth.*, *Bish.*; 'ordeyneth above,' *Wicl.*; 'addeth anything thereto,' *Tynd.* *Cov.* (sim. Test.), *Cran.*, *Gen.*; 'further disposeth,' *Rhem.*

16. *Were the promises, etc.*] Sim. *Rhem.*, *Wicl.*: 'and his seed were the promises,' etc., *Auth.* and the remaining Vv.

17. *Now this*] 'And this,' *Auth.*, *Gen.*, *Rhem.*; 'but,' *Wicl.*, *Cov.* (Test); *Tynd.*, *Cov.*, *Bish.*, omit δέ. The translation of δὲ is here somewhat difficult. Though 'now' has just preceded, it must appy. be adopted again as the only translation which seems to preserve the resumptive force. *A covenant*] '*The* covenant,' *Auth.* and the other Vv. except *Wicl.* and *Cov.* (both), 'this.' *Hath been before confirmed*] 'Was confirmed before,' *Auth.*, *Tynd*, *Cov.*, *Cran.*, *Gen.*; 'was given,' *Cov.* (Test.); 'the test. being confirmed,' *Rhem.*; *Wicl.*,

God [for Christ], the law, which was four hundred and thirty years
after, doth not invalidate, that it should make void the promise.
18 For if the inheritance *be* of the law, *it is* no more of promise:
but to Abraham God hath freely given it THROUGH PROMISE.

19 What then is *the object of* the law? It was added because of
the transgressions, till the Seed should come to whom the promise
hath been made; *and was* ordained by means of angels, in the
hand of a mediator. 20 Now a mediator is not a *mediator* of one,
but God is one. 21 *Is* the law then against the promises of GOD?
God forbid! for if there had been given a law which could have
given life, verily by the law would righteousness have come.
22 But, on the contrary, the Scripture shut up all under sin, that
the promise by faith in Jesus Christ might be given to them that
believe. 23 Now before that faith came, we were kept in ward

wholly inverts. *By God, etc.*] 'Of God in Christ,' *Auth.* *Doth not, etc.*] Sim. *Tynd., Cran., Bish.*: 'cannot disannul,' *Auth., Gen.*; 'makith not veyn,' *Wicl.*; 'is not disannulled,' *Cov.*; 'makith not void,' *Rhem.*; *Cov.* (Test.), confuses. *Make void*] Similarly *Wicl.* ('to avoide away') and *Cov.* (Test.): 'make the promise of none effect,' *Auth., Tynd., Cov., Cran., Gen., Bish.*; 'to frustrate,' *Rhem.*

18. *But to Abraham, etc.*] 'But God gave *it* to Abraham by promise,' *Auth.* and the other Vv. except *Cov.*, 'gave freely;' *Wicl.*, 'grauntide.' *Through*] 'By,' *Auth.* and all the other Vv.

19. *What then, etc.*] 'Wherefore then serveth,' *Auth., Tynd., Cov.* (sim. Test.), *Cran., Gen., Bish.*; 'what thanne the law,' *Wicl.*; 'why was the law then,' *Rhem.* *The transgressions*] *Auth.* and all the other Vv. omit the article; in a passage, however, of this dogmatical importance, it ought appy. to be retained. *Hath been made*] 'Was made,' *Auth., Tynd., Cran., Gen.*; 'He hadde made beheest,' *Wicl.*; 'He had promised,' *Cov.* (Test.), *Rhem.* *And was*] 'And it was,' *Auth.* *By means of*] 'By,' *Auth.* and the other Vv. except *Cov.*, 'of angels.'

21. *Given a law*] 'A law given,' *Auth.* *Verily by the, etc.*] 'Verily (*Wicl.*) righteousness should have been by the law,' *Auth.*; 'then no doute,' *Tynd., Cov., Cran., Gen., Bish.*; 'shuld have come,' *Tynd., Gen.*

22. *But on the contrary*] 'But,' *Auth.* and all the other Vv. The addition of the words "on the contrary" seem *here* required in translation to preserve the true force of ἀλλά, and to show clearly the nature of the reasoning. *Shut up all*] Similarly, as to the omission of 'hath,' *Tynd., Cran.*, 'concluded all things:' '*hath* concluded all,' *Auth., Bish.*; 'hath concluded all things,' *Wicl., Gen., Rhem.* *Faith in*] 'Faith of,' *Auth.* and the other Vv. except *Cov.*, 'faith on.'

23. *Now*] 'But,' *Auth.* and the other Vv. except *Wicl.*, 'and;' *Tynd.* and *Cov.* omit. *Before that*] So *Tynd., Cran.*, and similarly *Wicl.*, 'to for that;' *Cov.* (Test.), 'afore that:' 'before,' *Auth.* and the remaining Vv. *Kept in ward, etc.*] 'Kept under the law shut up,' *Auth.*; 'kept under the lawe, en-

shut up under the law for the faith which afterwards was to be
revealed. 24 So then the law hath been our schoolmaster unto
Christ, that we may be justified BY FAITH.

25 But now that faith is come, we are no longer under a schoolmaster. 26 For ye are all sons of God through the faith in Christ
Jesus. 27 For as many of you as were baptized into Christ put on
Christ. 28 There is among *such* neither Jew nor Greek, there is
neither bond nor free, there is no male and female: for ye all are
one in Christ Jesus. 29 But if ye *be* Christ's, then are ye ABRA-
HAM'S SEED, heirs according to promise.

closid,' *Wicl.;* 'kept and shut up, etc.,' *Tynd.*, *Cov.*, *Gen.;* 'kept under the law and were shut up,' *Cran.*, *Bish.*
For] 'Unto,' *Auth.* *Afterwards was, etc.*] 'Which should aft. be rev.,' *Auth.*, *Gen.*, *Bish.;* sim. *Tynd.*, *Cov.*, *Cran.* ('be declared').

24. *So then*] 'Wherefore,' *Auth.*, *Tynd.*, *Cran.*, *Gen.*, *Bish.;* 'and so,' *Wicl.;* 'thus,' *Cov.;* 'therefore,' *Cov.* (Test.), *Rhem.* *Hath been our schoolmaster unto*] 'Was our schoolmaster *to bring us* unto,' *Auth.*, *Gen.;* 'undir maister in Christ,' *Wicl.;* 'scolemaster unto the time of,' *Tynd.;* 'scolemaster unto,' *Cov.* (both), *Cran.*, *Bish.;* 'pedag. in,' *Rhem.* There is much difficulty in fixing on the most suitable translation of this word. The term 'schoolmaster' certainly tends to introduce an idea (that of teaching) not in the original and also serves to obscure the idea of *custodia* ('custos incorruptissimus,' Hor. *Sat.* I. 6. 81), which seems the prevailing one of the passage. Still as the same objection applies in a greater or less degree to 'pedagogue' (ed. 1) and 'tutor,' it will be perhaps better, in so familiar a passage, to return to *Auth.* *May be*] 'Might be,' *Auth.:* change to preserve what is called the succession of tenses, Latham, *Engl. Lang.* § 616 (ed. 3).

25. *Now that*] 'So *Cov.:* 'after that,' *Auth.* and the other Vv. except *Cov.* (Test.), 'whan the fayth did come;' *Rhem.*, 'when the faith came.'

26. *Sons*] So *Tynd.*, *Gen.: Auth.* and the remaining Vv., 'the children.' *Through the faith*] 'By faith,' *Auth.*, *Gen.*, *Bish.*, *Rhem.;* 'thorugh bileue,' *Wicl.;* 'by the fayth which is in,' *Tynd.*, *Cov.* (Test.); 'because ye believe in,' *Cran.*

27. *Were baptized*] 'Have been baptized,' *Auth.;* 'are baptized,' *Tynd.* (*Wicl.*, 'ben') and all the remaining Vv. *Put on*] 'Have put on,' *Auth.* and the other Vv. except *Wicl.*, 'ben clothid.'

28. *There is among such, etc.*] 'There is neither, etc.,' *Auth.* *No male and female*] 'Neither male nor female,' *Auth.* None of the other Vv. seem to have marked the change. *All are*] 'Are all,' *Auth.* and the other Vv. except *Rhem.*, 'al you are.'

29. *But*] So *Cov.* (Test.): 'and,' *Auth.*, *Wicl.*, *Rhem.* The rest omit the particle. *Heirs*] So *Rhem.:* * 'and heirs,' *Auth.*

CHAPTER IV

Now I say, That the heir, as long as he is a child, differeth in
nothing from a bond-servant, though he be lord of all; 2 but is
under guardians and stewards until the time appointed of the father.
3 Even so we, when we were children, were kept in bondage under
the rudiments of the world: 4 but when the fulness of the time
came, God sent forth His Son, born of a woman, born under the
law, 5 that He might redeem them that were under the law, that
we might receive the adoption of sons. 6 And to show that ye ARE
SONS, God sent forth the Spirit of His Son into our hearts, crying,
Abba Father. 7 So then thou art no more a servant, but a son;
and if a son, an heir also through God.
8 Howbeit, at that time, truly, not knowing God, ye were in

CHAPTER IV. 1. *In nothing*] 'Nothing,' *Auth.*, *Wicl.*, *Cov.* (Test.), *Bish.*, *Rhem.*; 'differeth not,' *Tynd.*, *Cran.*, *Gen.*; 'there is no diff.,' *Cov.* *Bond-servant*] 'Servant,' *Auth.* and all the other Vv. It seems desirable to keep up the idea of 'bondage' and 'slavery' which pervades the whole simile.

2. *Guardians*] 'Tutors,' *Auth.* and the other Vv. except *Wicl.*, 'kepers;' *Cov.*, 'rulers.' It seems desirable to make a change in translation to preserve a distinction between ἐπίτροπος here and παιδαγωγὸς in the preceding chapter. *Stewards*] 'Governors,' *Auth.* and the other Vv. except *Wicl.*, 'kepers and tutores.'

3. *Kept in bondage*] 'Were in bondage under,' *Auth.* and the other Vv. except *Wicl.*, 'serueden undir;' *Cov.* (Test.), *Rhem.*, 'were seruynge under.' *Rudiments*] So *Gen.*, *Bish.*: 'elements,' *Auth.*, *Wicl.*, *Rhem.*; 'ordinances,' *Tynd.*, *Cran.*; 'tradicions,' *Cov.* (both).

4. *Came*] So *Wicl.*, *Rhem.*: 'was come,' *Auth.* and sim. the remaining Vv. *Born . . . born*] 'Made . . . made, *Auth.*, *Wicl.*, *Rhem.*, *Bish.* ('and made under'); 'born . . . made bonde unto,' *Tynd.*, *Cran.*; 'borne and put under,' *Cov.*; 'made . . . made bonde unto,' *Gen.* The meaning preferred by Scholef. (*Hints*, p. 96), 'made subject to the law,' involves a change of meaning in γενόμενον, which does not appear necessary or natural.

5. *That he might*] So *Rhem.*, and sim. *Wicl.*, *Cov.* (Test.): 'to redeem,' *Auth.* and the remaining Vv. Here as in ch. iii. 14 it seems most exact to indicate the repeated ἵνα by the same form of translation.

6. *To show that*] 'Because,' *Auth.* and the other Vv. except *Wicl.*, 'for ye ben;' *Cov.*, 'forsomuche then as.' *Sent forth*] Sim. *Wicl.*, *Cov.* (Test.), 'sente:' 'hath sent forth,' *Auth.*; 'hath sent,' *Tynd.*, *Cov.*, *Cran.*, *Rhem.*; 'hath sent out,' *Gen.* *Our hearts*] '* Your hearts,' *Auth.*

7. *So then*] 'Wherefore,' *Auth.*, *Gen.*, *Bish.*; 'and so,' *Wicl.*; 'wherefore now,' *Tynd.*, *Cov.*, *Cran.*; 'therefore,' *Cov.* (Test.), *Rhem.* *An heir, etc.*] 'Then an heir * of God through Christ,' *Auth.*

8. *At that time, etc.*] 'Then when ye know (*sic* in Bagst.) not,' *Auth.*; 'thanne ye unknowynge,' *Wicl.*; 'when ye knewe not,' *Tynd.*, *Cov.*, *Cran.*, *Gen.*, *Bish.*; 'but then truely not knowynge,' *Cov.*

bondage to them which by nature are not gods. [9] But now that
ye have come to know God, or rather have been known by God,
how *is it that* ye turn back again to the weak and beggarly rudiments, whereunto ye desire to be again anew in bondage. [10] Ye
are carefully observing days, and months, and seasons, and years.
[11] I am apprehensive of you, lest haply I have bestowed upon you
labor in vain.

[12] Brethren, I beseech you, become as I *am*, for I also have
become as ye are. Ye injured me in nothing: [13] yea ye know
that it was on account of weakness of my flesh that I preached the
gospel unto you the first time; [14] and your temptation in my flesh
ye despised not, nor loathed, but received me as an angel of God,
yea as Christ Jesus. [15] Of what nature then *was* the boasting of

(Test.); 'then in deede knowing,' *Rhem.* The change in the translation of τότε is to prevent 'then' being mistaken for the inferential particle. *Were in bondage*] 'Ye did service,' *Auth.* *Not gods*] *'No gods,' *Auth.*

9. *Now that ye have come to know*] 'Now, after that ye have known,' *Auth.* *Have been known*] 'Are known,' *Auth.* and the other Vv. except *Gen.*, 'are taught.' *By God*] 'Of God,' *Auth.*, and all the other Vv. *How is it that*] So *Tynd.*, *Cov.*, *Cran.*, *Gen.*: 'how,' *Auth.*, *Wicl.*, *Cov.* (Test.), *Bish.*, *Rhem.* *Ye turn back*] So *Cov.*: 'turn ye,' *Auth.* and the other Vv. except *Gen.*, 'are turned backward unto.' *Rudiments*] So *Bish.*: 'elements,' *Auth.*, *Wicl.*, *Rhem.*; 'cerimonies,' *Tynd.*, *Gen.*; 'tradicions,' *Cov.* (both); 'ordinaunces,' *Cran.* *Again anew*] Sim. *Tynd.*, *Cov.*, *Cran.*, *Bish.*, 'againe afresshe:' 'again,' *Auth.*, and sim. *Cov.* (Test.), *Rhem.*; 'as from the begynnyng ye wil be in bondage backwardly,' *Gen.*

10. *Carefully observing*] 'Observe,' *Auth.* and the other Vv. except *Wicl.*, 'taken kepe to.' *Seasons*] 'Times,' *Auth.* and all the other Vv.

11. *Am apprehensive*] 'Am afraid,' *Auth*; 'I drede,' *Wicl.*; 'am in feare of,' *Tynd.*, *Cov.*, *Cran.*, *Gen.*, *Bish.*; 'feare me,' *Cov.* (Test.); 'fear,' *Rhem.*

12. *Become as, etc.*] 'Be as I *am*; for I *am* as ye are: ye have not injured me at all,' *Auth.*, *Bish.*; 'ye have not hurte me at all,' *Tynd.*, *Cov.*, *Cran.*, *Gen.*

13. *Yea ye know, etc.*] 'Ye know how through infirmity, etc.,' *Auth.* and the other Vv. except *Wicl.*, *Rhem.*, 'bi infirmyte;' *Cov.*, 'in weakness.' The slight changes made by substituting the simpler word 'weakness' for 'infirmity,' and 'my' for 'the,' seem to make the reference of the Apostle to some bodily affliction or illness slightly more apparent. *The first time*] 'At the first,' *Auth.* and the other Vv. except *Wicl.*, 'now bifor;' *Cov.* (Test.), 'a whyle ago:' this translation leaves the meaning ambiguous; see notes.

14. *Your*] *'My,' *Auth.*; see notes. *In my flesh*] So *Wicl.*, *Cov.* (Test.), *Rhem.*; 'which was,' *Auth.*, *Cran.* *Gen.*, *Bish.*, and sim. *Tynd.* *Loathed*] 'Rejected,' *Auth.*, *Rhem.*; 'forsaken,' *Wicl.*; 'abhorred,' *Tynd.*, *Cran.*, *Gen.*, *Bish.* *Yea*] So *Tynd.*, *Cov.* (Test.), *Gen.*: 'even,' *Auth.*, *Cov.*, *Cran.*, *Bish.*; *Wicl.*, *Rhem.* omit.

15. *Of what nature, etc.*] 'Where* is then the blessedness ye spake of,' *Auth.*;

your blessedness? for I bear you record, that, *if it had been* possible, ye would have plucked out your eyes, and have given them to
me. 16 So then, am I become your enemy, by speaking to you the
truth?

17 They pay you court in no honest way; yea, they desire to
exclude you, that ye may pay THEM court. 18 But *it is* good to be
courted in honesty AT ALL TIMES, and not only when I am present
with you . . . 19 My little children, of whom I am again in travail,
until Christ be formed in you, 20 I could indeed wish to be present
with you now, and to change my tone, for I am perplexed about
you.

21 Tell me, ye that desire to be under the law, do ye not hear the
law? 22 For it is written, that Abraham had two sons; one by the
bond-maid, and one by the free-woman. 23 Howbeit, he *who was*
of the bond-maid was born after the flesh; but he of the free-maid
was through the promise. 24 All which things are allegorical; for

'your blessynge,' *Wicl.;* 'how happy were ye then,' *Tynd.*, *Cov.;* 'your happynesse,' *Cov.* (Test.); 'your felicitie,' *Cran.*, *Bish.;* 'boasting of your fel.,' *Gen.;* 'your blessedness,' *Rhem.* *Your*] So *Wicl.*, *Cov.* (Test.), *Rhem.:* 'your own,' *Auth.* and the remaining Vv.

16. *So then*] 'Am I therefore,' *Auth.* and the other Vv. except *Wicl.*, *Rhem.*, 'thanne.' *By speaking*] 'Because I tell,' *Auth.* and the other Vv. except *Wicl.*, 'seiynge;' *Cov.* (Test.), *Rhem.*, 'telling.'

17. *Pay you court, etc.*] 'Zealously affect you, *but* not well,' *Auth.;* 'gelous over you amysse,' *Tynd.* and other Vv. except *Wicl.*, 'louen you not well;' *Rhem.*, 'emulate.' *Desire to*] 'Would,' *Auth.*, *Wicl.*, *Cov.*, *Rhem.;* 'intende to,' *Tynd.*, *Cran.*, *Gen.*, *Bish.;* 'wyll,' *Cov.* (Test.). *May pay them court*] 'Might affect them,' *Auth.*

18. *To be courted, etc.*] 'To be zealously affected always in a good thing,' *Auth.;* 'to be fervent,' *Tynd.*, *Cov.*, *Cran.;* 'to love earnestly,' *Gen.;* 'to be zelous,' *Bish.*

19. *Am again*] 'Travail in birth again,' *Auth.*

20. *I could indeed wish*] 'I desire,' *Auth.;* 'but I desire,' *Bish.;* 'I wolde I were,' *Tynd.*, *Cov.*, *Cran.*, *Gen.*, and similarly the remaining Vv. *Tone*] 'Voice,' *Auth.* and all the other Vv. *Am perplexed, etc.*] 'I stand in doubt of you,' *Auth.*, and similarly *Tynd.*, *Cov.*, *Cran.*, *Gen.*, *Bish;* 'am ashamed of you,' *Cov.* (Test.); 'am confoundid,' *Wicl.*, *Rhem.*

22. *One — and one*] So *Wicl.*, *Rhem.:* 'the one — the other,' *Auth.* and the remaining Vv. except *Cov.* (Test.), 'the one — and one.' *The bond-maid . . . . the free-woman*] Sim. *Rhem.:* '*A* bond-maid . . . *a* free-woman,' *Auth.*, and sim. the remaining Vv.

23. *Howbeit*] 'But,' *Auth.*, *Wicl.*, *Cov.* (Test.), *Rhem.;* 'yee and,' *Tynd.*, *Cran.*, *Gen.;* *Cov.* omits. *Bond-maid*] 'Bond-woman,' *Auth.* *Through*] 'By,' *Auth.*, and sim. remaining Vv. except *Cov.* (Test.), 'after.'

24. *All which, etc.*] 'Which things are an allegory,' *Auth.;* 'ben seide bi anothir

these women are two covenants, — the one from Mount Sinai,
bearing children unto bondage; and this is Agar. [25] For the word
Agar signifieth in Arabia Mount Sinai; — and she ranketh with
Jerusalem which now is, for she is in bondage with her children.
[26] But Jerusalem which is above is free, AND SHE is our mother.
[27] For it is written, Rejoice *thou* barren that bearest not; break
forth and cry, thou that travailest not: for many children hath the
desolate one more than she which hath an husband. [28] But ye,
brethren, as Isaac was, are children of PROMISE. [29] Still as then, he
that was born after the flesh persecuted him *that was born* after the
Spirit, even so *it is* now. [30] Nevertheless what saith the scripture?
Cast out the bond-maid and her son: for the son of the bond-maid
shall in no wise BE HEIR with the son of the free-woman. [31] Wherefore, brethren, we are not children of a bond-maid, but of the free-
woman. CHAP. V. Stand fast then in the liberty for which

understondinge,' *Wicl.;* 'betoken mystery,' *Tynd.;* 'betoken somewhat,' *Cov.;* 'are spoken by an allegory,' *Cran.*, and sim. *Cov.* (Test.), *Rhem.;* 'by the which thinges another thing is ment,' *Gen.*, *Bish.* *Two*] *'The two,' *Auth.* *These women*] So *Tynd.*, *Cov.;* 'these,' *Auth.* and the remaining Vv. except *Gen.*, 'these mothers.' *Bearing children, etc.*] 'Which gendereth to,' *Auth.* and the other Vv. except *Wicl.*, *Rhem.*, 'gendrynge;' *Cov.* (Test.), 'engendrynge.' *And this*] 'Which,' *Auth.*

25. *The word, etc.*] 'This Agar is Mount Sinai in Arabia,' *Auth.*, *Bish.* ('the mount'); 'for mounte S. is called A. in Arab.,' *Tynd.;* 'for Agar is called in Arabia the Mount Sin.,' *Cov.;* 'for Sin. is a mountaine in Ar.,' *Gen.*, *Cov.* (Test.), *Rhem.* *Ranketh with*] 'Answereth to,' *Auth.*, *Gen.;* 'is joyned to it,' *Wicl.*, *Cov.* (Test.); 'bordereth upon,' *Tynd.*, *Cran.*, *Bish.* (see notes); 'reacheth unto,' *Cov.;* 'hath affinitie to,' *Rhem.* *For she*] *'And she,' *Auth.*

26. *And she, etc.*] 'Which *is* the mother of us all,' *Auth.*

27. *For many more, etc.*] Sim. *Rhem.:* 'for the desolate hath many more children than she which hath,' *Auth.* *An husband*] So *Auth.* and all the other Vv. Idiom seems to require this less accurate translation.

28. *But ye*] 'Now *we,' *Auth.* *Children*] So *Tynd.*, *Gen.:* 'the children,' *Auth.* and the remaining Vv. except *Wicl.*, 'sones.'

29. *Still*] 'But,' *Auth.* and all the other Vv.

30. *Bond-maid* (bis)] 'Bondwoman,' *Auth.* *Shall in no wise*] So *Bish.* (ed. 2): 'shall not,' *Auth.* and all the other Vv. This seems one of the cases in which we may press the translation of οὐ μή: see notes *on* 1 *Thess.* iv. 15.

31. *Wherefore*] *'So then,' *Auth.* *A bond-maid*] 'The bondwoman,' *Auth.* and all the other Vv. *Free-woman*] 'Free,' *Auth.*

CHAPTER V. 1. *Then*] '*Therefore,*' *Auth.* and the other Vv. except *Wicl.*, *Rhem.*, which omit. *For which*] 'Wherewith,' *Auth.*, *Tynd.*, *Cran.*, *Bish.:* *Wicl.*, *Gen.*, follow different readings.

Christ made us free, and be not held fast again in a yoke of
bondage.
2 Behold, I Paul say unto you, that if ye be circumcised, CHRIST
will profit you nothing. 3 Yea I testify again to every man who
has himself circumcised, that he is a debtor to do the WHOLE law.
4 Ye have been done away with from Christ, whosoever of you are
being justified in the law; ye are fallen away from grace. 5 For
we, by the Spirit, are tarrying for the hope of righteousness from
faith. 6 For in Jesus Christ neither circumcision availeth anything,
nor uncircumcision, but faith working through love.
7 Ye were running well; who did hinder you that ye should not

Made us] 'Hath made,' *Auth.* *Held fast, etc.*] 'Entangled again with a,' *Auth.*, 'wrappe not yourselves in the,' *Tynd.*, *Cran.*, and sim. *Cov.*, *Gen.*; 'be not holden with (in the,' *Wicl.*), *Cov.* (Test.) *Rhem.*

2. *Will*] 'Shall,' *Auth.* and the other Vv. except *Cov.* (present); simple predication of result: 'in primis personis *shall* simpliciter prædicentis est, *will* quasi promittentis aut minantis; in secundis et tertiis personis *shall* promittentis est aut minantis, *will* simpliciter prædicentis,' Wallis, *Gr. Angl.* p. 106.

3. *Yea*] 'For,' *Auth.*, *Gen.*, *Bish.*; 'and,' *Wicl.*, *Cov.* (Test.), *Rhem.*; *Tynd.*, *Cov.*, *Cran.* omit. *Who has himself, etc.*] 'That is circumcised,' *Auth.*, and similarly *Tynd.*, *Cov.*, *Cran.*, *Gen.*, *Bish.*; 'circumcidith hym silf,' *Wicl.*; sim. *Cov.* (Test.), *Rhem.*

4. *Ye have, etc.*] 'Christ is become of no effect unto you,' *Auth.*; 'and ye ben voidid aweie fro,' *Wicl.*; 'are gone quyte from,' *Tynd.*, *Cov.*, *Gen.*; 'Christ is become but in veyne unto,' *Cran.*, *Bish.*; 'are evacuated from,' *Rhem.* Here idiom seems to require the English perfect: the pure aoristic translation, 'ye *were* done away with from Christ,' stands in too marked a contrast with the following present, and *to the English reader* too completely transfers the action to what is purely past; see notes *on* 1 *Thess.* ii. 16 (*Transl.*). *Are being justified*] 'Are justified,' *Auth.* and the other Vv. except *Cov.*, 'wyll be made ryghteous;' *Cov.* (Test.), 'are made ryghteous.' *In the*] So *Wicl.*, *Rhem.*: 'in the,' *Auth.* and the remaining Vv. *Fallen away*] 'Fallen,' *Auth.*

5. *By the Spirit, etc.*] 'Through the Spirit wait for the hope of right, by faith,' *Auth.*, *Bish.*; 'we loke for and hope in the sprite to be justified thorow,' *Tynd.*, *Cran.*; 'in the sprite of hope to be made ryghtuous by faith,' *Cov.*; 'in sprite by faythe we wayte for,' *Cov.* (Test.); 'we wayt for (by the Spirit through faith) the hope of,' *Gen.* *Are tarrying for*] 'Wait for,' *Auth.* *Cov.* (Test.), *Gen.* *Bish.*; 'abiden,' *Wicl.*; 'loke for,' *Tynd.*, *Cran.*; 'wayte,' *Cov.*; 'expect,' *Rhem.*

6. *Working*] 'Which worketh,' *Auth.* and the other Vv. except *Wicl.*, *Rhem.*, 'that worketh;' *Cov.*, 'which by loue is mighty.' The practice of inserting the relative before the anarthrous participle, even when idiom can scarcely be urged in its favor, is an inaccuracy that is not uncommonly found in the older Vv. Perhaps even in Eph. ii. 1, Col. ii. 13, it might seem better to adopt the concessive translation, 'though, etc.': see, however, notes *in locc.* (*Transl.*). *Through*] 'By,' *Auth.* and all the other Vv.

7. *Were running*] 'Did run,' *Auth.*,

obey the truth? 8 The persuasion *cometh* not of Him that calleth
you. 9 A little leaven leaveneth the whole lump. 10 I, for my
part, have confidence in you in the Lord, that ye will be none
otherwise minded; but he that troubleth you shall bear his judgment, whosoever he be. 11 But I, brethren, if I still preach CIR-
CUMCISION, why do I still suffer persecution? then is the offence
of the cross done away with. 12 I would that they who are unsettling you would even cut themselves off *from you.*

13 For ye were called unto liberty, brethren; only *use* not your
liberty for an occasion to the flesh, but by your love serve one
another. 14 For the whole law is fulfilled in one saying, *even* in
this, Thou shalt love thy neighbour as thyself. 15 But if ye bite and
devour one another, take heed that ye be not consumed one of
another.

16 Now I say, Walk by the Spirit and ye shall in no wise fulfil

Tynd., Cov., Cran., Gen., Bish.; 'runnen,' *Wicl.*; 'ranne,' *Cov.* (both), *Rhem.*

8. *The*] *Cran., Rhem.*; 'this,' *Wicl., Auth., Cov.* (Test.), *Gen.*; 'that,' *Tynd.*; 'such,' *Cov.* *That calleth*] So rightly *Auth.*: not 'called,' *Tynd., Gen.*, or 'is calling,' as the iterative force involved in the English present more nearly approaches to the idiomatic use of the participle than either the past tense or the resolved present; comp. notes *on Phil.* iii. 14, (*Transl.*), and Latham, *Engl. Lang.* § 578 (ed. 3).

10. *I for my part*] 'I,' *Auth.* and all the other Vv. *In*] So the other Vv. except *Auth., Gen.*, 'through the.'

11. *But I*] So *Cov.* (Test.): 'and I,' *Auth.* *Still* (bis)] 'Yet,' *Auth.* *Done away with*] 'Ceased,' *Auth.* and the other Vv. except *Wicl.*, 'voidid;' *Rhem.*, 'evacuated.'

12. *Are unsettling*] 'Trouble,' *Auth.* and the other Vv. except *Wicl.*, 'disturblen;' *Gen.*, 'do disquiet.' *Would even, etc.*] 'I would they were even cut off which trouble you,' *Auth.*, and similarly *Rhem.*; 'kutte aweie,' *Wicl., Cov.* (Test.); 'were seperated,' *Tynd., Cran.*; 'were roted out,' *Cov.*; 'were cut off from you,' *Gen.*

13. *For ye, etc.*] 'For brethren ye have been,' etc., *Auth*, and sim. all the other Vv. as to the forward position of 'brethren.' The aor. ἐκλήθητε is translated by different auxiliaries, 'ye are,' *Wicl., Cov.* (both), *Rhem.*; 'were,' *Tynd., Cran.*; 'have been,' *Gen., Bish., Auth.* *Your liberty*] So *Tynd., Cov.* (both), *Cran., Gen.*: 'liberty,' *Auth., Bish.*; 'fredom,' *Wicl.*; 'this liberty,' *Rhem.* *Your love*] 'Love,' *Auth.*, and the other Vv. except *Wicl., Rhem.*, charite; *Cov.*, 'the loue.'

14. *The whole*] 'All the,' *Auth.* and the other Vv. except *Wicl.*, 'everi lawe.' *Saying*] 'Word,' *Auth.* and the other Vv.

16. *Now I say*] '*This* I say then,' *Auth.*; 'I saye,' *Tynd., Cov., Cran.*; 'then ('and,' *Wicl.*) 'I say,' *Gen., Bish.* *By*] 'In the,' *Auth.* and the other Vv. except *Wicl., Cov.* (Test.), which omit the article. *Shall in no wise*] 'Shall not,' *Auth., Cov.* (Test.), *Gen., Bish.*; 'ye schalen not parfourme,' *Wicl.*;

the lust of the flesh. 17 For the flesh lusteth against the Spirit,
and the Spirit against the flesh: for these are opposed the one to
the other, that ye may not do the things ye may wish. 18 But, if
ye be led by the Spirit, ye are not under the law. 19 Now the
works of the flesh are manifest, of which kind are, — fornication,
uncleanness, wantonness, 20 idolatry, sorcery, hatreds, strife, jealousy, *deeds of* wrath, caballings, dissensions, factions, 21 envyings,
murders, drunkenness, revellings, and such like: of the which I
tell you beforehand, as I also told *you* beforehand, that they which
do all such things shall not inherit the kingdom of God. 22 But
the fruit of the Spirit is love, joy, peace, long-suffering, benevolence, goodness, trustfulness, 23 meekness, temperance: against all
such things there is no law. 24 Now they that are Christ's have

'and fulfill not' (imper.), *Tynd.*, *Cran.*; 'so shall ye not fulfyll,' *Cov.*; 'shal not accomplish,' *Rhem.*

17. *Are opposed*] 'Are contrary,' *Auth.* and all Vv. except *Wicl.*, *Rhem.*, 'ben adversaries togidre.' *That ye may not*] Comp. *Wicl.*: 'so that ye cannot do, etc.,' *Auth.* and the remaining Vv. except *Cov.* (Test.), 'that the thynges that ye will, ye do not the same;' *Rhem.*, 'that not what things soever you wil, these you doe.' *For*] * 'And,' *Auth.* *Ye may wish*] 'The things that ye would,' *Auth.*, *Gen.* ('the same'); 'that ye wyllen,' *Wicl.*; 'that which ye wolde,' *Tynd.*, *Cov.*; 'the thynges that ye wyll,' *Cov.* (Test.); 'whatsoever ye wolde,' *Cran.*; 'what ye wolde,' *Bish.*; 'what soever you will,' *Rhem.*

18. *By*] So *Wicl.*, *Cov.* (Test.), *Rhem.*: 'of,' *Auth.* and the remaining Vv.

19. *Of which kind are*] 'Which are these,' *Auth.* and the other Vv. except *Wicl.*, and *Cov.* (Test.), 'which are.' *Fornication*] * 'Adultery, fornication,' *Auth.* *Wantonness*] 'Lasciviousness,' *Auth.* and the other Vv. except *Wicl.*, *Cov.* (Test.), *Rhem* 'leecherie.'

20. *Sorcery, etc.*] 'Witchcraft, hatred, * variance, * emulations, wrath, strife, seditions, heresies,' *Auth.*, *Gen.*; 'witchecraft . . . variance, zele . . . sectes,' *Tynd.*, *Cran.*, *Bish.*

21. *Tell you beforehand*] 'Tell you before,' *Auth.* and the other Vv. (*Cov.* Test., 'afore') except *Wicl.*, 'seie;' 'foretell you,' *Rhem.* *Told you beforehand*] 'Have also told you in time past,' *Auth.*; 'haue told you to for,' *Wicl.*; 'haue tolde you in tyme past,' *Tynd.*, *Cov.*, *Cran.*; 'haue tolde you,' *Gen.*, *Bish.*; 'haue foretold you,' *Rhem.* *All such things*] 'Such things,' *Auth.* and the other Vv. except *Cov.* (both), 'such.'

22. *Benevolence*] 'Gentleness,' *Auth.*, *Tynd.*, *Cov.*, *Cran.*, *Gen.*, *Bish.*; 'benyngnite,' *Wicl.*, *Rhem.* *Trustfulness*] 'Faith,' *Auth.* and the other Vv. except *Tynd.*, *Cov.*, *Cran.*, 'faithfulness.'

23. *All such things*] 'Such,' *Auth.* and the other Vv. except *Wicl.*, 'suche thingis.'

24. *Now they*] 'And they,' *Auth.*, *Wicl.*, *Rhem.*; 'but,' *Cov.* (both); 'for,' *Gen.*; 'they truly,' *Bish.*: *Tynd.* and *Cran.* omit. *Have crucified*] So *Auth.* and all the other Vv. Here again it seems desirable to preserve the perfect in translation, as the *English* aor. tends to refer the crucifixion too exclusively to the past; see notes on verse 4.

crucified the flesh with the affections and lusts. 25 If WE LIVE by
the Spirit, let us also walk by the Spirit. 26 Let us not become
vain-glorious, provoking one another, envying one another.

CHAPTER VI.

1 BRETHREN, if a man should be even surprised in a fault, ye
which are spiritual restore such an one in the spirit of meekness;
considering thyself, lest thou also be tempted. 2 Bear ye one
another's burdens, and thus shall ye fulfil the law of Christ. 3 For
if a man think himself to be something, when he is nothing, he
deceiveth his own mind. 4 But let each man prove his own WORK,
and then shall he have his ground of boasting only in what concerneth himself, and not in what concerneth the other. 5 For each
man must bear his own load.

6 But let him that is taught in the word share with him that
teacheth in all good things. 7 Be not deceived; God is not
mocked: for whatsoever a man soweth, that shall he also reap.
8 For he that soweth unto his own flesh shall of the flesh reap

25. *By the . . . by the*] So *Wicl.* ('bi. Spirit'): *Auth.* and the remaining Vv. 'in the . . . in the.'

26. *Become*] So *Cov.* (Test.): 'be,' *Auth.*, *Tynd*, *Cov.*, *Cran.*, *Gen.*, *Bish.*; 'be made,' *Wicl.*, *Rhem.* *Vain-glorious*] So *Tynd*, *Cov.*: 'desirous of vain glory,' *Auth.* and the remaining Vv. except *Wicl*, 'coueitous of veyne glory.'

CHAPTER VI. 1. *Should be even surprised*] 'Be overtaken,' *Auth.*, *Cov.* (both); 'be occupied,' *Wicl.*; 'be fallen by chance,' *Tynd.*; 'be taken,' *Cran.*; 'by occasion,' *Gen.*, *Bish.*; 'be preöccupated,' *Rhem.*

2. *Thus shall ye*, etc.] *'So fulfil,' *Auth.*, *Tynd.*, *Cran.*, *Gen.*

3. *Deceiveth his own mind*] So *Cran.*; 'deceiveth himself,' *Auth.*, *Cov.* (both); 'bigilith hym silf,' '*Wicl.*; 'deceaveth hym silfe in his ymaginacion,' *Tynd.*, *Gen.*; 'in his own fansie,' *Bish.*; 'seduceth himself,' *Rhem.*

4. *Each*] So *Wicl.*; 'every,' *Auth.* and the remaining Vv. *His ground of boasting* etc.] 'Rejoicing in himself alone and not in another,' *Auth.*, and similarly, *Tynd.*, *Cov.*, *Cran.*, *Gen.*, *Bish.*; 'haue glorie,' *Wicl.*; 'so shall he rejoice only in himself,' *Cov.* (Test.); 'have the glorie,' *Rhem.*

5. *Each*] So *Wicl.*; 'every,' *Auth.* and all the remaining Vv. *Must bear*] 'Shall bear,' *Auth.* and all the other Vv. *Load*] 'Burden,' *Auth.* and the other Vv. except *Wicl.*, 'charge.'

6. *But let him*] So *Cov.* (both): 'let him,' *Auth.* and the remaining Vv. except *Rhem.*, 'and let him.'

8. *Unto his own flesh*] 'To his flesh,' *Auth.*, *Gen.*; 'in his fleisch,' *Wicl.*, *Tynd.*, *Coverd.* (Test.), *Cran.*, *Rhem.*; 'upon the fleshe,' *Cov.* *Unto the Sp.*] 'To the Spirit,' *Auth.* *Eternal life*] 'Life everlasting,' *Auth.* and the other Vv. except *Wicl.*, *Cov.*, (Test.), which preserve the more correct order 'everlasting

corruption; but he that soweth unto the Spirit shall of the Spirit
reap eternal life. 9 But let us not lose heart in well-doing; for in
due season we shall reap, if *now* we faint not. 10 Accordingly,
then, as we have opportunity, let us do what is good unto all *men*,
but especially unto them who are of the household of faith.

11 See in what large letters I have written unto you with mine
own hand. 12 As many as desire to make a fair show in the flesh,
THEY constrain you to be circumcised; only that they should not
suffer persecution for the cross of Christ. 13 For not even do they,
who are being circumcised, themselves keep the law; but they
desire to have YOU circumcised, that they may glory in your
flesh. 14 But far be it from ME to glory, save in the cross of our
Lord Jesus Christ, by whom the world is crucified unto me, and I
unto the world. 15 For neither doth circumcision avail any thing,

life.' It is not desirable to invert the order in English except when the adjective in the original occupies the emphatic, *i. e.* the *first* place; comp. Winer, *Gr.* § 59, 2, p. 464. On the translation of αἰώνιος, comp. notes on 2 *Thess.* i. 9 (*Transl.*).

9. *But*] 'And,' *Auth.*, *Wicl.*, *Cov.* (Test.); the rest omit δὲ in translation. *Let us not lose heart*] 'Let us not *be weary,' *Auth.*, and sim. *Tynd.*, *Cov.*, *Cran.*, *Gen.*, *Bish.*; 'faile,' *Wicl.*, *Rhem.*; 'faynte,' *Cov.* (Test.) *If now*] 'If,' *Auth.*, *Gen.*, *Bish.*; 'not failynge,' *Wicl.*, *Rhem.*; 'without werynes,' *Tynd.*, *Cran.*; 'without ceassynge,' *Cov.*; 'not ceassynge,' *Cov.* (Test.).

10. *Accordingly then*, etc.] 'As we have therefore,' *Auth.*; 'therefor while,' *Wicl.*, and similarly the remaining Vv. *What is good*] 'Good,' *Auth.* *But especially*] So *Rhem.*, *Coverd.* ('specially'), and sim. *Wicl.*, 'but moost;' *Cov.* (Test.), 'but moost of all:' 'and specially,' *Tynd.*, *Cran.*, *Gen.*; *Auth.*, *Bish.* alone omit δὲ in translation. If by the fine idiomatic turn 'of the household,' etc., nothing more be meant than close and intimate union, it may be advantageously retained: see, however, notes.

11. *See*] So *Wicl.* ('se ye'), *Rhem.*: 'ye see,' *Auth*, *Cran.*, *Gen.*, *Bish.*; 'beholde,' *Tynd.*, *Cov.* (both). *In what*, etc.] 'How large a letter,' *Auth.*, *Tynd.*, *Cran.*, *Gen.*, *Bish.*; 'with how many words,' *Cov.*; 'with what manner of letters, *Rhem.*, and sim. *Wicl.*; 'with what letters,' *Cov.* (Test.).

12. *That they*, etc.] 'Lest they should,' *Auth.*, *Cov.* (both), *Cran.*; 'that thei suffre,' *Wicl.*; because they wolde not,' *Tynd.*, *Gen.*; 'that they may not,' *Rhem.*

13. *Not even*, etc.] 'Neither they themselves who are circumcised,' *Auth.* and all the other Vv. 'The circumcision-party,' is far from an improbable translation; see notes. *They desire*] 'Desire,' *Auth.*

14. *Far be it*] So *Wicl.*, *Cov.*, (Test.): 'God forbid that I should glory,' *Auth.* and the remaining Vv. *To glory*] 'That I should glory,' *Auth.*, *Bish.*, *Rhem.*; 'to haue glorie,' *Wicl.*; 'that I shuld rejoyce,' *Tynd.*, *Cov.*, *Cran.*, *Gen.*; 'to rejoyce,' *Cov.* (Test).

15. *For neither*, etc.] 'For *in Christ Jesus neither circumcision availeth,' *Auth.*

nor uncircumcision, but a new creature. 16 And as many as walk
according to this rule, peace *be* upon them, and mercy, and upon
the Israel of God. 17 Henceforth let no man trouble me: for I
bear in my body the marks of Jesus.
18 The grace of our Lord Jesus Christ *be* with your spirit,
brethren. Amen.

16. *Upon*] So *Cov.*, *Rhem.*: 'on, *Auth.* and the remaining Vv. except *Cov.* (Test.), 'unto them;' *Gen.*, 'shal be to them.

17. *Henceforth*] 'From henceforth,' *Auth.* and the other Vv. except *Wicl.*, 'and here aftir.' *Of Jesus*] 'Of the * Lord Jesus,' *Auth.*

18. *The grace*] 'Brethren, the grace,' *Auth.* and the other Vv. except *Wicl.*, *Cov.* (Test.), *Rhem.*, which adhere to the order in the original.

THE END.

WORKS OF MOSES STUART, late Professor in Andover Theological Seminary.

COMMENTARY ON THE EPISTLE TO THE ROMANS. Third Edition. Edited and revised by PROF. R. D. C. ROBBINS. 12mo. pp 544. $2.25.

"His Commentary on the Romans is the most elaborate of all his works. It has elicited more discussions than any of his other exegetical volumes. It is the result of long-continued, patient thought. It expresses, in clear style, his maturest conclusions. It has the animating influence of an original treatise, written on a novel plan, and under a sense of personal responsibility. Regarding it in all its relations, its antecedents and consequents, we pronounce it the most important Commentary which has appeared in this country on this Epistle.—*Bib. Sacra.*

"We heartily commend this work to all students of the Bible. The production of one of the first Biblical scholars of our age, on the most important of all the doctrinal books of the New Testament, it deserves the careful study, not only of those who agree with Prof. Stuart in his theological and exegetical principles, but of those who earnestly dissent from some of his views in both respects."—*Watchman and Reflector.*

"This contribution by Prof. Stuart has justly taken a high place among the Commentaries on the Epistle to the Romans, and, with his other works, will always be held in high estimation by the student of the Sacred Scriptures."—*New York Observer.*

COMMENTARY ON THE EPISTLE TO THE HEBREWS. Edited and revised by PROF. R. D. C. ROBBINS. 12mo. pp. 570. $2.25.

"It is a rich treasure for the student of the original. As a commentator, Prof. Stuart was especially arduous and faithful in following up the thought and displaying the connection of a passage, and his work as a scholar will bear comparison with any that have since appeared on either side of the Atlantic."—*American Presbyterian.*

"This Commentary is classical, both as to its literary and its theological merits. The edition before us is very skilfully edited by Professor Robbins, and gives in full Dr. Stuart's text, with additions bringing it down to the present day."—*Episcopal Recorder.*

"We have always regarded this excellent Commentary as the happiest effort of the late Andover Professor. It seems to us well-nigh to exhaust the subjects which the author comprehended in his plan."—*Boston Recorder.*

COMMENTARY ON THE APOCALYSE. 2 vols. 8vo. pp. 504, 504. $4.

COMMENTARY ON THE BOOK OF PROVERBS. 12mo. pp. 432. $1.75.

"This is the last work from the pen of Professor Stuart. Both this Commentary and the one preceding it, on Ecclesiastes, exhibit a mellowness of spirit which savors of the good man ripening for heaven; and the style is more condensed, and, in that respect, more agreeable, than in some of the works which were written in the unabated freshness and exuberant vigor of his mind. In learning and critical acumen they are equal to his former works. No English reader, we venture to say, can elsewhere find so complete a philological exposition of these two important books of the Old Testament."—*Bib. Sacra.*

COMMENTARY ON ECCLESIASTES. Second Edition. Edited and revised by R. D. C. ROBBINS, Professor in Middlebury College. 12mo. pp. 346. $1.50.

The Introduction discusses the general nature of the book; its special design and method, diction, authority, credit, and general history; ancient and modern versions, and commentaries. The Commentary is strictly and minutely exegetical.

MISCELLANIES. pp. 369. 12mo. $1.00.

CONTENTS.—I. Letters to Dr. Channing on the Trinity.—II. Two Sermons on the Atonement.—Sacramental Sermon on the Lamb of God.—IV. Dedication Sermon.—Real Christianity.—V. Letter to Dr. Channing on Religious Liberty.—VI. Supplementary Notes and Postscripts.

HEBREW GRAMMAR; Translated from Gesenius. 8vo. $1.00.

GREEK GRAMMAR OF THE NEW TESTAMENT DIALECT. Second Edition. Corrected and rewritten. 8vo. Reduced to $1.00.

HEBREW CHRESTOMATHY. Third Edition. pp. 231. 8vo. $1.

COMMENTARIES (*Critical and Grammatical*) OF C. J. ELLICOTT, Bishop of Gloucester and Bristol.

The Commentaries of Prof. Ellicott supply an urgent want in their sphere of criticism. Prof. Stowe says of them, in his Notice to the Commentary on the Galatians: "It is the crowning excellence of these Commentaries that they are exactly what they profess to be, — *critical* and *grammatical*, and therefore in the best sense of the term, *exegetical* . . . . . His results are worthy of all confidence. He is more careful than Tischendorf, slower and more steadily deliberate than Alford, and more patiently laborious than any other living New Testament critic, with the exception, perhaps, of Tregelles."

"They [Ellicott's Commentaries] have set the first example in this country [England] of a thorough and fearless examination of the grammatical and philological requirements of every word of the Sacred Text. I do not know of anything superior to them, in their own particular line, in Germany; and they add, what, alas! is so seldom found in this country, profound reverence for the matter and subjects on which the author is laboring; nor is their value lessened by Mr. Ellicott's having confined himself for the most part to one department of a commentator's work, — the grammatical and philological."—*Dean Alford.*

COMMENTARY ON GALATIANS. With an Introductory Notice by C. E. STOWE, Professor in Andover Theological Seminary. 8vo. pp. 183. $1.75.

"We have never met with a learned commentary on any book of the New Testament so nearly perfect in every respect as the 'Commentary on the Epistle to the Galatians,' by Prof. Ellicott, of King's College, London — learned, devout, and orthodox."—*Independent.*

"We would recommend all scholars of the original Scriptures who seek directness, luminous brevity, the absence of everything irrelevant to strict grammatical inquiry, with a concise and yet very complete view of the opinions of others, to possess themselves of Ellicott's Commentaries."—*American Presbyterian.*

COMMENTARY ON EPHESIANS. 8vo. pp. 190. $1.75.

COMMENTARY ON THESSALONIANS. 8vo. pp. 171. $1.75.

COMMENTARY ON THE PASTORAL EPISTLES. 8vo. pp. 265. $2.50.

IN PRESS.

COMMENTARY ON PHILIPPIANS, COLOSSIANS, AND PHILEMON.

HENDERSON ON THE MINOR PROPHETS. THE BOOK OF THE TWELVE Minor Prophets. Translated from the Original Hebrew. With a Commentary, Critical, Philological, and Exegetical. By E. HENDERSON, D.D. With a Biographical Sketch of the Author, by E. P. BARROWS, Hitchcock Professor in Andover Theological Seminary. 8vo. pp. 490. $4.00.

"This Commentary on the Minor Prophets, like that on the Prophecy of Isaiah, has been highly and deservedly esteemed by professional scholars, and has been of great service to the working ministry. We are happy to welcome it in an American edition, very neatly printed." — *Bib. Sacra.*

"The American publisher issues this valuable work with the consent and approbation of the author, obtained from himself before his death. It is published in substantial and elegant style, clear white paper and beautiful type. The work is invaluable for its philological research and critical acumen. The notes are learned, reliable, and practical, and the volume deserves a place in every theological student's library."—*American Presbyterian, etc.*

"This is probably the best Commentary extant on the Minor Prophets. The work is worthy of a place in the library of every scholar and every diligent and earnest reader of the Bible." — *Christian Chronicle.*

MISCELLANEOUS.

WORKS OF LEONARD WOODS, late Professor in Andover Theological Seminary: comprising Lectures, Letters, Essays, and Sermons. 5 vols. 8vo. $12.00.

LECTURES ON INFANT BAPTISM. By Leonard Woods, late Professor in Andover Theological Seminary. Boards. 35 cents.

AUGUSTINISM AND PELAGIANISM. By G. F. WIGGERS, D.D. Translated from the German, by PROF. R. EMERSON, D.D. pp. 383. 8vo. $1.50.

DÖDERLEIN'S HAND-BOOK OF LATIN SYNONYMES. Translated by Rev. H. H. Arnold, B.A., with an Introduction by S. H. TAYLOR, LL. D. New Edition, with an Index of Greek words. 16mo. pp. 267. $1.25.

"The present hand-book of Döderlein is remarkable for brevity, distinctness, perspicuity, and appositeness of its definitions. It will richly reward not merely the classical, but the general student for the labor he may devote to it. It is difficult to open the volume, even at random, without discovering some hint which may be useful to a theologian. . . . . From the preceding extracts it will be seen that this hand-book is useful in elucidating many Greek as well as Latin synonymes." —*Bib. Sacra.*

"This little volume, mentioned above, introduced to the American public by an eminent Scholar and Teacher, Samuel H. Taylor, LL. D., is one of the best helps to the thorough appreciation of the nice shades of meaning in Latin words that have met my eye. It deserves the attention of teachers and learners, and will amply reward patient study." — *E. D. Sanborn, late Professor of Latin in Dartmouth College.*

RUSSELL'S PULPIT ELOCUTION. Comprising Remarks on the Effect of Manner in Public Discourse; the Elements of Elocution applied to the Reading of the Scriptures, Hymns and Sermons; with Observations on the Principles of Gesture; and a Selection of Exercises in Reading and Speaking. With an Introduction by PROF. E. A. PARK and Rev. E. N. KIRK. 413 pp. 12mo. Second Edition. $1.50.

"Mr. Russell is known as one of the masters of elocutionary science in the United States. He has labored long, skilfully, and successfully in that most interesting field, and has acquired an honored name among the teachers and writers upon rhetoric. It is one of the most thorough publications upon the subject, and is admirably addressed to the correction of the various defects which diminish the influence of pulpit discourses. It is already an established authority in many places." — *Literary World.*

HEBREW ENGLISH PSALTER. Containing the Hebrew and English, in parallel colmuns, versified in both languages. The Hebrew text is according to Hahn, versified according to Rosenmüller; the English is the common version, but arranged line for line with the Hebrew, forming a very convenient manual for those wishing to become familiar with the Hebrew. 16mo. $1.50.

HEBREW PSALTER. This is the smallest pocket edition, and is altogether the most convenient, Hebrew Psalter ever published in this country. It is printed in very clear type. 32mo. Morocco. $1.00.

THE POLYMICRIAN NEW TESTAMENT. With Notes and References in a centre column, and Maps. A very convenient Testament for Sabbath-School Teachers and Scholars. 32mo. 45 cents.

CODEX VATICANUS. *Η ΚΑΙΝΗ ΔΙΑΘΗΚΗ.* Novum Testamentum Graece, ex antiquissimo Codice Vaticano edidit Angelus Maius, S. R. E. Card. 8vo. $3.00.

WINER'S CHALDEE GRAMMAR. Translated by PROF. H. B. HACKETT. 8vo. Reduced to 75 cents.

THE FOLLOWING WORKS ARE IN PREPARATION AT THE ANDOVER PRESS.

Stuart on the Old Testament Canon. Being a Critical History and Defence of the Old Testament Canon. 12mo.

Archbishop Whately's Works. On some of the Difficulties in the Writings of St. Paul," "On some of the Peculiarities in the Christian Religion," and others.

Reprinted from revised copies furnished (solely to W. F. D.) by the Author.

W. F. DRAPER, Andover, Mass.

www.ingramcontent.com/pod-product-compliance
Lightning Source LLC
LaVergne TN
LVHW011221110826
845150LV00006B/1492

9781425516116